NEGLIGENCE IN HEALTHCARE

Clinical Claims and Risk in Context

By Vivienne Harpwood

ISBN 1 843 110 15 6

Published by Informa UK Limited
6th Floor, Mortimer House
37-41 Mortimer Street
London
W1T 3JH

Printed in Great Britain by
Hobbs the Printers of Southampton

Layout designed and set by Palmer Desktop Publishing.
Tel 01284 724227.

About the Author

Vivienne Harpwood is a Reader in Law at Cardiff Law School, where she directs the LLM (Legal Aspects of Medical Practice) degree course. She is also a qualified barrister not currently in practice. Contact over many years with doctors, claimants and lawyers who are involved in various ways with clinical negligence claims has given Vivienne important insights into the concerns of each of these groups, and her teaching, research and legal practice have equipped her with the knowledge necessary to write this book. She has written extensively on medical law and civil litigation matters and writes and edits the monthly newsletters *Medical Law Monitor* and *Health Law*. Her books include *Legal Issues in Obstetrics* and *Principles of Tort Law* and she has written numerous articles on clinical negligence and related matters. She edits Butterworth's medico-legal reports and the journal *Medical Law International*. In addition to lecturing in the UK and overseas on clinical negligence Vivienne was a member of the Wilson Committee on NHS complaints and continues as a member of the Silicone Gel Breast Implant Review Group.

About this Book

Never has there been a more pressing need for up-to-date information about the legal framework relating to clinical negligence. There has been a rapid increase in the number of clinical negligence claims in recent years, culminating in a report of the Audit Commission in the year 2000 estimating that one in fourteen patients suffer from an adverse event such as a diagnostic error. In 2001 the cost of defending claims and paying compensation was believed to equal the sum required to build 16 new hospitals. The figures were published in the wake of a series of healthcare scandals that are still pre-occupying the media. This book aims to provide details of the basic legal framework to inform healthcare professionals, potential claimants and students of medical law, and to update lawyers on recent case law. Themes explored in the book include changes in the standard of care in clinical negligence, trends in the law on consent to treatment, and the relationship between NHS complaints and litigation. Recent changes in the structure of healthcare delivery, the introduction of clinical governance and the increasing regulation of the quality of healthcare are analysed, together with their implications for law and policy development. Human rights issues are increasingly prominent in UK law with the advent of the Human Rights Act 1998 and a chapter is devoted to assessing the likely impact of this innovation on clinical negligence claims. The reasons for the increase in claims are outlined in the book, and various possible responses to the current litigation crisis are discussed. The legal developments are considered in the context of policy issues in the delivery of healthcare and professional regulations.

Preface

This book has been written at a time when the structure and delivery of healthcare are in the process of continuous change. Almost every month there are new developments that give rise to even greater complexity in the regulation of healthcare, and clinical governance is now a routine part of the overall structure. Even as the book was going to press, the Health and Social Care Act 2001, which introduces still more structural changes, received the Royal Assent. Meanwhile, medical science is developing new technologies, and ever more complex treatments are being made available. The revolution in communications and information technology has facilitated access to medical information for members of the public, and allows guidance about new treatment regimes to be disseminated to healthcare professionals. Medical errors and scandals are given great prominence by the media, and ever more complex monitoring of the healthcare professions is being introduced. At the same time, partnerships between public and private healthcare provision are being encouraged, and the independent healthcare sector is being subjected to more rigorous scrutiny than ever before. Against this background, and coupled with procedural changes in the conduct of claims, and the implementation of the Human Rights Act 1998, the common law of clinical negligence continues to develop. For that reason, the book deals not only with the legal framework within which claims are made, and the basic rules of law, but also with the political and social context within which the law is developing.

The first eight chapters set out in detail the law relating to clinical negligence, evaluating recent trends and developments. Chapter 9 deals with clinical negligence and human rights, and Chapter 10 covers developments over the past decade or so in legal procedure and the funding of claims. Chapter 11 explores recent developments in the structure and delivery and monitoring of healthcare – a process that is likely to continue for some time, and Chapter 12 attempts to foresee future trends and developments in medical practice that could affect the law of clinical negligence.

The law is stated as at 24 May 2001.

Vivienne Harpwood
Reader in Law
Cardiff Law School
Barrister.

Contents

Chapter 1

Introduction to Clinical Negligence

This chapter, which is an introduction to the law of clinical negligence, provides an overview of the figures relating to the number of clinical negligence claims brought against the NHS, and considers some of the possible reasons for the growing litigation problem. The basic conceptual framework of a negligence claim is explained in outline to set the scene for more detailed discussion in the chapters that follow.

The Increasing Volume of Clinical Negligence Claims

The recent rapid increase in the number of claims against the NHS is of great concern to the healthcare professions and the Government. In the thirty years after World War Two there was evidence of a gradual steady increase in claims against healthcare professionals, and by the mid-1970s there was a rapid acceleration in that trend. In 1989, the last year of the old system for funding the defence of claims for medical negligence, the Medical Defence Union paid almost £30 million in damages and costs, more than twice what was paid in 1985[1]. One single case[2] was settled for just over £1 million, a figure that was 97% greater than the amount paid out in damages and settlements for the entire year in 1975. Similar trends were reported by the Medical Protection Society, with costs of claims increasing four-fold between 1976 and 1985, and the number of claims against its members increasing from around one thousand in 1983 to more than 2,000 by the year 1987[3]. This trend was accompanied by a large increase in subscription-rates for members of the two doctors' defence organisations in the UK, and the proposal that high risk areas of medical practice should attract higher subscription rates. This led to the introduction of NHS indemnity just before the healthcare system was restructured in the early 1990s[4].

As specialist firms of solicitors began to develop greater expertise in handling medical negligence claims in the 1990s[5], and after changes in professional regulation that permitted solicitors to advertise their services, members of the general public became more aware of the possibility of obtaining compensation for medical injuries. This also gave patients the idea of complaining about their dissatisfaction

---

1　See Annual Reports of the Medical Defence Union.
2　The name of this unreported case has been withheld.
3　See Kennedy and Grubb, *Medical Law*, 3rd edition, Butterworths, 2000 p537.
4　HC(89)34 relieved hospital medical practitioners from their obligation to join a defence organisation, and district health authorities were instructed to assume responsibility for new and existing claims for negligence.
5　Not only has expertise in clinical negligence increased. The number of solicitors in practice has also increased – from 32,700 in 1986 to 75,000 in 1999 (Centre for Policy Studies April 1999).

with the services they were receiving from the medical profession and those who administered it. The rise in claims continued towards the end of the twentieth century, despite the fact that by the late 1980s litigation was well beyond the financial means of the majority of people who might have wished to bring claims for clinical negligence. Of those patients who bring claims, (usually supported by Legal Aid, now called Community Legal Service funding), a relatively small percentage are successful[6].

Claims for clinical negligence are still increasing rapidly every year, and could be regarded as part of a more general consumer culture of claims awareness. The problem resurfaced in the national media following a report of the Audit Commission in April 2000, which suggested that much of the recent cash injection into the NHS will be wiped out by defending clinical negligence claims and the cost of paying damages. The report by Sir John Bourn, Comptroller and Auditor General, claimed that thousands of patients die or are seriously injured every year as a result of medical errors, and that one in every 14 patients suffers an adverse event such as a diagnostic error. According to the report, in the year 2000 there was an estimated 36% increase in the cost of outstanding clinical negligence claims in England[7]. A small survey reported in the BMJ in March 2001[8] concluded that 10.8% of patients experience an adverse event in hospital, and that half of these events are preventable. An estimated one-third of these adverse events led to death or serious injury. In April 2001 the National Audit Office estimated that the clinical negligence bill had grown to £4 billion, about 10% of the annual NHS budget.

There has also been a very large increase in the claims which are being brought against GPs, according to figures published by the Medical Protection Society in March 1999. During the decade settlements increased dramatically in cases concerning GP negligence. In 1998 the highest settlement was £1,675,000. What is particularly significant is the fact that GPs are 13 times more likely to be sued successfully by their patients than they were in 1989, and are 33 times more likely to be confronted with what the Society, which represents 45% of GPs in the UK, describes as *'spurious'* claims. The Medical Protection Society spent around £7 million defending GP cases in the five years to 1999 which have been dropped after it became apparent that there was no basis for them. As many of these were legally aided, the money spent in the early stages of defending them could not be recovered by the Society.

It is not only the number of claims that has increased. The amount paid in damages to injured patients is now higher than in the past, especially in cases involving victims who require substantial future care since the decision in *Wells v Wells*[9]. The case of *Heil v Rankin*[10] has inevitably meant that awards of general damages are increasing[11].

This rise in claims against the NHS has been attributed to changed attitudes towards life's misfortunes, as Ham *et al* said:

---

6   In 1996 Michael Jones cited 25% as the number of clinical negligence claimants who are successful. Jones M, *Medical Malpractice In England and Wales – A Postcard from the Edge* (1996) European Journal of Health Law 109.

7   Although the estimate is a *'worst case scenario'* based on figures suggested by the bodies responsible for dealing with the defence of claims, and final figures may be lower than those suggested, there is still cause for alarm.

8   Vincent C, at al, *Adverse Events in British Hospitals: Preliminary Retrospective Record Review*, BMJ 2001; 322 3 March, 517-519.

9   [1999] 1 AC 345.

10   [2000] 3 All ER 138.

11   These important cases are discussed at length in the chapter dealing with quantum.

'One possibility is that there may have been a cultural change towards greater insistence on the right to be compensated for life's misfortunes and an increased distrust of the assumed skill and honour of professionals[12].'

Many complex reasons have been suggested for the increased volume of medical litigation, and there is no single factor that can be blamed for the rapid increase in claims. Among the other reasons that have been identified are increased patient expectation, greater technical complexity in diagnostic and therapeutic procedures, the introduction of new technologies, greater patient expectation and demands, and a deterioration in the relationship between doctors and patients[13].

Healthcare litigation should be analysed in the context of changing attitudes towards claims in society as a whole. The closing years of the twentieth century have witnessed a *'compensation culture'* across the whole spectrum of professional services[14] in Western Europe, America and the UK, though it is in healthcare that the largest rise in claims has occurred. *'Consumerism'* in general terms began to develop in Western Society after the Second World War, when collective action by consumers, along with the operation of market forces[15], brought about changes in the law to afford greater protection to individual consumers of goods and services[16]. The setting up of the NHS in 1948 probably sowed the seeds for a change in the attitudes of patients towards doctors. For the first time, healthcare was provided free at the point of delivery, and this became regarded as the *'right'* of every individual. In the decades that followed, assisted no doubt by the mass media and inspired by serious documentary television programmes identifying medical mistakes, the quality of healthcare became an issue for general public debate. By 1974 the NHS was called upon to accept responsibility publicly for its policies and errors, and to welcome debate[17]. Another catalyst was Ian Kennedy's Reith Lectures in 1980,[18] through which he generated a movement towards greater patient involvement in medical decision-making. In 1991 the Patients Charter[19] was introduced, and although it did not have the force of law, it succeeded in raising patients' expectations. The NHS was regularly criticised if it could not keep its promises.

The Thatcher reforms in the early 1990s spelled the beginning of the end for the traditional approach, by creating competitive internal markets for healthcare provision[20], and new management structures within the NHS, and by giving a central focus to patients[21] as consumers. The structure of healthcare delivery within the NHS was fundamentally reorganised, and greater emphasis was placed on local decision-making.

It became clear that patients required full information about available treatments, about matters such as the performance and competence of their doctors, success rates for surgery, and general state of the NHS. However, despite the progress towards establishing rights of access by patients to their medical records through common

---

12   Ham C, Dingwall R, Fenn P, Harris D *Medical Negligence: Compensation and Accountability* (1988).

13   See Giesen D, *Medical Malpractice and the Judicial Function in Comparative Perspective*, Medical Law International, Vol 1:1 pp3-16 at p4.

14   See Ham C, Dingwall R, Fenn P, Harris D, *Medical Negligence: Compensation and Accountability* (1988). See also Vincent C, et al *Why Do People Sue Doctors? A Study of Patients and Relatives Taking Legal Action, Lancet* 1994; 343; 1609-13.

15   See Cranston R, *Consumers and The Law*, London: Weidenfeld and Nicholson, 1984, p10 et seq.

16   eg The Unfair Contract Terms Act 1977, The Supply of Goods and Services Act 1982.

17   Klein R, *Accountability In the Health Service*, Political Quarterly 1974.

18   Kennedy I, *The Unmasking of Medicine*, London: George Allen and Unwin, 1981.

19   An off-shoot of the Citizens' Charter introduced on the initiative of John Major in 1991.

20   See Longley D, *Diagnostic Dilemmas: Accountability in the National Health Service*, 1990 Public Law 527.

21   As is demonstrated by the White Paper that preceded the 1990 legislation was entitled *Working for Patients*.

law developments, statutory provisions[22], and quasi-statutory intervention[23], there were by 1990, and still are, despite further reforms, some circumstances when information about health status can be withheld[24]. It was not until the start of the twenty-first century that progress towards greater openness was furthered in the UK by the implementation of the Human Rights Act 1998[25].

All the late twentieth century developments have contributed to the view that healthcare is a competitive industry, and have reinforced the notion of the ideology of healthcare as the ideology of the market, in which the concept of accountability attends the rhetoric of consumer choice. One much trumpeted objective of the reforms of the 1990s was to create a culture of *'patient-centred care'* within the NHS. That aim has been repeated on many occasions since the reorganisation of the NHS, and is still being highlighted as a major policy objective[26]. On John Major's initiative, the Patients Charter, reflecting the notion of the *'empowered client'* in the related Citizens Charter, encouraged patients to complain by asserting their so-called *'rights'* in healthcare. The NHS Complaints System, better access to information and consumer culture and media interest have all been contributory factors in the drive towards a greater volume of litigation.

The National Audit Office, in the April 2000 report, placed part of the blame for the increasing cost of litigation on the fact that cases are being processed more quickly since the introduction of legal aid franchising which demands specialist expertise from claimants' solicitors. David Davis, who chairs the Commons Public Accounts Committee, is on record as saying:

'Successful claims for negligence mean that there is less cash available to treat patients.'

This statement echoes Frank Dobson's famous comment in 1998 that *'The best place for a lawyer is on the operating table'* because lawyers are *'Milking the NHS of millions of pounds every year'*. However, lawyers representing patients argue that they encounter many examples of crass negligence in the cases they observe, and that the blame lies with the healthcare professions.

There is, of course, a possibility that healthcare professionals are becoming more negligent. This is unlikely, and there is no hard evidence that it is the case. However, it is possible that more errors are being detected and admitted in the NHS. Patients are now more likely to have access to their records, and internal monitoring does lead to admissions of responsibility for medical mistakes.

As will be seen the Government has attempted to tackle the litigation problem[27] in a variety of different ways, though not usually explicitly – more often under the guise of improving quality in healthcare on a uniform basis throughout the UK and ending the practice of *'postcode prescribing'*.

---

22   Data Protection Act 1998; Access to Health Records Act 1990; Access to Medical Reports Act 1988.

23   A Code of Practice on Openness was introduced in the NHS on 1 June 1995, by which patients may request access to medical records and to other information held by NHS bodies.

24   For example, Data Protection Act 1998 Part IV; also *R v Mid Glamorgan Family Health Services Authority, ex parte Martin* [1995] 1 All ER 356 CA.

25   The European Convention on Human Rights, Article 8(1) states that every individual has a right to respect for his family life, and in *Gaskin v United Kingdom* this was held to include personal information relating to health. Clearly, the right of access to medical records cannot be absolute, but there is a potential problem if the gatekeepers of records are doctors themselves. In *Gaskin*, where access to information provided in confidence to social services had been sought, it was held that there had been a breach of Article 8, because there was no system of independent review by which access, (or its denial), could be monitored, when consent of the person providing the information had not been obtained.

26   The NHS Plan published in 2000 claims to be designed to give patients *'more power, protection and choice than ever before'*.

27   It has been argued that the threat of litigation is more perceived than real. See Mulcahy L. *The Challenge of Medical Negligence Cases in Law and Medicine*, ed Freeman M and Lewis A, OUP, 2000, 81-105.

Clinical Negligence

There follows a brief overview of the basic legal framework in clinical negligence cases. It is within this framework that recent developments in the law will be discussed in later chapters.

Definitions and Background

Negligence belongs to an area of civil law that is primarily concerned with compensating people who have suffered harm as a result of breaches of duties imposed by law. Unlike criminal law, tort is not concerned with punishing wrongdoers for criminal offences. However, there are some circumstances in which a tort has been committed when there may also be a criminal prosecution. For example, gross negligence resulting in death may be prosecuted as manslaughter. This is extremely rare in cases involving medical malpractice[28].

The tort of negligence, of which clinical negligence is just one example, cannot be defined simply. It does not merely involve careless behaviour. Negligence is the breach of a legal duty to take reasonable care in relation to another person as a result of which there is damage to that person. Not every medical mishap or adverse incident gives the patient the right to sue for damages. In order to succeed in a claim for clinical negligence, the injured person must satisfy the complex requirements of the tort of negligence. Clinical negligence is a very specialised area of law, and differs from other forms of negligence in a number of ways. Expert medical evidence must usually be obtained, fault is difficult to prove, and the procedural rules governing the way in which claims must be brought are highly technical. The criteria that must be satisfied in order for a person to succeed in a negligence claim are outlined in the material that follows. There are many practical and procedural matters that influence decisions about whether cases are settled out-of-court or proceed to trial. Even before the implementation of the new Civil Procedure Rules in April 1999, the vast majority of cases were settled out-of-court. Figures published in the Health Service Journal in 1997 suggested that only 3% of medical negligence cases were reaching trial.

The Legal Framework of Clinical Negligence

In order to succeed in a claim for clinical negligence the claimant must prove that:

1. s/he was owed a legal duty of care by the defendant healthcarer;
2. the defendant was in breach of that duty of care in failing to reach the standard of care required by law;
3. the breach of duty caused or materially contributed to the damage suffered, and the damage was not *'too remote'* in legal terms.

The claimant has the legal burden of proving each of the above elements on a balance of probabilities, (ie that it was more probable than not that there was negligence), and the entire claim will fail unless the claimant succeeds at every point. There are relatively few disputes about whether or not a duty of care is owed, but those cases which have been decided on this point tend to be given prominence because many are decisions of the higher courts. While a large number of cases turn on the questions of breach of duty and/or causation, many of these cases concern factual matters, and do not give rise to important issues of law. A high percentage of cases are settled out-of-court, on the basis of what is, in fact a business decision by claims managers and lawyers. The high cost of

---

28   But see *R v Adomako* [1995] 1 AC 171.

defending claims rarely justifies a court battle, particularly if the claim is small[29]. Some aspects of a claim may be agreed between the parties at an early stage, and there may only be a dispute about one or two issues. The practical considerations raised by the Civil Procedure Rules influence this process, as will be seen in a later chapter. Equally, many claims are discontinued when the claimant is advised by medical experts and lawyers that the chances of success are relatively low[30].

Each stage in the above framework may give rise to matters of dispute, but in many cases some of the issues will be agreed. For example, the parties may agree that there was a duty of care owed by the healthcare professional concerned, and that there had been a breach of that duty, but that the breach of duty did not cause the injuries suffered by the claimant.

Defences to Clinical Negligence

The defendant may raise one or more defences to the claim. Defences are inherent in the framework of negligence. Thus the defendant might argue that there was no duty of care owed to the claimant, or that there had been no negligence in the circumstances of the case, or that the breach of duty did not cause the injury.

It could be argued that the injury occurred because the claimant was negligent in not following medical advice, for example, by not taking medication or failing to return for a check up, or that he or she had consented to run the risk of injury. Here, complete defence may be relied upon, as where the claimant is alleged to have agreed to take a particular risk. The partial defence of contributory negligence may be raised and would apply when the claimant is alleged to have taken too little care for his or her own safety – for example by returning to work too soon after surgery. In such a case, the damages payable would be reduced according to the percentage of the injury that the court considers was attributable to the conduct of the claimant.

A further defence is usually available if the claim is brought after too long a time has elapsed since the claimant discovered that he or she had suffered injury, or ought reasonably to have discovered that a legal claim might be available. This is known as the limitation defence and the Limitation Act 1980 determines what happens in any particular case. This highly technical legal matter is discussed in a later chapter.

Quantum

If the claimant succeeds in proving that there was negligence the judge must assess quantum – what the injury or damage is worth in money terms – and order a remedy accordingly. The parties are frequently in agreement that a breach of duty occurred that it caused injury to the claimant, but there may then be a disagreement about quantum. Medical experts are called upon to testify as to the likely course that the claimant's illness or injury might follow. The way in which quantum is assessed in clinical negligence cases is discussed in a later chapter.

Structural Changes in the Delivery of Healthcare and Legal Services

The past decade has witnessed many significant changes in the way in which healthcare is delivered. Indeed the 1990's were the years in which healthcare delivery changed the most since the foundation of the NHS in 1948. Coupled with technological developments, these structural changes have altered healthcare services

---

29   This is furthered by the Civil Procedure Rules 1999.

30   It was reported in the Health Services Journal in May 1997 that 75% of claims are dropped after the claimant has seen the medical records.

to a major extent. At the same time there has been an important change in the delivery of legal services and the procedures in the civil courts, driven by Lord Woolf, who is now Lord Chief Justice.

The Human Rights Act 1998 has altered the way in which those responsible for the organisation and delivery of legal and medical services approach their tasks. The combination of these transformations has meant that the practice of law and medicine and clinical negligence litigation are no longer as they were a decade ago. The developments and achievements of the 1990s will be discussed in a later chapter devoted to assessing the impact of the new era.

Failings in the Litigation System

Commentators have been in agreement for some time that the use of the law, and the tort system in particular, is not the most satisfactory way of dealing with claims for compensation against doctors and other healthcare professionals. Litigation is very expensive for both parties, and doctors fear that they may be adopting defensive practices in order to avoid the risk of being sued. Indeed, it could be argued that the litigation crisis has had an indirect impact on medical practice which is impossible to measure. Other more acceptable means of compensating patients in deserving cases have been suggested, and the Government is already experimenting with new ways of monitoring medical practice to prevent adverse incidents. These matters will be discussed in the concluding chapter of this book.

Chapter 2

Duty of Care in Clinical Negligence

The concept of duty of care is important in any negligence claim, because if no duty of care exists in a given situation, then even though it is obvious that there has been carelessness or negligence on the part of the defendant the claim cannot succeed. In fact there are now relatively few disputes about the existence of a duty of care because most of the situations in which a duty of care exists are settled law, as can be seen in the decided cases. Thus, for example, a motorist owes a duty of care to other road users, a teacher owes a duty of care to pupils in school, and a doctor owes a duty of care to patients. However, there are some instances in which the precise scope of the duty is unclear or has not previously been determined by a court, and it is in these grey areas and novel situations that disputes arise.

The leading case providing guidance on this matter is *Caparo Industries plc v Dickman*[1]. In that case the House of Lords reviewed the test for determining the existence of a duty of care. A duty arises when:

- it is foreseeable that the claimant would be affected by the acts or omissions of the defendant;
- there is sufficient proximity between the parties;
- the court considers that it would be fair, just and reasonable to impose a duty in all the circumstances of the case.

This last element allows the courts considerable discretion to make decisions on grounds of policy, and in some instances to limit the number of successful claims.

The criteria established in *Caparo v Dickman* are referred to in many of the more controversial and difficult cases that come before the courts, and provide useful guidance to judges in arriving at their conclusions. It is acknowledged that at times judges do not always reach their decisions purely on the basis of applying the law to the facts of the cases before them, and decisions may be influenced by one or more policy factors. In effect, the concept of duty of care in UK law is used by judges to determine the boundaries of liability though this process is not always fully articulated by the courts. When it is, lawyers are greatly assisted in determining the likely success or failure of later cases by the clarity and frankness of some of the judges. Current examples of this in practice can be found in the law relating to psychiatric injury, as discussed below.

---

1   [1990] 2 WLR 358.

Judicial policy was defined by a leading academic writer in the following way:

'The use of the word policy indicates no more than that the court must decide not merely whether there is or is not a duty, but whether there should or should not be one, taking into account both the established framework of the law, and also the implications that a decision one way or the other may have for the operation of the law in our society[2].'

From the cases it is apparent that the factors influencing judicial decisions on duty of care and breach of duty include economic and social policy[3], loss allocation[4], insurance[5], notions of social justice[6], moral and ethical considerations, practical matters, such as the need for manufacturers to be able to plan for the future, fear of too rapid and too wide an expansion of liability[7], fear of opening the floodgates to an escalation of claims[8], the perceived need to protect members of certain professions, including the legal and medical professions, and the respective roles of Parliament and the courts[9]. Human rights issues are also relevant to judicial policy.

Duty of Care and Human Rights

Although the Human Rights Act 1998 only came into force on 2 October 2000, UK judges had already been hearing and considering arguments about human rights issues for some time when dealing with certain medical law matters, with a view to ensuring, as far as possible, consistency between the common law and the Convention. This position was formalised by the Human Rights Act 1998 under which the European Convention on Human Rights is incorporated into UK law.

As far as the duty of care in negligence is concerned, the implementation of the Human Rights Act 1998 could mean that some of the past decisions made on the basis of judicial policy are likely to be challenged. In particular, cases involving the scope of the duty of care in negligence might result in established lines of precedent being demolished, particularly where the law is in a state of change or development. In addition, if there is no existing tort remedy equivalent to a Convention right, the judges would be required, by Article 6, to develop one.

The provisions of this Act and its potential impact on medical law, especially in the area of healthcare negligence, are discussed in Chapter 9 together with some of the recent cases concerning duty of care in negligence.

---

2   Winfield and Jolowicz in Tort, ed Rogers.

3   For example, in *Heil v Rankin* The Times 20 June 2000, the question of the cost of litigation to the NHS was considered at length.

4   *Donoghue v Stevenson* [1932] AC 562.

5   *Nettleship v Weston* [1971] 2 QB 691.

6   *Caparo v Dickman* [1990] 2 WLR 358.

7   *Goodwill v British Pregnancy Advisory Service* The Times 29 January 1989.

8   *McLoughlin v O'Brian* [1983] AC 410.

9   *McLoughlin v O'Brian* [1983] AC 410.

Duty of Care in the Healthcare Setting

The claimant's first task is to establish that he or she was owed a duty of care by the defendant. In the healthcare context this is not usually difficult, and in many cases it is assumed without further argument that a duty of care was owed. Nevertheless, there are some circumstances when the scope of the duty is unclear. In other instances it has been firmly established by courts that there is no duty owed at all – though as explained earlier these cases are likely to come under increasing scrutiny under the Human Rights Act 1998.

There are precedents establishing that in most healthcare situations a duty of care is owed to patients, and it almost goes without saying that this is the case[10]. If, however, a novel situation arises, the judge must decide whether there is a duty of care owed.

When a Clear Duty of Care is Owed

People within the carer/patient relationship

A duty care arises as soon as the healthcarer takes responsibility[11] for treating the individual concerned. Thus GPs, their nursing staff, receptionists and other staff owe a duty of care to patients accepted onto their lists, and hospital doctors and other hospital staff owe a duty of care to people accepted as out-patients or admitted to hospital.

Once the extension to the prescribing power of nurses under the Health and Social Care Act 2001 is implemented, the duty of care owed by nurses to patients will also be extended. A consultation paper suggests training around 10,000 nurses to extend their ability to prescribe treatment for a broader range of medical conditions, including minor injuries and ailments such as burns, cuts, and hay-fever; chronic disease management including asthma and diabetes and palliative care. Until the Act, only nurses who are working as qualified district nurses or health visitors, or who hold a district nurse or health visitor qualification and are working as GP practice nurses or in Walk-In Centres, are eligible to train to prescribe. By early October 2000, nearly 16,000 district nurses and health visitors had already trained to prescribe from the current Nurse Prescribers' Formulary. The consultation followed the Government's acceptance of the main recommendations of the Review of Prescribing, Supply & Administration of Medicines on 13 March 2000. The response was generally favourable.

People of all ages and unborn children

A duty of care is owed to patients of all ages, whether or not they are legally or mentally competent, and to unborn children[12], once a doctor accepts responsibility for the care of the patient. Under the Congenital Disabilities (Civil Liability) Act 1976 a person can bring a claim after birth in respect of injuries sustained by negligence before or during birth[13]. For example, if drugs are negligently prescribed to a pregnant woman, as a result of which the foetus suffers injury, the negligent doctor could be sued for damages. The Act also protects claimants who are injured during the birth process. A further right of action was introduced by the Human Fertilisation and Embryology Act 1990[14]. This extends the right of action under the 1976 Act to claims

---

10   See Brazier, M *Medicine, Patients and the Law* Penguin, 2 ed 1992 pp117-118.

11   In *R v Bateman* (19250 94 LJKB 791 (CCA). Although this was a criminal case, Lord Hewart CJ explained the nature of the situation that gives rise to the duty of care.

12   Congential Disabilities (Civil Liability) Act 1976.

13   This Act only applies in relation to births after 22 July 1976.

14   See Lee R and Morgan D *Human Fertilization and Embryology* Blackstone Press 2001.

arising out of disabilities caused by selection, storage or use of embryos or gametes in the course of fertility treatment. In all cases the action by the child is derivative in that it cannot be sustained unless the parent concerned can establish that he or she was owed a duty of care by the defendant. The action under both statutes is only available if the child was born alive. (No claim can lie against the mother of a child unless it is alleged that her negligent driving caused the injury.) If the parents knew before the child was conceived that there was a risk that the child would be born with disabilities, there would be a defence to a claim under the Act. However, if the defendant is the father and he alone was aware of the risk, then no such defence would apply. If one of the parents was contributorily negligent, the damages payable to the child would be reduced accordingly[15]. The common law (the law developed through the cases, outside the legislation) has also acknowledged the existence of a duty to unborn children, on the basis that this duty *'crystallises'* on the birth of the child to give rise to an action[16].

Accident and emergency patients

A patient who arrives at an Accident and Emergency Department of a hospital is probably owed a duty of care on being accepted for treatment[17]. A medical history of the patient and the circumstances of any accident are recorded on admission, and it is the patient's responsibility to inform the doctor of any medication he is currently taking. The planned introduction of electronic health records to be available throughout the NHS, at any time for every patient, will make the task of Accident and Emergency staff easier[18].

Who owes the duty of care?

A duty of care is owed by any healthcarer, (including a para-medic and alternative medical practitioner), who takes responsibility for treating a patient. Duties are also owed to patients by porters, cleaners and auxiliary staff. The NHS Trust, Health Authority or private healthcare provider may, in certain unusual circumstances, be primarily liable for negligence, and will almost always be vicariously liable for the wrongs of their employees.

Ambulance services

A duty of care is owed by ambulance services to the patients whom they transport to hospital and in certain cases, treat, provided relevant staff are given full information about the name and address of the patient and the nature of his or her condition – *Kent v Griffiths and the London Ambulance Service*[19]. In this case the issue on appeal was whether an ambulance service owed any duty of care to a member of the public on whose behalf a 999 call was made if, because of negligence, it failed to arrive within a reasonable time. On 16 February 1991 the claimant, then aged 26 and pregnant, called a doctor to her home. She suffered from asthma, and on the day in question, she felt particularly wheezy and called her GP. The GP telephoned the Ambulance Service using the 999 service, asked for an ambulance and was assured that one would be sent. On two more occasions within a short space of time, the claimant's husband telephoned the Ambulance Service, and was told that the ambulance was on its way. Eventually the ambulance arrived, but considerably later than would have been

---

15   Section 2 of the Act.
16   *B v Islington Health Authority* (1990) 6 BMLR 13.
17   *Barnett v Chelsea and Kensington Health Authority* [1969] 1 QB 428.
18   This is facilitated by the Health and Social Care Act 2001.
19   (2000) 2 All ER 474.

expected, and on the way to the hospital, a journey taking about six minutes, the claimant was given oxygen intermittently. However, shortly before her arrival at the hospital she suffered a respiratory arrest that resulted in serious brain damage and a miscarriage. The claimant sought compensation from the defendants. The Court of Appeal had, on an earlier occasion, ruled that there was an arguable case on the facts, and that the proceedings should not be struck out for failing to disclose a cause of action.

In the High Court, the London Ambulance Service had argued that the only duty owed in private law by the emergency services to an individual member of the public was not to create an additional danger which caused injury to the patient. This submission was based on the earlier cases of *Capital and Counties plc v Hampshire County Council*[20] and *Alexandrou v Oxford*[21]. The Ambulance Service also argued that negligence in the performance of a statutory duty, or in the exercise of a power, could only give rise to liability if the three requirements established in *Caparo v Dickman*[22] were met. They contended that here the second requirement (proximity) did not exist. The claimant argued that the unchallenged findings of the judge as to fact were sufficient to establish proximity and that the earlier cases could be distinguished.

Dismissing the Appeal by the Ambulance Service against a finding of liability in the High Court, the Court of Appeal held that the London Ambulance Service was under at least a public law duty to exercise its discretion to provide an ambulance, as this was its statutory function. Ambulances were paid out of public money and it was wholly inappropriate to regard the Service and its employees as volunteers who owed no duty of care. The Court of Appeal took the view that when a statute only established a power for a body to act in a particular manner, that body could still be liable in negligence if there was also a common law duty created on the particular facts of the case. In the present case it would have been irrational not to have accepted the request to provide an ambulance for the claimant. The London Ambulance Service was providing a healthcare service, and the ambulance staff were in the same position as doctors or nurses. Unlike the police and fire services, the ambulance service usually owed a duty to the individual patient rather than to the public at large *(Capital & Counties and Alexandrou v Oxford* (supra) were distinguished here). It was the claimant alone for whom the ambulance had been called, and it was an important feature of the case that there was no question of lack of ambulance availability or a conflict in priorities.

As there were no circumstances which made it unfair, unreasonable or unjust that liability should exist, there was no reason why there should not be liability if the arrival of the ambulance was delayed for no good reason. The trial judge had found that there had been an unacceptable delay. The acceptance of the call established the duty of care and the delay caused the further injuries. In the view of the Court of Appeal, the reaction of the trial judge to the facts of this case accorded with the likely reaction of any well-informed member of the public. Turner J had summed up this reaction as follows:

> '*I should have found it offensive to, and inconsistent with concepts of common humanity if, in circumstances such as the present, where there had been unreasonable and unexplained delay in providing the services which the ambulance service were in a position to meet, and had accepted that it would supply an ambulance, the law could not in its turn provide a remedy.*'

---

20   ibid.
21   (1993) 4 All ER 328.
22   (1990) 2 WLR 358, see the start of this chapter for details.

The claimant was awarded £362,377 for the brain damage and related losses that she had suffered.

It appears, on analysis of the *Kent* case, that in order to establish liability on the part of an Ambulance Service a claimant must be able to prove that a call had been made to the Emergency Services or Ambulance Service, giving details of the name and address of the patient, and of the medical condition requiring urgent attention. It is also necessary for a claimant to convince the court that he or she was relying on the timely arrival of the ambulance. It might still be possible to defend claims against Ambulance Services if claimants are unable to meet these criteria, although it is common practice for the GP or other person calling for an ambulance to give details identifying the patient and the medical condition, and these are routinely recorded. A situation that is rather more complicated was anticipated by Lord Woolf in the Court of Appeal when he remarked that the case might well have been decided differently if the question of resources, or the lack of them, on the part of the Ambulance Service had been raised.

Duty to 'primary victims' in psychiatric injury cases

It is possible to claim compensation for psychiatric injury as well as physical injury. In the case of psychiatric injury, for what are essentially policy reasons aimed at restricting the number of claims, the law divides claimants into *'primary'* and *'secondary'* victims. It has been established through the cases that there is a duty of care not to cause psychiatric injury to people classified as primary victims of negligence. The scope of the duty of care in negligence in relation to secondary victims of psychiatric injury is somewhat limited.

A *'primary victim'* is a person who is a participant in an accident or other traumatic event. Primary victims experience the event at first hand, and frequently, though not always, suffer physical injury. A *'secondary victim'* is someone who is not present at the heart of the traumatic event, but who witnesses it, or evidence of it, at a distance or soon afterwards. It has long been accepted that in general the victim of physical injuries caused by negligence also has a claim for any psychiatric harm which ensues. As long as physical injury is foreseeable, even if only slight physical injury is in fact suffered, and even if the claimant is especially vulnerable because of his or her personality, there will also be a duty of care not to cause psychiatric injury[23]. In *Gibblet v P & N E Murray Ltd*[24] the Court of Appeal ruled that the claimant would have been able to recover damages for a psychiatric condition which made her incapable of having sexual relations and children of her own, if physical injury in the road accident she was involved in was foreseeable. In this case the reasoning in *Page v Smith* was followed by the Court of Appeal. This issue also involves the question of causation, and the test is *'Did the accident, on the balance of probability, cause or materially contribute to or materially increase the risk of the development or prolongation of the symptoms of the pre-existing psychiatric illness?'*

It is always necessary for the claimant to prove that he or she is suffering from a recognised psychiatric illness. Short-lived distress will not be compensated. For example, in *Reilly v Merseyside Health Authority*[25] the defendants were not liable when the claimants were trapped in a lift at a hospital and suffered temporary

---

23   *Page v Smith* (1994) 20 BMLR 18.
24   TLR 25/5/99.
25   (1994) 23 BMLR 26.

symptoms of claustrophobia followed by chest pains and insomnia. They had not succeeded in establishing that they had suffered a recognisable long-term psychiatric illness.

Psychiatric injury manifests itself in a variety of different ways. In the early cases psychiatric injury was described as *'nervous shock'* because successful early claims recognised symptoms such as physical manifestations of shock, including miscarriage, and symptoms including depression[26], personality change[27] and panic attacks. As more sophisticated diagnostic procedures became available, the symptoms were recognised as part of the general condition known as post traumatic stress disorder (PTSD). This serious medical condition can be distinguished from temporary feelings of grief or shock, or *'normal human emotions'*. PTSD was first recognised in the *Diagnostic and Statistical Manual of Mental Disorders* of the American Psychiatric Association in 1980, and in the *Glossary of Mental Disorders in the International Classification of Diseases* in 1987. According to the first of these publications, PTSD must be traceable to a traumatic event outside the *'normal'* range of human experience. Symptoms include the mental reliving of the event, nightmares, irritability, lack of interest in life and lack of emotional response. Medical opinion suggests that an individual is more likely to suffer PTSD if he or she is actually present during a traumatic event or observes injury or death suffered by a close relative as a result of such an event.

In the case of primary victims, the slow appreciation over a long period of time, of the possibility of having been infected, negligently, by a frightening illness, is sufficient for a claim to succeed. In *The Creuzfeldt-Jakob Disease Litigation: Andrews & Others v Secretary Of State For Health (1998)*[28], Mr Justice Morland held that a claimant could recover compensation, whether he was a person of ordinary fortitude, or one with a vulnerable personality, provided he could prove that his psychiatric illness was caused by his becoming aware of the risk that he might already be infected with CJD, and that he suffered a psychiatric illness. He also took the view that there was no reason why foreseeability for shock and psychiatric injury should be limited to a period of time contemporaneous or almost contemporaneous with the negligent event. If the psychiatric injury was foreseeable it should be untrammelled by spatial, physical or temporal limits[29].

Problems can arise when a claimant takes many years to develop symptoms of psychiatric injury, and a claim could well fail for limitation reasons if the claimant does not begin proceedings until a long period of time has elapsed since the negligent event. (For example, *Crocker v British Coal Corporation*[30], a claim brought by a victim of the 1966 Aberfan disaster.) Similar problems can also arise in the cases of individuals who have suffered physical or sexual abuse as children.

A recent example of a successful claim in a case involving clinical negligence is *Farrell v Merton Sutton and Wandsworth Health Authority*[31] the claimant brought an action for damages for personal injuries which she claimed she had suffered as a result of negligence of hospital staff employed by the defendants during the birth of her son on 24 May 1990. In separate proceedings there was a settlement in favour

---

26   *Chadwick v British Railways Board* [1967] 1 WLR 912.
27   *McLoughlin v O'Brian* [1983] AC 410.
28   (1998) 54 BMLR 111.
29   See Schedule 2 *Claimants v Medical Research Council* (1998) 54 BMLR 92.
30   Unreported 1995.
31   (2001) 57 BMLR 158.

of the child, who suffered serious and irreversible brain damage at or around the time of his birth. The defendants admitted breach of the duty of care owed to the claimant, in that the operation was carried out without effective anaesthesia and with questionable aseptic technique. The judge noted that the management of the antenatal care given to the claimant, and delivery of her child, had fallen below minimum standards of competence. The claimant had undergone an emergency caesarean section operation, during which she was aware and in pain. She later suffered an infection following the operation because she had not been given antibiotics as instructed. After she recovered from the operation, regaining full consciousness at 10 pm, she was shown a Polaroid photograph of the baby lying on a mattress, but was not informed at that time that he was on a ventilator and was seriously ill. In fact he had been intubated when he was one minute old, his heart rate being nil, and had suffered convulsions during the night. The baby was moved to another hospital for specialist care, and the claimant was told that she was too ill to travel there with him. When eventually she did see her son late the next evening, the claimant was informed that he had suffered irreversible brain damage.

The claimant sought damages, not only for the physical effects of badly managed birth and the emergency caesarean section, but also for psychological injury suffered as a result of the trauma of the birth, and/or learning of her baby's poor condition. She alleged that she had suffered a psychiatric illness, loss of amenity and a back injury caused or exacerbated by lifting the child, who was unable to care for himself as he grew older. The main issue in this case was the question as to whether the defendant owed a duty of care to the claimant in respect of psychiatric injury, as a primary victim, or whether their duty of care was to the child, and the claimant was merely a secondary victim.

In this case, the judge was satisfied that there was no break in the chain of causation, as in her view, the trauma of the birth encompassed not only what had occurred in the operating theatre but also the events leading to, and including, the claimant's first sight of her baby, and her realisation of the disability. It followed that the claimant was a primary victim. The judge was satisfied that the claimant was suffering from a recognised psychiatric illness caused by the trauma of her son's birth. However, she held that the back injury was not directly attributable to the trauma of the birth, although it was directly associated with his condition. On that basis, no damages would be awarded for F's back injury. The claimant was awarded a total of £75,000 general damages, including a sum to cover loss of amenity for *'the loss of her private life, far beyond the constraints of bringing up a healthy child'*.

Again, in *Tredget v Bexley Health Authority*[32] both parents of a child who suffered exceptional distress when they witnessed the frightening circumstances surrounding the death of their baby, who was delivered negligently, recovered damages. They were able to prove psychiatric injury caused by the events and were primary victims of the negligence of the defendants because they were present when the events took place.

On occasion, secondary victims can also succeed in obtaining damages for psychiatric injury in medical cases. In *Powell v Boldaz*[33] the mother of a child whose death was hastened by misdiagnosis, received a substantial settlement containing an award for the psychiatric injury which she suffered as a result of her child's illness and early death. The principles established in *Alcock v Chief Constable of South*

---

32   (1994) 5 Med LR 178.
33   (1997) 39 BMLR 35.

Yorkshire[34] govern secondary victims. These are outlined below in the section dealing with circumstances when usually no duty of care is owed.

Primary duty of care owed by healthcare providers

Primary liability arises as a result of direct responsibility for a negligent act or omission. Vicarious liability arises when a person or organisation is liable for the negligence of other people. It has been suggested that there are two different types of primary liability[35]. The first arises in the form of a very obvious duty to provide a reasonable system of care through the services of staff, equipment, systems and facilities. The second arises as a non-delegable duty, an overriding and continuing duty to discharge the obligations owed by an institution to its patients – a duty to ensure that care is taken in the provision of services to patients. There is some blurring here of the distinction between primary and vicarious liability, though this is usually entirely academic because in most cases the distinction is of no real practical importance in its consequences. In almost every instance of clinical negligence a health provider will be vicariously liable for the negligence of its staff. The exceptions are explained later in this chapter.

In *Bull v Devon Area Health Authority*[36], an example of the first type of duty, the Court of Appeal held that the health authority owed the claimant a direct duty of care. Mrs Bull brought a claim against the defendants on behalf of herself and her son. She alleged that her son was disabled as a result of birth asphyxia caused by the negligence both of the health authority and of its staff. The hospital was based on two separate sites, and when the delivery of Mrs Bull's son was imminent there was no doctor available on her site to assist her, as the communications system for calling doctors had broken down. This case and others in which systems operated by healthcare providers have failed, fall within the ambit of direct primary liability. System failures, especially communications failures like that which occurred in *Robertson v Nottingham Health Authority*[37] discussed below are now likely to be an accepted form of negligence, and will become of greater significance since the introduction of clinical governance[38] which has at its heart the requirement that satisfactory systems for avoiding accidents be put in place by healthcare organisations. The decision of the European Commission in *Tavares v France*[39] supports this approach. However, in that instance the Commission rejected a complaint that there had been negligence because the hospital in question had procedures in place and these had been followed.

In terms of the second type of primary liability, there is a direct non-delegable duty of care owed by health authorities and NHS Trusts to provide adequate care to patients. This principle, established in *Cassidy v Minister of Health* in 1951[40], was re-explored and confirmed in *M v Calderdale and Kirklees Health Authority* in 1998[41]. In that case the health authority, through one of its doctors, made a contractual arrangement with a private hospital, for a patient to have a termination of pregnancy. It was held that the duty of the health authority to provide the patient with

---

34   [1991] 4 All ER 907.

35   Picard E, *The liability of Hospitals in Common Law Canada* (1981) 26 McGill LJ 997.

36   [1993] 4 Med LR 117 (CA).

37   *Robertson v Nottingham HA* [1997] 8 Med LR 1 (CA), see Chapter 4.

38   See Chapter 3.

39   Appl 16593/90 (1991) unreported.

40   [1951] 2 KB 343.

41   [1998] Lloyd's Rep Med 157.

an effective termination of her pregnancy could not be delegated, and the health authority remained responsible when the claimant discovered that she was still pregnant as a result of the negligence of staff at the private hospital. This decision is of great importance in the light of proposals to encourage more public/private partnerships in healthcare.

When a Duty of Care May not be Owed

Borderline cases

In some borderline cases there may be doubt as to whether a person is owed a duty of care. It may not always be clear precisely when the relationship between the particular healthcare professional and the patient begins. It may be difficult to pin-point the exact time that the doctor assumed responsibility for the patient[42]. In the case of a formal admission of a patient to hospital via a GP, nurses, doctors, administrators, porters and others might assume responsibility at different times. In these instances much turns on the particular situation involved. For example: at what point is a patient, who has been referred by a GP and admitted to hospital, owed a duty of care by the consultant who will be in charge of his treatment? This is a question of fact for the court to decide in each case, and the answer depends upon the point at which the particular consultant assumed responsibility for the patient[43]. Another borderline area is dealt with below. That concerns psychiatric injury suffered by people who are not directly involved in traumatic events (*'secondary victims'*), who are only owed a duty of care in certain restricted circumstances.

When a Duty of Care is not Owed

Good Samaritans

There is no duty in UK law at present to act as a Good Samaritan[44], for example, at the scene of an accident. A healthcarer has no obligation to go to the rescue of a person in need of medical attention if the sick person is not one of his or her existing patients, though there are some exceptions relating to midwives and to GPs[45] in their own practice area. Although there may be sound policy reasons for this rule[46], it is possible that this situation could change in the light of the Human Rights Act 1998, which incorporates into UK law the European Convention on Human Rights[47]. If a doctor, nurse or first-aider does decide to assist an injured person at the scene of an accident, or a heart attack victim in a hotel for example, a duty of care arises as soon as the doctor assumes responsibility for the care of the injured person. If the treatment provided by the doctor or nurse is negligent, he or she could be liable for damages. That is one reason why hospital doctors are still advised to become members of one of the defence organisations.

Doctors employed by third parties

There is probably no duty of care owed by a doctor to a patient on whom he or she carries out a pre-employment medical examination at the request of a third party (the

---

42   One view is that it will arise somewhere along the continuum which begins with the patient being at home and ends with the doctor embarking on the first *'laying on of hands'*. See Kennedy and Grubb *Medical Law*, Butterworths 2000, at p280.

43   See Lord Nathan in *Medical Negligence* (1957), cited in Kennedy and Grubb in *Medical Law*, Butterworths, 2000 at p280.

44   *The Ogopogo* [1971] 2 Lloyds Rep 410.

45   See Nurses, Midwives and Health Visitors Act 1997 and the National Health Service (General Medical Services) Regulations 1992 relating to general practice and Directions to Health Authorities Concerning the Implementation of Pilot Schemes 1997.

46   See the discussion in the Australian case of *Lowns v Woods* (1996) Aust Tort Reports 81-376 (NSWCA).

47   It has been suggested that Article 2 of the Convention might be engaged, if someone was to deny a person life-saving treatment in an emergency – see Chapter 9.

employer). However, the picture is not absolutely clear. In *Baker v Kaye*[48] it was held that there was a duty of care owed to a person on whom a pre-employment medical was carried out, but there was no negligence on the facts of the case. In *Kapfunde v Abbey National plc and Others*[49] the Court of Appeal held that a doctor engaged to assess the medical questionnaires of applicants for posts, did not owe a duty of care to an applicant who had completed a pre-employment questionnaire. The claimant had completed a medical questionnaire and the report was sent to Dr Daniel, Abbey National's occupational health adviser. Dr Daniel advised that her medical history suggested that she was likely to have a higher-than-average absence level from work and she was not accepted for the post. Drawing a parallel with the case of *X v Bedfordshire County Council*, and applying the criteria established in *Caparo v Dickman* (supra), this was not a case in which it was appropriate to extend the scope of the duty of care in negligence. Here there was no *special relationship* between Ms Kapfunde and Dr Daniels. There may well be a contract between the commissioning body and the doctor who produces the report, but contractual duties do not extend to third parties in cases like this.

The Court of Appeal in *R v Croydon Health Authority*[50], a wrongful birth case, drew their conclusions on the tacit assumption basis that a duty of care was owed by a radiologist to a woman who was required to undergo a pre-employment medical examination. This case should not be regarded as authority for the proposition that a duty of care is owed to those who undergo pre-employment medicals, because there was no reasoned judgment on that particular point. However, the approach taken by the Court of Appeal to the other issues in the case is worth examining. Part of the medical examination was a chest X-ray that ought to have alerted the radiologist to the fact that the claimant was suffering from a rare condition known as primary pulmonary hypertension. That condition was a significant abnormality that should have been reported to the claimant's GP. It can reduce life-expectancy, especially if a sufferer becomes pregnant. Mrs R did become pregnant and suffered psychiatric injury on learning that her life expectancy was reduced. In addition to a claim for general damages she sought compensation for the cost of bringing up her baby who was born healthy. Breach of duty was admitted and most of the argument in the case turned on quantum.

What is interesting about this case is that it appears from the reports that the argument that no duty of care was owed to the claimant was not presented. There were arguments turning on the *scope* of the duty, (eg whether it extended to warning that pregnancy should be avoided), but these arguments proceeded on the assumption that a duty of some kind was owed to the claimant. The trial judge had concluded that pregnancy and its consequences were the kind of damage from which the defendant health authority must take care to save a claimant suffering from such a serious medical condition. After acknowledging the strong interrelationship between duty of care, breach and damage in negligence, Chadwick LJ dealing with the question of remoteness of damage, commented:

> '*In my view, a proper examination of the facts in the present case leads to the conclusion that, whatever the duty of care owed to the plaintiff by the health authority as her prospective employer, the scope and extent of that duty stopped short of responsibility for the consequences of the decision by the plaintiff and her husband that she should become pregnant.*'

---

48   (1996) 39 BMLR 12.
49   (1998) 46 BMLR 176.
50   (1997) 40 BMLR 40.

The Court of Appeal concluded that it was important to bear in mind the relationship between the claimant and the defendants, which was that of employer and prospective employee. The claimant's domestic circumstances were of no concern to the radiologist even though the defendant was required to take the victim as he found her. There was no award for the cost of bringing up the child in these circumstances (though damages were awarded to cover pain and suffering in connection with the heart catheterisation which could have been avoided if an earlier diagnosis had been made) any complications of the hysterectomy that the claimant had undergone and the exacerbation of reactive depression. The case suggests[51] that a duty of care is more likely to be owed if the claimant is physically examined by a doctor and some serious medical condition is overlooked, so that physical illness rather than economic loss is suffered as a consequence. Much would depend upon the precise facts of the case and the view of the court on application of *Caparo v Dickman* (supra).

Diana Kloss[52] argues that the decision in *Spring v Guardian Assurance*[53] means that by analogy there is a duty of care owed by doctors carrying out pre-employment medical examinations to those who are examined. This view is certainly tenable, and the implementation of the Human Rights Act 1998 suggests that there are strong grounds for arguing that there is a duty to disclose the existence of a life-threatening disease.

A worrying decision on a related point is that in the case of *London Borough of Hammersmith & Fulham v Farnsworth*[54] as it has far-reaching consequences for occupational health physicians. Ms Farnsworth was offered a post as a residential social worker for the local authority, but the offer was subject to a satisfactory medical examination. She completed a health questionnaire that revealed a history of depression including several admissions to hospital, the last one for four days approximately 18 months before the job offer was made. The council's occupational physician, Dr Cooper examined her, and requested further information from Ms Farnsworth's own doctor, having obtained consent to do so using a standard form. Ms Farnsworth's general practitioner stated that her health had been good during the past year, but the occupational physician wrote to the employers saying that he was concerned that she might be liable to further recurrences of illness. The letter continued: *'If such a recurrence were to occur her performance and attendance at work could be affected.'*

The council, relying on this, withdrew their offer of employment, and Ms Farnsworth took the matter to the Employment Tribunal on the grounds that she had been discriminated against because of her disability and that the council was in breach of the Disability Discrimination Act 1995. The ET found in her favour and the council appealed, stating that they could not be held to have known that Ms Farnsworth had a disability because that was not disclosed to them by Dr Cooper, on the basis that she was under a duty of confidentiality to Ms Farnsworth. She had advised the council only in general terms. This point was considered on appeal and it was held that Dr Cooper was not bound by any duty of confidence owed to Ms Farnsworth not to disclose details of her medical condition to those who needed to

---

51   See Grubb A, 6 Med Law Rev 364.

52   *Pre-employment Health Screening* in *Law and Medicine*, Current Legal Issues, Volume 3, ed Freeman M and Lewis A, OUP 2000. This article examines the law in other jurisdictions.

53   [1995] 2 AC 296. This case concerned the duty to take care when writing a reference for employment purposes.

54   [2000] IRLR 1691.

know about it in order to make a decision about her future employment. The view was that the health questionnaire and the consent form completed by Ms Farnsworth were headed *'London Borough of Hammersmith and Fulham'*. It should have been clear that she was consenting to information being collected on behalf of the council despite the fact that the questionnaire contained the statement that *'All information will be treated as strictly confidential'*. It therefore appears that even if there was a duty of care owed to the patient in negligence, that duty may not coincide with a concurrent duty of confidentiality[55].

People belonging to an indeterminate class

There is no duty of care owed to people who are members of an *'indeterminate class'* of potential victims. In theory, such individuals would not be foreseeable to the defendant, and there would be insufficient proximity between the parties, as required by the second of the criteria stated in *Caparo v Dickman*. In *Goodwill v The British Pregnancy Advisory Service*[56] a patient, M, had arranged through the BPAS to undergo a vasectomy operation. They had advised him in 1985 that as the operation had been a success he did not need to use any form of contraception in future. In 1988 M began a new sexual relationship with the claimant and in reliance on the advice given to M in 1985, no contraception was used. She became pregnant by M, and gave birth to a healthy daughter. The claimant sought damages from the defendants for the delivery and upbringing of the child on the basis that she had relied upon the negligent advice given by them to M. It was held by the Court of Appeal that no duty of care was owed by the defendants to the claimant in advising M. They could not at that time have known that their advice would have been acted on by the claimant, as she was a member of an indeterminate class of women who might one day become sexual partners of M. There was therefore insufficient proximity in the relationship between the claimant and the defendants to justify imposing a duty of care. It is likely however, that the duty of care would have been owed to M's current sexual partner when the advice was given, as long as the doctor was aware of her existence. Gibson LJ explained that the *'... Doctor is concerned only with the man, his patient, and possibly with that man's wife or partner if the doctor intends her to receive, and she receives advice from the doctor in relation to the vasectomy and the subsequent tests'*.

Wrongful life

There is no duty of care owed in relation to *'wrongful life'*. This means that the courts have ruled that on the grounds of public policy, no-one can claim damages on the basis that they should never have been allowed to be born. Wrongful life cases should be distinguished from *'wrongful birth'* cases which are legitimate claims arising from unwanted pregnancies following sterilisation, missed abortion, or failure to warn about the risks of a pregnancy[57]. While damages are awarded for wrongful birth, their scope has recently been drastically restricted.[58]

McKay v Essex Area Health Authority[59] is an example of a claim for wrongful life. An action for damages was brought on behalf of a child who had been born with severe deformities. It was claimed that her mother had been given negligent treatment and testing during early pregnancy when she was suffering from rubella,

---

55   See Waldron A, *Health Law*, April 2001, p1.

56   [1996] 2 WLR 161.

57   *R v Croydon Health Authority* (1997) 40 BMLR 40.

58   *McFarlane v Tayside Health Board* [1999] 3 WLR 1301.

59   [1982] QB 1166.

and that she had not been informed early in her pregnancy that her baby was likely to be born with deformities. The mother stated that she would have requested a termination of the pregnancy if she had been properly counselled at an early stage. The Court of Appeal rejected the claim. However, the mother of the child was able to bring an action in her own right for damages to cover for the personal and financial harm which she had suffered as a result of giving birth to a handicapped child.

By contrast, the highest French appeal court has ruled that a teenager was entitled to an award of damages for wrongful life. The claimant, Nicolas Perruche, was born severely mentally and physically disabled, and was the son of a woman who had contracted rubella when she was pregnant with him. Despite tests, her illness had not been diagnosed at the time, but she was able to convince the court that she would have requested an abortion had she been found to be suffering from rubella.

Third parties

There is no duty of care owed to people outside the immediate doctor/patient relationship. Predictably the courts have been reluctant to extend the duty of care beyond the person who is receiving the medical treatment, even when in reality, it is foreseeable that a third party would suffer as a result of any negligent treatment. An exception lies in the cases involving psychiatric injury suffered by close relatives of patients who are present when the negligent treatment is given, and who witness its effects at first hand.

The question of whether there is a duty to tell relatives of a patient the truth about medical conditions from which their loved-ones are suffering was considered by the Court of Appeal in *Powell and another v Boldaz and others*[60]. Parents of a ten-year-old boy brought an action against five GPs who had allegedly hidden the truth about the circumstances surrounding their son's death. The claimants had brought an action for damages under the Law Reform (Miscellaneous Provisions) Act 1934 and the Fatal Accidents Act 1976. The boy had died of Addison's disease which is rare, could have been treated successfully if it had been dealt with at an early stage. The claimants alleged that failure to diagnose the illness amounted to negligence. The claim for negligence against the health authority had been settled out-of-court, and the settlement included a substantial sum in connection with psychiatric injury suffered by the boy's mother. However, the claimants continued to pursue the claim in respect of an alleged *'cover-up'* of the truth after the boy's death, which had involved the removal of documents from the medical records and their substitution with further papers. These events, they claimed, had caused economic loss, psychiatric injury to the boy's father and an exacerbation of the mother's psychiatric injury.

The case before the Court of Appeal was an appeal against the order of Butterfield J to strike out parts of the claimants' statement of claim under Order 18 r19 of the Rules of the Supreme Court on the grounds that they failed to disclose a reasonable cause of action, and were scandalous, frivolous or vexatious and amounted to an abuse of process. The appeal was dismissed on the grounds that any duty of care had been owed by the doctors to the boy and not to his parents. This was based on the view that when a doctor informs the relatives of a deceased person of the death, he does not assume a doctor-patient relationship towards them even if they are registered as his patients. Nor in general terms is there a duty of candour which exists separately from the doctor-patient relationship. No duty in respect of bereavement counselling had been established on the facts of the case, and there was insufficient

---

60   (1997) 39 BMLR 35.

proximity between the doctors and the claimants to establish a duty of care in relation to psychiatric injury, which was not reasonably foreseeable[61].

Stuart-Smith LJ concluded: *'I do not think that a doctor who has been treating a patient who has died and who tells relatives what has happened thereby undertakes the doctor-patient relationship towards the relatives. It is a situation that calls for sensitivity, tact and discretion. But the fact that the communicator is a doctor does not mean he undertakes the doctor-patient relationship.'*

Although there are those who would argue that the ethical principle of veracity should be supported in the context of healthcare generally, it would have been very surprising if the Court of Appeal had been prepared to acknowledge the existence of a legal *'duty of candour'* to relatives outside any doctor-patient relationship. As Stuart-Smith LJ explained: *'This would involve a startling expansion of liability.'* Nevertheless, there is an argument that the relationship between counsellor and client is one of sufficient proximity to give rise to a duty of care in certain circumstances and the decision in this case might not preclude the possibility of successful actions in later cases if the facts warrant this[62].

The Health Service Commissioner has commented in several of his reports that many justifiable complaints arise from poor communication between staff, patients and their relatives, especially in the context of bereavement counselling. The Royal College of Physicians has published a report entitled *Improving Communication Between Doctors and Patients*, recommending that doctors be given better training in communication skills, especially in relation to breaking bad news. They suggest *that training should begin in medical school and be interwoven throughout the curriculum. It recommends that guidance be obtained from other professional groups who have experience in this field. It is clear from the report of the Redfern Inquiry into the retention of organs and tissue at Alder Hey Childrens' Hospital that bereaved families suffer great distress if they are given inaccurate or incomplete information about their dead children. That report recommends that healthcare staff should receive counselling about how to deal with the bereaved.*

Secondary victims of psychiatric injury: special requirements

While the law has little difficulty in recognising the existence of a duty of care to primary victims who are directly involved in traumatic events, the position of secondary victims is more tenuous. A secondary victim is *'a passive and unwilling witness of injury to others'* – perhaps a bystander or a rescuer, or a relative who identifies a loved-one shortly after an accident. In *Cullin and Others v London Fire & Civil Defence Authority*[63] the Court of Appeal held that the issue as to whether the claimants were primary or secondary victims was a question of mixed fact and law. Claims by secondary victims are frequently ruled out by the courts on the basis that there is insufficient proximity[64] between the victim and the person who caused the injury.

Traditionally, courts have been sceptical about claims by secondary victims for psychiatric injury partly because in the early years of the twentieth century, when claims of this kind first began to arise, little was known about the nature of psychiatric illness, and it was feared that some individuals might try to fake symptoms in order to secure compensation. There was a certain amount of scepticism about expert

---

61 This case is of interest in the light of claims by relatives of deceased children against Alder Hey Hospital who were not informed that organs and tissue had been removed.

62 See Kennedy and Grubb, *Principles of Medical Law* Butterworths London, para 5.8.

63 Unreported 1999.

64 ie under the second of the criteria stated in *Caparo v Dickman* (supra).

psychiatric evidence which could be very contradictory, and the judges were concerned about ensuring fairness to defendants[65] and about the cost of funding compensation and its effect on insurers[66]. In more recent cases, although it is recognised that some people do suffer psychiatric injury as a result of witnessing horrific events, judges have taken the view that there is a risk that litigation is sometimes an unconscious disincentive to rehabilitation,[67] and that to open the floodgates by allowing too many situations in which a duty of care is owed for psychiatric injury would result in an unacceptably high number of claims[68]. The courts have taken the view that it is difficult to distinguish between acute grief and psychiatric injury, and to expand the scope of recognised claims might provoke further claims and impose disproportionate liability on defendants in situations where physical harm to the claimant could not reasonably have been foreseen.

The first hurdle for the claimant, (whether a primary or secondary victim), is to establish that he or she is suffering from a recognisable psychiatric condition as outlined above, and not simply from grief, distress or some transient medical condition[69]. In *Fraser v State Hospital Board For Scotland*[70] a claim was made by an employee as a secondary victim for psychiatric harm suffered in the course of employment. The Court of Session, Outer House, held that the condition suffered by the employee in this case amounted to no more than unpleasant emotions. This had not involved any physical injury, and psychiatric injury was not foreseeable. It followed that the claim failed.

A crucial difference between the claims of primary and secondary victims has developed. The criteria for determining whether a duty of care is owed to the secondary victim of psychiatric injury are set out in the case of *Alcock v Chief Constable of South Yorkshire*[71]. These are as follows:

- There must be sufficient proximity in time and space between the claimant and the scene of the accident. If the person claiming is not directly involved in the incident he or she must have seen or heard the incident or come upon it in the *'immediate aftermath'*.

- There must be a close relationship – a tie of love and affection between the claimant and the person who is injured or killed in a traumatic event.

- The shock must be experienced by the claimant through his or her own senses.

Further, it has also been established that for a secondary victim to succeed in a claim for psychiatric injury, it must have been foreseeable to the defendant that a person of normal fortitude would have suffered a similar injury[72]. For a primary victim to succeed, it need only be established that physical injury of some kind was foreseeable[73].

Staughton LJ restated the rationale for the *Alcock* principle in these terms in *Sion v Hampstead Health Authority*[74]:

> *'It is ... recognised almost universally that the common law ought to impose some limit on the circumstances in which a person can recover damages for the*

---

65   For a discussion of the policy issues involved see *McLoughlin v O'Brian* [1983] AC 410.

66   *McLoughlin v O'Brian* [1983] AC 410.

67   See Lord Hoffmann's speech in *White v Chief Constable of South Yorkshire* [1998] 3 WLR 1510.

68   See Lord Steyn's speech in *White v Chief Constable of South Yorkshire*]1998] 3 WLR 1510.

69   See Lord Bridge in *Alcock v Chief Constable of South Yorkshire*, op cit.

70   The Times 12 December 2000.

71   [1991] 4 All ER 907.

72   This was reiterated and explained by Lord Slynn in *W v Essex County Council* The Times 17 March 2000.

73   *Page v Smith* [1994] 4 All ER 522.

74   (1994) 5 Med LR 170.

negligence of another. The common law has to choose a frontier between those whose claims succeed and those who fail. Even the resources of insurance companies are finite.'

The effect of the Alcock case has been to restrict the number of successful claims for psychiatric injury. For example, usually only close relatives are now successful and then only if they can prove a tie of love and affection with the accident victim. Rescuers who witnessed scenes of horror used to succeed in claims for psychiatric injury[75], but will now only be successful if they can prove a tie of love and affection[76]. There is continued emphasis on the need for a secondary victim to be present at the scene of the accident or to arrive in the immediate aftermath. In *Taylor v Somerset Area Health Authority*[77] a widow whose husband had suffered a heart attack because of the failure of a doctor to diagnose his condition, was unsuccessful in her claim. She was not present when he died, nor did she see him in the *'immediate aftermath'* of what can properly be regarded as a *'traumatic event'*. Even though she had identified his body within an hour of death, she did so at her own request to satisfy her disbelief, and there were no visible marks on the body.

The case of *Sion v Hampstead Health Authority* suggests that for a claimant to succeed there must usually be a single sudden shock rather than a steady accumulation of events culminating in psychiatric injury. The claimant in that case suffered a psychiatric illness as a result of attending intensive care and realising that medical negligence had caused the injuries suffered by her loved-one. Peter Gibson LJ said:

'A psychiatric illness caused not by a sudden shock but by an accumulation of more gradual assaults on the nervous system over a period of time is not enough.'

Despite the recent restrictions on the scope of the duty owed in relation to psychiatric injury, the case of *W v Essex County Council and Another*[78] indicates that the courts are prepared to contemplate extending the scope of the duty of care and that the law in this area is still developing. The claimants were specialist adolescent foster carers. They had explained when they were approved by the local authority that they were unwilling to foster any child suspected of sexually abusing another. The council placed a 15-year-old boy, G, in the family. G had been cautioned by the police for an indecent assault on his own sister and was being investigated for an alleged rape. The claimants were not informed of these facts, even though there was a record of them on the council's files and despite the fact that they were known to the social worker concerned.

G allegedly committed serious acts of sexual abuse against the claimants' children (who were also claiming against the council) over a period of one month in 1993 after the boy had arrived at the foster home. Both parents and their four children claimed that they had suffered injury as a result of what had happened. The parents' claim was based on psychiatric injury alone. They alleged that when they discovered the sexual abuse on their children, including anal and vaginal penetration and oral sex, they suffered psychiatric illness including severe depression and post-traumatic stress disorder.

The defendants applied to strike out the claims, and at first instance the judge did strike out all the claims made by the parents, but refused to strike out the claims of

---

75   *Chadwick v British Railways Board* [1967] 1 WLR 912.

76   *White v Chief Constable of South Yorkshire* [1998] 1 WLR 1510.

77   (1993) 4 Med LR 94.

78   The Times 17 March 2000.

the children. The Court of Appeal, on 2 April 1998, upheld the judge's order in respect of the children's claim in negligence, and unanimously upheld the order in respect of the parents' claim. By the time of the House of Lords hearing, the defendants had accepted that the claim by the children should proceed. The parents argued that the claim for their own injury should proceed to trial, contending that the defendants were negligent in placing a known sex abuser in their home when they knew of G's history and of the foster parents' understandable anxiety not to have a sex abuser in their home with four young children.

Lord Slynn explained that the power to strike cases out must be exercised with care, but that it would not be necessary to prove at this stage that the parents' claim would definitely succeed if the case came to trial. Lord Browne-Wilkinson said that where the law is not settled, but is in a state of development (as in the present case), it is normally inappropriate to decide novel questions on hypothetical facts. In *Barrett v Enfield London Borough Council*[79] Lord Browne-Wilkinson had repeated what he had said in *X (minors)*. In the same case, Lord Slynn had himself taken the view that the question whether it is just and reasonable to impose liability for negligence is not to be decided in the abstract for all acts or omissions, *'but is to be decided on the basis of what is proved'.*

The defendants argued that only if the parents were within the range of foreseeable physical injury were they primary victims. They contended that the parents were not *'participants'* in the traumatic events. The injury was to their children, and it was not foreseeable that if G was placed with the family the parents would suffer injury. On that basis they argued that the parents were only secondary victims, and a duty of care would only be owed to them in relation to psychiatric injury if it was foreseeable that a person of normal fortitude would suffer such injury in the same circumstances. Although the parents had the necessary ties of love for their children, the defence argued strongly that they were not close enough in time or space to the acts of abuse, and they did not have direct visual or oral perception of the incident or its aftermath – the parents only knew about the incidents after they had happened.

The defendants also rejected any suggestion that the parents could claim to be entitled to damages because they felt that they had participated in, or contributed to or laid the foundation for the commission of the acts of abuse on their children by arranging for G to be brought into their home. The parents, argued the defence, are in the same position as a person who suffers shock on being told of the death of a loved one – a claim not recognised by the law.

Lord Slynn concluded that the claim in *W v Essex* was arguable on the facts that had been alleged and should not be struck out. The parents had made it clear that they were anxious not to put their children at risk by having a known sex abuser in their home. The council and the social worker knew this and also knew that the boy concerned had already committed acts of sex abuse. The risk was obvious and the abuse actually happened. Whether the court should recognise an actionable duty of care, and whether there was a breach of the duty depended on an investigation of the full facts of the case. It was important, in his Lordship's opinion, in the present case, to bear in mind all of the relevant policy factors, together with the limitations stipulated in *Alcock*. However, Lord Slynn said that it is right to recall that in *McLoughlin v O'Brian* Lord Scarman recognised the need for flexibility in dealing

---

79   [1999] 3 WLR 79 In this case, the House of Lords concluded that the question whether it is just and reasonable to impose a duty of care should not be decided in the abstract for all time, but each case should be considered on its own facts.

with new situations not clearly covered by existing case law, and that in *Page v Smith*[80], Lord Lloyd said that once it is accepted that a defendant could foresee that his conduct would expose the claimant to personal injury *'there is no justification for regarding physical and psychiatric injury as different "kinds of damage"'*

The House of Lords took the view that the psychiatric injuries sustained by the parents amounted to more than *'acute grief'*. The parents' happy marriage had broken up, and both had suffered reactive depression and could no longer act as foster parents. Their sex lives had been ruined. The effect on the entire family had been devastating.

The question of whether the parents were primary or secondary victims was not absolutely clear, and the categorisation of primary and secondary victims was not finally closed. If the psychiatric injury suffered by the parents flowed from a feeling that they brought the abuser and the abused together or that they had a feeling of responsibility that they did not detect earlier what was happening, that did not necessarily prevent them from being primary victims. Indeed, in *Alcock* Lord Oliver said:

> *'The fact that the defendant's negligent conduct has foreseeably put the claimant in the position of being an unwilling participant in the event establishes of itself a sufficiently proximate relationship between them and the principal question is whether, in the circumstances, injury of that type to that claimant was or was not reasonably foreseeable.'*

The House of Lords unanimously dismissed the appeal by the local authority.

It is important to recognise that the law concerning psychiatric injury is still developing and the courts must proceed incrementally (*Caparo Industries plc v Dickman*). *W v Essex County Council* is a case which suggests that there is considerable scope for clarifying and even developing the law, especially in the light of the Human Rights Act 1998 and the jurisprudence of the European Court of Human Rights. There are several matters in relation to psychiatric injury that still require clarification, and this claim highlights some of them. They include: the precise scope of the category of *'primary victims'*; the extent of the limitation as to time and space placed on claims of secondary victims; whether it is possible to include in the category of those entitled to succeed, individuals who believe that they have failed in their responsibility to primary victims; the justification for distinguishing between foresight of physical and psychiatric injury.

Law Commission proposals

The Law Commission Report, number 249, accompanied by a draft Bill, recommended legislation to reform the law on damages for psychiatric injury. The present law, as established in the leading case of *Alcock v Chief Constable of South Yorkshire Police*, limits the circumstances under which people who suffer psychiatric illness as a result of negligent injury to relatives or friends, can claim damages. The Law Commission Report recognises the inequities of the present rules which mean that some people who suffer disabling psychiatric conditions are excluded from the present narrow category of claimants. Such distinctions are regarded by the Law Commission as arbitrary and unjust, but it also acknowledges the concerns of those who fear too wide a sphere of potential liability and the opening of the litigation floodgates.

---

80   [1996] 1 AC 155.

The report recommends that the most rational way of limiting the potential flood of claimants is to extend the possibility of making a claim for psychiatric injury to all those who are able to prove a close tie of love and affection with the primary accident victim, while removing the restrictions based on proximity to the accident and direct perception of it through the senses.

Victims of psychiatric patients

The cases decided to date in UK law suggest that there is no general duty of care owed to previously unidentified victims of criminal acts carried out by psychiatric patients. However, it is possible, in the light of more recent developments, that a future court could find that a duty arises if the particular victim is known by the doctors concerned to be at serious risk, and it is foreseeable that the patient is likely to inflict injury on the victim.

Victims of psychiatric patients can be classified within the general category of people who are regarded as members of an indeterminate class. The question of whether a public body owes a duty of care in negligence to the potential victim of a sick person under its care, was raised by the case of *Palmer v Tees Health Authority and Hartlepool and East Durham NHS Trust*[81]. In that case the mother of a murdered child sought damages from the health authority caring for the murderer at the time of the crime. In 1994 Rosie Palmer, a four-year-old girl, was abducted, sexually assaulted and murdered by a psychiatric patient living in the community. The man, who has now been convicted of the offences, had been released into the community and housed on a council estate despite warnings from a senior social worker that he was likely to be a danger to children. Mrs Palmer brought a claim on behalf of the estate of her dead child under the Law Reform (Miscellaneous Proceedings) Act 1934 for the pain and suffering endured by her before her death, and on her own behalf for post traumatic stress disorder and pathological grief disorder. She contended that defendants had been negligent in failing to diagnose the real, substantial and serious risk that S would sexually abuse children.

The case raised interesting issues of foresight and proximity, which suggested from the outset that it would be difficult for the claimant to succeed. There was a definite reluctance on the part of the English courts, for policy reasons, to find public authorities liable to the victims of crimes committed by people for whom they are responsible[82]. Mrs Palmer, in her own claim as a secondary victim suffering post traumatic stress disorder, faced substantial difficulties as a result of the ruling in *Alcock v Chief Constable of South Yorkshire*[83]. The most difficult hurdles for secondary victims like Mrs Palmer to surmount, are those concerned with establishing proximity in time and space between their relative and the traumatic event. In cases where there has been a public inquiry into an incident it may be easier to establish liability, but in this case the inquiry had concluded that despite the fact that the authorities had been at fault at several points, the particular risk was not foreseeable.

The trial judge had ruled that the claim should be struck because there was insufficient proximity between the mother of the murdered child and the defendants. On appeal, Mrs Palmer argued that the decision in *Barrett v London Borough of Enfield*[84] had brought about a change in the courts' approach to striking out claims on the basis that the facts pleaded did not give rise to a duty of care.

---

81   (1999) Lloyd's Rep Med 351.
82   In *Hill v Chief Constable of West Yorkshire Police* (1988) 2 WLR 1042 the police were held not liable for the death of Jacqueline Hill, the last victim of the Yorkshire Ripper.
83   (1991) 4 WLR 907.
84   (1999) TLR 18 June.

In the event, the Court of Appeal held that for the mother of the murdered child to succeed in an action alleging a breach of a duty of care by a health authority treating an outpatient sex offender, it was necessary to show that the murder of the child was foreseeable and that there was a sufficient proximity between the child and the health authority. The Court of Appeal took the view that *Hill v Chief Constable of West Yorkshire*[85] was critical to the case of Rosie Palmer and her mother. Although the facts in that case differed from those in the present case, in *Hill* the crucial point was that there had been no relationship between the defendant and the victim. In this case the victim (and her mother) were not identifiable as persons who might suffer damage, and were not foreseeable as identifiable individuals. There was no proximity between them, the murderer and the respondents, who could not have known to have warned them about the danger, even if it had been realised. Accordingly, the Court of Appeal took the view that the trial judge had correctly decided that there was no proximity as between the respondents and the murdered child, and the action failed. The appeal was dismissed.

The White Paper[86] on the reform of mental health law anticipates that greater powers will be given to doctors to treat patients compulsorily in the community, and there is a possibility that in future their responsibilities to people living in the community with their patients might increase.

The American case of *Tarasoff v The Regents of the University of California*[87] suggests there is room for an expansion of the scope of the duty of care to cover situations similar to that in the *Palmer* case. There a student patient had informed his psychiatric counsellor that he intended to kill a woman student. The psychiatrist did not warn the woman concerned and she was killed by the patient. It was held that the psychiatrist had been negligent. The case is distinguishable from *Palmer* because the claimant was identifiable.

Wrongful Birth: There is no duty of care in relation to the cost of bringing up a healthy child born as a result of a failed vasectomy or unsuccessful female sterilisation *(McFarlane v Tayside Health Board 2000)*. If a child that is born as a result of negligence is disabled, the duty only extends to the cost of providing for the disability, and not for the cost of other aspects of child-rearing (*Carver v Hammersmith and Queen Charlotte's Special NHS Hospital Trust*[88]).

In *McFarlane v Tayside Health Board*[89], the House of Lords ruled that the cost of bringing up a child born after an unsuccessful sterilisation operation was an *'economic loss'*. There is a large body of case law dealing with the question of whether a duty of care is owed not to cause economic loss – but the matter had seldom been considered before the higher courts in the context of healthcare. In *McFarlane*, the claimants, who were married, had been assured by doctors employed by the Health Board, that the husband was no longer fertile after his vasectomy operation. However, the wife became pregnant, and gave birth to a healthy daughter in May 1992. Mr and Mrs McFarlane claimed general damages of £10,000 for the pain and distress suffered by Mrs McFarlane during the pregnancy and birth, and also a sum of £100,000 to cover the cost already incurred and likely to be incurred in

85   [1998] 2 WLR 1049.
86   HMSO December 2000.
87   (1976) 131 Cal Retr 14 (Cal Sup Ct).
88   2000 unreported.
89   [1999] 3 WLR 1301.

the future in bringing up the child. The parents had accepted the child into the family, even though, for economic reasons, they had not wanted another baby.

The House of Lords reviewed the earlier cases in the UK and in other jurisdictions dealing with damages for failed sterilisation. It was recognised by all but Lord Millet that the claim by the mother for the pain and inconvenience of child-bearing should be compensated. Although different approaches were taken by each judge to the question of compensation for the cost of rearing the child, they were unanimous in their view that these expenses should not be recoverable in law.

Lord Slynn regarded the claim as one within the broad category of economic loss, and treated it cautiously, because of the traditional reluctance of judges to find that there is a duty of care in relation to pure economic loss, where there is no closer link between the act and the damage. His Lordship concluded that it would not be fair, just and reasonable to impose a duty on the doctor or his employer in this case *(Caparo Industries v Dickman*[90]*)*.

Lord Steyn did not consider the question of duty of care in depth, but concentrated on the question of distributive justice, taking the view that law and morality are linked inextricably, and although there might be some objections to the fact that the House of Lords acts, on occasion, as a court of morals, positive justice should be regarded. He approached the matter from the perspective of the *'notional commuter on the Underground'*, concluding that such a person would not be in favour of compensating the parents for the cost of bringing up the child to her 18th birthday. His Lordship was anxious not to perpetuate the practice of masking the true reasons for the decision with formalistic propositions by denying a remedy on the grounds that there was no foreseeable loss or no causative link between the act of negligence and the damage, saying:

> *'Judges ought to strive to give the real reasons for their decisions. It is my firm conviction that where judges have denied a remedy for the cost of bringing up an unwanted child, the real reasons have been grounds of distributive justice ... Judges' sense of the moral answer to a question, or the justice of the case, has been one of the great shaping forces of the common law.'*

Lord Hope attempted to strike a balance between the intangible benefits to parents of love and affection, and in later life, support from their children, and the burdonsome cost of child-rearing. He was of the view that it would not be fair, just or reasonable to leave these intangible benefits out of the balance. As it is impossible to calculate the cost of those benefits in money terms and set them off accurately against the cost of bringing up the child, he argued that the costs to the parents of meeting their obligations to the child during her childhood were not recoverable as damages.

Lord Clyde took the traditional approach of tort law, pointing out that damages should put the injured party in the same position as he would have been in if he had not sustained the wrong. In this instance, without giving up their child, the parents could not possibly be put into the same position as they would have been in had the negligent act never been committed. To relieve the parents of their financial obligations towards the child did not seem reasonable because it would be going beyond what should constitute *'reasonable restitution'*.

Lord Millett explained that the admissibility of any head of damages is a matter of law, and if the law took the approach that an event was beneficial, claimants could

---

90   [1990] 2 AC 605.

not make it a matter for compensation, simply by arguing that they had not wanted that event to happen. In his view:

'Claimants are not normally allowed, by a process of subjective devaluation, to make a detriment out of a benefit ... The law must take the birth of a normal healthy baby to be a blessing, not a detriment.'

This sentiment echoes the decision in the earliest case on this point to be decided by a UK court – *Udale v Bloomsbury Health Authority*[91]. There the judge observed that although this world be a vale of tears, the birth of a child is *'a blessing and an occasion for rejoicing'*. It was not until two years later that the case of *Emeh v Kensington and Chelsea Health Authority*[92], established that claims for the cost of bringing up a child could succeed. Many couples who had been able to establish negligence in failed sterilisation cases have since received the benefit of large settlements or court awards. The ruling in the *McFarlane* case is to be welcomed, because the law in this area is now certain, at least if the child is born healthy.

It is surely correct that the woman who has to carry the child, suffer the discomfort of pregnancy, and undergo the pain of labour and delivery should be compensated in a case of this kind. Only Lord Millett, who regarded pregnancy and birth as natural processes, took the view that such personal discomfort did not deserve compensation. The £10,000 awarded to Mrs McFarlane for pain and suffering was substantially higher than that suggested in the Judicial Studies Board guidelines of £3,000 to £4,000.

The *McFarlane* approach was confirmed in *Rand v East Dorset Health Authority*[93] where the defendants admitted that their negligence had resulted in the wrongful birth of a disabled child. In January 1988 doctors negligently failed to inform Mr and Mrs Rand of the results of a prenatal scan that indicated the likelihood that Mrs Rand was pregnant with a Down's Syndrome baby. The defence agreed that this negligent omission had deprived the couple of the opportunity to have this pregnancy terminated, and that if they had known of the Down's baby the wife would have had the pregnancy terminated. The parents claimed for the financial consequences flowing from that negligence. The judge accepted that the claim was based on the principle in *Hedley Byrne & Co Ltd v Heller & Partners Ltd*[94] for the financial consequences due to the defendant's negligence, limited to the consequences of a child's disability. The claim for the cost of care for the child was a claim for pure economic loss, because it included the claim for loss of profits of a residential care home run by the claimants.

These cases are also discussed in relation to quantum in a later chapter. See also *Greenfield v Flather*[95], and *Parkinson v St James and Seacroft University Hospital NHS Trust*[96].

Treatment in the community

There is no common law duty on health authorities to treat patients in the community with reasonable care and skill. In *Clunis v Camden and Islington Health Authority*[97] the claimant had been diagnosed as suffering from schizophrenia, and had been

---

91   [1983] 1 WLR 1098.

92   [1985] 1 QB 1012.

93   (2000) 57 BMLR 158.

94   [1963] 3 WLR 101.

95   The Times 6 February [2001] EWCA Civ 113 and *Health Law* May 2001, p1.

96   The Times 24 April 2001.

97   The Times 10 December 1997.

convicted of manslaughter after he had killed a stranger during an unprovoked attack. He brought a claim against the health authority for breach of the duty to treat him with reasonable care and skill while he was living in the community. The Court of Appeal held that there is no common law duty running parallel with the statutory duty of a health authority to provide aftercare services under the Mental Health Act 1983[98] and his claim was unsuccessful. It should be noted that now both the Health Act 1999 and the Care Standards Act 2000 will impose additional duties on healthcarers to ensure that the uniformly high quality care is delivered to all patients throughout the country. These duties are superimposed on any common law duty of care that might be owed.

The Secretary of State and individual patients

Claims against the Secretary of State usually arise as judicial review cases if there is an allegation that the Secretary of State has acted *ultra vires*. There is usually insufficient proximity between the Secretary of State and the individual patient to give rise to the existence of a duty of care in common law negligence[99]. In *Danns v Department of Health*[100], Roch LJ explained the rationale of this in these terms:

> *'The Department did not owe the claimant a duty of care at common law to take reasonable care, for the reason that there did not exist as between the claimant and defendants that degree of proximity which the law requires.'*

Although it is apparent that the courts are reluctant to enter into an evaluation of the exercise of political or administrative discretion, there are a few cases where the courts have accepted that there may be some merit in considering whether a duty of care in negligence might arise[101].

However, as will be seen in the section that follows, an action for breach of statutory duty may be available if the Secretary of State exercises a statutory power in a manner that is *ultra vires* (beyond the powers given in the statute or statutory instrument).

Dealing with the Grey Areas

It follows from the above outline that there are certain *'grey areas'* in which it is difficult to predict the outcome of cases. In such instances, the judges allow themselves considerable discretion, and frequently arrive at their decisions on grounds of public policy (see the criteria in *Caparo v Dickman*, above). Certainty in the law is important, but it is a feature of our legal system that the law is able to adapt and develop according to changing conditions and new developments such as the Human Rights Act 1998. It is important to bear this in mind when faced with difficult cases.

If, for example a case were to arise based on a novel set of facts, a judge would be required to apply the criteria in *Caparo v Dickman* and also to take into account human rights issues. It is possible to envisage such a novel situation arising in relation to the question of whether there is a duty of care in negligence to disclose that a colleague is incompetent and is putting patients' lives in danger or exposing them to inhuman and degrading treatment[102]. In the light of the European Convention on Human Rights, and

---

98   Section 117.

99   But see Re: *HIV Haemophiliac Litigation* (1990) 41 BMLR 171.

100   *Danns v Department of Health* [1998] PIQR 226 (CA).

101   Re *HIV Haemophiliac Litigation* (1990) 41 BMLR 171; [1996] PNLR 290.

102   For example, it appears that colleagues of the surgeons at the Bristol Royal Infirmary Paediatric Cardiac Unit who were struck off the Medical Register as a result of incompetence, knew that children may have been at risk. The question is whether they had a duty to disclose information about their suspicions to a competent person in authority. As far as negligence claims are concerned the question is academic because there would be vicarious liability on the part of the NHS Trust if there had been negligence on the part of the surgeons. At the time of writing the Inquiry into what happened at Bristol has not reported its findings.

the current climate of openness in the NHS, and taking into account developments outside the law of negligence in clinical governance and professional regulation, it is arguable that a court would find that it is fair just and reasonable to impose a duty to disclose such information to a competent person in authority.

Negligence and Breach of Statutory Duty

Most claims in healthcare cases are for negligence, and in these cases the duty of care arises at common law, as explained above. However, in rare circumstances, when a statute also gives rise to duties in tort[103], an action for breach of statutory duty may be brought.

Breach of statutory duty

If a patient wishes to bring an action for breach of statutory duty, the court will be required to scrutinise the particular statute in question. The main object of the statute forming the basis of the claim could well be the imposition of a regulatory or criminal law framework of liability, but in some circumstances a claimant may succeed in a civil action for damages even though the defendant is in breach of a duty imposed by a statute which was not primarily intended to create liability in tort. There is now a substantial body of regulatory law covering a wide range of healthcare activities. We are not concerned here with the many regulations relating to health and safety at work and employers' liability, which form the basis of claims by health service employees. The chief concern in this book is with the doctor-patient relationship and with the provision of services to patients. Most of the regulations relating to health and safety have as their main purpose the prevention of accidents, rather than compensation for injury suffered by accident victims. It is unusual for a regulatory framework to create a right of action in civil law.

The tort of breach of statutory duty, like the tort of negligence, offers a private law remedy, but the two torts are entirely separate. However, in appropriate cases it is common to plead both negligence and breach of statutory duty, and there are many cases in which both torts are discussed. The distinction between negligence and breach of statutory duty was explained in *X v Bedfordshire County Council*[104] by Lord Browne-Wilkinson, and in *London Passenger Transport Board v Upson*[105] by Lord Wright when he said that it ought:

> '*Not to be confused in essence with a claim for negligence. The statutory right has its origin in the statute, but the particular remedy of an action for damages is given by the common law in order to make effective for the benefit of the injured party his right to the performance by the defendant of the defendant's statutory duty. It is not a claim in negligence in the strict or ordinary sense.*'

Because this area of law concerns duties and powers conferred by statute there may be an overlap with public law, for which there is yet another entirely separate conceptual framework, the principles of which are explained later in this chapter. The law can be traced back to the case of *Anns v Merton Borough Council*[106] (which has subsequently been overruled on different points), which established that there may be an action for common law negligence where a local authority or other public body negligently exercises powers given to it under a statute. In the healthcare

---

103   For detailed discussion of the tort see Stanton, *Breach of Statutory Duty* (1986); Buckley, *Liability in Tort for Breach of Statutory Duty* (1984) 100 LQR 204.
104   [1995] 3 WLR 152.
105   [1949] AC 155. See also *Caswell v Powell Duffryn Collieries Ltd* [1940] AC 152.
106   [1978] AC 728.

setting it is important to ensure that a distinction is drawn between the tort of breach of statutory duty and the action for negligence that can arise as a result of the inadequate exercise of a statutory power. There are three leading cases in recent years in which the House of Lords explored the possibility of a claim for damages in private law when the defendant has a statutory power to exercise a particular function. These are *X (Minors) v Bedfordshire County Council*[107], *Stovin v Wise*[108] and *Barrett v Enfield London Borough Council*[109].

Where both negligence and breach of statutory are pleaded

Some of the discussion that follows concerns common law negligence arising out of the careless exercise of a power or discretion provided by a statute which may also be a public law matter (see below). Cases involving healthcare and related matters such as child care, may concern the question as to whether a duty exists, either under the statute, where the issue is determined by the interpretation of the statute, or in the common law of negligence, where the test for the existence of a duty, formulated in *Caparo Industries v Dickman*[110] applies to determine whether a duty exists.

It is clear that where the claimant argues that the defendant's duty of care in negligence arises from a statutory power there can be no action for negligence in tort unless the exercise of that power (or the failure to exercise the power) is *ultra vires*[111] – beyond the power conferred by the statute in question. Thus the initial hurdle to be surmounted by the claimant in a claim for negligence is to establish that the defendant acted *ultra vires*. The next step is for the claimant to invite the court to apply the criteria set out in the three-stage test in *Caparo v Dickman*[112]. If the Court considers that these criteria are satisfied, only then will a duty of care be owed[113]. It is becoming apparent from recent decisions[114] that a purported breach of a statutory duty will not readily give rise to a cause of action in private law for damages by individuals who are adversely affected by the breach. However, in the light of the *Human Rights Act 1998* the courts are now reluctant to find that there is no duty of care owed without probing the facts, as to do so would be to impose a blanket ban on liability.[115]

The propositions that can be drawn from Lord Browne-Wilkinson's speech in *X v Bedfordshire* (subsequently overruled in part) that concerned both common-law negligence and breach of statutory duty by a local authority are as follows:

1. A breach of statutory duty does not automatically give rise to a private law claim. To prove that it does give rise to a claim, the claimant must demonstrate that the statutory duty was imposed for the protection of a limited class of the public, and that Parliament intended to confer a right of action in private law for breach of the duty imposed in relation to the class. Regulatory or welfare legislation should not be treated as being for the benefit of individuals, but for society at large. This factor restricts considerably the possibility of success in claims involving healthcare.

---

107   [1995] 26 BMLR 15; [1995] 3 All ER 353.
108   [1996] 3 All ER 801.
109   [1999] 3 All ER 193.
110   [1990] 2 AC 605.
111   *Home Office v Dorset Yacht Company* [1970] AC 1004.
112   supra.
113   *Stovin v Wise supra, Danns v Department of Health* [1998] PIQR 226.
114   *Clunis v Camden and Islington Health Authority* (1997) 40 BMLR 181 which concerned the provision of after care duties to patients under the Mental Health Act 1983.
115   *Barrett v Enfield LBC supra.*

2. If statutory powers and/or duties are exercised carelessly, the claimant must prove that the circumstances of the case gave rise to a duty at common law. Here, a distinction was made between a discretion and a duty imposed by statute. Most statutes imposing duties on local authorities and other public bodies also give them a discretion as to how, and to what extent, the statutory duty in question is to be performed. The case-law makes it clear that a public body may be liable merely for doing what Parliament has authorised. Lord Browne-Wilkinson continued[116]:

    'However, if the decision complained of is so unreasonable that it falls outside the ambit of the discretion conferred upon the local authority, there is no a priori reason for excluding all common law liability.'

    This view followed the reasoning of Lord Reid in *Dorset Yacht Co Ltd v Home Office*[117] where he said:

    'There must come a stage when the discretion is exercised so carelessly or unreasonably that there has been no real exercise of the discretion which Parliament conferred.'

3. The courts cannot consider the legality of policy matters where social values or the allocation of resources or similar issues are concerned.

    'If the decision complained of falls outside the statutory discretion, it can (but not necessarily will) give rise to common law liability. However, if factors relevant to the exercise of discretion include matters of policy, the court cannot adjudicate in such policy matters and therefore cannot reach the conclusion that the decision was outside the ambit of the statutory discretion. Therefore, a common law duty of care in relation to the taking of decisions involving policy matter cannot exist.'

In *X v Bedfordshire* a distinction was drawn between omissions to act in decision-making cases, where the *way in which* a discretion was exercised is challenged, and cases in which the *implementation* of a statutory discretion is challenged. Lord Browne-Wilkinson, changing the scope of the earlier House of Lords' decision in *Anns v Merton*, explained that anything which a local authority does within the scope of its statutory discretion will be immune from challenge at common law, but that if a local authority decision falls outside the statutory discretion it could give rise to liability at common law. However, if the exercise of a discretion includes policy matters, the courts cannot adjudicate on them and cannot even reach a conclusion as to whether a decision is within the scope of the statutory authority (*intra vires*) or outside it (*ultra vires*).

To sum up – the questions to be decided in such cases are: first, whether the alleged negligence in the exercise of the discretion granted by statute involved policy considerations – if so the matter would not be considered at all by the court as part of a private law claim; and second, whether the acts which formed the basis of the cause of action fall within the scope of the statutory discretion. If they do not do so, the question as to whether it would be fair, just and reasonable to impose a duty of care (*Caparo v Dickman*) should be considered.

Although most medical law cases are decided in negligence, and are of only marginal relevance in relation to breach of statutory duty, it should be noted that the common law of negligence is still developing in ways which might assist those

---

aggrieved by incompetent execution of statutory functions[118]. For example, the House of Lords, distinguishing the *X* case, held in *Barrett v London Borough of Enfield*[119], that a claim by a person who alleged that he had not been properly cared for while in local authority care under the Children Act 1989, should not be struck out, and that he should have the right to have his case in negligence heard by a court. Cases of this kind will at least be given proper consideration on their own facts in the light of the relevant statutory framework, and a series of claims can be expected by people who allege that they have suffered physical or psychological injury at the hands of local authorities or other public bodies such as healthcare organisations.

If the Secretary of State chooses to exercise a statutory power, a negligence action may be available if it is alleged that the duty was exercised negligently. On the other hand, if the Secretary of State chooses not to exercise a power at all, in very exceptional cases, it may be possible to argue that a claim for negligence arises. In any event, in both instances the test in *Caparo v Dickman* would have to be applied to ascertain whether a duty of care is owed. However, recent high-level decisions[120] indicate that in future it will not be routine for the court to strike out a claim as disclosing no reasonable cause of action, without further argument, on the basis of generalisations based on previous decisions.

The prerequisites of liability for breach of statutory duty

Case law relating to breach of statutory duty is concerned with issues of statutory interpretation. At almost every point in establishing a claim, the parties must consider the wording of the statute or regulation in question, and basic principles of statutory interpretation apply.

The claimant must prove that:

- The statute was intended to create civil liability, so that a duty of care arises under the statute.
- The statutory duty was owed to the particular claimant.
- The duty was imposed on the defendant.
- The defendant was in breach of the statutory duty.
- The breach of duty was of a type contemplated by the statute.
- The breach of duty caused the damage of which the claimant complains.

In the context of healthcare provision, the relevant statute is the National Health Service Act 1977, s3(1) of which provides that the Secretary of State has a duty to provide, throughout England and Wales, to such extent as he considers necessary, to meet all reasonable requirements:

(a) hospital accommodation;

(b) other accommodation for the purpose of any services provided under the Act;

(c) medical, dental, nursing and ambulance services;

(d) other such facilities for the care of nursing and expectant mothers and young children as he considers appropriate as part of the health service;

(e) such facilities for the prevention of illness, the care of persons suffering from illness and the aftercare of persons who have suffered from illness as he considers are an appropriate part of the health service;

---

118   See Chapter 17.
119   17 June 1999.
120   *Barrett v Enfield London Borough Council* [1999] 3 All ER 193, *W v Essex County Council* [2000] 2 All ER 237.

(f) such other services as are required for the diagnosis and treatment of illness.

There are other legislative powers that enable these wide powers to be delegated to health authorities and NHS Trusts and others. It is the service provider (eg the Trust) who would be sued if the claim was brought in negligence, but it has also been suggested[121] that claims might be brought directly against the Secretary of State for breach of statutory duty in appropriate circumstances. However, there are no examples of this remedy being sought successfully[122], and it seems that the only possibility is a public law remedy, and as will be seen, such actions rarely succeed because of the very broad discretion given to the Secretary of State and others as to how their duties are exercised.

The Use of Public Law Remedies in Medical Law Cases

Judicial review

In rare cases, for example those which arise when it is claimed that the Secretary of State has failed in his duty to provide a service to patients, there may be an action for judicial review in public law. It is important, for practical reasons, to distinguish between the claims in negligence and breach of statutory duty discussed above, and actions for judicial review, as different criteria must be satisfied before a challenge can succeed. It is only in the most unusual circumstances that a claim for anything other than common law negligence will succeed. The usual method of challenging the decisions of public bodies or ministers is by judicial review. The Court of Appeal in *Credit Suisse v Borough Council of Allerdale*[123], explained that significant differences do exist between public and private law proceedings[124].

Judicial review is exercised by the Administrative Court of the Queen's Bench Division[125], and the jurisdiction of the Administrative Court in exercising judicial review is supervisory. Judicial review does not challenge the merits of the decision or actions of a public body or Government minister. It is concerned with the form, procedure and appearance of decisions rather than their substance, and the courts regularly emphasise that the purpose of judicial review is not to allow the courts to usurp the functions of the decision maker. This was explained by Lord Hailsham in *Chief Constable of North Wales Police v Evans*[126].

> *'The purpose of judicial review is to ensure that the individual is given fair treatment by the authority to which he has been subjected ... it is no part of that purpose to substitute the opinion of the judiciary or individual judges for that of the authority constituted by law to decide the matter in question.'*

Its purpose is to ensure that public bodies keep within the limits of their powers when they make decisions affecting the rights of others, and it is used in medical law cases as a possible alternative to negligence claims if what is involved is a challenge to a decision of a minister, an NHS Trust or other public body on a healthcare matter such as waiting times or allocation of resources for treatment. A full analysis of the use of public law remedies in the context of healthcare is beyond the scope of this book, but the basic principles are outlined briefly below.

---

121   See Nathan *Medical Negligence* (1957).
122   *Re HIV Haemophiliac Litigation* (1990) 41 BMLR 171; *Danns v Department of Health* [1998] PIQR 226.
123   (1996) The Times, 20 May.
124   See the explanation offered by Hobhouse LJ.
125   Supreme Court Act 1981, s31 and Rules of the Supreme Court Order 53.
126   [1982] 1 WLR 1155.

Public Law Challenges

There are three basic heads under which a public law challenge could be made. Decisions may be challenged on the grounds of illegality, irrationality and/or procedural impropriety[127].

Illegality

It is a basic principle of public law in that a public body is not entitled to act in excess of its powers (*ultra vires*). If a statutory power is not exercised in good faith, it is exercised unlawfully and this is said to be substantive *ultra vires*. Moreover, a public body must exercise the powers given to it only for the purpose granted[128]. In the case of guidance, local authorities and other public bodies must have regard to it, but are not required invariably to follow it precisely, as departures from the guidance may be justifiable as long as there are good reasons[129]. However, directions are mandatory. They have the force of law and are set out in the same manner as a statutory instrument.

Procedural ultra vires

Where statute prescribes a particular procedure this must be observed by the relevant bodies. Failure to do so could result in a challenge before the Divisional Court.

Irrationality

The test for irrationality was established in the case of *Associated Provincial Picture Houses v Wednesbury Corporation*[130]. This test is very difficult for a complainant to satisfy, because *'Wednesbury unreasonableness'* means that a decision is so outrageous in its defiance of logic or accepted moral standards that no sensible person who had applied his mind to the question to be decided could ever have arrived at it.

The basic rule is that a public body entrusted with a discretion must act reasonably. It must direct itself properly in law, and should consider those matters which it is required to consider. It must not take irrelevant considerations into account, and must ensure that it does not act so unreasonably that no reasonable decision-maker in that position would take such a decision.

Procedural impropriety

Public bodies have a duty to act impartially and fairly. Procedural impropriety is more than the mere failure to observe basic rules of natural justice (*'audi alteram partem'*, *'nemo judex in causa sua'*), or failure to act with procedural fairness towards the person affected. The term covers failure by an administrative tribunal to observe procedural rules which are laid down in the statute or statutory instrument by which it is given its jurisdiction, even where such a failure does not involve a denial of natural justice.

Public Law Remedies

Certiorari: is a prerogative order issued to remove a decision taken contrary to law to the High Court and quash it. The original decision is set aside, with effect from the time when the order is granted. However, the court cannot substitute its own decision for that of the body concerned, as the case simply goes back for the decision to be revised in accordance with the court's interpretation. If the court is satisfied that there

---

127   See Lord Diplock in *Council of Civil Service Unions v Minister for the Civil Service* [1985] AC 374, 410-411.

128   eg in *Bromley LBC v Greater London Council* [1983] 1 AC 768 *'fares fair'* scheme was held to be unlawful because the fare structure had to promote the statutory purpose of organising an *'economic service'*.

129   See Sedley J in (*R v Islington LB ex parte Rixon*, The Times 17 April 1996).

130   [1948] 1 KB 223.

are grounds for quashing the decision, the court may, in addition to quashing it, remit the matter to the court, tribunal or authority concerned with a direction to reconsider it, and reach a decision in accordance with the findings of the court.

Prohibition: is a remedy granted to prevent an inferior court or person charged with a public function from exceeding the limits of their jurisdiction in the future, or from making a decision until certain parties have been consulted.

Mandamus: is an order which requires a person charged with a public duty to perform that duty.

Injunction: is an order that a party do or cease to do some act, and this is rarely granted in public law field.

Declaration: The court states the correct position in law on the basis of given facts. A Declaration can only be granted in relation to rights which are the subject of genuine dispute, as in the *Gillick* case[131] where a Declaration was sought to establish the validity of advice given in a non-statutory circular by a Government department.

Damages: are only available in conjunction with public law action if the applicant can show that he had a private law cause of action, and an award of damages is discretionary. Under Order 53 rule 7, the court *may* award damages if it is satisfied that the applicant could have been awarded damages if he had commenced a private law action.

Some healthcare cases turn on the question of whether there has been a proper allocation of resources for caring for patients. This question might involve a challenge to the provision of a service by the Secretary of State or by another body that has been delegated with the task of allocating services. The Secretary of State has a duty to provide healthcare services under s1 of the National Health Service Act 1977, as amended. The Secretary of State has a *'duty to continue the promotion of a comprehensive health service designed to secure improvement (a) in the physical and mental health of people ... and (b) in the prevention, diagnosis and treatment of illness and for that purpose to provide or secure the effective provision of services in accordance with this Act.'*

A detailed discussion of these matters is beyond the scope of this book. However, it should be noted that the courts have proved reluctant to enter into the debate about the adequate provision of services, partly because this is perceived to be a political question. In the leading case of *R v Secretary of State for Social Services ex parte Hincks*[132] the Court of Appeal took the view that when the Secretary of State is exercising his judgement about the provision of a service, he is entitled to take into account resources that are available for healthcare. This line of reasoning was followed in the cases of *R v Secretary of State for Health, ex parte Walker*[133] and *R v Secretary of State ex parte Collier*[134], both of which concerned patients waiting for life-saving treatment in hospital. In general the courts will only interfere with an administrative decision if it is judged to be *'Wednesbury unreasonable'* – that is, so unreasonable that not reasonable person or body in the position of the defendant could ever arrive at such a decision in all the circumstances of the case. However, there is evidence that a more critical approach to Government decision-making is developing in recent cases. In *R v Cambridge Health Authority ex parte B*[135], the

---

131   [1986] AC 112.
132   [1980] 1 BMLR 93.
133   (1992) 3 BMLR 32.
134   1988, unreported.
135   [1995] 2 All ER 129.

Court of Appeal was prepared to hear evidence on the clinical aspects of the case, and in *R v North Derbyshire Health Authority ex parte Fisher*[136] the decision of the defendants not to provide beta interferon treatment to a patient suffering from multiple sclerosis was regarded as so unsatisfactory that it was overturned by the Court. In *R v North and East Devon Health Authority ex parte Coughlin*[137] the Court of Appeal was prepared to enforce a promise that a home would be provided *'for life'* to a group of patients. The decision was based in part on the notion of *'legitimate expectations'* of the patients concerned. More recently the case of *North West Lancashire Health Authority v AD and G*[138] confirmed that courts are prepared to order that a decision not to provide certain treatment should be quashed if it fails to conform to stated policies of a health authority.

Difficulties arise when a case concerns both the provision of a service and the exercise of a legal duty of care by the healthcare provider (see *Bull v Devon Area Health Authority* above). These are discussed in the section dealing with a primary duty of care owed by the Secretary of State and other health providers.

It remains to be seen whether challenges by patients on the basis that essential treatment has not been made available to them are likely to be successful since the coming into force of the *Human Rights Act 1998*. The implementation of the *Human Rights Act 1998* and the consequent relevance of the jurisprudence of the European Commission and European Court of Human Rights, suggests that if life saving treatment is denied to a patient there could be a breach of Articles 2 or 3 of the European Convention. The Commission has expressly refused to exclude the possibility that the lack of proper medical care when a patient is suffering from a serious illness could in certain circumstances, amount to a breach of Article 3 of the Convention[139].

Vicarious Liability

Under the principles of vicarious liability employers are liable for the wrongful acts of employees committed in the course of their employment. Vicarious liability extends beyond the tort of negligence, and employers may be liable, for example, for batteries, breaches of confidence and defamation committed by their employees. For an employer to be vicariously liable for an employee, two criteria must be satisfied. First, the individual who committed the wrongful act must be an employee rather than an independent contractor. Second, the employee must have been acting in the course of employment at the time the wrongful act was committed.

The employment relationship
People working on a full[140] or part-time basis[141] in almost any capacity for NHS Trusts and health authorities have long been regarded as employees rather than independent contractors. The usual tests to determine an individual's employment status are based on factual matters such as who pays the salary, what type of contract exists between the parties, and who stipulates the hours of work and holiday periods. This matter is a factual question that can be determined by looking at all the circumstances of the employment, including the contract of employment. If the wrongdoer is employed by a firm of contractors, such as cleaners or caterers, the

---

136   [1997] 8 Med LR 327.
137   [1999] Lloyds Rep Med 306; (1998) 47 BMLR 27.
138   [1999] Lloyd's Rep Med 399.
139   *Tanko v Finland Appl* 23634/94 (1994) unreported, and *Association X v UK* (1978) 14 DR 31.
140   *Gold v Essex County Council* [1942] 2 KB 293.
141   *Roe v Minister of Health* [1954] QB 66, *Cassidy v Minister of Health* [1951] 2 KB 343.

healthcare provider would not be liable because liability would then fall upon the direct employer of the wrongdoer. It has long been thought, though never expressly established, that consultants are employees even if they are working only on a part-time basis. They work as an integral part of the organisation, and have a particular employment status at the apex of the hierarchy of NHS employees[142]. The same basic principle would apply in the case of nurses, radiographers, physiotherapists, porters and others, provided they are direct employees of the healthcare provider and can be regarded as part of the NHS organisation.

NHS Trusts and health authorities may also be vicariously liable for staff supplied by agencies. This situation is very common in the case of nursing staff. The NHS body would probably be liable if it controlled the work of the employee in question, though much would turn on the terms of business agreed between the NHS body and the particular agency. If it appears, on construction of the contract between the NHS organisation and the agency, that the individual members of staff remain employees of the agency, the position would of course be different. There is also the possibility that the NHS organisation might be directly liable for breach of the non-delegable duty that it owes to patients[143].

General practitioners, dentists, opticians and other primary care providers are similarly vicariously liable for the wrongs of their practice staff, including receptionists and nurses. GPs and their staff are not employees of health authorities, and as independent contractors they are liable for the staff that they employ. Each GP in a partnership would be jointly and severally liable for the wrongful acts of other partners[144]. In practice, GPs subscribe to one of the doctors' defence organisations. However, GPs are not usually liable for the wrongs of locums who provide temporary cover on their behalf, though if the GP is negligent in choosing a particular locum, he or she would be directly liable to any patient injured as a result of the negligence of the locum[145].

The course of employment

As the employer will only be liable for wrongs committed by staff in the course of their employment, it is crucial to examine the facts of a case to determine whether in fact the employee was acting within the scope of employment at the time the act was committed. There is little authority on this matter in the healthcare context, though in the field of social care, the House of Lords has ruled that in principle employers could be liable for acts of sex abuse committed by an employee on boys in his care[146]. However, it is clear that hospital employees who assist sick or injured individuals outside hospital, in an emergency or other voluntary situation, would not be acting within the course of their employment, and could not rely on NHS indemnity should they be negligent in giving medical assistance. They are therefore advised to belong to a defence organisation. If, for example, a hospital doctor offered voluntary assistance on a regular stand-by basis to a lifeboat station, he or she would be advised to join one of the doctors' defence organisations.

---

142 Consultants' appointments are in fact governed by statutory instrument.
143 *M v Calderdale and Kirklees Health Authority* [1998] Lloyd's Rep Med 157.
144 Partnership Act 1980.
145 See Kennedy and Grubb, *Principles of Medical Law*, 1998, Butterworths.
146 *Lister v Helsey Hall*, 3 May 2001.

Conclusion

The comparatively large volume of care-law relating to the question of whether a duty of care exists in the healthcare setting belies the fact that this aspect of clinical negligence probably gives rise to fewer claims than the questions of breach of duty, causation and quantum. Obviously, there are aspects of the duty question that give rise to very difficult legal problems, and that means that certain cases frequently come before the Court of Appeal and House of Lords. This level of decision-making affords the duty principle greater prominence than it deserves on the over-all scheme of clinical negligence.

One important principle that can be extracted from the cases on the duty of care is that it is difficult to establish the existence of a duty outside the immediate doctor-patient relationship. Another point worthy of note is that judicial policy has played a crucial part in shaping the law relating to the duty principle, and it is important for lawyers to keep abreast of developing trends in judicial policy so that they can attempt to predict the outcome of cases and advise their clients accordingly.

Negligence is not the only claim that may be brought by people injured on healthcare premises. There are many claims brought every year for breach of the duty owed by NHS bodies and other healthcarers, as occupiers, to all their lawful visitors, as a result of accidents on healthcare premises. This is governed by the Occupier's Liability Act 1957. Lawful visitors include patients, employees and contractors. There are also duties owed to trespassers, in relation to known hazards on premises, by the Occupier's Liability Act 1984. In addition, many claims are made by employees (usually supported by Trade Unions), who suffer injuries or illness contracted in the workplace. The Health and Safety at Work etc Act 1974 and related regulations are crucial in this field of employers' liability, as they impose a framework for ensuring safe working conditions.

Scientific technology and many aspects of medical treatment are regularly being revised and updated, and the law will need to address new duty issues as they emerge. For example, the medical profession is in the process of developing *'telemedicine'*. This involves care and treatment of patients at long distances – even across continents – by means of communication technologies. Legal problems, as yet unidentified, are likely to arise concerning the scope of the duty of care in such novel situations.

Chapter 3

Breach of Duty: The Standard of Care

Once it has been established that the defendant owed the claimant a duty of care, if the matter is not admitted, and case proceeds to trial, the judge must rule on whether the defendant has met the required standard of care in the given situation. The claimant must prove that the defendant was at fault in failing to meet the standard of care required.

Healthcare professionals are not necessarily legally liable whenever anything goes wrong with a particular treatment or a patient is dissatisfied with the outcome. The claimant can only be successful if he or she can prove that the healthcare professional did not achieve the required professional standard of care in all the circumstances of the case.

In every negligence claim there are two issues involved in determining whether there has been a breach of duty. First it must be decided what standard of care applies in the circumstances of the case. That is – how a person in the defendant's situation should have acted. This involves establishing the correct standard of care against which to judge the defendant's conduct. This is a matter of law. Second, on the basis of the evidence, it must be decided whether the defendant met that required standard. This is a question of fact. It is not unusual for the two issues to merge and be decided as if they were a single point.

This chapter deals with the first of these matters – the standard of care in clinical negligence cases. The next chapter catalogues specific cases dealing with negligence in various healthcare settings, and examines the operation of the principles set out in this chapter in the context of selected areas of healthcare.

The Standard of Care in the General Law of Negligence

In the general law of negligence, the standard of care is traditionally the standard of the *'reasonable man'* the *'man on the Clapham omnibus'*, or more recently, the standard of the *'person using the London underground'*[1]. This is at least on the face of it, an objective test, based not on how the particular individual ought to have behaved in a given situation, but on what would have been expected of the notional reasonable person in the same circumstances. In *Glasgow Corporation v Muir*[2], Lord Macmillan explained the approach in this way:

---

1   *McFarlane v Tayside Health Board* [1999] 3 WLC 1301.

2   [1943] AC 448.

'The standard of foresight of the reasonable man eliminates the personal equation, and is independent of the idiosyncrasies of the particular person whose conduct is in question.'

Although the theoretical standard of care in the general law of negligence is objective as far as possible, there is evidence that in practice, like the concept of duty of care, the notion of the reasonable man has been used by the courts as a policy device to enable judges to arrive at decisions that they consider to be fair and just in the particular circumstances of the case before them[3]. Factors that might influence a judge are the question of whether the defendant was insured, the impact that a particular decision might have on future cases of the same type, and the implications of a particular decision for future practice in a particular industry or profession, or for society as a whole.

In what might be described as the *'ordinary law of negligence'*, some general propositions emerge from the case law, but it is clear that what the courts regard as reasonable behaviour varies according to the particular circumstances of each case, depending upon the act or omission that occurred. It is regarded as reasonable for a person to consider the risks involved in a course of action, and to balance them against the cost and difficulty of taking precautions to prevent harm occurring[4]. The reasonable person is not expected to take extreme precautions to prevent a risk which is very unlikely to materialise[5]. The ordinary reasonable man is not expected to have special skills or knowledge and will be judged only against the standard of other lay-people when carrying out specialist activities. For example, in *Phillips v Whitely*[6], it was held that a jeweller, when piercing ears, is not expected to meet the standard of care that would be expected of a surgeon.

A different standard of care is applied in situations involving professional people, including healthcare professionals. The standard of care required of doctors was settled in 1957 in the case of *Bolam v Friern Hospital Management Committee*[7]. In that case, McNair J set out the test for determining the standard of care in clinical negligence cases. He explained the standard of care in his direction to the jury[8] as follows:

'The test is the standard of the ordinary skilled man exercising and professing to have that special skill. A man need not possess the highest expert skill; it is well established in law that it is sufficient if he exercises the ordinary skill of the ordinary competent man exercising that particular art. A doctor is not guilty of negligence if he has acted in accordance with a practice accepted as proper by a responsible body of medical men skilled in that particular art ... a doctor is not negligent if he is acting in accordance with such a practice, merely because there is a body of opinion which takes a contrary view.'

McNair J cited with approval the view expressed by Lord Clyde in *Hunter v Hanley*[9] when he said:

---

3   See Atiyah P, *Accidents, Compensation and the Law*, ed Cane, Weidenfeld and Nicholson, London, 4th ed 1998.
4   *Bolton v Stone* [1951] AC 850; *Hilder v Associated Portland Cement Manufacturers Ltd* [1961] 1 WLR 1434; *Haley v London Electricity Board* [1965] AC 778.
5   *Latimer v AEC* [1953] AC 643.
6   [1938] 1 All ER 566.
7   [1957] 1 WLR 583, (91957) 1 BMLR 1.
8   Juries are no longer used in negligence cases. *Ward v James* [1966] 1 QB 273.
9   (1955) SLT 213.

'In the realm of diagnosis and treatment there is ample scope for genuine differences of opinion, and one man clearly is not negligent merely because his conclusions differ from those of other professional men.'

Although the *Bolam* case was decided at a relatively low-level within the court structure, the test formulated by McNair J was later approved and adopted by the Court of Appeal and the House of Lords[10], and it soon became known as the *"Bolam"* test. It is based on a peer group standard, focusing on what a responsible body of doctors would have done in the same or similar circumstances, and was quickly extended to other professions and experts. In the healthcare context, negligence means failure to meet the standards of reasonably competent healthcare workers at the time of the alleged wrongful act. Practitioners are not expected to meet higher standards determined by later more advanced medical knowledge[11].

Under the *Bolam* test[12] the conduct of the defendant would be examined against the standard of a doctor practising in the same field of medicine, and a doctor who professed to exercise a special skill was required to exercise the ordinary skill of his specialty. Thus the same standard of expertise would not be expected of a GP and a hospital consultant[13]. This is still the basic rule.

If there were at the relevant time, two or more schools of thought or opinion among doctors about a particular procedure, diagnosis, treatment or other matter, a doctor would be justified in following one of them, provided it could be regarded as acceptable to a *'responsible body of medical opinion'*. In *Maynard v West Midlands Regional Health Authority*[14] the House of Lords stated that it is not for the courts to choose between two bodies of medical opinion. As long as the defendant could demonstrate that one such body of opinion had been followed the claimant could not succeed. Thus judges were not able to examine medical standards effectively.

From a practical perspective the peer approach makes good sense. Medical science is complex, and doctors take many years to learn the theoretical issues and practice the procedures they carry out. Judges are not expected to be fully conversant with technical medical matters, and require advice from experts when they hear clinical negligence cases. Medical experts advise the lawyers acting for both parties, and trials involve the examination and cross examination of eminent expert medical witnesses. However, the *Bolam* test meant it could be difficult for the claimant to establish that a doctor or other healthcare professional had been negligent if the defence called responsible experts to give evidence[15].

In theory, the *Bolam* test allowed for differences of medical opinion and permitted the exercise of professional discretion. It prevented doctors being found negligent if they had carefully and reasonably considered how they should act in the particular case in the light of accepted medical practice and opinion. However, in practice, as lawyers with experience in this field would recognise, the *Bolam* test was renowned for creating a situation in which claimants appeared to have the balance of justice in clinical negligence cases weighted against them. There were very few cases in which

---

10   eg *Whitehouse v Jordan* [1981] 1 WLR 246.

11   See Lord Bridge in *Sidaway v Governors of Bethlehem Royal Hospital* [1985] 1 All ER 643 at p660.

12   The test has recently been modified by the House of Lords in the case of *Bolitho v City* and *Hackney Health Authority* (1997) 30 BMLR 1.

13   The standard of care is that of reasonably competent members of the profession who have the same rank and profess the same specialisation as the defendant – see Powers and Harris *Clinical Negligence* 3rd ed, Butterworths para 1.8.

14   [1985] 1 All ER 635.

15   Although the number of experts has been reduced since the introduction of the Civil Procedure Rules in April 1999, the use of expert evidence is essential in clinical negligence cases.

judges were prepared to find that a body of opinion supported by an eminent expert could be negligent. In 1978 the Pearson Commission expressed concern that very few plaintiffs in medical negligence cases, as compared with all other negligence actions, were successful[16].

Criticisms of the Bolam Test

After the Pearson Report the *Bolam* test continued to be the subject of critical comment, especially by claimants' lawyers and academics. For many years after the *Bolam* test was formulated it was relatively easy to find doctors willing to give expert testimony in favour of the defendant doctor, but more difficult to find experts for the claimant[17]. The duties of expert witnesses were eventually spelled out in case-law[18], but had not yet been formulated in the rigorous manner of the Civil Procedure Rules. The duty of expert witnesses is now stated clearly as a duty to the court, but before 1999 there were some experts who considered that it was their duty to support the person who paid them.

The test had been identified almost as soon as the *Bolam* case was decided, as too protective of the medical profession in that it was not, (like the test for standard of care in ordinary negligence cases,) a normative test, based on what *ought to have been* done, but a sociological test based on what *is* done in practice by doctors[19]. Making full use of the *Bolam* test Lord Denning acted vigorously in his decision-making in the Court of Appeal to support the interests of the medical profession. In his book, *The Discipline of Law* he commented:

'*As a result of this case (Cassidy v Minister of Health), the medical profession became alarmed. It seemed to have opened the door to many groundless charges of negligence. This became known to us – from articles in journals and periodicals and so forth. The Courts are, I find, always sensitive to criticism. So in the next case, we sought to relieve the anxieties of the medical men[20].*'

Despite receiving support from the judiciary, the formulation of the *Bolam* test continued to be criticised for its vagueness. The term '*responsible body of medical opinion*' required clarification. How many doctors were required to hold an opinion for it to be regarded as responsible? This varied according to the view of the judge. For example, in the much later case of *De Frietas v O'Brien and Conolly*[21] the Court of Appeal held that despite the fact that there was clear evidence that only 11 out of 1,000 surgeons working in a particular field would have operated in the circumstances which arose in this case, it was still open to the trial judge to conclude that the surgeon in question had met the required standard of care. There is extensive case law on this subject which indicates that the courts were consistently reluctant to define a '*responsible body of medical opinion*'. The term was frequently interchangeable with '*reputable*', '*respectable*', '*reasonable*' or '*competent*'.

The *Bolam* test was also criticised because it endorsed practices which were merely on the fringe of what was acceptable medically, and it allowed the medical profession rather than the judge to set standards. In the *Bolam* case itself for instance, a patient to whom ECT was administered, sustained fractures. No relaxant drugs or

---

16   Royal Commission on Civil Liability and Compensation for Personal Injury 1978, Vol 1.

17   AVMA (Action For Victims of Medical Accidents) is a registered charity that was established to assist claimants to find expert witnesses and competent lawyers to held them to claim against healthcare professionals.

18   *The Ikarian Reefer Case* [1993] 2 Lloyd's Rep 68.

19   Montrose (1958) 25 MLR 259.

20   *The Discipline of Law*, Butterworths, London 1979, at p 241.

21   [1995] 4 Med LR 251.

manual restraints were used. At the time there were two bodies of opinion within the medical profession, one in favour of the use of relaxant drugs and one against, and there were also two opinions as to whether, in the absence of relaxants manual control should be applied. When the patient brought a claim, the doctor concerned was absolved from negligence, despite the fact that there were clear indications in the medical literature at the time of the dangers of adopting the chosen course of action.

Bolitho: The Modification of Bolam

One of the most important recent decisions in medical law is *Bolitho v City and Hackney Health Authority*[22]. In this long awaited case the House of Lords reassessed *Bolam* and reformulated the test for the standard of care in clinical negligence cases. Although the test is essentially a modification of the long-established *Bolam* test, it provides the opportunity for a new approach to expert evidence for determining the standard of care. The case dealt with two issues relating to liability for clinical negligence – the first concerned proof of causation[23] when there is an omission as opposed to a positive act, and the second concerned the approach to professional negligence laid down in *Bolam v Friern Hospital Management Committee*.

The events occurred in 1984 when a two-year-old boy, Patrick Bolitho, was admitted on 11 January to St Bartholomew's Hospital in London, suffering from croup. He was treated under the care of Dr Horn, senior paediatric registrar, and Dr Rodger, senior house officer in paediatrics. Patrick was discharged from hospital on 15 January, but was readmitted on 16 January when he was experiencing further difficulties in breathing. Arrangements were made for Patrick to be nursed on a one-to-one basis by a specialist nurse. The following morning he appeared much better, but in the afternoon his experienced nurse became concerned because he was wheezing badly and had become very white. The sister was extremely worried about Patrick's condition, and bleeped Dr Horn who promised to attend as soon as possible. However, when sister Sallabank returned, Patrick again appeared much improved, and Dr Horn did not need to attend.

At about 2.00pm a second episode occurred, and sister Sallabank was again very worried about Patrick's breathing. She telephoned Dr Horn who was in clinic at the time, and who informed her that she had asked Dr Rodger to see Patrick instead of her. However, Dr Rodger did not see Patrick, her evidence being that the batteries in her bleep were flat and that she did not receive the message from Dr Horn. Meanwhile, Patrick's condition again improved and his nurse reported that he was chatty and very active. At 2.30pm sister Sallabank became concerned yet again and telephoned the doctors. The emergency buzzer indicated that Patrick was experiencing breathing difficulties and a cardiac arrest team was immediately called. It appeared that Patrick's respiratory system had become entirely blocked and there was a period of ten minutes before cardiac and respiratory functions were restored. In consequence, Patrick suffered severe brain damage. He required intensive nursing for some time. A claim was brought on behalf of Patrick, but he died shortly after the High Court hearing. His mother continued proceedings as administratrix of his estate.

The causation element
It is also necessary to explain the causation point briefly at this point.

---

22   (1997) 39 BMLR 1; [1998] 1 Lloyd's Rep Med 26.
23   This aspect will be dealt with more fully in the chapter on causation.

The defendant accepted that there had been a breach of duty by Dr Horn on the basis that she should have attended Patrick or should have ensured that a deputy did so. The outcome of the case therefore turned on causation. In this instance what was under consideration was the correct approach which should be adopted when damage is caused by a negligent omission as opposed to a negligent act. It was agreed between the parties that intubation to provide an airway would have ensured that Patrick's respiratory failure and cardiac arrest did not occur, and that if it was to be done, intubation should have been carried out before the final catastrophic episode took place. The trial judge took the view that if Dr Horn would have intubated the patient had she attended him, the claim should succeed. If she would not have intubated him, the claim could only succeed if it could be established that such failure was contrary to accepted medical practice – that is the application of the *Bolam* test to *causation* in the event of a negligent omission. The trial judge found that Dr Horn would not have intubated had she attended Patrick. He also ruled that the *Bolam* test should apply to determine whether a reasonable doctor would have intubated the child. The House of Lords found that the judge had been correct in is approach. He had no option but to follow *Bolam* because of the system of precedent in UK law that requires judges in lower courts to follow decisions of higher courts in earlier cases on the same point.

The standard of care

The House of Lords again found that the trial judge had been correct to ask what course of action would have been followed by a reasonably competent medical practitioner in the same circumstances. Evidence was given by eight experts, five for the claimant who gave the opinion that any competent doctor would have intubated. The three experts for the defence thought intubation would not have been appropriate. Because Patrick had not died immediately, there was no post mortem at this early stage to determine what exactly had happened. The claimant's experts based their views on the premise that there had been a gradual decline into respiratory failure in the two hours before the catastrophic event. The defence experts argued that there was sudden blockage of the respiratory system, probably by a mucous plug, and that Patrick's condition was inconsistent with that of a child passing through stages of gradual progressive hypoxia.

Not surprisingly, the trial judge had found that there were two opposing bodies of medical opinion, each representing responsible views. Relying on *Maynard v West Midlands Regional Health Authority*[24] he concluded that he was in no position to choose which of these opinions he preferred[25]. The much-quoted approach urged by Lord Scarman in that case is as follows:

> *'I have to say that a judge's preference for one body of distinguished opinion over another, also professionally distinguished, is not sufficient to establish negligence in a practitioner ... For, in the realm of diagnosis and treatment, negligence is not established by preferring one respectable body of professional opinion to another.'*

Accordingly, the trial judge in *Bolitho* decided that it had not been proved that the breach of duty by Dr Horn caused the damage in question. The House of Lords agreed with the majority in the Court of Appeal in accepting that the trial judge had been correct to direct himself in the way in which he had. He had asked himself the

---

24   [1985] 1 WLR 634.
25   ibid, at page 639.

correct questions and on the correct basis. Lord Browne-Wilkinson, delivering the judgment of the House, explained the position in this way:

> 'The two questions which he had to decide on causation were (1) What would Dr Horn have done, or authorised to be done, if she had attended Patrick? And (2) if she would not have intubated would that have been negligent? The Bolam test has no relevance to the first of those questions but is central to the second.'

The challenge to Bolam

In *Bolitho*, counsel for the appellant had argued that the judge had been wrong to treat the *Bolam* test as requiring him to accept the view of an expert which did not persuade him in its logic. He submitted that it was for the court to decide the standard of care in a particular case involving professional negligence. The House of Lords accepted this argument to some extent, and Lord Browne-Wilkinson considered the correct interpretation of the meaning of *'a practice accepted as proper'* by a *'responsible body of medical men'*.

Their Lordships concluded that the court is not bound to allow a doctor to escape liability for negligence on evidence from a number of experts that his opinion accorded with medical practice. Lord Browne-Wilkinson put the position in the following way:

> 'The use of these adjectives – responsible, reasonable and respectable – all show that the court has to be satisfied that the exponents of the body of medical opinion relied upon can demonstrate that such opinion has a logical basis. In particular in cases involving as they so often do, the weighing of risks against benefits, the judge before accepting a body of opinion as being responsible, reasonable or respectable, will need to be satisfied that, in forming their view, the experts have directed their minds to the question of comparative risks and benefits and have reached a defensible conclusion on the matter'.

In support of this view, his Lordship cited two highly persuasive cases in which it had been held that there could be a finding of negligence despite the existence of a body of opinion that endorsed the acts of the professional person in question. In *Hucks v Cole*[26] the Court of Appeal found a doctor negligent when he had not treated a patient with penicillin when he knew she was suffering from a condition which could lead to puerperal fever. In *Edward Wong Finance Co Ltd v Johnson Stokes and Master*[27] the Privy Council had held that although the defendants had acted in accordance with a practice universally adopted in Hong Kong, they had been negligent because that practice was not reasonable[28].

It is significant that Lord Browne-Wilkinson made the point that in the vast majority of cases the fact that distinguished experts in a certain field are of a particular opinion will demonstrate that the opinion is reasonable, and only in rare cases would it be possible to demonstrate that the professional opinion does not withstand logical analysis.

In this case the House of Lords unanimously decided that this was not such a situation. The views of the leading defence expert, Dr Dinwoody, could not have been dismissed as illogical. The trial judge heard evidence that intubation is not risk free. It is a major invasive procedure, associated with mortality, and involves

---

26   [1993] 4 Med LR 393.

27   [1984] 1 AC 296.

28   In citing this case, which appears to have little relevance to clinical negligence, but which does deal with the matter of the standard of care in cases involving experts, the House of Lords demonstrated that it is regarded as important to find, at the highest available level, authority for a proposition, especially if the law is to be changed or modified.

anaesthetising a young child – a difficult and dangerous procedure in itself. The appeal failed.

The decision in this case is potentially of great significance in that it is the first in which the House of Lords has expressed serious reservations about the *Bolam* test. The case also has far-reaching implications for all professional negligence claims. Although the departure from *Bolam* is guarded, it does permit the court to choose in appropriate cases between two bodies of opinion. This can only happen when the judge is unable, as a matter of *'logic'* to accept one of the opinions. Such cases are, by their very nature, likely to be rare, according to the House of Lords, as experts are specially selected for their eminence and do not normally give opinions which are insupportable in logic. Lord Browne-Wilkinson explained:

> *'It is only where a judge can be satisfied that the body of expert opinion cannot be logically supported at all that such opinion will not provide the benchmark by reference to which the defendant's conduct falls to be assessed.'*

A *'reasonable opinion'* involves the *'balancing of risks and benefits'*. This is regarded as necessary in a case of this kind by the House of Lords, and the assessment of medical risks is a matter for clinical judgment which the judge would not normally be able to make without expert evidence. This must mean that the judge is in a position simply to apply logic and identify situations in which the expert evidence, although honest, does not withstand logical scrutiny. Experts must be prepared to give reasons for their views, which can be scrutinised by the judges for coherence, rationality and logic. Their opinions must be logically defensible. That is the new definition of *'a responsible body of medical opinion'*.

Several peripheral points of interest are raised by the case in addition to the central focus on causation and the *Bolam* test. First, the House of Lords adopted a risk management approach. The *'balance of risks and benefits'* was regarded as a crucial element in medical decision making. Risk management is an essential part of healthcare planning and quality control and it also influences clinical decisions. It has become increasingly important since the introduction of clinical governance and the Health Act 1999 reinforces this. The Clinical Negligence Scheme for Trusts insists upon the implementation of risk management by its members. Second, issues relating to the choice of experts in clinical negligence cases are raised in this case. The trial judge had emphasised the need for expert evidence focused directly upon the point in issue. He paid special attention to the experts in the narrow field of paediatric respiratory diseases. Practising lawyers are becoming increasingly aware of the need to select the correct expert, and this decision provides an important lesson that could lead to the saving of costs. This has since been further reinforced by the Civil Procedure Rules, considered in Chapter 10.

It can be concluded tentatively that the approach to the standard of care in clinical negligence cases introduced in *Bolitho* holds little prospect for the success of many claimants in future cases. The decision is a modification of *Bolam* rather than a radical departure from it. A flood of successful cases can probably be discounted, but the case is evidence of a new approach and it is likely that deviation of sound accepted practice may in future amount to negligence unless there are logical reasons for departing from it.

Developments since Bolitho

There have been very few cases dealing with the question of the standard of care on the application of *Bolitho* since November 1997 when that case was decided, though there have been several in which the *Bolitho* test on causation has been applied.

However, it is impossible to discover how many claims have been settled because the modified test in *Bolitho* has meant that they are not worth fighting. As Lord Browne-Wilkinson suggested in *Bolitho*, it is only on very rare occasions that a judge will have the opportunity to reject a body of medical opinion on the grounds that it is not logically defensible. Nevertheless, the role of the judiciary in determining whether the appropriate standard of care has been met is reaffirmed by the new approach, and doctors will be subjected to greater scrutiny in future[29].

As Andrew Grubb points out:

'There is every reason to believe that this [the Bolitho case] will have a salutary effect on expert witnesses and perhaps, also on professional practice thereafter[30].'

In *Marriott v West Kent Health Authority*[31] the Court of Appeal ruled that the trial judge had been correct to choose between two opposing bodies of medical opinion when reaching her conclusion. This was an appeal against a finding of liability in the High Court on 29 August 1997, whereby there was judgment for the plaintiff against three defendants. The claimant had fallen downstairs at his home and had collapsed in an unconscious state on 3 October 1984. He was admitted to Burton District Hospital for observation. Staff concluded incorrectly on the basis of X-rays, that the plaintiff had not sustained a skull fracture, and he was discharged the next day still complaining that he felt ill. When he arrived home he was very drowsy, and would not eat or drink that day or the next. As he also appeared unresponsive to his surroundings, his wife telephoned Burton District Hospital, but was reassured by a doctor. Five days later she contacted Dr Patel, the GP, and asked him to call at the house. There was a conflict of evidence as to what had been said and done during that visit, but the trial judge found that the claimant's wife had informed Dr Patel of the case history surrounding the accident, including the unconsciousness and subsequent headaches, drowsiness and lack of interest in food. Dr Patel had been alert to the possibility of an extra dural or subdural lesion. The judge found that he had carried out tests but had not detected any neurological signs, and had ruled out any neurological problem. He prescribed paracetamol for the headaches.

The claimant's condition did not change until the night of the 15 and 16 October when he awoke with a headache and began to lose consciousness. He was taken to Burton District Hospital and transferred to Stoke for a CT scan. This indicated an extra dural collection in the left temporo-parietal region with compression of the left lateral ventricle and marked mid-line shift. Surgery was performed, and although he recovered from the operation he suffered permanent brain damage. The claimant argued that he had been discharged prematurely from hospital without any proper advice or follow up arrangements. It was argued on his behalf that had he not been discharged, or had he been properly followed up, the defendants would have realised that he was suffering from an extra dural haematoma, and could have taken prompt steps to operate. This would have prevented the catastrophic collapse and led to his full recovery. The claimant alleged that Dr Patel had been negligent in failing to refer the plaintiff back to hospital for readmission.

The trial judge ruled that Dr Patel had been negligent in failing to give proper weight to the complaints which had been made to him by assessing the plaintiff's

---

29   See *Wszniewski v Central Manchester Health Authority* [1998] Lloyd's Rep Med 223; and *Brown v Lewisham and North Southwark Health Authority* [1999] Lloyds Rep Med 265.

30   Kennedy and Grubb *Medical Law*, Butterworths London, 2000 p445 where the Canadian developments are examined where there is a broadly similar approach to that in *Bolitho*.

31   [1999] 1 Lloyd's Rep Med 23.

condition by reference only to his neurological tests, and in failing to refer the patient back to hospital for readmission. Dr Patel appealed. The Court of Appeal held that the judge had correctly directed herself in applying the test formulated in *Bolam* and *Maynard v West Midlands Regional Health Authority*[32] and had been correct in stating that *'it would not be open to the court, when considering the standard of care to be expected. simply to prefer the expert evidence of one body of competent professional opinion over that of another where there is a conflict in the evidence between the experts'*. The expert for each side had done no more than state what approach he would have taken in the circumstances, and the judge had come to her conclusions correctly. The court had to be satisfied that the body of opinion relied upon had a logical basis, and although the risk of the haematoma had been small, the judge had been entitled to approach the issue on the basis of the seriousness of the consequences to the plaintiff. Where proper scanning facilities had been available in hospitals, Dr Patel had been negligent in not admitting the plaintiff to hospital. Accordingly the appeal was dismissed.

Although the original trial had taken place before the House of Lords had made their ruling in the case of *Bolitho v City and Hackney Health Authority* the Court of Appeal approached the question of the standard of care in this case in the spirit of the *Bolitho* test. Under the *Bolitho* ruling a judge must be satisfied, before accepting a body of opinion put forward by an expert as being reasonable or responsible, *'that in forming their views, the experts have directed their minds to the question of comparative risks and benefits and have reached a defensible conclusion on the matter'*. At the time of the trial, High Court judges, being bound by the *Bolam* test, as explained in *Maynard v West Midlands Health Authority,* were not permitted to choose between two bodies of expert opinion, both equally responsible. However, it appears that in this particular case, the judge had been able to choose because the experts were not putting forward bodies of opinion to support one side or the other. They were simply stating what they would have done themselves in the circumstances. The judge had therefore been free to reject the evidence of the defendant's experts, and this case is not a direct application of *Bolitho*, as might be thought, as the Court of Appeal was able to decide the issue without the necessity of dealing with *Bolitho*.

There is scope for considerable conceptual confusion in attempting to identify when there has been an application of *Bolitho* in the relation to breach of duty. That is because judges can choose, and indeed frequently do choose between the opinions of experts when making a preliminary ruling on the factual matter as to what happened in a particular fact situation. A case in which it has been claimed that *Bolitho* was applied is *Penney and Others v East Kent Health Authority*.[33] However, the issue in the case was not the question of breach of duty, but disagreement between the parties on what had actually happened – matters of fact. The case concerned the right of the judge to decide between two versions of the facts propounded by expert witnesses. Pill LJ, in the Court of Appeal, explained that *Bolam/Bolitho* applies only to matters of professional opinion in relation to breach of duty, and not at this earlier stage when the court is taking expert advice on matters of fact. At that stage the judge has always been entitled to choose which version of the facts is correct.

The defendants were appealing against the decision of a High Court judge, in which he found in favour of the claimants on the question of breach of duty, in their

32   [1984] 1 WLR 634.
33   The Times 25 November 1999.

claims for negligence arising out of the reading of cervical smears taken from the three claimants between 1989 and 1992. The smears had been reported by the primary cytoscreeners as being negative, but the claimants later developed invasive adenocarcinoma of the cervix, and needed to undergo radical surgery. The claimants argued that the slides had revealed abnormalities which no reasonably competent cytoscreener could, with absolute confidence, treat as innocent. However, the smear tests were declared clear, and there was no adequate follow up or diagnostic or therapeutic intervention.

The parties had agreed that not every condition would be detected by cervical smear, because suspect cells might not have been collected for analysis when the smear was taken from the cervix, and it was also agreed that even in the best laboratories mistakes would happen which were not necessarily negligent mistakes. It was also agreed that no smear should be given a negative result unless it could be said *'with absolute confidence'* that no actual or suspected abnormality was revealed. If there was an abnormality, the smear should be submitted for further review or analysis. The judge had found that the slides revealed abnormalities which no reasonably competent cytoscreener would have treated as innocuous, and that negative (*'clear'*) test results could not have been justified. The defendant challenged the judge's findings of fact, and what conclusions ought to have been drawn from what was to be seen on the slides.

The Court of Appeal held that the judge was entitled to prefer the evidence of the claimants' experts. It was his duty to decide as a matter of fact which experts were correct. There were three questions. First – what was to be seen on the slides? Second – could a reasonably responsible screener, exercising reasonable care, fail to see what was on the slides? Third – could a reasonably competent screener treat the slides as negative?

The trial judge had found as a fact that the slides showed abnormalities, and had applied the agreed *'absolute confidence'* test. An appellate court is merely a court of review, and is only entitled to interfere if it was satisfied that there had been an injustice. The Court of Appeal took the view that where the judge was required to make findings of fact *Bolam*, as modified by *Bolitho*, had no application, and the appeal was dismissed.

A case involving similar issues is *Starcevic v West Hertfordshire Health Authority*[34]. This appeal was brought against the dismissal of a claim for clinical negligence, on the grounds that the trial judge should have preferred evidence presented by the claimant that the defendant's medical staff failed to detect a deep vein thrombosis in her husband's leg before surgery, which resulted in his death.

The case turned on conflicts of evidence as to the facts – as to what actually happened before the deceased underwent surgery. It did not concern, as was the case in *Bolitho v City and Hackney Health Authority*[35], the question as to which of two expert opinions concerning medical practice was correct.

The *Bolitho* case is important because it is the first time the House of Lords has been prepared to acknowledge that there may be flaws in the deeply entrenched *Bolam* test. The modification of the *Bolam* test introduced in *Bolitho* is very guarded and in future a judge will only be able to choose between two bodies of medical opinion if he or she is satisfied *'that the body of expert opinion cannot be logically supported at all'*. Although it is small, this concession creates the opportunity for

---

34   [2001] EWCA Civ 192.

35   Supra.

establishing a more objective approach to determining the standard of care in clinical negligence cases, based on a normative framework derived from evidence-based medicine. Such a framework could be constructed from the emergent culture of guidelines and protocols increasingly formulated by professional bodies and endorsed by Government policies for the delivery of quality in healthcare.

Bolitho and NHS Changes

During the 1990s there were significant changes in the structure of the NHS and the regulation of medicine. As a result of the changes, medical care is now monitored and audited on a regular basis, and league tables are produced on the performance of hospitals. One the most important of these developments in healthcare is the Health Act 1999, one of the objectives of which is to ensure that uniformly high standards of care are delivered to all patients regardless of where they live within the United Kingdom. The means for monitoring of standards and the quality of medical practice are dealt with in sections 18 to 25 of the Act. Similar provisions for monitoring private healthcare have been introduced by the Care Standards Act 2000.

There is a statutory duty of quality under the Act imposed on all NHS Trusts and Primary Care Trusts, and this duty operates alongside the duty of care owed to patients at common law in the law of negligence. NHS Trusts and Primary Care Trusts must establish plans for monitoring and improving the quality of the care they provide to patients. A central feature of the changes is *'clinical governance'* – effectively a system of risk management, which must be implemented within the NHS.

The Government requires all healthcare organisations to implement clinical governance, assisted by two newly created bodies, the National Institute for Clinical Excellence, (NICE) and the Commission for Health Improvement (CHI)[36]. Guidelines commissioned by NICE will determine what *ought to be done* in various healthcare situations, and will bring the standard of care in clinical negligence closer to the objective standard in the general law of negligence. The implementation of these guidelines is being monitored by CHI. NICE is already commissioning guidelines on the treatment of certain medical conditions from the Royal Colleges. In future it may be difficult for a doctor who does not follow such guidelines to argue that he or she has met the required standard of care, unless there are very strong reasons for departing from them. A deviation from NICE guidelines might not be logically defensible under the *Bolitho* test. Indeed, Sir Michael Rawlins, the first Chairman of NICE, recently informed a conference that:

> *'NICE guidelines are likely to constitute a reasonable body of opinion for the purposes of litigation', and that 'doctors are advised to record their reasons for deviating from guidelines.'*

He advised that in a clinical negligence case, a doctor who does not, without good reason, follow NICE guidelines, might be found to have fallen below the standard of care.

In 1995 the Scottish Office had warned that clinical guidelines would be used to an increasing extent to resolve questions of liability. A further indication of the importance of guidelines lies in the fact that they are used by claimants' solicitors at an early stage in the processing of claims to assist in the decision whether to proceed with litigation.

---

36   The Health Act 1999.

The crucial question is what view the courts will take of this matter. Even before NICE was established, the courts were prepared to accept that guidelines could, on occasion, determine the correct standard of care in clinical negligence. For example, in *Thomson v James*[37] in 1996, a GP was held to be have been negligent because he had ignored Department of Health guidelines on childhood immunisation (though the decision was reversed on appeal on another point – the issue of causation).

This view is supported by a decision of the European Human Rights Commission in which an application for a ruling that there had been clinical negligence on the part of a hospital was rejected because the hospital in question had in place procedures or protocols, and those procedures had been followed[38].

One important aspect of the implementation of clinical governance is risk management and the setting up of systems to reduce or prevent the likelihood of mistakes and accidents occurring. If there is no effective system in place, or a system that has been established is not adhered to by the staff required to follow it, there might be a successful claim for negligence by any patient who suffers injury as a result. This is what happened in *Robertson v Nottingham Health Authority*[39] where there was a series of communications systems failures in an obstetrics case, as a result of which there was the potential for primary liability to be imposed on the defendant health authority. Although the claim failed on causation, the words of Brooke LJ should be heeded:

> *'If an effective system had been in place ... for ensuring that so far as reasonably practicable, communications breakdowns did not occur ... the health authority would be vicariously liable for any negligence on the part of its servants or agents who did not take proper care to ensure, so far as reasonably practicable, that the communications systems worked efficiently. If on the other hand no effective systems were in place at all ... then the authority would be directly liable in negligence for this lacuna.'*

The implication of this approach is that there may be a claim at some future date for primary liability in clinical negligence arising from the failure of an NHS Trust to implement clinical governance in accordance with the statutory duty of quality imposed on chief executives by the Health Act 1999.

Communication systems are especially important in the healthcare setting as the *Bolitho* case demonstrates, and good note taking and record keeping is essential in the interests of patients and to avoid liability in the event of a claim. In *Collins v Hertfordshire County Council*[40] there is an early example of a successful claim as a result of a communications breakdown. A surgeon had told a junior medical officer to ensure that a patient was given an injection of procaine, but as this instruction was given over the telephone the junior doctor misheard and prescribed cocaine. The pharmacist dispensed what was an exceptionally large dose of cocaine and the patient died as a result of being injected with it. It was held that the surgeon and his junior were negligent and that the hospital was also liable for not having a safe system for dispensing medication. Although the events that led to this case occurred many years ago, similar errors occur today and measures to prevent harm to patients through such mistakes are being taken through clinical governance.

---

37   (1996) 31 BMLR 1; (1997) 41 BMLR 144.

38   *Tavares v France* Appl 16593/90 (1991) unreported, cited by Starmer K in European Human Rights Law; and see also *X v Germany* (1985) 7 EHRR 152.

39   [1997] 8 Med LR 1.

40   [1947] 1 KB 598.

The Standard of Care Required of Doctors in Specific Cases

The legal standard of care that applies in negligence is now settled law. What is regarded as *'reasonable'* behaviour varies according to the circumstances of each case, and the standard of care usually relates to the activity being carried out by the defendant rather than to his or her personal characteristics. As has been seen, negligence may take the form of an omission as well as a positive act. The House of Lords has warned against relying too heavily on previous cases to decide what behaviour can be regarded as meeting, or failing to meet, the appropriate standard of care, but it is possible to find useful guidance from the cases. The discussion that follows explains the general principles of law in relation to breach of the duty of care in clinical negligence. In the next chapter specific cases illustrating the standard of care required in various clinical situations are catalogued.

In general terms, if the defendant has an opportunity to reflect on what action should be taken, he is expected to carry out a basic assessment of risks[41]. Lord Reid explained the position in the following way in a case that did not concern clinical negligence but which did raise the issue of balancing risks[42]:

'Reasonable men do in fact take into account the degree of risk, and do not act upon a bare possibility as they would if the risk were more substantial.'

Precautions are generally regarded as reasonable if they are commensurate with the risk and with the possible consequences[43], but there may be some situations in which the reasonable person need take no precautions at all, because the law does not expect people, including doctors, to guard against remote occurrences or outrageously improbable events. The reasonable medical practitioner is expected to consider the likely consequences of particular actions and weigh them against the precautions which are necessary to avoid injury. In *Coles v Reading and District Management Committee*[44] there was a finding of negligence when a patient was not given an anti-tetanus injection – a simple precaution that could have prevented serious illness. A defendant who can show that sensible consideration has been given to the implications of particular activities or decisions is less likely to be found negligent than one who has not. The introduction of risk management and clinical governance provides a valuable means of reflecting on past problems, assessing risks and acting upon that information. If it is possible to demonstrate that sound systems exist within an organisation for managing risk it may be possible to escape liability – or to settle an obvious case of negligence at an early stage before the claim becomes too expensive.

The standard of care required of healthcare professionals in different situations has been considered by the courts on many occasions. Some of the issues that have been raised are discussed below.

Can there be a breach of duty if a particular risk was not known at the time?

The standard of knowledge required of a healthcare professional defendant is that which was current at the time of the alleged negligence. The defendant is judged in the light of knowledge available at the time of the alleged negligent act and not according to scientific knowledge that has emerged at a later date. The same basic proposition has been included as a statutory defence under the Consumer Protection Act 1987.

---

41 *Bolitho v City and Hackney Health Authority* (supra).
42 *Bolton v Stone* [1951] AC 850.
43 *Darley v Shale* [1993] 4 Med LR 161.
44 (1963) 107 SJ 115.

A doctor cannot be negligent for being unaware of something unknown to medical science at the time. In *Roe v Minister of Health*[45], the claimants suffered pain and permanent paralysis from the waist down. They had been admitted to hospital for minor surgery and had been given spinal anaesthetic. The defence succeeded in escaping liability because they were able to convince the court that medical science at the time was unaware it was possible for minute invisible cracks to appear in glass ampoules in which the anaesthetic, nupercaine, was stored, and for the nupercaine to be contaminated by the phenol solution in which the ampoules were stored[46]. The court took the view that as it is impossible to guard against an unknown risk there cannot be liability in a situation of this kind.

This principle applies to protect the healthcare professions from impossible claims, but it should be noted that as soon as a risk is suspected the matter should be investigated and reappraised. This might be especially relevant in the case of clinical trials and the use of new treatments and products.

Roe v Minister of Health was relevant in claims concerning defective medical products which were the subject of litigation in the case of patients who contracted CJD from infected human growth hormone. *N v United Kingdom Medical Research Council; sub nom Creutzfeldt Jakob Disease Litigation*[47] is one of a series of claims concerning the transmission of CJD through human growth hormone treatment. This form of CJD is not the new variant contracted from beef, but the established human variant found sporadically in older members of the general population. Human growth hormone was obtained from pituitary glands extracted by mortuary attendants after post mortem examinations. Some of the individuals from whom the human growth hormone was extracted would have been suffering from this form of CJD.

The defendants had begun clinical trials of human growth hormone (HGH) with the agreement of the Department of Health. There were four different methods of dispensing the drug to the children suffering from growth retardation who were the trial subjects. In 1976 the defendants were considering the possibility that HGH might cause CJD after they had received a warning to that effect, and in 1977 an investigation suggested the need to explore this possibility further in relation to two of the methods of dispensing HGH. A number of the people who contracted CJD after receiving HGH by these methods had died, and the plaintiffs claimed that the defendants had been negligent in 1973 and again in 1977 in not demanding a thorough reappraisal of HGH and a halt to use of the product until it could be declared safe. It was held that there had been negligence on the part of the defendants in not carrying out a full reappraisal of HGH early in 1977. If this had been done, failure to suspend the use of the product would have been negligent. Claims by patients who developed CJD would be successful subject to the production of adequate evidence in each case. Thus in *N v UK Medical Research Council*[48] the judge found that there had been negligence when the defendants failed to carry out a full reappraisal of the use of human growth hormone as soon as it was suspected that it might transmit CJD to patients injected with it.

---

45   [1954] 2 QB 66.

46   This version of events has since been doubted and it is thought to be more likely that the contamination was caused by the failure to clean descaling solution from sterilising equipment.

47   (1996) 54 BMLR 85.

48   (1996) 54 BMLR 85.

The Court of Appeal gave a ruling on the relevant dates of infection with CJD for the purposes of medical negligence claims arising from treatment with human growth hormone. The crucial date is 1 July 1977. It was held that cases arising from treatment which began after 1 July 1977 were caused by negligence, but those arising from treatment which ended before that date were not. Patients whose treatment straddled the relevant date could adduce evidence in order to establish whether they had received an infecting dose of human growth hormone before or after that date. The *Consumer Protection Act 1987* does not apply in these cases because it was not in force at the relevant time and it was necessary to prove negligence on the part of the Department of Health.

It has to be accepted that to some extent ground breaking new medical procedures have, in some cases, to be learned by trials on patients. However, doctors are urged to be cautious and should audit and monitor the results of new forms of surgery to ensure that they are not putting patients at unnecessary risk[49]. Clinical governance and the publication of the results of surgery and success rates at all hospitals in the UK should help to ensure that procedures that prove too experimental or risky are halted before too much damage is done. It is hoped that the situation that arose at the Bristol Paediatric Cardiac Unit would be avoided under this new regime.

Do limited resources justify taking risks?

In the general law of negligence outside the sphere of clinical negligence, it has occasionally been argued, with some success, that limited resources made it impossible for defendants to take precautions necessary to prevent harm. In *Smith v Littlewoods Ltd*[50] the House of Lords held that there was no breach of duty in a situation where, although the monitory loss involved was substantial, the likelihood of the damaging events occurring was small. In *Overseas Tankship (UK) Ltd v Miller Steamship Co Ltd, the Wagon Mound (No 2)*[51] the Privy Council took the view that a reasonable man may ignore a very small risk as long as there is a valid reason for doing so, but he should not ignore a small risk if the elimination of that risk was a simple and cheap matter (*Coles v Reading and District Management Committee*[52]). In *Hucks v Cole*[53] Sachs LJ warned that even if a practice involving great risks is widely accepted as appropriate in the medical profession, it should be examined carefully, particularly if the consequences of the risk could be death or serious illness, and cost of preventing the risks was small.

In the healthcare setting where life and bodily integrity as opposed to property may be threatened, it is more difficult to base a defence on lack of financial or other resources. In *Selfe v Ilford and District Hospital Management Committee*[54] the claimant was admitted to a hospital ward after a suicide attempt, and was accommodated in a ward on the ground floor with three other patients who were also known to be suicide risks. He climbed through the window that had been left unlocked, and jumped out in another suicide attempt, suffering serious injuries. The judge did not accept arguments relied upon by the defence that scarce resources

---

49 See *Hepworth v Kerr* [1995] 6 Med LR 139 in which an anaesthetist was found negligent when carrying out an experimental procedure because he had not researched what was possible within the realms of safety.
50 *Smith v Littlewoods Organisation* [1987] AC 241.
51 *The Wagon Mound* [1967] 1 AC 617.
52 (1963) Sol J 115.
53 (1968) [1993] Med LR 393 at p397.
54 (1970) 114 SJ 935.

prevented proper staffing, and the claim was successful. He ruled that there had been a breakdown in communication between nursing staff on this occasion.

Nevertheless, arguments based on lack of resources did succeed in *Thorne v Northern Group Hospital Management Committee*[55], where a depressed patient walked out of a general hospital, (not a specialist psychiatric centre), went home, and soon afterwards committed suicide. It was held that there had been no negligence on the part of the staff at the general hospital, as in this case constant supervision of the patient would not have been appropriate.

In *Hyde v Tameside Area Health Authority*[56] the plaintiff was not admitted to hospital as a psychiatric patient, but for tests on a painful shoulder. He erroneously believed that he had cancer and in a suicide attempt he jumped from a window on the third floor of the building, suffering serious injuries. It was alleged on his behalf that medical staff should have recognised that he required psychiatric treatment and should have taken proper care of him accordingly. The Court of Appeal held that there had been no negligence. Many patients experience anxiety and require reassurance, and it might not be helpful to tell a patient that he needs psychiatric treatment as well as treatment of physical injuries.

In *Jamieson v Royal Hospitals NHS Trust*[57], a 26-year-old man suffering from schizophrenia threw himself from the third floor of a multi-story car park and sustained serious physical injuries. His claim for negligence was based on the failure of the defendants to section him and treat him compulsorily under the Mental Health Act 1983. He had refused to stay in hospital as a voluntary patient, against his doctor's advice. The case was settled out-of-court for £167,500 damages. The settlement figure had been reduced by 25% to allow for contributory negligence.

Similarly in *Hunter-Blair v Worthing Priority NHS Trust*[58], the claimant, at the age of 19, was diagnosed as schizophrenic, and had since then had periods of in-patient treatment. In January 1996 his condition deteriorated. After admissions to two other hospitals, he was transferred to the Homefield Hospital in the Extra Care Area. At transfer, he was noted as being a paranoid schizophrenic with a history of absconding from hospital, and that he needed to be constantly observed. The nursing plan at Homefield recorded *'absconding risk'*. On the 10 October 1996 he attempted to leave the ward, and on the 11 October 1996, inexplicably, he was able to leave the unit unobserved and unhindered. When he absconded, he made his way to a multi-storey car park and jumped from a great height, in a presumed suicide attempt, breaking both ankles and injuring his back.

Liability was disputed, in effect, on the basis that the claimant would have been able to abscond anyway. It emerged, on examination of the records, that the claimant was not monitored for 35 minutes, and probably there were rather more intervals between observation than the 5 minutes recommended in the Care Plan. The case was eventually settled for £40,000. There were in fact no significant special damages because the claimant did not lose appreciable earnings[59].

---

55   (1964) 108 SJ 484.

56   (1986) 2 PN 26.

57   (1999) unreported.

58   (2000) settled out-of-court.

59   Based on a casenote submitted by the claimantls solicitors: Julian Bobak, George Ide, Phillips, Chichester.

In *Knight v Home Office*[60] it was held that the higher standard of care to be expected in hospitals in relation to patients at risk of committing suicide did not apply to remand prisons. Pill J said:

> '*To take an extreme example, if the evidence was that no funds were available to provide any medical facilities in a large prison, there would be a failure to achieve the standard of care appropriate for prisoners. In a different context, lack of funds would not excuse a public body which operated its vehicles on the public roads without any system of maintenance for the vehicles, if an accident occurred because of lack of maintenance'.*

Must doctors keep up-to-date?

In 1953 it was judicially stated that a doctor was not expected to be aware of every recent development in medical science. In *Crawford v Charing Cross Hospital*[61] the claimant suffered brachial palsy because of the position an arm during an operation. The Court of Appeal held that although attention had been drawn to this possibility in an article in *The Lancet* some six months before it happened, it would impose too great a burden on the defendant to expect him to read every article in the medical literature . However, it was pointed out that there might come a time when a procedure suggested in the medical literature became '*so well proved*' and so '*well accepted*' that it ought to be adopted. Recent developments in information technology and the advent of monitoring and guidelines mean that in some areas of medicine this position would already have been reached in the near future in relation to treatments that have been approved by NICE.

The GMC advice about keeping up-to-date is as follows:

> '*You must maintain the standard of your performance by keeping your knowledge and skills up-to-date throughout your working life. In particular you should take part regularly in educational activities which relate to your branch of medicine. You must work with colleagues to monitor and improve the quality of healthcare. In particular you should take part in regular and systematic clinical audit. Some parts of medical practice are governed by law. You must observe and keep up-to-date with the laws which affect your practice*[62].*'*

The introduction of revalidation, annual appraisals of all doctors, compulsory continuing education and compulsory retraining of incompetent doctors, are incentives to all doctors to keep up-to-date. In addition, it would be difficult to defend a claim involving an allegation that a doctor had failed to observe the most recent guidelines issued by the National Institute for Clinical Excellence (NICE).

While it is recognised that it may not be possible for healthcare professionals to be up-to-date in every aspect of medical practice, they should make every effort to keep \abreast of developments in their own field of practice. This is relatively easy for people within specialist areas of medicine but it would be far more difficult for general practitioners to keep up-to-date in every aspect of their practice. The law allows for this by setting the standards of knowledge and expertise required at a level that can reasonably be expected of others practising in the same area of medicine. In *Gascoine v Ian Sheridan and Co*[63] it was held that a '*shop floor*' gynaecologist had a responsibility to keep well-informed on the main changes in diagnosis and treatment by reading mainstream literature, including leading textbooks and journals.

---

60   [1990] 3 All ER 237.
61   (1953) The Times 8 December.
62   *Duties of A Doctor* 1995.
63   [1994] 5 Med LR.

Can junior or inexperienced doctors be negligent?

The standard of care in any given field is that of the ordinary competent specialist, not that of the highest and most expert practitioner in the field[64]. Even very inexperienced practitioners may be in breach of duty if they make errors in the course of carrying out specialist tasks. This rule applies even to novices in the medical profession and indeed in any field[65]. In *Jones v Manchester Corporation*[66] an inexperienced junior doctor caused the death of a patient by administering an excessive dose of an anaesthetic. The Court of Appeal was of the view that it was no defence to a negligence action to argue that the doctor was too inexperienced to undertake the job assigned to him. The case also gave rise to the question of direct primary liability of the hospital authority (see Chapter 2).

In *Wilsher v Essex Area Health Authority*[67] a case that will be discussed later in connection with causation, the situation was that a junior hospital doctor had administered excessive oxygen to a premature baby by taking an oxygen reading from a vein instead of an artery. He had failed to notice that the catheter was in the wrong position. Although he had consulted a more senior colleague, that doctor had also failed to notice that there was a mistake. As a result the baby suffered retrolental fibroplasia and became blind. Although the members of the Court of Appeal expressed rather different views, and were sympathetic towards the junior doctor, it was held that the law required a trainee to be judged by the same standard as more experienced colleagues, and that inexperience could not be a valid defence to clinical negligence[68].

This case introduced the concept of team negligence in the clinical setting. It is a well-established practice for doctors and other staff to work as part of a firm or team when caring for patients in hospital, and the same principle would be carried, in theory, beyond the hospital setting to cases where patients are cared for in the community. It is advisable for all doctors and other healthcare professionals within a team to be aware that they might have gaps in their knowledge and experience and to seek advice when appropriate. In the *Wilsher* case the junior doctor was held not to have been negligent because he had taken the precaution of asking his more senior colleague the registrar for advice. In the event, the Registrar was found to have been negligent.

The National Confidential Inquiry into Perioperative Deaths has revealed that in 1995/6 one-fifth of operations on weekday evenings were performed by senior house officers who were apparently usually unsupervised by more experienced staff. The report outlines the usual patterns of surgical activity occurring in 1995/6 in 355 UK hospitals, involving 51,000 cases. The figures reveal that although only 6.1% of weekday surgery is done outside conventional working hours, 93.4% of this is emergency surgery. However, some of the operations were being carried out because of the need to reduce waiting lists and were not emergencies in the true sense. In most instances both surgeons and anaesthetists tended to be inexperienced junior staff working with no supervision whatsoever. The specialist registrars involved in the preparation of the report expressed the view that junior staff planning to operate during the night should take advice from consultants before embarking upon the

---

64   *Bolam v Friern Hospital Management Committee* (supra).

65   *Nettleship v Weston* [1971] 2 QB 691.

66   [1952] 2 All ER 125.

67   [1986] 3 All ER 801.

68   See Glidewell J at page 831.

surgery. The report, which was supported by the Royal College of Surgeons, recommends that all hospitals admitting patients for emergency surgery must be large enough to provide twenty-four hour operating rooms and other critical care services, and that all hospitals should have emergency surgery lists and an arbitrator in theatre to prioritise cases for surgery. That person *'should perhaps be a consultant'* according to the recommendations.

From the perspective of medical negligence litigation the findings in this report are rather worrying. It is clear from the case of *Wilsher v Essex Area Health Authority*[25], that a junior doctor doing his or her inexperienced best may be found negligent. The Court of Appeal in *Wilsher*, concluded that a junior doctor should seek advice if necessary from a more experienced colleague. If no such person is available there could be a finding of primary liability on the part of the Hospital Trust[69] for not providing the necessary senior support staff. Alternatively, the consultant in charge could be found negligent for not ensuring that someone in a senior position was available to advise and preferably to supervise surgical procedures.

The question of the standard of care required of junior staff was raised in *Sherlock v North Birmingham Health Authority*[70]. This was an appeal against the decision of Owen J who had dismissed the claim against the health authority. The appellant had been admitted to hospital when she was a few months old, and at that stage was incorrectly diagnosed as suffering from pneumonia. In fact she had contracted myocarditis, a progressive viral infection of the heart muscles which is usually treated by allowing the illness to run its course. She was examined by a paediatric senior registrar who told staff to call him if her condition deteriorated. At 12.30am the senior house officer was called but did not seek advice from the paediatric senior registrar. The same senior house officer was called at 2.00am and 5.00am, and because there was concern about the baby's condition, a blood test was taken. While they were still awaiting the results she suffered a partial collapse and was transferred to the intensive therapy unit at 5.45am, but during the transfer she suffered a cardiac arrest, as a result of which she was left permanently brain damaged. There was no spontaneous cardiac output for 15 minutes, and the judge found, as a fact, that the appellant would have suffered no significant brain damage if that interval had been only up to eight minutes duration. It was held at first instance that the senior house officer had been negligent in failing to consult the paediatric senior registrar at 2.00am, though the case failed on causation because there had been no negligence in not transferring the appellant to the IT unit sooner. The Court of Appeal held that the appellant would have suffered a cardiac arrest even if she had been ventilated, and there was no defect in the judge's reasoning. The case illustrates the importance of team co-operation and the need for junior staff to be trained to understand the point at which it is necessary to consult a senior colleague for advice.

Developments like the Bristol Paediatric Cardiac Unit cases have made it clear that the Department of Health is anxious to encourage staff to expose colleagues who might be placing patients in danger through incompetence in their professional practice. This will assist in preventing legal claims by patients who are dissatisfied with their treatment and should also prevent doctors acting inappropriately. After a nurse, Amanda Jenkinson, was sentenced to five years imprisonment for causing grievous bodily harm to a patient in intensive care, the Department of Health announced that it was encouraging members of the healthcare professions to inform

---

69   *Jones v Manchester Corporation* [1952] QB 852.

70   3 October 1997, Court of Appeal.

the authorities if they believe that the health and safety of patients may be threatened by the behaviour of a colleague. This process is facilitated by the Public Interest (Disclosure) Act 1998. An inquiry found that healthcare professionals are reluctant to inform on colleagues and recommended that clear reporting guidelines be established to ensure greater frankness. Improvements were also recommended in recruitment procedures used by the NHS, including the introduction of a probationary period of employment, a standardised system for obtaining and writing references and a permanent occupational health record for each employee.

What is the standard of care expected outside mainstream healthcare?

Some healthcare professionals work outside the mainstream healthcare setting, for example, in occupational health within schools and companies, in prisons, and at sports events. A duty of care is owed in each of these situations[71] and if there is insufficient care taken in the carrying out of medical procedures there is the potential for a negligence claim. The standard of care will vary in accordance with the particular circumstances of each case. For example, in *Knight v Home Office*[72] a claim was brought against the prison authorities following the suicide of a prisoner. It was held that a prison doctor cannot be expected to exercise as high a standard of care as a doctor working in a hospital. By contrast in *Brooks v The Home Office*[73] it was held that a woman prisoner who is pregnant can expect the same standard of obstetric care as would be available outside prison, though this might be subject to some limitations connected with transport to hospital in appropriate cases[74]. Alternative medical practitioners are in a rather difficult position, although they are acting in a similar way to doctors and other more conventional healthcare practitioners, in holding themselves out as offering diagnoses and even cures, they may not have the training and expertise of a qualified healthcare practitioner. There is very little case law authority on this subject, but it appears that the courts are prepared to take a tough approach and to demand high standards in appropriate cases. This matter is discussed in Chapter 4.

Can a doctor be negligent when giving advice as opposed to treatment?

Negligence may occur in the course of all aspects of medical care, including consultation, diagnosis, diagnostic testing, clinical trials, the giving of advice about treatment, and during all forms of medical care. Negligence has been found to have occurred when there are omissions to treat or delays in giving treatment, and cases of negligence have arisen in most fields of healthcare.

In *Burke v Leeds Health Authority*[75], the Court of Appeal explored the question of the standard of care required when doctors are advising patients. In this case it was held that the failure by two consultant oncologists to explain fully to the claimant's parents that there could be a short delay in the commencement of treatment did not give rise to a breach of duty on their part. The facts are set out in Chapter 5.

In this case it seems at first sight that the Court of Appeal takes a different approach to that of the differently constituted Court of Appeal in *Pearce v United Bristol Healthcare Trust*[76], in which the test that was applied was related to *'the risks that a reasonable patient would consider significant'*. The approach in the case of

---

71   Though there is no duty to rescue (see Chapter 2).
72   [1990] 3 All ER 237.
73   (1999) unreported.
74   Although breach of duty was established in this case the claim failed on causation.
75   [2001] EWCA Civ 51.
76   (1998) 48 BMLR 118. See Chapter 7.

Burke v Leeds Health Authority was summed up by the Court of Appeal in the following words:

> *'Clearly what a doctor must tell a patient or his parents at what point and with what force are matters of clinical judgement for the doctor. Much will depend on what the patient's or his parents' worries are.'*

While doctors must be expected to exercise common sense and sensitivity when providing information and advice about medical treatment, this decision may be a retrograde step for patient autonomy, as it appears to reassert the dominance of clinical judgement in determining what information should be given to patients when seeking consent to medical procedures.

Can a doctor be negligent for failure to warn of risks and side effects?

This question is dealt with more fully in the chapter on Consent to Medical Procedures. The question of how much a doctor should tell patients about the risks and side effects associated with particular drugs and other forms of treatments has been the subject of some controversy. As in the case of giving advice (see above), the UK courts traditionally approached the matter by supporting medical paternalism, and ruling that a doctor will not be negligent providing he has not departed from the *Bolam* standard of care. Providing the doctor gave broad information about the nature of the treatment and its side effects, according to what information in his judgement it was necessary to provide, there would be no negligence.[77] However, there is now evidence of a more patient-orientated approach[78], and this will be discussed in detail later.

Res Ipsa Loquitur

In the majority of cases the burden is on the claimant to gather all the appropriate evidence, and to prove that the defendant has failed to meet the required standard of care. However, occasionally, in special circumstances, there is a shift of emphasis away from the claimant. Here the *maxim res ipsa loquitur* (the situation speaks for itself) applies. This can operate to the claimant's advantage when an accident happens which should not occur if adequate care is taken, and the full details of precisely what occurred are not clear. This doctrine will apply if the defendant had some control over the situation denied to the claimant at the time. In these circumstances the court is prepared to treat the accident/untoward incident itself as evidence of negligence, and the defendant will be liable unless he can provide a satisfactory explanation of what occurred, and demonstrate that he or she was not negligent. The pleadings often state specifically that the claimant will rely if necessary on the doctrine of *res ipsa loquitur*, but the case is heard in the normal way with the plaintiff adducing whatever evidence of negligence he or she can gather. Thus the application of the doctrine does not in practice shift the onus of proof to the defendant, as is sometimes claimed. It does give rise to an inference of negligence on the part of the defendant.

Res ipsa loquitur in clinical negligence cases

Although the application of the doctrine of *res ipsa loquitur* is a convenient way of assisting a claimant when the exact circumstances surrounding what occurred are difficult to ascertain, it is only rarely that it is raised successfully in clinical negligence cases. This is somewhat surprising, because the doctrine will apply if the

---

77   *Sidaway v Governors of Bethlem Royal Hospital* (1985) 1 BMLR 32.

78   *Pearce v United Bristol Healthcare Trust* (supra).

defendant had some control over the events, which was denied to the claimant at the time – often the precise situation in medical cases[79].

In *Ratcliffe v Plymouth and Torbay Health Authority, Exeter and Devon Health Authority*[80] the effect of the *maxim res ipsa loquitur* was explained in depth after it had been examined by the Court of Appeal. Hobhouse LJ said:

'*Res ipsa loquitur is not a principle of law; it does not relate to or raise any presumption. It is merely a guide to help identify when a prima facie case is being made out. When expert or factual evidence has been called on both sides at a trial, its usefulness will normally have long since been exhausted.*'

Res ipsa loquitur is usually invoked in cases involving failure to remove instruments or swabs after surgery. In *Mahon v Osborn*[81] an early case involving a claim for clinical negligence, the judge ruled that a surgeon has overall responsibility to ensure that swabs are removed and that sound procedures are adopted in respect of this. Most cases of this kind are settled out-of-court in any event. However, some are considered worth fighting, and in *Mahon v Osborn* it was accepted that in an emergency it may be necessary to dispense with usual procedures. In *Hucks v Cole*[82] Lord Denning, ever the champion of the medical profession[83], said that *res ipsa loquitur* should only apply against a doctor in extreme cases, and in 1978 the Pearson Committee[84] which was established by the Government to review accident compensation, rejected the general application of the doctrine in medical cases.

In *Bull v Devon Area Health Authority*[85] the claimant brought an action for negligence when one of her twins suffered a birth injury. There had been an interval of about 68 minutes between the delivery of the twins. Mustill LJ adopted the following approach, taking the view that the use of the doctrine did not advance the case for the claimant:

'*I do not see that the present situation calls for recourse to an evidentiary presumption applicable in cases where the defendant does, and the plaintiff does not have within their grasp the means of knowing how the accident took place. Here all the facts that are ever going to be known are before the court. The judge held that they pointed to liability and I agree.*'

However, Slade LJ took the view that here the extent of the delay between the two deliveries was so great that it placed on the defendants the evidential burden of justifying what had happened. As they could not explain the delay the majority view was that they had been in breach of their duty of care.

In *Jacobs v Great Yarmouth Health Authority*[86] there was an appeal by the claimant against a decision that she had not been injured by the negligent administration of preoperative anaesthesia before she underwent a hysterectomy. The basis of her claim was that the anaesthetist had missed a vein and, although she had a later injection of a drug which temporarily paralysed her, she was conscious during the operation. She argued that the judge was wrong to conclude that her memory was likely to be

---

79   In *Wilsher v Essex Area Health Authority* [1998] AC 1074, the House of Lords rejected the suggestion of the trial judge that there should be a broader application of *res ipsa loquitur* in clinical negligence cases.

80   February 1998, unreported.

81   [1939] 2 KB 14.

82   (1968) [1993] 4 Med LR 393.

83   Lord Denning described the negligence action as '*like unto a dagger at the doctor's back*' in *Hatcher v Black*, (1954) The Times 2 July, see also his comments in *The Discipline of Law* Butterworths, London 1979

84   Royal Commission on Civil Liability and Compensation for Personal Injuries.

85   [1993] 4 Med LR 117.

86   [1995] 6 Med LR 192.

unreliable after the operation. She contended that if the recollection which she had of the event was pre-operational, the doctrine of *res ipsa loquitur* should apply. The Court of Appeal dismissed her appeal on the grounds that there was sufficient evidence presented to the trial judge for him to conclude that a person's memory could be unreliable after having been given various drugs. The evidence presented by the claimant had been answered by the defendant so this was not a case in which there could be an inference of negligence, and *res ipsa loquitur* did not apply.

In *Ratcliffe v Plymouth and Torbay Health Authority, Exeter and North Devon Health Authority* the claimant argued on appeal that the trial judge should not have dismissed the possibility of applying the *res ipsa loquitur* doctrine. The basis of the appeal was that the judge had misunderstood the so-called doctrine of *res ipsa loquitur* and had not applied it correctly. Counsel asked the Court of Appeal to give guidance on the appropriate approach to the doctrine in clinical negligence cases. There followed a careful analysis of the medical law cases involving the doctrine, and this case is extremely useful as a reference source for medical lawyers. Cases include those involving unexplained cardiac arrest during surgery[87], untoward consequences of surgery and anaesthesia[88], and awareness under anaesthesia[89], are discussed in course of the explanation. The Court of Appeal took the view that it is not safe to raise an inference that there has been negligence merely because the medical evidence is difficult to understand. The claimant was aged 48 at the time of the incident. He underwent surgery for a triple arthrodesis of his right ankle, and was given a spinal anaesthetic in addition to a general anaesthetic. Although the surgery was a success he suffered a serious and permanent neurological defect on his right side, and the claimant alleged that the spinal anaesthetic had been administered negligently, and had been given without consent because insufficient preoperative advice and explanation had been given. The trial judge was not satisfied that the evidence of the medical experts supported the claimant's case. He was unwilling to accept that *res ipsa loquitur* applied. He found that the claimant had been given an explanation in broad terms about the treatment, and that this was adequate for the purposes of obtaining consent.

The Court of Appeal concluded that it would be unfair to medical practitioners to presume that there had been negligence merely because a patient had suffered an unexpected adverse outcome. It was explained that the burden of proving negligence is on the plaintiff and *res ipsa loquitur* is merely a convenient phrase to cover situations when it is possible to conclude that there has been sufficient proof of the facts to establish an inference of negligence. Even then, if it is decided that there is an inference of probable negligence, it was still open to a defendant to convince the court that he did take reasonable care in all the circumstances of the case. The Court of Appeal went on to consider further the nature of the *'doctrine'* of *res ipsa loquitur*. It was not to be regarded as a principle of law, nor did it raise a presumption. The conclusion was that the judge at first instance had been correct to deal with the issues in the case in the way he had, and that he could not be criticised for his approach. The appeal was dismissed.

---

87   *Saunders v Leeds Western Health Authority* [1993] 4 Med LR 355; *Glass v Cambridge Health Authority* [1995] 6 Med LR 91.

88   *Bentley v Bristol and Western Health Authority (No 2)* [1991] 3 Med LR 1; *Moore v Woking Health Authority* [1992] 3 Med LR 431; *Howard v Wessex Regional Health Authority* [1994] 5 Med LR 57; *Ritchie v Chichester Health Authority* [1994] 5 Med LR 187.

89   *Ludlow v Swindon Health Authority* [1989] 1 Med LR 104.

When There is No Need to Prove Breach of Duty

It has long been recognised that the claimant is at a disadvantage in relaying solely in the law of contract[90] or the law of tort as the basis for a claim. One of the main drawbacks in the law of tort is the requirement that fault or breach of duty must be proved before a claim can succeed. Another is that tort offers no protection to consumers of goods that are merely shoddy rather than dangerous to health. Although contractual remedies may be available without the need to prove fault, in many medical law cases the law of contract would not be applicable. The Consumer Protection Act 1987 was passed on the initiative of the EU to overcome some of these difficulties in all member states. The Act also provides a comprehensive framework for regulating product safety.

The Consumer Protection Act 1987 makes producers liable regardless of fault for injury caused to consumers by their defective products. This means that the injured consumer can bring a claim against the producer without having to prove that there was a breach of duty. Liability under the Act is joint and several, allowing consumers to bring claims against one or more of the potential defendants in the chain of supply. Although the scope of the protection afforded by the Act is more limited than it appears at first sight, a recent review indicates that in the UK consumer claims are being settled early, and that there has been no increase in the number of claims.

Defective Medical Products

It has been established[91] that if a patient suffers illness or injury as a result of a defective medical product, a claim may be brought under the Consumer Protection Act 1987. In many instances where medical products are involved, it would be easier for the claimant to pursue a claim under the Act than to rely on the law of negligence, because in creating strict liability[92] the Act eliminates the need to prove breach of duty. Detailed discussion of the scope and application of the Act is not possible here, but a brief outline of some of the relevant points follows.

The definition of a *'product'* is very wide and includes any goods and electricity as well as component parts of other goods. Medical products which have been put through a process of some kind would be included in the definition. Such products as pharmaceutical products[93], products derived from the human body[94], blood and blood products[95], prostheses such as artificial hips and breast implants, condoms[96], heart valves. Surgical instruments and medical equipment of various kinds would all be included. Primary agricultural produce was originally excluded from the operation of the Act, but the position has changed partly as a result of concerns about beef and the vCJD crisis. A proposal for a European Parliament and Council Directive amending Council Directive 85/374/EEC of 25 July 1995 concerning the law in member states governing primary agricultural produce, was published on 7 November 1997 and the UK had until 4 December 2000 to remove the exemption[97].

---

90   See Teff H in Kennedy and Grubb *Medical Law* Butterworths, London, 3rd ed p1612-1614.

91   In a decision on 26 March 2001 it was held that blood products contaminated with the hepatitis C virus were defective products for the purposes of the Consumer Protection Act 1987.

92   Section 2(1).

93   See Mullany K, *Pharmacy Law and Practice*, Blackstone Press, London 2000.

94   eg human growth hormone that was obtained from pituitary glands of corpses during post-mortem examinations.

95   See Grubb A and Pearl D *Blood Testing AIDS and DNA Profiling* 1990. However, the UK courts, in 2001 decided that blood was in fact a product for the purposes of the Act. *A v National Blood Authority* April 2001.

96   *London Rubber Co v Richardson* 2000 (unreported).

97   The relevant Council Directive is 99/34.

A product is *'defective'* if its safety is not such as persons generally are entitled to expect in all the circumstances[98], and the Act therefore covers only unsafe goods and not goods that are merely substandard but carry no risk to health. The Court of Appeal held in *Abouzald v Mothercare (UK) Ltd*[99], that the defectiveness of a product must be determined by reference, not to its fitness for use, but to its lack of safety that the public are entitled to expect. It was irrelevant whether the hazard causing the damage had come, or ought reasonably to have come to the attention of the producer of the product before the accident occurred.

The claimant has the burden of proving that the damage in question was caused by a defect that made the product unsafe. Much depends upon the facts of the particular case. The courts take into account matters such as the adequacy of the labelling of products and information enclosed with them, such as warnings, product leaflets and information about the safe use of the product[100]. Any information provided about the safe use of a product must be clearly written and easily understood by the lay person, as is the case under the common law[101]. In *Worsley v Tambrands*[102] a woman suffered toxic shock when using a tampon. The court found that there had been adequate warnings in an information leaflet about the dangers of developing this condition, and about how the risks might be reduced. In the case of pharmaceutical products the product information sheet may be an important factor. The court will also consider what consumers might reasonably be expected to do with the product. Another important factor in deciding whether a product is defective is the timing of its supply. When there is a chain of distribution a product may begin its journey along the chain in a safe condition, and only become defective after changing hands on several occasions.

It is not usually necessary for a manufacturer to provide information directly to the consumer of medical products which are to be used under the supervision of an expert. It has been held in North America[103] that there is no obligation to take steps to inform the patient if the product is being used under the supervision of a doctor or other *'learned intermediary'* who has been warned of any risks or side-effects, including possible allergic reactions[104]. It is, however, necessary for manufacturers to ensure that doctors are supplied with all the relevant literature on which to base their advice to patients. In the UK there is no case law directly on the *'learned intermediary'* point, but the same principle is implicit in the UK rules governing the use and approval of pharmaceutical products.

The Act provides that there is strict liability on the part of the *'producer'* of unsafe goods. This term includes not only the manufacturer but also the importer into the EU, an *'own brander'*, and other person or body in the chain of distribution of the defective product in question, though the immediate supplier has a defence if he can identify the person or body who supplied him with the product[105]. The imposition of strict liability should in theory, of course, provide claimants with a considerable advantage since it does away with the need to prove negligence. However, in practice

---

98 Section 3(2).

99 The Times 21 December 2000.

100 *London Rubber Company v Richardson* (2000) unreported in which one of the circumstances to be taken into account when a claimant sued because a condom had split during use, was the fact that emergency *'morning after'* contraception could have been used to prevent pregnancy.

101 *Devilez v Boots* (1962) 106 Sol J 552.

102 2000 unreported.

103 *Sterling Drug Inc v Cornish* 370 F 2d 82 (8th Cir) (1966), *Buchan v Ortho Pharmaceuticals Canada Ltd* (1986) 25 DLR (4th) 658.

104 For a discussion see *Hollis v Dow Corning Corp* (1995) 129 DLR (4th) 609 Can Sup Ct.

105 The regulatory authorities (eg the MDA) responsible for approving or monitoring products would almost certainly not be caught by the Act – see Barton A, *Pharmaceutical Medicine and the Law* 1991.

the problems involved in establishing causation frequently mean that defendants escape liability.

A serious drawback for claimants in the legislation is the *'development risks'* defence[106]. In UK law this means that manufacturers and others will not be liable if they can demonstrate that the state of scientific and technological development at the time the product was put into circulation was not such that a producer of a product of the same description as the product in question might be expected to have discovered if they had existed in his products while they were under his control[107]. Although the wording of the UK Act does not follow the Directive precisely, it has now been settled that it does not infringe the Directive[108]. The effect of the development risks defence is that manufacturers and producers of products which are discovered to be defective within the meaning of the Act will not be strictly liable until such time as the defect is confirmed in the industry as a whole nor indeed would they be liable in negligence (*Roe v Minister of Health*[109]). Indeed it is very unlikely that they would be liable in negligence either (*Roe v Minister of Health*[110]).

An example of the potential application of the defence can be found in the situation involving defective artificial hips that were implanted in some patients between 1991 and 1997. It appears that one type of artificial hip used in some hip transplant operations has now been found to be so defective that they are a possible source of damage to the bone and tissue in the surrounding area. The artificial hips were implanted after the *Consumer Protection Act 1987* came into force, and consequently there would have been strict liability on the part of the manufacturer and others in the chain of distribution for any injury sustained by patients as a result. If however, the manufacturers could rely on the development risks defence, claimants would be no better off than under the ordinary law of negligence, and the manufacturers would escape liability.

Defences under the Consumer Protection Act

There are several defences available under the Consumer Protection Act 1987, and some writers have suggested that the protection afforded by the Act is little better than the common law protection for consumers because one or more of numerous defences might be applicable in any given case. The defences are as follows:

- The defect was attributable to compliance with a statutory or EU requirement.
- The defendant did not supply the product and the defendant can identify the supplier.
- The immediate supplier (eg a retailer), will only be secondarily liable and can escape liability by identifying his immediate supplier. This makes it necessary for NHS Trusts, pharmacists and others who supply goods to keep accurate records of the resources of supply and batch numbers[111].
- The product was not supplied in the course of a business.
- The defect did not exist at the relevant time.
- The development risks defence might apply.
- The defect was in the subsequent product and not in a component part.

---

106   See Mildred M and Howells G *Comment on Development Risks: Unanswered Questions* (1998) 61 MLR 570.
107   Section 4(1)(e).
108   *EC Commission v United Kingdom (Re Product Liability Directive).*
109   [1954] 2 QB 66.
110   [1954] 2 QB 66.
111   This was an important issue in relation to the supply of blood products contaminated with HIV to haemophiliacs.

– Limitations: there is a ten year cut-off point from the date that the defendant supplied the product after which no claims can be brought under the Act.
– The Act does not apply to small property damage worth less than £275.
– The Act does not cover damage to the product itself, but only damage caused by a defect in the product.

Medical devices
New medical devices in the UK, from June 1998 are now required to comply with European-wide standards before being placed on the market and there are procedures for checking compliance. Manufacturers need to prove that medical devices are fit for the functions for which they are intended and products must not place at risk the health and safety of patients. They are expected to have quality systems in place to ensure that their products conform to approved standards, and must establish written policy statements and procedures.

The European Directives[112] provide detailed information on these requirements and are comprehensive in scope. They apply to medical devices and their accessories. A *'medical device'* is defined as *'any instrument, apparatus, material or other article, whether used alone or in combination, including the software necessary for its proper application intended by the manufacturer to be used for human beings'* for the purpose of diagnosis, prevention, monitoring and alleviation of disease, injury or handicap, investigation, replacement or modification of the anatomy or of a physiological process, or the control of conception, which does not achieve its principal intended action in or on the human body by means of pharmacological, immunological or metabolic means, but which may be assisted in its function by such means.

The Directives should ensure that there is a successful means of ensuring that medical devices will be properly tested and their use monitored on a systematic basis to the benefit of patients.

Variant CJD and HIV infected blood: the consumer protection implications
The National Blood Authority had always advertised that British blood was the safest in the world, but in 1998, doubts were first cast over the safety of British blood and products derived from it. What the Department of Health describes as *'precautionary measures'* had to be introduced to protect patients against the *'theoretical risk'* that vCJD may be contracted from blood and blood products derived from British donors. Other countries, such as America, now no longer use blood donated by people who have travelled to or lived in the UK. This follows the discovery that blood has been donated by four donors who have subsequently developed vCJD. The precautionary measures were announced on the advice of the UK Committee on the Safety of Medicines, which has considered all available data, including the conclusions of the Committee on Proprietary Medicinal Products (CPMP). Up to 35,000 people a year are believed to receive blood products.

Whole blood used for transfusions was not affected by the announcement, but blood products manufactured from plasma were withdrawn at the time of the announcement. These products include Factors VIII and IX used to treat haemophiliacs, as well as immunoglobulins used to treat immunodeficiency, and a range of other products including those which are used in certain vaccines and in the treatment of pregnant women who are rhesus negative. Although the official statement was vague and

---

112   The Active Implantable Medical Devices Directive; the Medical Devices Directice, and the In Vitro Diagnostic (IVD) Medical Devices Directive. For a detailed discussion see Longley D, (1998) *Medical Law International*, pp319-345.

defensive, further investigation of the products suggests that a large number of patients could be involved, despite the fact that relatively few cases of vCJD have so far been confirmed in the UK. For example, doubts have been expressed about the safety of some childhood vaccines, as suspect plasma was used until as recently as 1994 in their manufacture. Media Oral Polio, last produced in 1991 was used until 1994, contained UK albumin, and some manufacturers of the MMR vaccine used UK sourced albumin until 1992, according to the Health Services Directorate. It is impossible to assess the risks involved with accuracy. Blood products are made from pools of plasma derived from between 20,000 and 60,000 donations, and only those products which are known to contain plasma donated by people suffering from CJD have been withdrawn as a precautionary measure.

It emerged in the year 2000 that 3,000 patients may have been given vCJD infected blood. The blood was taken from a donor who died from the disease, but none of the patients concerned is to be informed because it is thought that the risk of any of them developing the disease is very small indeed. The identities of all the patients who were injected are known, but as there is still no evidence that vCJD can be blood-borne, it is thought that it would cause unnecessary anxiety to inform the people involved. The blood product is of a type used in investigating lung disease and hospitals were asked to return the blood product concerned.

Other problems have beleaguered the Blood Service in the UK. Three people have been infected with the AIDS virus after receiving infected blood given by a donor who was HIV-positive. It appears that the donor, who was new to the system, had either lied about his or her lifestyle in the interview which was routinely carried out before donation, or was unaware of having just become HIV-positive. A so-called 'fool-proof' system of interviews accompanied by testing, which was established in 1985 to prevent contaminated blood being given to patients, appears to have a loophole of about 30 days. If the donor has only been infected for that short time, the test is not sufficiently sensitive to detect the presence of the AIDS virus. A more sensitive but much more expensive test is available but the cost is prohibitive. However, now that the 30-day window has been exposed in the conventional test, there is a need to rethink the procedures in the light of current knowledge.

If injury is suffered as a result of defective blood products a consumer would have a claim under the *Consumer Protection Act 1987*, but as explained above, there is a defence if it can be shown that *'the state of scientific and technological development at the time the product was put into circulation, was not such that a producer of a product of the same description might be expected to have discovered the defect if it had existed in his products while they were under his control'.*

Despite this defence, it has been announced that patients who have been infected with hepatitis C through blood products are to receive compensation. A High Court judge has ruled that blood is a *'product'*[113] for the purposes of the Consumer Protection Act 1987, and that patients in six test cases are to receive between £10,000 and £210,000, and the total cost to the Government of compensating all the potential claimants is believed to be likely to exceed £7 million. Mr Justice Burton concluded that a total of 114 patients were entitled to compensation, and this is the first multi-party action to reach trial under the Consumer Protection Act 1987. All of the claimants in the test cases were infected since 1 March 1988, as a result of blood or blood products infected by the virus, which affects the liver and can cause serious

---

113   This point had not been judicially decided before that date in the UK. See *A and Others v National Blood Authority*, The Times 4 April 2001.

illness later in life and premature death. It was held that the infected bags of blood were non-standard and defective because the public was entitled to expect that they would not be infected with hepatitis C.

Vaccine Damage

It is not necessary for fault to be proved in order for a claimant to obtain compensation for injuries caused by vaccines. There is a statutory compensation scheme to cover vaccine damage under the Vaccine Damage Payments Act 1979 as recommended by the Pearson Commission in 1978[114]. The scheme allows for payments to be made to those whose health has suffered as a result of vaccination against diptheria, tetanus, whooping cough, polio, measles, rubella, tuberculosis and, if the vaccination was carried out before 1971, smallpox. The scheme has been extended to cover the haemophilius type b (hib) vaccine[115], and there is power to extend it further by statutory instrument. In June 2000 there was an announcement by the Government that it would facilitate compensation by increasing maximum payments to £100,000 under the scheme, and by lowering the threshold for claiming to include people who suffer from a disability level of 60% instead of the previous 80%. The new arrangements will allow people to claim up to the age of 18.

However, it is still necessary for claimants to prove that the vaccine was the cause of the illness or injury of which they complain, a very difficult task[116]. In the related case of the injuries sustained by patients whose mothers had taken the drug thalidomide during pregnancy, a settlement was only achieved after a major campaign by *The Sunday Times* and it was clear in those cases that causation would have been difficult to establish in many of the cases if they had come to trial.

Before the recent changes in compensation thresholds, parents of 100 children who suffered brain damage following routine vaccinations decided to sue the pharmaceutical companies concerned in an attempt to obtain more compensation than was then available under the Vaccine Damage Payments legislation. In some instances it may be possible to obtain compensation at a higher level by bringing a claim in negligence instead of relying on the statutory scheme. In *Best v Wellcome Foundation Ltd*[117] it emerged that the plaintiff had suffered brain damage because the vaccine used in his case had been particularly toxic.

Conclusion

This chapter has covered the law determining whether a healthcare professional is in breach of duty. New developments relating to the determination and application of the standard of care in clinical negligence claims have been explored and the prospects for patients wishing to bring claims appear to be more promising than they were under the old regime. There are many web sites providing advice to patients about clinical negligence and how they can set about bringing legal action if they suffer illness or injury in the course of receiving healthcare. The claims industry is clearly highly competitive. Against this, it is necessary to consider the cost to the NHS of defending claims made against healthcare professionals, the need to ensure that sound risk management procedures are implemented through clinical governance, and to monitor practice in healthcare in order to identify areas of medicine that might present particular difficulties.

---

114   1978 Cmnd 7054.

115   SI 1995 No 1164.

116   See Lee R, *Vaccine Damage: Adjudicating Scientific Dispute* in Howells G (ed) *Product Liability, Insurance and the Pharmaceutical Industry: An Anglo-American Comparison* (1991).

117   (1992) 17 BMLR 11.

Chapter 4

The Standard of Care in Specialist Areas of Healthcare

The previous chapter concerned the standard of care required of healthcare professionals, and dealt with the *legal* decision as what standard of care applies in the healthcare setting. That standard of care has been determined by the House of Lords, and applies in all cases involving healthcare. Cases in which the courts have considered whether the defendants have achieved the appropriate standard of care in various areas of healthcare are outlined in this chapter. Each of the cases discussed here turns on its own special facts, and involves consideration of whether there was breach of the duty of care in the particular circumstances. This involves a *factual* inquiry, and readers are cautioned against treating the conclusion reached by the court in any individual case, on hearing evidence as to the facts, as a precedent for later cases[1]. However, the cases discussed in this chapter do provide useful guidance about what the courts have found to be appropriate or inappropriate behaviour by healthcare professionals. They illustrate some of the pitfalls involved in providing medical care. That information may indicate to potential claimants, healthcare professionals, claims managers and lawyers acting for the parties, how a claim might best be managed. For example, it is apparent from some of the cases that errors are made as a result of poor record keeping and inadequate communication between healthcare professionals. The Government has recommended that those working in healthcare throughout the UK should learn from past mistakes and that adverse incidents should be reported and recorded with that aim in view[2]. This and other examples of Government intervention that attempt to improve healthcare are referred to briefly from time to time in this chapter.

It is impossible in this volume to catalogue all the decided cases on negligence in healthcare. However, a selection is made of cases decided since 1995 that illustrate significant points, and the two specialist sets of law reports covering medical law should be referred to for further examples. These are *Butterworth's Medico-Legal Reports* and the *Medical Law Reports* – now *Lloyd's Law Reports Medical*.

There are numerous examples of the application of the *Bolam* test which can be drawn from these cases. Cases outlined in this chapter that were decided before the House of Lords modified the *Bolam* test in *Bolitho v City and Hackney Health*

---

1   See the view of the House of Lords in *Qualcast (Wolverhampton) Ltd v Haynes* [1959] AC 743 per Lord Keith at p755.
2   *An Organisation with a Memory*, Department of Health June 2000.

Authority[3] must now be considered in the light of that development. Readers are invited to consider whether they would have been decided differently if they had post-dated the House of Lords' ruling in *Bolitho*. Some cases dealing with duty of care and causation are also discussed here if they are relevant, may be given fuller treatment in the chapters covering those topics.

It will be observed that some of the awards given to successful claimants run into millions of pounds and the Government has announced that it is to require all doctors and dentists including those in private practice, to be fully insured following cases where patients have been unable to claim compensation when they have received negligent treatment at the hands of uninsured clinicians.

Anaesthetics

Anaesthetics is an area which gives rise to many claims for clinical negligence, and was identified in 1990 as one of the areas for special concern by the Medical Protection Society. Anaesthetists are faced with specialised medical problems that can easily lead to litigation. In some cases the consequences of a mistake by an anaesthetist may be devastating for the patient. The burden of proving that the doctor in question was negligent is on the claimant, and this is not an easy task as is demonstrated in the cases outlined here.

In *Delaney v Southmead Health Authority*[4] the claimant had undergone a successful operation under routine general anaesthesia. However, three or four days later she noticed that she had a pain in her left hand and fingers and it transpired that she had suffered a lesion of the brachial plexus. The claimant alleged that this lesion was caused by the anaesthetist's negligent failure to take account of an earlier injury which had left her susceptible. Alternatively, she contended that the lesion was caused by the incorrect positioning of the arm during surgery. Her action failed. The trial judge had decided on the evidence presented to him that the anaesthetist had followed the correct procedure and the Court of Appeal refused to interfere with that finding.

Brock v Frenchay Healthcare Trust[5] concerned the question of causation in a case involving an anaesthetist. The claimant appealed from the order of Sedley J dismissing his claim against the defendant Trust in negligence. The claimant had been admitted to hospital after an accident during which he had hit his head. He was discharged, and a few hours later, was readmitted as an emergency case. The main issue on appeal concerned the delay in administering the drug *'Mannitol'* to alleviate pressure on his brain, and whether earlier administration would have made a substantial difference to the injury that he sustained. The Court of Appeal held that Mannitol would have taken effect 15 minutes after it had been administered, and the claimant's argument that the 25-minute delay in administering the drug caused the significant disability suffered by the claimant was hard to sustain. The trial judge had been aware of the intuitive conclusion which one neurosurgeon reached, and had carefully explained the reasons in his judgment. The crucial question which one of the neurosurgeons had to answer was: *'If the drug had been administered earlier would the claimant still have developed the uncommon neurogenic pulmonary*

---

3   (1997) 39 BMLR 1.
4   [1995] 6 Med LR 355.
5   Court of Appeal 17 May 1999.

oedema?' The answer was that it was difficult to predict what might have happened as this was such an unusual occurrence. It was possible that the pressure might not have risen to the level which it did, but there was no certainty one way or another.

In the view of the Court of Appeal, the judgment had contained a remarkably clear analysis of both the facts and the evidence in this case and, with reference to that judgment, at no time was it determined that the claimant would have gained any benefit from an earlier administration of Mannitol. The appeal was dismissed.

In *Muzio v North West Herts Health Authority*[6] the claimant alleged that an anaesthetist had pierced the dura when administering a spinal anaesthetic in preparation for a Caesarean section operation. She also claimed that her postoperative care had been unsatisfactory because she was not given a simple treatment to clear the spinal headaches which she was experiencing. It was held that the anaesthetist had not been negligent and that the postoperative treatment had not amounted to negligence because it was deliberately conservative and not out of line with current practice.

Skelton v Lewisham and North Southwark Health Authority[7] was a case concerning causation. The claimant alleged that his injury was caused by the negligent acts or omissions of anaesthetists at the defendant's hospital. The claimant was born in 1982, and it was apparent that he was suffering from a congenital disorder, Williams' Syndrome, which caused a narrowing of the aorta. Surgery to correct this was carried out at the defendant's hospital in November 1983. Although the object of the surgery was achieved, neurological symptoms appeared after the surgery and it became obvious that the claimant had suffered perioperative hypoxic or ischaemic brain damage. As a result of that damage, he exhibited features of severe mixed cerebral palsy. It was argued that the brain damage had been caused by the anaesthetists' negligence in the pre-operative period, and that the poor and sparse contemporaneous notes were evidence of a poor standard of anaesthetic care.

The judge held that on a balance of probabilities the senior anaesthetist was not present in theatre in the early stages of surgery, although it was probable that he was called and did attend in the later stages of the process. In the crucial period just before surgery the only anaesthetists involved were a senior registrar and another more junior doctor. Unfortunately, the registrar's notes fell significantly below the prevailing standards of 1983, as they were extremely brief, unsigned and did not include a record of key events and pressures. Although this had not caused the damage, it was indicative of an unexplained carelessness. The duration of hypotension necessary to cause such damage was probably at least 20 minutes. Such an episode was the only possible explanation for the administration of certain drugs as recorded in the notes, and was probably profound and severe. It was probable that a large dose of Fentanyl was given concurrently with maintenance by Enflurane. It was this inappropriate combination, because of the inexperience of the doctors responsible, which negligently caused the hypotensive episode. The anaesthetists negligently failed to notice what was happening and respond to it earlier. The claim succeeded.

Jacobs v Great Yarmouth Health Authority[8] concerned the alleged negligent administration of preoperative anaesthesia before a hysterectomy. The appellant contended that the anaesthetist had missed a vein when giving her an injection, and that after a later injection of a drug which temporarily paralysed her, she was

---

6   [1995] 6 Med LR 42.
7   (1998) 4 Lloyd's Rep Med 324.
8   (1995) 6 Med LR 192.

conscious during the operation. She argued that the judge had been wrong to conclude that her memory was likely to be unreliable after surgery, and that if the recollection which she had of the event was preoperational, the doctrine of *res ipsa loquitur* should apply. The Court of Appeal dismissed her appeal on the grounds that there was sufficient evidence presented to the trial judge for him to conclude that a person's memory could be unreliable after having been given various drugs. The evidence presented by the claimant had been answered by the defendant so this was not a case in which there could be an inference of negligence, and *res ipsa loquitur* did not apply.

In *Hepworth v Kerr*[9] an anaesthetist was held negligent in unnecessarily reducing a patient's blood pressure to 40mmHg for 1.5 hours where no proper scientific validation of that technique was provided. The claimant was aged 40, and was a reasonably heavy smoker. His blood pressure was recorded as 150 over 100 on admission and some atheroma was noted. He had undergone a mastoid operation in 1979 with the defendant as anaesthetist. The claimant alleged that the paraplegia he had suffered since his surgery was caused by the defendant's use of hypotensive anaesthetic techniques involving reduction of blood pressure to a point lower than required for haemostasis, in order to give the surgeon a relatively blood-free operating field in middle ear. It was argued that such hypotension was excessive and prolonged, and resulted in lack of adequate blood supply to the spine, leading to anterior spinal artery syndrome. It was held that the claimant's blood pressure was probably reduced to 40mmHg (or lower), possibly for 1.5 hours. The defendant could not reasonably have reduced the claimant's blood pressure to such a low level for such a period in 1979, as he knew that the technique had never been attempted routinely before, and there was no scientific validation of the technique. For such a fundamental departure from conventional practice, minimal investigations following each of 1,500 operations in which he had used it were entirely inadequate. It was recognised in 1979 that the lower limit of autoregulation for the brain was 60mmHg; the defendant had routinely gone well below that level, without regard to haemostasis. The anaesthetist had been negligent in this instance, having breached the duty not to expose a patient to unnecessary risks during surgery.

The judge found that the deliberate hypotension had caused or materially contributed to the claimant's condition, and although the specific risk was not one which ought to have been foreseen by a reasonably competent anaesthetist in 1979, the risk of major organ under-perfusion was reasonably foreseeable. The patient's injury was simply a variant of what was foreseeable.

In *Taylor v Worcester and District Health Authority*[10] the patient claimed that she was awake and suffered pain and distress during a Caesarean section operation. She alleged that there had been negligence in that she was inadequately anaesthetized. The claim was successfully defended when the anaesthetist, assisted by her anaesthetic chart, was able to convince the judge that she had followed her normal procedure. The judge found that the claimant's description of her awareness was consistent with events taking place at the reversal stage both individually and sequentially. There were no features of recall in the claimant's description at or about the time of birth, and there were no clinical signs whatsoever of pain and distress during the operation.

---

9   (1995) 6 Med LR 139.
10   (1997) 2 Med LR 215.

Dental anaesthesia

General anaesthetics administered in dental surgeries have given rise to special concern over the past few years, and revised guidelines have been drafted to deal with the problem. An inquiry in Scotland investigated the events which led to the death of ten-year-old Darren Denholm in October 1998 during a routine anaesthetic at a dental practice the Peffermill Clinic in Edinburgh. Darren suffered heart failure and died under the general anaesthetic. The anaesthetist, Dr Evans-Appiah, who had been practising anaesthesia since 1976, admitted that on the day after Darren had died he had made false entries on the sheet recording blood-pressure readings. Dr Evans-Appiah agreed that he had made a mistake, but claimed that he had tried to rectify it as soon as he discovered what had happened. It emerged during the inquiry that the same doctor had been dismissed from his previous employment in 1993 after he had injected the wrong drug into a woman who had just given birth. Instead of giving her the routine drug to induce uterine contractions in order to hasten the third stage of labour, he had administered a drug which caused temporary paralysis. On that occasion he had been disciplined by the GMC. Dr Evans Appiah has now been struck off the Medical Register after being found guilty of serious professional misconduct. He was found guilty of 17 charges of incompetence and neglect, including the incident that led to the death of the 10-year-old boy. Another patient described to the Professional Conduct Committee of the GMC the pain and distress she had suffered when she had not been properly anaesthetised by John Evans Appiah when she underwent a Caesarean section operation in 1998.

Dr Pradhaker Gadgil, a consultant anaesthetist, pleaded guilty to manslaughter and admitted killing a boy whom he had anaesthetised for a tooth extraction, has been sentenced to a term of imprisonment. Neville Bainbridge, the dentist who removed the patient's milk tooth, denied manslaughter and was released after the prosecution decided that the charge should be left on the file. The death occurred at Mr Bainbridge's surgery, and during the course of the trial it was pointed out the attempted extraction should not have been carried out under anaesthesia in the surgery because there was no equipment on the premises for dealing with emergency situations. The boy died in October 1997 after he had been given nitrous oxide instead of oxygen to assist his recovery after the anaesthetic. He had not been fitted with a pulse oxymeter to monitor his oxygen levels, so the error was not detected in time. He was in any case not a suitable patient for anaesthetic treatment outside a hospital because he had a condition which meant that he had restricted airways.

An extreme example of negligence in anaesthesia is *R v Adomako*[11] (1990), a criminal case in which gross negligence by an anaesthetist was found to constitute manslaughter. The Court found that it is the duty of an anaesthetist at all times, to watch and monitor the patient. The defendant who had failed to recognise disconnection from the ventilator for a period of six minutes was criminally negligent and was found guilty of manslaughter after the patient died following a cardiac arrest.

Obstetrics

Litigation is an ever present fear for obstetricians and gynaecologists, and it has been claimed that most specialists in these fields of medicine retire early because of the stress of their practice[12]. Obstetrics was the first medical discipline to introduce

---

11   (1993) 15 BMLR 13.
12   NICE is working to improve standards in obstetrics and has approved guidelines on Induction of Labour.

voluntary national adverse event reporting systems[13]. In future these are to be mandatory, as part of the Government's nationwide programme designed to improve the quality of healthcare. The law reports contain many cases concerning negligence in obstetrics and gynaecology, including several in which midwives are the main target of the negligence claim. As medical techniques become more sophisticated, so the potential for injury increases, whether or not that is attributable to the fault of a healthcare professional. Much emphasis is placed on CTG traces as evidence of the state of the fetus before delivery, and a claim by a brain-damaged infant has a better chance of success if there is evidence that the CTG trace has not been reviewed on a regular basis throughout labour. It has become routine for CTG traces to be kept for up to thirty years in case of litigation.

High levels of awards

An obstetrics claim may involve one or more of three potential claimants, the mother, the baby, and more rarely, the father of the child, and some of the awards made to the victims of obstetric negligence can be very high indeed. As will be seen in a later chapter, recent changes in the ways in which damages are calculated have resulted in greatly increased awards since 1998[14] especially in cases where serious brain damage is caused by oxygen starvation during delivery.

In *Alayan v Northwick Park and St Marks NHS Trust*[15] the claimant was five years old at the date of the trial. During the later stages of delivery at the defendant's hospital, the claimant had suffered brain damage as a result of oxygen starvation. She suffers from cerebral palsy, cannot move without assistance, and suffers from cortical blindness. She has profound learning difficulties and attends a special school. Intensive 24-hour care was being provided by her mother who assumed the role of principal carer. The claimant would never have the capacity to work, marry or manage her own affairs. The award amounted to £1,129,313 total damages, but as the claimant had rejected an offer of £1,250,000 made on 21 December 1998 she was liable for all costs incurred from that date.

In *Mansell v Dyfed Powys Health Authority*[16] the claimant, an 11-year-old boy, received £3,281,199.10 for injuries sustained at or around the time of his delivery, when there were two unsuccessful attempts to deliver him using forceps. Eventually, after a Caesarean section was performed, the baby was found to be severely brain damaged, and now that he is older he still requires 24-hour care, hence the very high award. In *Choudry v Hillingdon Health Authority*[17] the claimant, who was a woman aged 28 at the time of the settlement, received £1,990,000 for the cerebral palsy she suffered around the time of her birth, allegedly as a result of a negligently managed delivery at the defendant's hospital. During the course of her delivery she suffered oxygen starvation, and was born severely asphyxiated. It was alleged that the hospital staff had been negligent in the way they had managed her delivery. They had failed to intervene and carry out a Caesarean section earlier, despite the fact that there had been a fall in the foetal heart rate. The claimant was severely handicapped as a result of what had happened, and needed constant care. Her mother was her primary carer, and she spent her nights on a travel bed beside her daughter. Her condition was

---

13   The National Confidential Enquiries Into Maternal Deaths.
14   *Page v Sheerness Steel, Wells v Wells, Thomas v Brighton Health Authority* (1998) 43 BMLR 99; *Barry v Aberlex*, The Times 22 March 2000.
15   QBD 9 February 1999.
16   Reported on BBC television news 23 October 1998.
17   QBD 7 May 1999.

permanent and she would continue to require 24-hour care. Liability was disputed. There was an approved settlement of £1,990,000 total damages. £200,000 was to be paid to the claimant's family in respect of the care they had already provided for her.

Laws v Kingston and Richmond Health Authority[18] is another case in which the award was very high indeed. The claimant was eight years old at the time of the trial. She suffered oxygen starvation during delivery, which she claimed was caused by the negligence of medical staff in that they had failed to monitor her mother's labour, or her own condition properly and had not detected obvious signs of foetal distress. It was argued that if a proper monitoring system had been in place, the claimant would have been delivered earlier, either by Caesarean section or forceps delivery, and she would not have suffered the injuries. Liability was disputed. The claimant had limited control over her limbs, and suffered involuntary writhing movements. She had difficulties with speech, and needed special equipment to communicate, but her mental faculties remained unaffected and she was fully aware of her condition which was not likely to improve. She would require care and support for the rest of her life. It was expected that she would reach the age of 50 years. The award was £2,350,000 damages.

In *Butt v Ealing, Hammersmith and Hounslow Health Authority*[19], a 21-year-old man received £2,740,000 for the brain damage he sustained after his birth, allegedly as a result of the hospital's errors both during and after his delivery. He had suffered severe physical and mental disability and had learning difficulties. In *Jenks v West Kent Health Authority*[20] the claimant was an eight-year-old boy. When his mother was in labour the hospital staff failed to notice signs of foetal distress. The midwife relied only on the foetal heart rate as a monitor of the claimant's condition, and discounted the signs of foetal distress. As a result the delivery was delayed, and the claimant subsequently suffered oxygen starvation. The claimant brought an action against the defendant alleging negligence in delaying his delivery, which caused his injuries, and liability was admitted in 1995. The claimant suffered from cerebral palsy. In addition to suffering severe cerebral palsy, his mental condition was seriously impaired. He was believed to have the mind of a 12-14-month-old baby, and had low insight into his injuries. However, despite his terrible injuries, the claimant could smile, enjoy himself and laugh, and he was very responsive to those around him. He could not speak, but he communicated by means of eye movements. The claimant's bodily functions were severely restricted and he had limited movement. The disabilities were permanent and he would require 24-hour care and supervision for the remainder of his life. His condition was expected to improve slowly, as better aids and equipment became available. His life expectancy was agreed at 50 years. An out-of-court settlement of £2,600,000 total damages was approved.

An award of almost £3 million was made to a child who suffered brain damage around the time of delivery, in *Aston v Mid Essex Hospital Services NHS Trust*[21]. The claimant's mother discovered that she was pregnant in July 1992, and the pregnancy proceeded normally until 2 January 1993 when she developed pain across the top of her back. The GP examined her at home and prescribed pain-relieving drugs for a pulled muscle. The next day, she observed traces of blood in her urine and attended hospital, where it was noted that she had a high temperature. It was difficult to detect a foetal heart rate, and the mother confirmed that she had not felt her baby move for

---

18   QBD 3 February 1999.
19   QBD unreported 1 November 1999.
20   QBD unreported 23 October 2000.
21   QBD 5 July 1999.

several hours. An examination revealed that she was in labour, and her progress was carefully monitored. The foetal heart was still hard to detect, and the CTG traces were abnormal. On delivery, the claimant was severely hypoxic. He based his action on the allegation that the hospital had been negligent in overseeing his delivery, arguing that he should have been delivered 37 minutes sooner, as this would have avoided the compromising situation which led to irreversible brain damage.

The claimant had sustained severe brain damage and suffered athetoid cerebral palsy. He was completely dependent on others for ongoing care and assistance in his daily life. Although his intellect was not damaged, he was severely physically handicapped. He could communicate with the aid of a computer, and would need more advanced technology to assist further as he grew up. There was an approved settlement of £2,900,000 damages.

Twin births

Twin births can be difficult and give rise to concerns about potential claims. For example, in *Riordan v Hammersmith and Hounslow Health Authority*[22], the claimant aged 12 at the date of the trial, was the second baby to be born in a twin delivery after an induced labour. His sister's birth had been normal, but he was delivered in the breech position. Immediately after delivery he was experiencing breathing difficulties which appeared so serious that staff abandoned attempts to resuscitate him, but when it was realised that he had a heart beat, he was taken to a special care unit, and he did eventually recover. However, he suffered mild cerebral palsy, some intellectual impairment, and impaired motor functions. It was likely that he would suffer a handicap on the labour market. He received £500,000 total damages in an approved settlement.

In *Wildsmith v Berkshire Health Authority*[23], the claimant was one of twins, but suffered severe brain damage at birth because medical staff had failed to identify that her mother was carrying twins. After the first baby, Andrea, was delivered, ergometrine was administered to ensure delivery of the placenta, and this compromised the birth of the second twin, Lesley, who was delivered by emergency Caesarean section 40 minutes after her sister. The twins are now aged 26. Andrea is a graduate who holds a Masters degree and has a high-flying career, but Lesley, although intellectually capable, requires constant care, and finds it difficult to concentrate for long periods. Lesley received damages of £4.9 million.

Mismanagement of labour

Failure to monitor the mother and baby appropriately during labour is a regular complaint, as in *Rayment v Ministry of Defence*. The claimant's mother, in July 1985, was admitted to a military hospital to give birth to him. Her labour was uneventful in the early stages, and the CTG traces were normal. However, it later became apparent that the cervix was not dilating as quickly as expected, and that delivery of the baby would be delayed. Monitoring was continued and the foetal heart rate was decelerating. The baby began to show signs of foetal distress. Eventually, after a labour of 16 hours, the cervix was sufficiently dilated to enable the baby to be delivered, but he had become fixed in a occipito-anterior position. An attempt was made to deliver the baby by three firm pulls with the forceps, but this was unsuccessful, and his mother was transferred to theatre for an emergency Caesarean section. The claimant was born severely distressed requiring intubation.

---

22   QBD 1 February 1999.
23   The Times, 20 February 2000.

An action was brought alleging that the mother's labour and the claimant's birth had been mismanaged. It was argued that there had been insufficient regard to the signs of foetal distress, and to the slow progress of the cervical dilation, which suggested that there was a possibility that the baby would suffer injury. He contended that a Caesarean section should have been carried out far earlier. Liability was admitted. The claimant, who was aged 15 years at the date of the settlement, had suffered severe brain damage and dystonic quadriplegia, as a result of which he had no control over his limbs and was prone to dystonic spasms. He was permanently in a wheelchair and was doubly incontinent. His communication skills were basic and he had no understandable speech. He could not dress or care for himself at all, and required constant supervision. He attended a school for children with special needs. The claimant's condition was permanent, and the settlement was based on a life-expectancy of 43 years. The approved settlement consisted of £1,295,000 capital payment, plus an annual income of £50,000 linked to the Retail Prices Index for the rest of his life.

In *Trayfoot v Riverside Health Authority*[24] the claimant was aged 12 years at the time of the settlement, and alleged that he had suffered brain damage caused by oxygen starvation in the course of his negligent delivery at the defendant's hospital. Although his intellect was unaffected, he could not speak and communicated by means of facial expression and by writing on a computer screen. The claimant could not walk or move around, and was dependent on a wheelchair for mobility, but he had an unusually acute intellect. The claimant was progressing well at school and had taken a keen interest in his father's business. Had it not been for his disabilities, it was likely that the claimant would have pursued a full-time career in that business. However, his physical disability was permanent and he would need constant care for the rest of his life. His main carers had been his parents, and the family had moved into a new home which was specially adapted to meet the claimant's specialist needs. There was an approved settlement of £2,750,000 total damages.

The claimant's perspective in obstetrics cases
Despite the impression created by some of the well-publicised successful claims, it is not a simple matter for a claimant to prove that the defendant was negligent, and it can be very difficult to obtain the finance required for an expensive claim. Information can be difficult to secure and even if there is evidence that something went wrong in the course of obstetric treatment, that does not necessarily mean that the claim will succeed, because the case could fail on the question of causation. Many claimants give up when their funds are depleted, and some, who have suffered ill-health, lose the will to continue the fight for compensation.

Cord accidents
Medical accidents such as cord problems do not necessarily amount to negligence, and there are many instances of unsuccessful claims. One example is *Corley v North West Hertfordshire Health Authority*[25]. The claimant had been born suffering from hypoxia caused by the undisputed evidence that the umbilical cord had been compressed around her neck during delivery. In the period immediately after her birth the baby had been seriously ill with convulsions and an inability to maintain independent respiration. Although she later made good progress she was found to be suffering from cerebral palsy. The issue of causation was important,

---

24   QBD 11 May 1999.
25   [1997] 8 Med LR 45.

because it was difficult for the claimant to establish, on a balance of probabilities, that her injury was caused or materially contributed to by the negligence of the defendant.

It was argued on behalf of the claimant that the medical staff who delivered her had failed to have sufficient regard for the fact that labour had been induced because of an ante-partum haemorrhage suffered by the mother, and that this induction placed the baby in a high risk category. It was further contended that there had been signs of bradycardia in the fetus during the labour and that midwives had failed to maintain the cardiotachograph for a sufficiently long time and had not monitored the labour properly. They had thus failed, it was argued, to call for urgent help from an obstetrician or paediatrician at the crucial time, and to ensure that the baby was delivered by forceps as soon as difficulties were apparent. It was also alleged that there had been insufficient specialist help available at short notice when it was known that this was likely to be a problem case. The main allegations of negligence were made against the midwives in charge of the delivery.

After hearing the evidence and summarising it in detail, the judge found that it was most likely that the foetal condition was normal until the crowning of the head of the foetus and that there was no evidence of foetal bradycardia during the labour. He also found that it was not a high risk delivery, because although labour had been induced, syntocinon had not been used and it was only in those circumstances that continuous CTG monitoring was necessary throughout labour. Following ante-partum haemorrhage the growth of the foetus had been satisfactory. The judge rejected the allegations that the midwives had failed to appreciate that there was an urgent need for prompt intervention. He found that the midwives did monitor the foetal heart accurately. He described this as a *'rare cord accident case'* and concluded that the damage had probably occurred at a very late stage during delivery, but that there was nothing to suggest that any action could have been taken in the circumstances to prevent it. Accordingly, the claimant failed to establish liability. The judge commented at the outset that in fairness to all the parties concerned, the case should have been brought long ago.

Another example is *Hoque v Sheffield Health Authority*[26], where the claim was again unsuccessful. The claimant's mother was seen at an antenatal clinic at the defendant's hospital on 27 September 1998, and told to return a week later. By 2 October 1988 she went to the hospital in an anxious state, believing that she was in labour and giving a history of contractions since 9pm. She was admitted at 11pm and observed overnight, but was discharged by the obstetric senior registrar early on 3 October because it was not considered that labour was established. On 4 October, she was readmitted following a spontaneous rupture of the membranes, and gave birth to the claimant at full term plus either 12 or 13 days. The claimant was born with the umbilical cord around his neck and despite being expertly resuscitated by the obstetric senior house officer, he was found to have suffered severe permanent hypoxic brain damage.

The child brought a medical negligence claim by his litigation friend alleging that his condition had been caused by the mismanagement of his mother's labour. Five distinguished experts gave evidence at the trial. It was held that the obstetric senior registrar, in deciding to discharge the claimant from hospital, had acted logically, and in accordance with practice accepted in 1988 as proper by a responsible body of skilled

---

26   QBD 19 July 2000.

medical opinion. Although the mother's greater age did present some risks - she was in her late thirties at the time of the claimant's birth, those risks related to pregnancy rather than labour. She had remained healthy throughout her pregnancy and there was no evidence that the foetus would be more adversely affected by labour. The judge emphasised that even if it were wrong to find that the obstetric senior registrar was entitled to discharge the mother when he did, it could not be shown that had she been in hospital at spontaneous rupture of the membranes. Had a cord problem then occurred, it would reasonably have been detected. Further, it could not be shown that maternal movement or Caesarean section would have been sufficient to avert the danger, and could have been performed in time. Accordingly the claim was dismissed.

Abortion

In *Barr v Matthews*[27], the claimant had visited her GP to seek an abortion in December 1988. Although she satisfied the grounds for abortion, she claimed that unbeknown to her, the defendant was philosophically opposed to the termination of a pregnancy. According to the claimant's account, the defendant presented matters in such a way as to prevent her from obtaining an abortion. She alleged that she was advised that the pregnancy was too far advanced to be carried out, and that this advice was wrong, improper and in breach of the defendant's duty of care to a young and vulnerable patient. An important question in this case was whether the discretion available under s33 Limitation Act 1980 should be applied, to allow the claim to proceed. It was common ground that the claimant had the requisite knowledge to bring a claim from mid-January 1989 and that primary limitation expired in mid-January 1992. The writ was not issued until April 1996.

The defendant denied absolutely the conduct and remarks which the claimant had attributed to her. However, the claimant alleged that the consequence of the defendant's advice was an unwanted pregnancy, a severe ante-partum haemorrhage, and a catastrophically brain-damaged child. She argued for the exercise of the court's discretion in relation to the limitation period, admitting her own delay but stating that the crucial facts in the case were either agreed or firmly refuted by the defendant, and that the defendant had been aware of the issues in 1991 before the primary limitation period had expired. The defendant argued that there was no reason why the action could not have been commenced within the primary limitation period, and that as a result of the delay the cogency of the evidence had been diminished. The entire process of the claim had been dilatory, and had the claimant really believed the defendant was seeking to dissuade her from having an abortion, alternative advice would have been easy to obtain.

The Court of Appeal held that at the hearing the judge had correctly ruled that the claimant's account of what had occurred could not prevail over contemporaneous notes and the evidence of the defendant. In particular, the judge rejected the claimant's evidence that the defendant had said it was too late in the pregnancy for an abortion. Therefore, the defendant had not denied the claimant an abortion and, on the evidence before the court, the claim failed.

Pre-eclampsia

Pre-eclampsia is a relatively rare condition involving high blood pressure. The condition is experienced by about 2% of women, and is tested for routinely during antenatal care. It can be treated very effectively, and prevented from developing into eclampsia by careful monitoring, bed-rest and by inducing labour early or by

---

27   (2000) 52 BMLR 217.

carrying out a Caesarean section. Failure by a doctor or midwife to take prompt action once warning signs of raised blood pressure and protein in the urine are recorded is very difficult to defend. It is estimated that the condition causes the deaths of approximately seven women and 1,000 babies in the UK every year.

The need to take urgent action when a patient is suffering from pre-eclampsia is vividly illustrated by the case of *Moor v Bryce-Taylor*[28]. The claimants were the partner and son of a woman who had suffered an eclamptic fit and who subsequently died. In August 1994, the deceased was pregnant with her son when she suffered an eclamptic fit and lost consciousness. She was rushed to hospital, and the baby was delivered several weeks premature by emergency Caesarean section. The mother suffered a brain haemorrhage and after two days was declared to be brain stem dead. She had been a language teacher, and she had set up a translating and interpreting business shortly before her death. The claimants brought an action for negligence against the general practitioner who treated the deceased just before her admission to hospital, alleging that warning signs of the onset of eclampsia were not noticed or acted upon. In this case there was an approved settlement in this case of £110,000 total damages. The claimant received £40,000 for loss of dependency and £10,000 for psychiatric shock; their son received £60,000 for the loss of the love, care and attention of his mother.

Again, in *O'Sullivan v Barking, Havering and Brentwood Health Authority*[29] the claimant was a 33-year-old widower who received a total sum of £200,000 in a settlement following the death of his wife from renal failure caused by the negligence of her doctors. The claimant's wife had died a week after the birth of her second child as a result of renal failure and asphyxia, following an attempt to insert a catheter into her neck. It was argued on behalf of the claimant that the defendant should have performed a Caesarean section on his wife at 34 weeks of pregnancy, when there was clear evidence of pre-eclampsia. Instead she went full term, and after giving birth she suffered renal failure. This could have been avoided, had the obstetrics department followed the terms of a protocol on treating pre-eclampsia, and had they ensured that a strict fluid balance was maintained. The defendant administered excessive fluid and potassium, failing to note a significant rise in serum urate levels, which indicates that there is renal impairment.

In *Peoples v Greenwich District Area Health Authority*[30] the basis of the claim was that the defendant had failed to take note of or act upon the results of an ultra sound scan carried out on the mother, indicating that foetal development was four weeks ahead of the clinically estimated time of delivery. The defendant did not diagnose a rise in the mother's blood pressure or the presence of protein in the urine and did not ascertain whether the baby's head could enter the pelvis. The defendant failed to diagnose pre-eclamptic toxaemia in the claimant's mother. Liability was admitted, and the judge approved a settlement of £2,200,000 total damages.

On occasion the Coroner can be involved in obstetrics cases, as in *R v Her Majesty's Coroner's Court of Saint Pancras; R v Her Majesty's Coroner for Inner North London District, ex parte Touche*[31]. This was an application for the judicial review of the refusal by the Inner London Coroner to hold an inquest on the death

---

28   QBD 8 June 1999.
29   QBD 20 October 1998.
30   QBD 9 November 1999.
31   (2000) COD 439.

of Laura Touche, and for an order under s13 Coroners Act 1988 that such an inquest be held.

Laura Touche had died of a sub-acute intra cerebral haemorrhage soon after her twins had been delivered by Caesarean section. It seems that she had been suffering from raised blood pressure, a symptom of pre-eclampsia, and the applicant, the husband of the deceased, had complained of a delay in administering medication which would have reduced her blood pressure. The coroner had refused an inquest on the basis that he had been satisfied that the deceased had died of natural causes. The coroner gave evidence to the effect that he had concluded that the defects and human fault complained of did not lift the case out of the category of *'natural'* and into the category of *'unnatural death'*. The applicant obtained a preliminary report from an expert in obstetric anaesthesia who was critical of the poor recording of events relating to the periods before and after surgery. In particular he found that there had been a failure to monitor and record vital signs and described the level of neglect as starkly apparent. He also obtained a second opinion from a practitioner in high risk obstetrics who was an expert in preclampsia. He concluded that the severe hypertension was responsible for the cerebral haemorrhage, and that this could have been prevented by timely diagnosis and treatment. The applicant submitted that the coroner had failed to address himself to the correct line of inquiry in this case.

It was held that the law concerning when an inquest was to be held was set out in s8(1) of the Coroners Act. In *R v Poplar Coroner, ex parte Thomas*[32] where it was held that there was no general discretion for a coroner to hold an inquest, and that remained the case even if the cause of death was rare. Although in this case the coroner did not take an obviously incorrect approach, it would have been more appropriate had he specifically addressed the issue as to whether there were grounds to suspect that the wholly inadequate post-operative monitoring, with its consequential loss of opportunity to provide timely treatment, had been an effective cause of death. The second expert report provided clear grounds to suspect that the post-operative failure to monitor and treat was an effective cause of death. In these circumstances, the coroner had been wrong to refuse to order an inquest. The coroner had reached a conclusion that was irrational in the sense defined by *Associated Provincial Picture Houses Ltd v Wednesbury Corporation*[33]. Accordingly, the coroner's decision was set aside and an order for an inquest was made.

Maternal infections following childbirth

Fortunately there has been a dramatic reduction in maternal deaths since the founding of the NHS in 1948, and serious life-threatening infections can be dealt with rapidly and efficiently by antibiotics. *Clayton v Milton Keynes General NHS Trust*[34] is one of the very few tragic cases of maternal death and stillbirth that are seen under modern conditions. The claim was brought by a widower, under the *Fatal Accidents Act 1976* and under the *Law Reform (Miscellaneous Provisions) Act 1934*. His wife had been admitted to the defendant hospital for the birth of her child, after a difficult pregnancy. She had a retro-placental blood clot that had haemorrhaged, and her labour was complicated. Despite the efforts of medical staff, the baby was stillborn, and soon after the delivery the mother began to develop symptoms of infection and disseminated invascular coagulation. The placenta was foul smelling,

---

32   [1993] 2 WLR 547.
33   [1948] 1 KB 223.
34   QBD 11 October 1999.

and the midwife on the labour ward had been warned of this. A blood test had been conducted and this indicated a raised white cell count which led the midwife to call a doctor. The mother was prescribed antibiotics at around 5pm with the unusual instruction that they were not to be given until 10pm. In the event, the drugs were not administered as intended and treatment was not in fact commenced until some time later. By that time her condition was too far advanced for her life to be saved.

The claim for negligent post-natal care succeeded. Medical experts agreed that antibiotics would, if they had been administered at 10pm, have delayed the progress of the uterine infection, and the onset of fulminant infection would have been sufficiently delayed to allow the clinicians to take appropriate action. They also agreed that had effective antibiotic therapy been started at 10pm., the deceased would have survived without even having to undergo a hysterectomy. Liability was disputed, but the case was settled for a total of £150,000 damages.

Ectopic pregnancies

There are serious risks involved with ectopic pregnancies, and occasionally patients die if they are not treated appropriately. In *Bagan v Chelsea and Westminster Healthcare NHS Trust*[35], the claimant's wife died during surgery. She had been admitted to hospital with a suspected ectopic pregnancy, for laparascopic exploration and removal of the ectopic pregnancy, if that was found. She had died as a result of a perforation of her right common iliac artery. The claimant was 42 years old at the time of the settlement which was approved by the court, and had three young daughters. He had felt bound to give up his work as a mechanic in order to bring up his daughters in the way he thought was best for them. He received a total of £170,000 damages.

Keyhole surgery to deal with ectopic pregnancy can be extremely hazardous if it is carried out by someone who lacks the necessary skill, as the case of *Scarratt v Portsmouth and South East Hampshire Health Authority*[36] illustrates. The claimants received £160,000 total damages in an out-of-court settlement for the loss of a wife and mother due to alleged negligence during an ectopic pregnancy. The deceased bled to death on an operating table when a junior doctor attempted keyhole surgery to extract an ectopic pregnancy. The doctor concerned was an obstetrics registrar, and had been on a course in keyhole surgery techniques shortly before he operated on the deceased. He attempted to use various forms of instrument to extract the pregnancy and in doing so, ruptured a major blood vessel.

According to the Medical Defence Union, claims for negligence in performing keyhole surgery have increased by 50% over seven years. A quarter of claims which involve this type of surgery concern the perforation of intestines or blood vessels. It is well-recognised that keyhole surgery requires particular skills, and it is inevitable that there will be claims for negligence unless surgeons receive specialist training. Another case in which a surgeon was held to have been negligent when performing keyhole surgery is *Burrows v Forest Healthcare NHS Trust,* though this was not an obstetrics case. The procedure was carried out by a senior registrar who used only two laparoscopic ports of entry into the abdomen. One of these was for the laparoscope, and the other was for instrumentation. He discovered an adhesion in the bowel, where there was a scar from previous abdominal surgery, and decided to divide the adhesion. However, when he did so, he cut through a loop of the small

---

35   QBD 25 January 1999.
36   QBD 30 March 1998.

bowel. This damage was not discovered until post-operatively, when the plaintiff developed purulent peritonitis. She was given an emergency laparotomy. The claimant had an unsightly and uncomfortable scar, and she claimed damages on the grounds that the surgeon had been negligent not using a three-port technique. It was held that the failure to use a third port amounted to a breach of duty and held that the breach was causative of the injury.

Systems failure in obstetrics

If a hospital has in place a system for managing events during labour and delivery and that system is not followed by the staff responsible for caring for the patient, there may be a finding of breach of duty[37]. However, the claim will fail if it cannot be proved that the negligence caused the injuries in question. That was the case in *Robertson v Nottingham Health Authority*[38] where there were several communications failures but the Court of Appeal concluded that the negligence did not cause the serious brain damage suffered by the baby when she suffered hypoxia.

This case has far-reaching implications because it suggests that failure to implement clinical governance as required by the Government could not only amount to the breach of duty to ensure quality in healthcare[39], imposed on chief executives, but could also result in a successful claim for negligence by an injured patient if the systems failure could be proved to have caused or materially contributed to the claimant's injury. These implications are discussed in Chapter 3.

Incompetent administration of vitamin K

In *Mughal v Ealing Hospital NHS Trust*[40] the claimant was six years old at the time of the trial, and had been born in hospital and remained there for a while for observation. A few days after her birth, as is usual practice, a midwife administered vitamin K orally to the claimant. However, it was argued for the claimant that she had not taken the full dose, as it had trickled out of her mouth. It was alleged that this had not been noticed by the medical staff, who had been negligent in not having a proper system in place to ensure that babies took the correct dose of vitamin K. A short time after this the baby developed diarrhoea and vomiting, and tests at Ealing Hospital indicated that she was suffering from anaemia. Vitamin K deficiency was diagnosed, and a CT scan at Great Ormond Street Hospital indicated a large intraventricular haemorrhage. Immediate treatment was necessary, and the claimant underwent surgery. Although she had recovered from the brain injury she had suffered as a result of vitamin K deficiency, the claimant's head area in general remained vulnerable and she had an increased risk of infection and intellectual impairment. However, her progress had been reasonably good, though she had been rather late reaching certain milestones in her development. A settlement of £27,500 was approved.

In *Abid v Riverside Health Authority*[41] the claimant suffered a severe nose bleed when she was only two weeks old. The medical staff who treated her did not try to discover the cause, and as a result, neither hepatitis nor vitamin K deficiency were diagnosed, and the onset of a brain haemorrhage was not discovered. The claimant contended that steps should have been taken to determine the reason for the nose

---

37   See also *Bull v Devon Health Authority* [1993] 4 Med LR 117.
38   [1997] 8 Med LR 1.
39   Health Act 1999.
40   QBD 1 February 1999.
41   QBD 13 April 1999.

bleed, and argued that if an investigation had been undertaken, her condition would have been discovered early enough to have prevented her suffering injury. As a result of the late diagnosis of the true condition, she suffered injury to her right arm and leg and significant brain damage. The claimant had the mental capacity of a four-year-old, although she was now aged eight years, and she was not developing at a normal rate. She required constant supervision and special assistance at school. Her short-term memory was impaired and she was prone to inadvertent injury. There was an approved settlement of £1,200,000 damages.

Psychiatric injuries incurred as a result of obstetric negligence

In *Farrell v Merton Sutton and Wandsworth Health Authority*[42] the claimant succeeded in obtaining £75,000 compensation for psychiatric injury suffered as a result of the negligent treatment that she and her baby had received. The facts of this case are stated in Chapter 2. This is one of a series of cases in which parents of infants injured as a result of negligent deliveries have succeeded in obtaining damages for psychiatric injury. The case of *Tredget v Bexley Health Authority*[43] involved a claim by the parents of a child who died two days after delivery. The pregnancy had been very difficult because of previous unsuccessful pregnancies and because the mother was diabetic. There was negligence in the delivery as a Caesarean section should have been performed sooner than it was, and the baby was born severely asphyxiated. His condition was so bad that he died within a couple of days. Both parents succeeded in their claims for psychiatric injury. The mother was, of course, present all the time, though she did not see the damaged baby immediately after he was delivered. The father was present throughout the labour and during the period of panic immediately before the baby was delivered, and as the judge explained *'both parents were directly involved in and with the event of the delivery'*. He had no difficulty in finding that they were primary victims and awarded them damages for psychiatric injury.

Giving advice

Obstetrics patients, perhaps more than any other group, are anxious to be involved in decisions about their care. This approach has been encouraged by midwives and by some obstetricians. *Pearce v United Bristol Healthcare Trust*[44] illustrates some of the difficulties that can arise if the patient is not informed about aspects of her care and possible consequences. Mrs Pearce was expecting her sixth child. On 13 November 1991. The baby had still not arrived on 27 November 1991, when Mrs Pearce saw Mr Niven, the consultant at the respondent hospital. She was very distressed during the consultation, and begged to have an induced labour or a Caesarean section. Mr Niven, however, thought it appropriate for her to have a normal birth without any medical intervention. He explained that it would be risky to induce the birth, and that it would take longer for her to recover if she had a Caesarean section. The baby died in utero some time between 2 and 3 December, and the delivery of the stillborn baby was induced on 4 December. At the trial the judge considered the following issues: (1) Should Mr Niven have advised Mrs. Pearce that there was an increased risk of stillbirth as a result of the delay in delivery? (2) If Mr Niven should have done so would his advice have altered the decision made by Mrs Pearce to have a natural birth? The trial judge dismissed the claim, finding

---

42   (2001) 57 BMLR 158.

43   [1994] 5 Med LR 178.

44   (1998) 48 BMLR 118.

that there had been no negligence on the part of Mr Niven in not advising Mrs Pearce of the small risk attached to waiting for a natural labour to begin.

The Court of Appeal held that tests in *Bolam v Friern Hospital Management Committee*[45] and *Bolitho v City and Hackney Health Authority*[46] applied to cases which concern a complaint by a patient of being deprived of the opportunity to make a proper decision about treatment. If there is a *'significant risk'* attached to a particular treatment or course of action, which would affect the judgement of a reasonable patient, then the doctor is responsible for informing the patient of that risk. The doctor has to take into account all the relevant considerations when deciding how much to tell a patient, including the patient's physical and emotional state at the time, and his or her ability to comprehend information. However, in this instance, the risk involved in waiting for labour to begin naturally, even after the expected date of delivery, was so small as to be insignificant. Had the patient been informed of the risk she would, as far as could be ascertained from the evidence, reluctantly have agreed to follow the advice of the doctor and wait for a natural labour and delivery.

Screening
Modern techniques allow for extensive screening and even for diagnosis in the antenatal period, but these developments carry a risk of litigation. In *Carver v Hammersmith & Queen Charlotte's Special Health Authority*[47], the defendant health authority was held liable in negligence for the failure of its doctor to explain that the *'Bart's test'* for Down's syndrome was not a diagnostic test, unlike amniocentesis, but was only a screening test which could not detect one in three Down's syndrome foetuses. This case involved a claim for damages for the wrongful birth of the claimant's Down's syndrome child in 1989. As the claimant had worked with handicapped children she was determined not to have a handicapped child herself, so when she became pregnant she requested an amniocentesis at the defendant's hospital but was refused a test under the hospital's policy. However, she agreed to undergo the *'Bart's test'*. She believed, mistakenly, that this test would, like amniocentesis, determine whether or not her foetus had Down's syndrome or Spina Bifida. Although the test did not reveal this to be the case, the baby was born with Down's syndrome, and the claimant alleged that if she had known this she would have terminated the pregnancy.

Nelson J considered that the case turned on what advice had been given to the claimant by the defendant's doctor, and whether, if she had received correct advice, the claimant would have insisted on having an amniocentesis. Finally, if an amniocentesis showed that the baby she was carrying had Down's syndrome, whether she would have terminated her pregnancy. It was held, on a preliminary issue, that the entitlement of the claimant to damages in respect of the costs of bringing up a seriously disabled child went to quantum, and not liability (*Emeh v Kensington and Chelsea Health Authority*[48]). The leading case of *MacFarlane v Tayside Health Board*[49] dealt only with the case of a *healthy* but unwanted baby, and expressly reserved the situation where an unwanted child was born seriously disabled. The judge was satisfied that the claimant and her partner had made a clear

---

45   (1957) 1 BMLR 1; [1957] 1 WLR 582.
46   (1997) 39 BMLR 1; [1997] 3 WLR 1151.
47   QBD 25 February 2000.
48   (1985) QB 1012.
49   (1999) 3 WLR 1301.

decision not to have a handicapped child. Nelson J concluded that the claimant was fully aware of the risks of undergoing an amniocentesis, but such was her determination not to have a handicapped child that she was prepared to take the risk of losing a healthy baby, and if she discovered that she was carrying a handicapped child to have the pregnancy terminated. He concluded that the doctor had not explained the true nature of the *'Bart's test'* and as a result, the claimant left the consultation with the clear but mistaken view that the *'Bart's test'* would determine whether or not she had a handicapped child.

The judge concluded that the defendant's doctor's failure to advise the claimant correctly constituted a breach of duty. This breach of duty was the cause of the wrongful birth.

Rand v East Dorset Health Authority[50] concerned a woman who had not been warned that she might be pregnant with a foetus affected by Down's syndrome. The parents had not wanted to have a disabled child, and in view of the admitted negligence, the birth could appropriately be described as *'wrongful'*, but the child had, since birth, been loved, wanted and cared for in the family, though her disability had caused the parents distress and emotional turmoil. The parents were awarded damages to cover the additional cost of bringing up a disabled child[51].

Forceps deliveries – the standard of care

Nash v Kingston and Richmond Health Authority[52] concerned the use of Keilland's forceps. This case, concerning obstetric negligence which allegedly occurred in 1973, was heard when the claimant was 23 years of age. The claimant had suffered cerebral palsy during birth, but unusually she had not been intellectually damaged, though she was significantly physically disabled. The claimant's mother had been admitted to hospital in the early stages of labour in the morning. She was given oxytocin to augment her contractions and she also had an epidural block. After the cervix was fully dilated the baby's head was in the persistent occipito-posterior position and it was decided to try a forceps delivery as there was some evidence of foetal distress.

Mr May, the obstetrician on duty, decided to use Keillands forceps which have independent blades which can be locked together once in position. He used what is called the *'long wandering'* technique which involves passing the anterior blade of the forceps around the baby's head from the face and back over the ear. He inserted one blade, but one of the baby's arms became trapped in the fenestration – the opening of the blade, and he was unable to free it. This was a rare complication of the use of Keillands forceps. He then attempted to use the blade of a second pair of Keillands forceps but was unsuccessful and a Caesarean section was performed. Some time between 6.45pm when Mr May first saw the mother and 7.35pm when the baby was delivered, she suffered a short period of severe hypoxic stress which resulted in the damage.

The claimant's case was that the entanglement of the arm with the blade of the forceps would not have occurred at all if the long wandering technique had not been employed, and in any event the second attempt with forceps should not have been

---

50 (2001) 57 BMLR 158.

51 In later proceedings it was held that the negligent misrepresentation made by the health authority to the parents of this Down's syndrome child, in consequence of which they had recovered damages, was not an *'injury suffered'* by the parents within the meaning of s1(1) Social Security (Recovery of Benefits) Act 1997. However, the health authority's liability depended not on the child's disability, but upon the reasonable expenditure of the parents in connection with the child's disability. Therefore the invalid care allowance received by the parents in consequence of the child's disability should not be deducted from their compensation.

52 (1996) 36 BMLR 123.

made. But for the second pair of forceps, the claimant would not have suffered asphyxiation. The defendant's case was that the technique used was reasonable in the light of the circumstances taking into account the expert evidence, and that it was not unreasonable to try to deal with the entangled arm by further manoeuvring with the second forceps rather than carrying out an immediate Caesarean section. The judge preferred the evidence of the defendant. He found that taking into account the exact position of the head, the use of the long wandering technique was not unreasonable. Accordingly, judgment was given for the defendant.

The claimant in *Holdway v Kingston and Richmond Health Authority*[53] suffered prolonged oxygen starvation during a forceps delivery at the defendant's hospital in May 1976, and had not been expected to live. It was alleged that as a result of the defendant's negligence, the claimant had suffered severe brain damage. He was severely disabled by cerebral palsy and was completely dependent upon his parents for day-to-day care. He suffered from impaired memory, and had no comprehension of danger, thus being extremely vulnerable. Although he could do many things for himself he was effectively helpless if he was left alone, and although he was aged 22 years at the time of the settlement, he needed to be cared for at home. Part of his settlement was to provide him with his own home where he would receive support from full-time professional carers. His condition was permanent and he would need constant supervision for the rest of his life. Liability was disputed. There was an approved out-of-court settlement of £1,850,000 total damages.

Failing to perform a Caesarean section

A problem which arises from time to time in obstetrics lies in the dilemma as to whether, and at what point, it is appropriate to perform a Caesarean section and abandon attempts to deliver a baby vaginally. In the case of *Cowdie v Camberwell Health Authority*[54] a High Court judge concluded that the wrong decision had been made and that in the circumstances this amounted to negligence. An emergency situation had arisen in the course of delivering the infant claimant because one of his shoulders had become lodged above the mother's symphysis pubis (unilateral shoulder dystocia). The baby needed to be delivered as soon as possible in order to avoid hypoxia and consequent brain damage. Emergency procedures to deliver him vaginally had resulted in damage to his right brachial plexus affecting five nerves and severely weakening his right arm and hand. As a result, he sustained a fracture to his left humerus and damage to the left radial nerve. It was held on a balance of probabilities that if the baby had been delivered by emergency Caesarean section, all the injuries which he had suffered would have been avoided.

It has been suggested by some obstetricians that these problems can be avoided by making an assessment of the size of the baby's shoulders prenatally where there is a higher than average risk of unilateral shoulder dystocia. It seems that the condition is more common in infants from certain ethnic groups and that good risk management practices could reduce the incidence of emergency situations of the kind which arose in this case.

In *Simms v Birmingham Health Authority*[55] the court considered whether the failure to perform a Caesarean section amounted to a breach of duty. The claimant was born on 4 March 1982 at a maternity hospital in Birmingham. He was born suffering from

---

53   QBD 4 May 1999.
54   QBD 1 July 1997.
55   QBD 24 November 2000.

severe hypoxia, having been delivered by forceps delivery at 12.58pm, and was vigorously resuscitated. He subsequently suffered encephalopathy with renal impairment, and developed spastic quadriplegia. It was agreed that the cause of the claimant's disabilities was the prolonged period of chronic hypoxia during labour, but the defendants disputed the contention that delivery should have been by Caesarean section. It was agreed that the claimant had suffered irreversible brain damage from 12.30pm, and that a Caesarean section would only have been performed before that time if it had been ordered by 11.30am.

The claimant argued that the CTG trace was probably abnormal from the start, and probably disclosed beat to beat variability of the foetal heart and non-reassuring decelerations. The claimant also alleged that the artificial rupture of membranes performed at 10.30am had been ordered because the registrar was concerned by the trace he had seen at 9.30am. Undiluted meconium, a sign of foetal distress, was discharged at 10.30am during the artificial rupture of the membranes. A serious problem should have been recognised at this stage, and the senior house officer should have reported this to the registrar. As there was clinical evidence of foetal distress, and as there were no means of obtaining information from a foetal blood sample, a Caesarean section should have been ordered at approximately 11.30am and performed soon afterwards. The defendants argued that undiluted meconium in conjunction with an abnormal CTG would mean that a Caesarean was mandatory, but that in this case the CTG was not abnormal according to the standards of 1982 and a significant percentage of babies discharged meconium without subsequent harm.

The judge found that the presence of undiluted meconium should have been reported. Accordingly, the senior house officer had been in breach of his duty, and had fallen below the required standard, by leaving the midwife to interpret the trace in a high-risk situation. Had he read the trace himself and taken steps to ensure that the registrar read it, the reduced beat to beat variability would have been disclosed soon after 10.30am. Its presence, together with continuing decelerations, would also have alerted the registrar to the need to act promptly. The standard of care pertaining in 1982 demanded that a Caesarean section should have been ordered no later than 11.15am. If this procedure had been carried out the claimant would have been delivered at 12 to 12.15pm and would not have suffered irreversible brain damage. Quantum was agreed between the parties.

In *Woodward v Kingston and Esher Health Authority*[56] the claimants, a mother and her son, received £1,950,000 for the injuries they suffered as a result of an excessively long and traumatic labour. The baby was born with severe brain damage, considerable learning and behavioural difficulties and he required constant care. Although labour had progressed normally in the beginning, the mother's contractions became increasingly less powerful and her membrane was artificially ruptured at 9am. Entonox was administered shortly afterwards and the foetal heart rate began to regulate. The baby's head was still not engaged and there was no significant progress in labour between 4pm and 7pm and at 8.30pm. The mother was given an epidural anaesthetic. At 11.40pm there were signs of foetal distress and a series of late decelerations were noted. However, it was not until 5.50am on the following day that a decision was made to perform a Caesarean section. The operation was carried out one hour later but the baby was born severely brain

---

56   QBD 26 April 1999.

damaged. The claim was based on the allegation that the hospital had been negligent in the light of the warning signs, not to carry out a Caesarean section at an earlier stage in the labour. Liability was admitted.

If a caesarean section is carried out when the baby is in the breech position, injury to the child and a subsequent claim can sometimes be avoided. In *Mullen v Enfield and Haringey Health Authority*[57] the claimant, who was aged 13 years at the date of the settlement, was born severely brain damaged as a result of alleged negligence by hospital staff during his delivery. He had been in the breech position, but was born by conventional delivery. There was a period of 10-12 minutes between delivery of his body and his head during which time his brain was starved of oxygen. He suffered serious mobility problems, and several other disabilities associated with oxygen starvation at birth. He had behavioural problems, displaying characteristics of autism, and knowing no sense of danger, which meant he could be a danger to himself and possibly to others. This condition was permanent and he would require constant supervision for the rest of his life. Liability was disputed, but there was an approved out-of-court settlement of £900,000 total damages. Although the claimant's parents accepted the sum, taking into account the risks of litigation, it was submitted by the claimant's counsel that this only represented about 60% of the full value of the claim.

The defendant health authority was liable in *Miles v Redbridge and Waltham Forest Health Authority*[58], after there had been a misdiagnosis of foetal death in the course of delivery, and for negligence in administering Pethidine to the mother imminently before delivery based on that diagnosis. It was argued for the claimant that had it not been for the misdiagnosis of foetal death, a Caesarean section would have been carried out, and the brain damage to the baby could have been avoided. However, it was held that there was no negligence in the failure to carry out a Caesarean section, and that the defendant's doctor was not negligent in simply failing to locate the foetal heart. However, he was negligent to diagnose foetal death without identifying the heart and satisfying himself that it was not beating. If he was not able to be certain the foetus was dead, he should have proceeded on the basis that it was alive. But for the misdiagnosis, Pethidine would not have been given at 5.50am, immediately before delivery. The result of the injection of Pethidine at 5.50am was the transfer of a substantial quantity of Pethidine into the foetus and this caused the depression of D's respiration at birth, which itself led to the hypercarbia. The defendant was also negligent in delaying the commencement of ventilation to the child to *'blow away'* the hypercarbia caused by the Pethidine for a period of three-and-a-half hours. Judgment was given in favour of the claimant.

Home births

Changing approaches to childbirth in the past two decades have meant that as treatment patterns have changed, so medical intervention in childbirth has been

---

57   QBD 4 May 1999.
58   QBD 18 February 2000.

reduced[59]. More women are demanding to have their babies delivered in their own homes rather than in hospital, but this trend is not without risk, and the majority of deliveries still take place in hospital. A survey of 6,000 home births carried out by Professor Chamberlaine of University College London has found that about 40% of the first time mothers who had been booked for home deliveries were in fact transferred to hospital, in comparison with only 15% of women who were having their second or subsequent babies at home. The main reason given for transfer to hospital was prolonged labour.

A report produced during the lifetime of the Conservative administration revealed that babies born at home are up to three times more likely to die following birth complications than babies delivered in hospital. The report came at a difficult time for the Government which had encouraged home deliveries in *'low-risk'* pregnancies. The document *Changing Childbirth*[60] recognises the importance of patient autonomy and the right of women to choose the place and methods of delivery. The report of the *Confidential Inquiry into Stillbirths and Deaths in Infancy* reveals that babies are dying unnecessarily and their mothers are being put at risk because of the lack of readily available emergency equipment.

Government Intervention in Obstetrics and Related Medical Practice

Successive Governments have been anxious to improve the health and welfare of pregnant women and to reduce perinatal mortality. Such policies place additional burdens on healthcare staff and raise the possibility of claims if they fail to take notice of special requirements and guidelines issued by the Government.

Violence against pregnant women

People who work with pregnant women are advised to be extra vigilant for their safety, following a report dealing with violence to pregnant women. The relationship between health and social services was again highlighted in an alert to healthcare workers to recognise and report signs of domestic violence in pregnant women.

Speaking to the Royal College of Obstetricians and Gynaecologists at the launch of the report of the Confidential Enquiry into Maternal Deaths, the then Health Minister Baroness Hayman said that the report contained important health messages and recommendations for health professionals. The onus appears to be on healthcare professionals to recognise women who are at risk and who feel inhibited about seeking antenatal care. The report of the Confidential Enquiry into Maternal Deaths, covering the period 1994-96, deals for the first time with deaths from domestic violence, from road accidents, and those resulting from psychiatric illness. The enquiry noted that an estimated 30% of domestic violence starts during pregnancy, and urged all health professionals to recognise the importance of the problem, even recommending that enquiries about violence occur as a matter of routine included when a social history is being taken, and that local strategies should be developed to identify and help those most at risk.

The enquiry's findings were seen by the Government as endorsing their policies on cross-departmental strategies to tackle domestic violence and ill-health. The report also recommended a simple procedure in every antenatal clinic to identify

---

59   Honour P, *Review of Maternity Services 1996/7* District Audit Southampton.
60   Report of the Expert Maternity Group, HMSO London 1993.

women at risk of postnatal depression and self harm, and to establish adequate support services[61].

Folic acid campaign

The policy of this and the previous Government has been to improve public health by encouraging health education. This policy has born fruit in the important area of health awareness in pregnancy and childbirth. The target for this campaign is reached relatively easily in GP surgeries, antenatal clinics and women's magazines. The highly successful Folic Acid Campaign, organised by the Health Education Authority and funded by the Department of Health, has been awarded the *Health for All* certificate for the UK to commemorate the WHO's 50th Anniversary. One example is the three-year health promotion campaign that has raised women's awareness of the importance of taking folic acid before and until the 12th week of pregnancy. The Folic Acid Campaign was selected by the European Region of the World Health Organisation as an example of an effective national campaign for improving health status within the framework of the objectives of the Region's *Health for All* public health policy.

A research report, *Changing Preconceptions*, concluded that 49% of women of childbearing age are now aware of the importance of folic acid, compared with only 9% in 1995 when the campaign began. The research also reveals an increase in the percentage of pregnant, or recently pregnant, women who take folic acid. Since 1992, following the recommendations of an expert committee, the Government has recommended that women need to increase folic acid consumption in the months before conception and in early pregnancy to reduce the risk of having a baby with a neural tube defect. It is recommended that women eat foods fortified with folic acid such as some breakfast cereals and breads; eat foods naturally rich in folic acid such as leafy green vegetables; take 400 microgram folic acid supplement daily from the time they stop using contraception until the 12th week of pregnancy[62].

However, there is some evidence that despite this campaign to increase the number of women who take folic acid during pregnancy, the incidence of neural tube defects, such as spina bifida and anencephaly, has not been reduced. Data has been collected as part of a research project by Imperial College School of Medicine, London, the National Statistics Office and the University of Glasgow, which demonstrates that the number of babies born with neural tube abnormalities has remained roughly the same as it was before the campaign, and in some areas has even increased. It is difficult to find an explanation for this. Some researchers suggest that one reason might be that the women who are most at risk and most need to increase their folic acid intake are not planning their pregnancies or are unaware of the benefits of folic acid.

Risks and benefits

Pregnancy carries considerable risks even in the normal course of events, and this was emphasised in a Commons written reply, when Health Minister John Denham acknowledged that 104 deaths could be linked to the contraceptive pill since 1989. The Government is anxious to emphasise that in percentage terms these figures are very low, especially when the risks associated with pregnancy are taken into account.

---

61   The Report is available from the Stationery Office, price £16.95 (ISBN 0 11 322253X), and on their website on *http://www.the-stationery-office.co.uk*.

62   *Changing Preconceptions: The HEA Folic Acid Campaign 1995-1998*. Volume I (Summary Report) and Volume 2 (Research Report) price £15 each or £22.50 for both. Copies are available from Marstons Book Services Tel: 01235 465 565.

Three million women take the contraceptive pill in the UK every year, and the risks associated with this are much lower than the risks involved in pregnancy and childbirth. However, there were also 2,408 cases in which adverse effects had been associated with oral contraception.

Teenage pregnancies

Funding has been announced for teenage pregnancy advice projects. Britain has the highest rate of teenage pregnancy in Western Europe, and grants announced from the Department of Health's Local Implementation Fund are part of the cross-Government strategy which it is hoped will cut by 50% the number of women under 18 who become pregnant by the year 2010. Projects designed to prevent teenage pregnancies or help teenage parents avoid long-term deprivation have been given extra funding.

The Social Exclusion Report on teenage pregnancy, published in June 1999, set the goal of halving the rates of conceptions among under 18s by 2010. It also recommended that more teenage parents should go into education, training or employment to reduce the risk of long-term social exclusion. The report set out a 30-point Government-wide programme for meeting these targets. The projects which include the use of drama, photography and art and other methods to teach about sexual health, practical help to encourage teenage parents to return to school, the appointment of contraception advisers, and the use of peer advisers for young people living in hostels.

Meanwhile the morning-after pill is being offered free of charge in a pilot scheme in Manchester. Until now women have only been able to obtain the morning-after pill on prescription from GPs and Family Planning Clinics. The scheme raises legal concerns because of the problem of supplying these pills to women under the age of 16 years. However, pharmacists are being advised that they will be able to do so if they are satisfied that the young women who appear to be under 16 years old understand the consequences of their treatment. Women requesting emergency contraception are to be taken to a private area and asked questions and given advice based on a protocol used by the Brook Advisory Centres. They will be asked to sign consent forms. In the case of women under the age of 16 years, this procedure is of doubtful legality, as the *Gillick* criteria demand a high level of understanding on the part of the woman and careful and thorough counselling by doctors (and by analogy, pharmacists). It is also proposed to sell the morning after pill over the counter at pharmacies throughout the country, instead of on a prescription only basis. The Pregnancy Advisory Service considers that easier availability of emergency contraception would be a major advance, but the Pro life groups believe that the drug simply facilitates early abortion and that the health risks associated with it are being underestimated.

Government attempts to reduce low birth-weight

Promising a sustained attack on poverty, the Government acknowledged the link between poverty and poor health. A report, which runs into 168 pages, acknowledged that poverty is not necessarily about low income, which has been the traditional bench-mark. *'Poverty'* also encompasses poverty of opportunity, poor housing conditions and poor health. Although the Government has set out a large number of indicators and specific targets, the report has been criticised for being too vague, with too many conflicting targets. The aim was to reduce the proportion of low birth-weight babies (that is babies born weighing under 2,500 grams) by 5% in the year 2001/2. At present there are 7.4% of these babies born annually, and there is a strong connection between low birth weight and diseases in infancy and heart disease in later life. Another objective is to reduce by half the rate of conceptions among women under 18 by 2001. The report indicated that the number of children living in poverty has tripled during the past 20 years. The poverty line is officially defined as an income of £123 a week for a household – a figure of half the national average income[63].

HIV testing of pregnant women

The Department of Health is encouraging all pregnant women to undergo an HIV test. Research indicates overwhelmingly that identifying babies likely to be at risk, and taking appropriate measures at an early stage can reduce infection rates from mother to child by approximately two-thirds. Delivery by Caesarean section and not breast feeding are likely to reduce the risk of transmitting HIV by almost 20 times, and not only would testing prove to be offering hope to the children of HIV positive mothers, it would almost certainly be cost-effective, although the number of infected babies is currently very low – 25 boys and 43 girls out of a total of 600,000 births in 1998. The latest guidance issued by the Department of Health recommends strongly that women should be tested early in pregnancy at antenatal clinics, at around the time when they are routinely tested for rubella and other infectious diseases. Women will be informed that they are being tested for HIV, and will be asked to give their consent. While women are entitled to refuse the test, doctors are advised to point out the possible dangers of so doing. There has been some concern that women will be reluctant to consent to the HIV test, as they fear that it could affect life-insurance premiums and employment prospects.

Negligent Misdiagnosis

Several recent cases illustrate the consequences of failure to diagnose medical conditions correctly. Indeed, this is one of the most fertile areas for clinical negligence claims and some examples are discussed in this section. The cases again suggest that it can be very difficult for claimants to prove negligence on the part of their carers.

In *Scott v Northern Devon Healthcare Trust*[64] the claimant sought damages from the defendants for negligence that had allegedly occurred in the course of a consultation she had with a doctor at the North Devon and Exeter Hospital. She had a history of depression since 1980 but had recovered well by the early 1990s. In November 1991, when she was pregnant, she became concerned that her depression, which had previously been connected with pregnancy, might return. Medication was prescribed, but the symptoms continued beyond the pregnancy, and she increasingly suffered what she described as *'funny turns'*. In May 1993 the claimant was referred to a specialist by her GP, whose letter of reference noted frequent attacks of blurred vision, followed by loss of balance and brief numbness in her left leg. The frequency of the attacks was stated as being more than two a week, with one example of three in one day. After seeing the specialist in June 1993, the claimant had one more *'funny turn'* and subsequently suffered a stroke in August 1993. It became clear that she had in fact been suffering from Transient Ischemic Attacks for some time. At the trial, the claimant alleged that the specialist was negligent in failing to seek the advice of a neurologist who would then have advised him to carry out appropriate tests which, in turn, would have led to the discovery of antiphospholipid syndrome. Subsequent administration of high-dose warfarin would have prevented the stroke.

---

63   The report, entitled *Opportunity for All, Tackling Poverty and Social Exclusion,* can be accessed on *www.dss.gov.uk*
64   QBD 31 July 2000.

It was held that the case was difficult and unusual, because Transient Ischemic Attacks are rare in a woman of the claimant's age, (41 years old at the date of consultation), and antiphospholipid syndrome was extremely rare. Indeed, neither of the consultant physicians called by the parties had seen such a case in their combined experience of nearly 60 years in practice. Expert medical evidence given on behalf of the Trust suggested that there were several possible diagnoses available, and there was an insufficient risk of Transient Ischemic Attacks for the case to have been considered an emergency. Urgent reference to a neurologist would not have been expected. In the light of *Bolitho v City and Hackney Health Authority*[65] there was a logical and reasonable body of medical opinion to support the course of action taken by the defendant, so there was insufficient evidence to make a finding of negligence against him. Accordingly, the claim was dismissed.

Rare conditions can be very difficult to diagnose, but there are some examples of successful claims even in the case of very unusual medical conditions. In the case of *R v Croydon Health Authority*[66], Mrs R had been required to undergo a medical examination when she had applied for a post with the defendant health authority in October 1988. A radiologist had negligently failed to report a significant abnormality which if investigated would have revealed that Mrs R was suffering from primary pulmonary hypertension. This condition, which can be exacerbated by pregnancy and is untreatable, carries a risk of sudden death and limits life expectancy. After only four months as an employee of the defendants, Mrs R had become ill and primary pulmonary hypertension was diagnosed, but despite her illness a healthy baby girl was delivered by Caesarean section in November 1989. However, Mrs R had undergone two cardiac catheterisations and a hysterectomy after delivery. She developed reactive depression after being informed that her life-expectancy was then only three to ten years, and had retired on grounds of ill-health in May 1991. However, since then it had emerged that the primary pulmonary hypertension had been exacerbated only on a temporary basis by the pregnancy, and her life-expectancy was re-estimated at 20 years.

At first instance the judge had held that the pregnancy was a foreseeable consequence of failure to diagnose the illness as it was clear that pregnancy carried a very high risk of devastating consequences, and that risk *'should have been in the forefront of the mind of a competent radiologist'*. He had ruled that if there had been no negligence on the part of the radiologist the claimant would have been warned about the danger to her life which pregnancy entailed, and accordingly that there was no difference in principle between this case and the *'unwanted birth'* cases arising out of failed sterilisation operations. Included in the original award of damages was a sum to cover the cost of bringing up the child. However, the Court of Appeal accepted the argument of the health authority that in all the previous cases in which damages had been awarded for the upbringing of a child, the child had either been not wanted at all or had not been wanted because it was disabled; but that here the mother had wanted to become pregnant and had welcomed her healthy baby so that there was no occasion for awarding damages either for the normal expenses of pregnancy or the cost of bringing up the child[67]. Damages were therefore reduced to reflect this.

---

65   (1999) 39 BMLR 1.
66   The Independent 4 December 1997.
67   Note that the law on this has changed since this case was decided.

Two cases recently settled out-of-court indicate that there may be serious consequences if there is a misdiagnosis of mental illness.

In *Sheldon v East Norfolk Health Authority*[68], (settled out-of-court August 2000), after which the claimant was interviewed on BBC Radio 4's Woman's Hour[69], it was alleged that there had been misdiagnosis of a depression, and that the claimant had been given the wrong treatment. The allegations raise some serious concerns about the possibility that there can be misdiagnosis, and therefore the wrong treatment for psychiatric problems. Although liability was disputed, the BBC programme presented the situation as one of clear misdiagnosis, and this may have been somewhat misleading.

The claimant was a 37-year-old woman who received £57,919 for the prolonged depression she suffered as a result of the defendant's alleged misdiagnosis of her depressive illness as schizophrenia. She was treated for schizophrenia between 1986 and 1990, and claimed that she had suffered severe side effects as a result of the drugs that she was prescribed. During the years before the misdiagnosis was recognised the claimant was admitted to hospital seven times and was given anti-psychotic medication. She had attempted to commit suicide on three occasions. Only after the diagnosis of depression was made when a different psychiatrist examined her on her seventh admission to hospital, did the claimant's condition begin to improve.

Liability was disputed, with the defendants admitting that the claimant had periodically shown symptoms of depression, but alleging that she had been *'clearly psychotic'* throughout her admissions. It was agreed by experts for both parties that it was possible that the claimant could have been diagnosed with either severe depression or schizophrenia at any time up until her third admission.

In *Charley v Royal Surrey County Hospital and Healthlands NHS Trust*[70], the claimant received £40,000 in an out-of-court settlement. In June 1995, she lost control of the car when she was driving and had collided with a hedge. The police were called, and the claimant was breathalysed. She found that she could not speak at that time, and she was taken by ambulance to the defendant's hospital, where she could not communicate, except to say *'no'*. The claimant, who had brought her younger child to the hospital with her, dropped the carrycot onto the floor, and this was interpreted by staff at the hospital as an act of aggression. A casualty officer thought that the claimant was suffering from post-natal depression, and did not carry out any formal neurological or physical examination upon her. A few days later the claimant was examined by a consultant psychiatrist and admitted to a psychiatric hospital under s2 of the Mental Health Act 1983. She was kept in that hospital against her will for four-and-a-half days, and was subsequently transferred to another psychiatric hospital. The claimant was examined and diagnosed with an organic, rather than a psychiatric condition. It was then recognised that the claimant had suffered a left middle cerebral artery stroke. The claimant brought an action for negligence against the defendants, and liability was admitted in September 2000.

Misdiagnosis of cancer can lead to unnecessary and painful treatment, and there are several examples of this in the law reports. For example in one case, a young athlete was misdiagnosed as having bone cancer, and as a result her leg was amputated. The treatment she received may mean that she will never be able to have

---

68   August 2000 settled out-of-court.

69   8 February 2001.

70   Settled out-of-court 11 December 2001.

children. The case has been settled for around £1.2 million. In *Cormack v East London Health Authority* [71], the claimant, formerly a senior health visitor, was a 63-year-old woman, who was awarded £345,222 for unnecessary extensive surgery and resulting depression and anxiety, following the defendant's misdiagnosis of cancer. A pathologist at the defendant's hospital had incorrectly reported that the claimant had an invasive lobular carcinoma, leading to a misdiagnosis of breast cancer. Following the misdiagnosis, she had undergone thirteen operations, including a mastectomy and reconstructive surgery, over a period of thirteen years, and was left feeling mutilated, and a profoundly altered body image. She had taken a very high daily dose of Tamoxifen as part of the unnecessary breast cancer treatment, and this led to her having to undergo a hysterectomy as a result of unpleasant side effects of the drug regime. She suffered from depression and had a very low sense of self-esteem as a result of what had occurred, and had retired from work early, believing that her condition was terminal.

In 1994, the claimant was recalled to the defendant's hospital and was informed that her original breast cancer diagnosis had been incorrect. She was advised to stop taking the Tamoxifen immediately. In 1995, she underwent bilateral removal of the breast implants, one of which was found to have ruptured, and this required further unpleasant surgery. The claimant's second marriage was dissolved in 1990, and she believed that the divorce was caused partly by her mental state following the drastic surgery she had undergone, but she married again in 1992.

The claimant brought an action against the defendant alleging negligence in the original misdiagnosis of her with cancer. The defendant argued initially that the claimant's mastectomies were justified on prophylactic grounds due to her high risk factor for breast cancer, but liability and causation were admitted prior to trial. The judge commented that this was a case involving a serious and indefensible misdiagnosis. The award amounted to £345,222 damages.

In *Taylor v West Kent Health Authority*[72] a woman in her early thirties who eventually died of breast cancer, had been referred to the Kent and Sussex Hospital by her GP. Initial cytology had suggested that a biopsy needed to be carried out in order to arrive at a firm diagnosis. The cytology report, dated 10 January 1989, had stated: *'Blood and groups of mildly atypical epithelial cells possible from a fibroadenoma or fibrocystic disease. Consider biopsy to confirm'.* No biopsy was carried out at this stage and the diagnosis was stated to be fibroadenoma and/or fibroadenosis. The deceased woman had two reviews of her condition at six-month intervals and was reassured by two different registrars, but in February 1990, only a few weeks after the second review, she noticed that the swelling in her left breast was larger. Her GP referred her to a consultant surgeon who wrote *'probable carcinoma'* on her medical records. A pathology report, dated March 1990, stated *'Adenocarcinoma cells are present, consistent with breast primary'.* She was given radiotherapy commencing in May 1990, but unfortunately by late November 1990 metastasis was apparent. After further radiotherapy and then chemotherapy she died on 23 December 1991, aged 33 years. Kay J held that there had been negligence in 1989 when no further investigation had followed the first cytology report, and that investigation at that stage would probably have led to a diagnosis of carcinoma at that stage when it was still sufficiently early for the nodes to be unaffected. It was unlikely that she would have been offered chemotherapy in 1989, but there had been

---

71   QBD 6 October 2000.

72   (1997) 8 Med LR 251.

negligence in March 1990 in that she had not been provided with chemotherapy. The case was decided on liability alone. Damages are unlikely to be high because it was probable that the tumour from which the deceased was suffering was aggressive, and that she would have died close to the time of her eventual death in any event, even if properly diagnosed and treated in January 1989. After considering the opinions of five different experts, Kay J decided that she would have survived only for a further 18 months if the illness had been correctly diagnosed and treated.

In *Bateman v Industrial Orthopaedic Society and Others*[73] there was a failure to diagnose and treat colorectal carcinoma, in a woman who died at the age of 46 years. She left a husband and two children aged 14 and 19 years. Between the date of the negligent failure to diagnose her illness and her death, she had numerous medical investigations and two operations. During the last nine months of her life she was aware that she was terminally ill. Actions were brought on behalf of the estate of the deceased and also by her dependants in their own right. The judge decided that the award of general damages in cases of terminal illness, especially if the deceased was aware that life had been shortened, should be higher than awards for other illnesses or conditions which had been misdiagnosed.

In *Raven v Patel, Rao and Queen Mary's Sidcup NHS Trust*[74], the claimant was a 31-year-old woman who claimed damages for the death of her husband, allegedly caused by the negligent medical treatment he had received at the defendant's hospital. She brought her claim under the Fatal Accidents Act 1976 on behalf of herself and her son, and under the Law Reform (Miscellaneous Provisions) Act 1934 on behalf of the estate of the deceased. In August 1994, the claimant's husband had suffered injury while playing football. He attended a casualty unit, and later visited his GP complaining of severe headaches. He continued to suffer such headaches every day for two years. He also developed other symptoms, including nausea, dizziness and blurred vision. On 27 March 1995, the deceased's condition deteriorated seriously, and on the way to hospital in an ambulance, he suffered a respiratory arrest. He had a gross papilloedema in his right eye, and his left pupil was dilated. He was intubated and underwent a craniotomy. However, he died on 30 March 1995. A post-mortem examination indicated that he had suffered from brain stem compression as a result of raised intracranial pressure from a benign tumour.

The claimant alleged that the medical staff who had treated her husband were negligent in failing to appreciate the fact that the deceased's headaches had been so persistent and that they had not taken appropriate and urgent steps to determine the cause. She contended that if the case had been properly managed, his death would have been avoided. Liability was disputed but an out-of-court settlement of £135,000 total damages was approved, with the sum of £15,000 specifically allocated to the claimant's son.

Scotter v Queen Mary's Sidcup NHS Trust[75] concerned the death of a woman aged only 33 years, a few months after she had given birth to her second child. On 2 August 1994 the woman had been discharged from hospital after the birth of her second child, and on the same evening she had gone to bed early complaining of a severe headache. Her husband had found her lying on the bed at 10pm having an epileptic fit. She was unconscious and in obvious respiratory difficulty. She was

---

73   Quantum December 1997.

74   QBD 19 May 1999.

75   QBD 26 April 1999.

taken to the hospital run by the defendants for treatment, and an initial diagnosis suggested that she was suffering from a viral infection so a course of antibiotics was prescribed. A CT scan was arranged for the following day, and after that had been carried out the diagnosis was revised to one of meningitis. She was treated accordingly and was discharged from hospital on 15 August 1994, but received further treatment as an out-patient. Although the severity of her symptoms subsided over the following months, she still suffered from severe headaches and nausea, and in January 1995, she had severe pain in her neck and lost consciousness. She was admitted to the hospital where she died three days later. A post-mortem revealed that D had suffered three sub-arachnoid haemorrhages which had gone undetected, the first having occurred on 2 August the previous year. The claimants, the husband and children of the deceased, brought an action under the Fatal Accidents Act 1984 and the Law Reform (Miscellaneous Provisions) Act 1934 alleging that the defendant hospital was negligent in failing to diagnose the deceased's condition, on the basis that insufficient regard was given to the fact that there was blood visible in her brain in the CT scan of August 1994 and that the three aneurysms in the vertebro-basilar arteries should have been detected and treated. Liability was admitted, and a settlement of £150,000 total damages was approved, but the settlement figure represented a compromise between the parties, as there were causation difficulties for the claimants in this case, the defendant arguing that even if a correct diagnosis had been made in August 1994, the condition might still have been fatal because the course of treatment she would have undergone was attended by considerable risks and had a low success rate.

Reed v Sunderland Health Authority[76], involved the failure to diagnose a twisted and herniated small intestine. If diagnosed in time the condition could have been cured by a laparotomy, a relatively simple procedure to untwist and repair the intestine and repair the herniation. The claimant, then aged 18 years, spent three days in hospital suffering severe pain during which time she was not even seen by a consultant. It appears that nursing staff did not believe her symptoms. She was discharged without any proper treatment and was readmitted three days later when her abdomen was very distended. It was necessary to remove 131cm of small intestine which had by this time become necrotic, and 33cm of necrotic large intestine. She continued to suffer severe pain and diarrhoea. She also needed regular injections of vitamin B12. As a result of her experiences she suffered a serious psychiatric condition and became reclusive and depressed. She had attempted suicide on two occasions. Before her illness the claimant had been an outgoing teenager with normal interests and a bright future. She had been expected to go to university and to achieve a good grade in her degree, but as a result of the negligent treatment she had been unable even to complete her A level courses and was unlikely ever to find gainful employment. The claimant, who was aged 27 years when the case finally came to trial, was awarded general damages of £35,000, past loss of earnings of £49,000, loss of future earnings of £235,538, and additional special damages of £11,847.40.

A woman whose medical condition was misdiagnosed as gastro-enteritis when she was in fact suffering from appendicitis, was awarded £23,750 damages by the High Court. In *Daniels v Kay*[77] the claimant consulted her GP when she was suffering from stomach pains. She was told that she had gastro-enteritis and was

---

76   QBD December 1997.
77   QBD 1997.

prescribed treatment for that condition. Her GP also advised her that it was safe to join her husband in Paris and then to proceed to Singapore on holiday. By the time she arrived in Singapore the appendix had burst and she was admitted to hospital as an emergency. She was left with a sizeable scar and her recovery was delayed because the wound became infected.

Negligent Treatment

When negligent treatment is alleged, even though the claimant can prove that the treatment was substandard, the claim will not succeed unless the claimant can establish that the poor quality treatment caused the alleged injury. In *Temple v South Manchester Health Authority*[78] there was a claim for damages arising from the alleged negligence of a hospital registrar. The claimant, then nearly ten years of age, was referred by his GP to the defendant's hospital. There, a paediatric registrar correctly diagnosed him as suffering from diabetic ketoacidosis ('DKA') and began treatment. His condition was monitored during the night, but early next morning he lapsed into unconsciousness. Soon after that further treatment was administered by a consultant paediatrician, but the claimant had suffered cerebral oedema resulting in severe and permanent brain damage. The basis of the claim was that the paediatric registrar failed to seek advice from the consultant paediatrician shortly after the claimant's admission; had not monitored his condition properly; and had failed to make appropriate adjustments to his management during the night. It was argued that if the claimant had been managed differently, the cerebral oedema would not have developed, or would have been less severe.

It was held that the case turned entirely on whether the claimant could prove, on a balance of probability: first, that the way in which he was managed after he arrived at hospital fell below the standard reasonably to be expected of a competent hospital authority acting through its medical staff; and second, if it did, that as a result he had suffered injury and loss which would have been avoided had he been treated without negligence. The judge found that there had been negligence in not involving the consultant paediatrician in the claimant's management at an earlier stage. That was because the patient's condition was critical with the risk of fatal or other devastating complications; and also there was no protocol in use at the hospital for treatment of DKA. It was preferable to have two experienced minds at work in such a situation. The paediatric registrar's management of this case did reflect that which was considered appropriate practice in texts to which he had the opportunity to refer and which, although different in places, reflected the same basic approach to the necessary reduction in blood glucose before changing from an isotonic to a hypotonic solution. Nevertheless, having considered the credibility and evidence of three experts it could not be said on the balance of probabilities that the negligence found to be established had resulted in the development of cerebral oedema and its devastating consequences. Accordingly, the claim was dismissed.

Holder v Ealing Health Authority[79] was an appeal from an order giving judgment for the defendant, and the claimant appeared in person. The facts of the case are that between September 1991 and April 1992 the claimant attended the defendant's hospital on different occasions as both an in-patient and an out-patient, to receive treatment for severe retro-sternal pain. He complained that he had suffered severe chest pains which the defendant had failed to diagnose as coronary heart disease, and

---

78   QBD 19 July 2000.
79   Court of Appeal, 25 June 1999.

which eventually required heart bypass surgery. He claimed damages for unnecessary pain and suffering before a correct diagnosis was made. The defendants stated that all proper tests has been carried out, and that when an irregularity was discovered in April 1992 the claimant was immediately referred to a specialist hospital. Counsel for the defendant addressed the judge in the claimant's absence (he had to be taken to hospital at one point during the trial), as to the correct course to take in the circumstances, and the trial was adjourned. The claimant contended on appeal that discussions made in his absence had not been fair. He also complained that he was prevented from calling his GP to testify, and made particularly personal allegations against the recorder who heard the case, claiming that he was under the influence of alcohol because he had a red face and he wore his wig sideways.

It was held that all of the claimant's submissions were without substance. There had been a misunderstanding regarding the calling of the GP. Although a report from the GP was produced at trial there was little opinion expressed in it, and the recorder had a discretion whether or not to allow the GP to be called. Given the late introduction of the report, and the fact that no opinion was expressed in it, the Court of Appeal could not say that the exercise of this discretion had been wrong. The recorder had considered all the relevant facts, and had no evidence before him to show that the defendant's standard of care fell short of that required. The appeal was dismissed.

There have been several successful claims relating to poor quality of treatment in recent years. The problems involved in intubating infants suffering from croup were disused at length by expert witnesses in the case of *Bolitho v City and Hackney Health Authority*[80], in which the doctor concerned stated that even if she had attended the child, she would not have intubated him because of the hazards of that procedure. The case of *Fallios v Croydon Health Authority*[81] demonstrates these hazards. The claimant had been taken to the defendant's hospital as a young baby suffering from severe breathing difficulties caused by croup. The diagnosis was acute airways obstruction and the case was treated as an emergency. The claimant was intubated in an effort to assist his breathing. This involved sliding a tube down into his throat, but the tube used was too large in relation to his size, so although they saved the claimant's life, they also caused him injury. As a result of the large tube placed into his throat, the claimant's air passage became narrowed and he later required a tracheotomy to be in place for five years. This meant that he needed to make frequent return visits to hospital for monitoring and further treatment. There was an approved settlement of £83,000 total damages.

In *Beatham v Carlisle Hospitals NHS Trust*[82], the claimant was a married woman who was 30 years old at date of settlement. On 14 January 1996 she had suffered a severe asthma attack and attended the defendant's hospital for treatment. She had a history of asthma, and was admitted to a ward. However, the hospital took no steps to investigate her condition, or to ascertain her condition or monitor its progress. In particular, the standard procedure of monitoring the claimant's peak respiratory flow was not carried out. Whilst she was in hospital, the claimant suffered a respiratory arrest. She urgently required oxygen, but there was a delay in administering this until an oxygen mask could be located. She then subsequently suffered a cardiac arrest which resulted in severe brain damage. The claimant alleged that the defendants

---

80   (1997) 39 BMLR 1.
81   QBD 27 May 2000.
82   The Times 22 May 1999.

were negligent in the medical treatment provided, in that they had failed to prescribe appropriate medication or to ensure that essential equipment was available. She further contended that when it had become apparent that her condition was deteriorating there was a negligent delay in responding.

As a result of the negligence of the defendants, the claimant required 24-hour care, and was unable to walk or talk. At the date of settlement she was receiving care in an NHS hospice and was described as *'minimally aware'*, only being able to recognise her mother and father, who were frequent visitors. She had no real awareness of her surroundings, but she could make her carers aware that she was in pain or discomfort, by moaning, and could respond to some basic commands made by her father. The prognosis was poor as the claimant's condition was permanent and she would make only slight progress. It was agreed that she was expected to live to about the age of 42 and would continue to require intensive care. There was an out-of-court settlement of £1,700,000 total damages.

The judge went on to consider the question as to whether settlements should be approved in open court. He ruled that settlements made on behalf of children or mental patients should normally be held in public, despite the statement in para 1.8 of the Practice Direction relating to Part 21 of the Civil Procedure Rules, which provides that *'A hearing of an application under Part 21 will take place in private unless the court directs otherwise'*. Mr Justice Buckley ruled that there was a public interest in these cases and that he did not believe that the Practice Direction was intended to interfere with that.

In *Morris v Solihull Healthcare Trust*[83] there was a substantial award of damages to a woman who had suffered serious injuries in a suicide attempt. In May 1994 the claimant suffered concussion and a fractured femur when she fell from a horse in a riding accident. As she was recovering from her physical injuries in hospital her behaviour began to change. Although no brain damage was detectable on scans, it was later believed that the claimant had probably sustained such injury, possibly from an embolism or the anaesthetic. She was given medication and her condition appeared to be improving. However, by August 1994 she was suffering from depression and had spoken of suicide. On medical advice, she was admitted to the defendant hospital. Four months after the accident, in September 1994, hospital staff discovered that the claimant had tried to strangle herself by tying her tights to a radiator. She argued that she should have been kept under continuous observation rather than close observation and that had she received appropriate monitoring she would not have had the opportunity to harm herself. Liability was disputed by the defendants who denied that there was evidence that the claimant was intending suicide, and argued that medical staff had observed her more frequently than was required under the level of supervision that had been formally instituted. However, the 51-year-old woman received £800,000 for her severe brain damage.

Negligence in Surgery

Surgery carries many risks that could lead to litigation and to very large awards being paid to claimants. Fear of professional discipline as well as litigation can create an atmosphere of unease among surgeons. An announcement by the Royal College of Surgeons that it is to investigate the work of two more cardiac surgeons, has caused anxieties among the profession that many surgeons will only be prepared to operate in straightforward cases, and that risky surgery will simply not be undertaken. New

---

83   QBD 14 October 1999.

compulsory audit procedures will reveal mortality rates which are worse than average, and monitoring by the Commission for Health Improvement is likely to make the hope of surgery for high risk patients more remote.

Depending on the nature of the injury suffered by the claimant during surgery, awards are sometimes very high. In *Waddington v Lancaster Acute Hospitals NHS Trust*[84] a six-year-old boy received £1,900,000 for the brain damage he suffered during routine surgery to correct a testicular abnormality. He suffered a heart attack during the operation and his heart stopped beating. As a result, his brain was starved of oxygen, and he was severely disabled, unable to communicate and in need of 24-hour care.

In *Pineiro v Hammersmith and Queen Charlotte's Special Health Authority*[85] it was discovered almost immediately after his birth that the claimant was suffering from congenital cyanotic heart disease. When he was one day old he underwent emergency surgery as a temporary measure, and when he reached the age of almost six months he required further surgery, known as the *'Mustard Operation'*. During this procedure the claimant was attached to a cardio-pulmonary by-pass circuit, and staff failed to notice that blood had become clotted. A blood-clot lodged in his aorta and he suffered severe brain damage as a result. He had the mental abilities of a three-year-old, and experienced severe learning and behavioural difficulties which meant that he was very disruptive, requiring intensive one-to-one care. The claimant's condition had improved somewhat since he had attended a residential school where he could stay until the age of 19 years, after which he would probably be transferred to another residential institution and cared for by professional carers. He was likely to live for another twenty-five years. The total award of damages amounted to £1,723,216.

Post Operative Care

Newbury v Bath District Health Authority[86], provides an example of a situation in which the only negligence lay in post operative care although surgery was found to have been carried out competently. The claimant had undergone a three-hour spinal decompression and fusion operation in an attempt to alleviate the pain from which she had been suffering for some time. The judge ruled that she had not been misled into believing that the surgery was less hazardous than in fact it was. However, when she suffered a loss of sensation following surgery, and staff had not acted immediately, she had lost a 50% chance of making a full recovery. She has now lost much of the sensation in her lower body and suffers from sensations of numbness. Her marriage is under strain as a result of her depression and altered personality and she can no longer enjoy walking and cycling. She was awarded £200,000 damages.

In *Gray v Southampton and South West Hampshire Health Authority*[87] the claim arose out of events that had occurred in July 1984, when the claimant underwent surgery for the removal of a brain tumour. She had suffered epileptic fits from the age of two, but had been free of them for two years before the operation in 1984 at the defendant's hospital. Within an hour of the surgery she suffered an epileptic fit, and at some stage during the ensuing hours, she suffered severe and irreparable

---

84   QBD 18 October 1999.
85   QBD 29 January 1999.
86   QBD 21 January 1998.
87   QBD 3 June 2000.

generalised anoxic-ischaemic brain damage. As a result she was severely disabled and dependent on her parents.

It was held that what had happened involved a rare occurrence for which the number of possible causes was limited, the task of the experts was to eliminate incomplete evidence. It was clear from the good medical records available in this case that the damage was not caused to the claimant during the operation itself. The judge preferred the opinion of the claimant's expert on the course of the neurological events leading to the claimant's injuries, but it was a question of fact as to whether on a balance of probabilities her injuries were caused by want of care on the part of the defendant. Despite misgivings about shortcomings on the part of the doctor in charge of the claimant's care, and despite profound sympathy for her parents, there was insufficient evidence of the degree and nature of the relative hypotension or hypoxia to justify finding that it was caused by lack of proper management. Accordingly, the claim was dismissed.

There are many cases in which negligence is alleged when the result of surgery is not what was anticipated. The claimant in *Lavelle v Hammersmith and Queen Charlotte's Special Health Authority*[88] was a child who had been suffering from a serious congenital heart condition. Had the condition remained uncorrected he would have suffered brain damage or death through cyanosis, and a balloon atrial seprostomy was performed in an attempt to alleviate the condition. The surgeon, who was alleged to have carried out the procedure negligently, had since died. The claimant had suffered brain damage as a result of the rupture of two of the three sheaths of the right middle lobe pulmonary vein. This had caused blood to leak into the chest cavity. The injury was severe. He was left doubly incontinent, almost blind and unable to speak. He required constant care and physiotherapy. At first instance it had been contended for the claimant that the surgeon, although very experienced, had been working under great pressure and speed when the operation was performed. However, the judge had ruled at first instance, after hearing the expert evidence, that negligence had not been proved.

The Court of Appeal ruled that there were two equally speculative explanations of what might have happened in this case and that the trial judge had been entitled to conclude that the surgeon had relied on frontal screening when positioning the catheter, so that there had been no mistaken insertion of the catheter in the right middle lobe pulmonary vein. The claimant had therefore failed on the evidence to establish liability, and the judge had been correct to conclude that negligence had not been established in this case. The appeal was dismissed.

General Practitioners

GPs are expected to exercise the standard of care that would be expected of other doctors in general practice and not that of specialists. However, they are required to make difficult decisions about rare conditions, frequently in very testing circumstances, as the case of *Etheridge v Millar*[89] demonstrates. On 22 November 1989 the claimant made a suicide attempt, by inhaling carbon monoxide in his car. The attempt failed and the claimant was discovered lying outside his garage. When the evidence of the claimant's attempted suicide was discovered, he was taken to the first defendant, a general practitioner, who did not examine him, but recommended that he be taken home to be cared for, and see his own general practitioner in due

---

88   QBD January 1998.
89   QBD 27 November 2000.

course. The claimant was taken to his mother's house, and the next day, he was seen by the second defendant, his own general practitioner. This GP prescribed anti-depressant tablets and vitamins, and saw the claimant on each subsequent day until 27 November 1989, when he referred him to hospital because of continuing breathing difficulties. There, the claimant was diagnosed as suffering from carbon monoxide poisoning.

He brought an action against the defendants alleging that they were negligent in failing to refer him for specialist treatment for carbon monoxide poisoning. The claimant alleged that if he had been treated appropriately by the first defendant he would have made a substantial recovery, and that if he had been treated appropriately by the second defendant he would have made a recovery, but it would have been rather more limited. Liability was initially disputed, but following service of the defence, it was admitted that the first defendant should have referred the claimant to hospital on the morning of 22 November 1989 for treatment.

The claimant's injuries were extensive. He sustained severe brain damage, and he suffered from cognitive deficits and intellectual impairment. The severity of his injuries was increased as a result of the delay in his receiving the appropriate treatment. The claimant also suffered from profound amnesia as a result of his injuries. He could not care for himself or manage his own affairs, and required care and supervision from residential carers. The claimant would never work. He did not claim for a full recovery of damages, because he would have suffered some brain damage suffered before either defendant had an opportunity to provide treatment. There was an approved settlement of £585,000 total damages.

In *Sheppard v Moore*[90], the claimant succeeded in establishing that his doctor had been negligent. In January 1994 he attended the defendant GP's surgery complaining of acute chest pains. The claimant believed that the cause of his symptoms was indigestion and he told his doctor as much. He was prescribed indigestion medicine and sent home. However, soon after the claimant left the surgery, he had a severe heart attack and collapsed. The defendant was called outside to attend the claimant and made attempts to resuscitate his patient before he was taken to hospital where he recovered to some extent, but he suffered brain damage. The claimant brought an action against the defendant alleging that the GP had been negligent in failing to refer him immediately to hospital. He argued that the defendant knew about the claimant's family history of coronary heart disease, and should have known that he had an abnormally high cholesterol level, a history of cigarette smoking and was overweight. It was argued that the defendant should have responded appropriately to these risks by referring his patient to hospital and giving him an aspirin tablet. Whilst the claimant accepted that he would still have suffered a heart attack even had the defendant reacted to his symptoms correctly, he argued that he would not have suffered damage to his brain and would have been able to live a normal life. However, his intellect was impaired and his memory was reduced to 30% of normal. He was unable to work and could not return to his pre-accident career as a managing director of two food trading companies. The claimant needed to be given constant care. Liability was disputed. There was an approved settlement of £1,575,000 total damages.

In *Major v Wilcox*[91] there was an appeal from a decision in a claim arising out of the alleged negligence of a general practitioner. The action was brought by the

---

90   QBD 5 October 1999.
91   Court of Appeal 4 February 1999.

widow of a man who had consulted his GP during surgery hours on 2 November 1992 feeling unwell and feverish. The doctor examined him and made a note that his cervical glands were enlarged, but he prescribed no treatment, and the claimant's husband returned to work. On 7 November 1992, the patient and his wife again attended at the defendant's surgery, and the deceased was diagnosed as suffering fever, headache and sore throat. The GP explained that antibiotics would not be helpful because he believed the illness was viral rather than bacterial, so again, no treatment was prescribed. His condition deteriorated during the next day and by the Monday he had become very seriously ill. He died in hospital the same day, the cause of his death being stated as *'streptococcal septicaemia'*.

The Court of Appeal decided that the trial judge was entitled, on the evidence, to conclude that the defendant was in breach of his duty of care towards the deceased. He found that he should have advised him to seek further medical advice should his condition deteriorate during the weekend. The judge had carefully considered the evidence before him and had been correct in his conclusion that had the patient been correctly advised he would have probably acted in accordance with such advice, and had he been seen by a doctor on the Sunday, he would have been admitted to hospital and his death would probably have been avoided. Accordingly, the appeal was dismissed.

This case gives particular cause for concern because the events which led to the trial occurred in 1992. That was before the recent official guidance was given to GPs about prescribing antibiotics sparingly to reduce the risk of the development of more antibiotic resistant bacteria. The new approach to prescribing could lead to more cases like *Major v Wilcox*. GPs who decide not to prescribe antibiotics for what appear to be viral illnesses should make a point of advising patients to seek further medical assistance if the condition deteriorates, and to record the fact that they have given such advice in the patient's notes.

In *Marriot v West Midlands Area Health Authority*[92] it was held that a GP had been negligent when he did not arrange for a patient with signs of a serious head injury to be readmitted to hospital for further observation. This case is discussed in full in Chapter 3.

Accident and Emergency Services

The British Orthopaedic Association believes that in some areas up to 70% of deaths from accidents could be avoided by the provision of prompt and appropriate treatment. A survey reported in a recent article in the British Medical Journal found that many operations carried out in accident and emergency units throughout the UK were performed by doctors who had no experience of the particular procedures. Some of the doctors at these units are very inexperienced, and for many it is their first post after qualifying. Another report in *The Lancet* concludes that more than 2,000 deaths every year could be caused by lack of availability of intensive care facilities. A proper trauma system with a team of well-trained and experienced staff from consultants down is what is being demanded.

Ambulance services

Throughout the UK ambulance services are facing testing times, as members of the public are becoming more demanding. Recently published figures indicate that 999 calls to ambulance services have doubled over the last decade. During the year 2000

---

92   [1999] 1 Lloyd's Rep Med 23.

alone, demands on ambulance services rose by 7%. There were more than 4.1 million emergency calls made to ambulance services in England during 1999-2000, almost a million of these in London.

There has been a recent investment of £21 million to help ambulance services make improvements and they have been set an interim target of reaching 75% of life threatening calls within eight minutes by March 2001. The money is being used to provide extra front line vehicles and staff, and it is also intended that it will assist in improving operational efficiency, allowing ambulance services to work more closely with other parts of the health service.

There is some concern among ambulance staff that too many people demand an ambulance for patients who could have been more appropriately dealt with by ringing GP out of hours services or NHS Direct. In addition to transporting some 2.9 million victims of accidents or sudden illnesses to hospitals, the 32 English ambulance services also carried over a million patients requiring urgent attention, and made arrangements for transporting almost 15 million non-emergency journeys.

Statistics on a national basis prepared by the Government Statistical Service reveal that in 1999-2000, of the 20 ambulance services that had introduced call prioritisation by 31 March 2000, one service, Staffordshire, responded to 87% of category A (immediately life threatening) calls within eight minutes; seven services responded to between 60% and 70% of category A calls within eight minutes; and a further eight services responded to between 50% and 60% of category A calls within eight minutes. Fourteen services responded to 95% or more of category B/C (other emergency) calls within 14 minutes (urban services) or 19 minutes (rural services). Of the 12 ambulance services that had not introduced call prioritisation by 31 March 2000, five services (two rural and three urban) responded to 50% or more of emergency calls within eight minutes. One of the seven rural services responded to 95% or more of emergency calls within 19 minutes and none of the five urban services responded to 95% or more of emergency calls within 14 minutes.

In addition to the worrying pattern of unnecessary demands on ambulance services, there is evidence that the courts are prepared to find ambulance services liable for failing to attend a patient within a reasonable time. In *Kent v Griffiths, Roberts and the London Ambulance Service (No 2)*[93], the Court of Appeal ruled that an ambulance service owes a duty of care to an individual patient, providing that the patient has been clearly identified by name and address, and as long as the details of the patient's condition are given to the ambulance service. In this case the Court of Appeal upheld the decision of the trial judge, ruling that as the ambulance service had accepted the 999 call in respect of the particular patient, and as the ambulance failed, for no good reason, to arrive within a reasonable time, the service was liable for the injury suffered by the patient as a consequence. However, it was held that there is no general duty owed to the public by the ambulance service to respond to a telephone call for help. It is vital that a 999 call must have been accepted, and that the patient was relying on the timely arrival of an ambulance[94].

After this case, in order to protect themselves from legal claims, GPs who call for an ambulance would be well-advised to give careful details of the name, address and medical condition of the patient. This is common practice, and it is also usual for the person calling the ambulance to give some indication of the urgency of the situation. To enable the ambulance service staff to respond appropriately, it is of course,

---

93   [2000] 2 All ER 474.
94   See Chapter 2 for a detailed account of the facts of this case.

necessary for them to be given adequate information to enable them to recognise the urgency of the situation. It might be possible, in future cases, for an ambulance service to defend a claim based on late attendance if it can be proved that weather or traffic conditions prevented the ambulance reaching the patient in time or at all. Protocols should be drafted to take account of such contingencies. Lord Woolf, in the *Kent* case, expressed the view that there may be a defence on the issue of breach of duty in certain cases, and provided staff follow sound protocols an ambulance service might be able to escape liability.

Provision of Care Services in the Community

The tragic case of Christopher Clunis illustrates the difficulties for claimants in maintaining a claim on the basis of inadequate care in the community. Christopher Clunis was a mentally ill patient who murdered a stranger, Jonathan Zito, in a completely unprovoked attack at a London tube station. In *Clunis v Camden and Islington Health Authority*[95] the claimant sought damages from the health authority for failing to treat him and to prevent him killing someone. He had a long history of violent behaviour, and in June 1993 he had pleaded guilty to a charge of manslaughter on the grounds of diminished responsibility and was detained under s37 of the *Mental Health Act 1983*. A restriction order was made under s41 of the Act without limit of time. In a subsequent civil action he claimed that staff at Friern Hospital had done nothing to restrain him or to treat him even though his condition had deteriorated to such a point that the police were concerned about his behaviour. He argued that if he had been treated competently he would not have killed Jonathan Zito. However, he failed to establish that a cause of action arose and the claim was unsuccessful.

The White Paper on Mental Health published late in the year 2000 proposes the extension of powers to treat mentally ill people in the community, and there is likely to be a change in the law to allow compulsory treatment in rare cases when patients living in the community fail to take their medication and become a danger to other people. The question as to whether this new power will be attended by greater legal obligations towards patients and their potential victims has yet to be decided by a court. It has already been held, in the light of the Human Rights Act 1998, that blanket immunities from the duty of care in negligence are, in another context, unacceptable.

Hospital Acquired Infections

Studies of infections acquired in hospital have concluded that even in well-run wards the risk of cross-infection was higher than had previously been believed[32]. A study by the Public Health Service Laboratory for one year and conducted in 19 hospitals with 500 beds in England and Wales found that mothers in maternity wards were most at risk. Although collecting accurate data was complicated by poor note taking, and cases of infection were found to be misdiagnosed, the researchers found that many doctors and nurses did not follow basic rules about hand washing. The risk of infection was found to be considerably higher among people who were catheterised or fitted with other intrusive devices. With increasing litigation consciousness among patients it is likely that claims will arise in future as a result of infections which have been acquired in hospitals.

A report by the Office of Health Economics in 1997 concluded that hospital infections are responsible for 5,000 deaths a year and responsible in part for another

---

95   The Times 10 December 1997.

15,000. These figures give rise to particular concern because they exceed figures for road accident fatalities and injuries. While the fatalities from road accidents are decreasing annually, deaths from hospital infections are increasing, with correlative increases in the cost of healthcare. The report states that on average 1 in 16 people contracts an infection after being admitted to hospital, and that drug resistant bacteria are responsible for many of these infections. As a result many patients are required to stay in hospital for longer than expected, so dramatically increasing the overall cost of healthcare. Some patients are released from hospital before symptoms of infection develop and then need to be readmitted for further treatment. The report suggests that about one-third of these infections could be prevented and argues for the cost effectiveness of higher spending on infection-control nurses. A 32% drop in the incidence of hospital infections would, according to the report, reduce healthcare costs by £29.3m a year. Hospitals should be aware of the possibilities of prosecutions for breaches of health and safety legislation and of the possibility of negligence actions by patients who contract hospital infections.

The results of yet another survey published in the *Health Service Journal* indicate that one in three hospitals in England failed to pass basic checks for cleanliness, according to a national audit of hospital wards. The survey was conducted in nearly 700 hospital buildings, and of those inspected, 250 were given the lowest possible grading for basic sanitary conditions, including the state of wards, lavatories, litter collection, décor, freshness of linen and smells. In some hospitals toilets were found to be over-flowing, and soiled tissues were left lying about. Almost 300 hospitals fell into a middle category of institutions that could do much to improve. It is thought that up to 20 of the hospitals inspected were so dirty that the Government has demanded immediate action from them to improve their standards. Emergency *'hit-squads'* are to be used to provide assistance in these cases. In November 2000, a report submitted to MPs linked poor personal hygiene of staff with outbreaks of disease in hospitals. The first phase in the development of national evidence-based guidelines to prevent healthcare associated infections was commissioned in 1998.

The report, issued by the National Audit Office in the Summer of 2000, prompted measures to improve conditions of hygiene. There was an immediate investment of £31 million for cleaning purposes. All trusts were required to draft action plans for cleaning and were later inspected. Inspections were conducted by *'patient environment action teams'*, and standards were assessed on a traffic light grading system of red for poor, yellow for generally good but with some poor areas, and green for the most outstanding services. Fifty follow-up inspections have shown a dramatic improvement in standards in 41 Trusts, moving them from red to yellow status. A further £30 million will now be fast-tracked directly to hospitals from April to help ensure that targets are met.

National guidelines issued following the Audit Commission Report set standards of cleanliness for all hospitals to follow. These guidelines were intended to assist the fight against MRSA, (methicillin resistant Staphylococcus aureus), a potentially fatal infection suffered by some patients, which is believed to be carried by dust mites. Despite this Government action, Alan Milburn admitted that MRSA is now endemic in hospitals in England. In 1990 there were only 67 reported cases, as opposed to 3,110 in 1999. He blamed the problem on continuing poor sanitation, and declared that there would be a further set of unannounced inspections. Besides MRSA, among other infections that can be acquired in hospital are other skin infections, and gastro-intestinal infections causing diarrhoea and vomiting. Hospitals had been given until the end of March 2001 to ensure that they are meeting essential standards of cleanliness, and on 18 January 2001, the Government issued a more comprehensive set of guidelines to deal with the problem. From 1 April 2001 a national set of minimum standards came into force, and it has been suggested that league tables for hospitals should include ratings based on standards of hygiene.

In future, the responsibility for cleanliness on wards will rest with ward sisters, who are expected to play a new role in improving standards of cleanliness in NHS hospitals. There are also proposals to bring back Matrons. From April, ward sisters will have the authority to agree with managers to withhold payments from contract cleaning companies if standards are not reached. It is a widely held belief that since the contracting out of hospital cleaning services to firms outside the NHS, and the consequent devolving of responsibility from clinical staff to cleaning contractors, standards have fallen dramatically. In the days when the Matron was responsible for standards of cleanliness in wards and operating theatres ward sisters were able to exercise some authority over *'ward maids'* and cleaners employed directly by the NHS. The policy director of the NHS Confederation described the situation as *'a kind of Railtrack scenario, with no investment in the people needed to do the job'*.

The Government guidance is of particular importance to those concerned with risk management and legal claims. Some patients considering bringing claims for injuries and ill-health which they believe they have suffered as a result of hospital-borne infections, have had problems establishing causation. The Government has now admitted that the transmission of many of these infections is avoidable, and any institution which cannot demonstrate that it has met the minimum required standards may experience difficulty defending claims in individual cases, particularly if more than one patient on the same ward contracts the same kind of infection. The record of NHS hospitals in fighting hospitals acquired infections and so-called *'superbugs'* will be independently inspected and monitored. Both the Commission for Health Improvement and the Audit Commission would be involved in hospital inspections, and the two bodies would have a legal right to demand information on the level of hospital infection and, if they think appropriate, to publish it.

Hospital staff are also at risk from infections and as employers, Trusts should take seriously their responsibilities in relation to training and the maintenance of responsible standards of hygiene. In the context of healthcare, the Health and Safety at Work etc Act 1974 applies to employees and to visitors to their premises, including tradesman, as well as to patients.

Successful claim by patient who contracted MRSA

It can be difficult to establish causation when patients contract MRSA in hospital. However, in a recent case a 74-year-old woman succeeded in obtaining £400,000 in a settlement, from Whipps Cross Hospital after contracting MRSA virus. In 1994 she was admitted to Whipps Cross Hospital, Leytonstone, for a right hip replacement even though at the time Whipps Cross Hospital was in the grip of a major outbreak of a particularly virulent strain of MRSA which had already resulted in the temporary closure of one of its surgical wards. Soon after she had her operation she was found to have been infected with MRSA. However, there was a delay of eight days in administering appropriate antibiotics to treat the infection. By 1996, the prosthetic hip was found to have loosened as a result of the MRSA infection and was replaced. The claimant spent over three months in hospital on that occasion. In 1998, her prosthetic right hip was again found to be infected. It was removed, and could not be replaced because of the risk of further MRSA infection. The claimant then spent a further three months in hospital. Whipps Cross Hospital finally admitted full responsibility for causation of the intractable MRSA infection in November 2000.

The claimant obtained a settlement of £400,000 in damages for the negligent treatment she received at Whipps Cross NHS Hospital. The award is an unusually large sum, considering the age of the claimant, and demonstrates the potential cost to the NHS of MRSA[96].

Smear testing services

The NHS Cervical Screening Programme offers a cervical smear test at three-five yearly intervals to women aged 22-64. The programme screens over four million women each year in England, preventing up to 3,900 cases of cervical cancer each year according to expert estimates. Over 8,000 lives could have been saved by the Programme between 1988 and 1997. However, the screening programme has not been without its problems.

A report following an investigation into the shortcomings of the cervical cancer smear test programme at Kent and Canterbury Hospitals NHS Trust between 1990 and 1995, is critical of inefficient management and blames poor training, insufficient staffing and fragmentation of services after the introduction of the NHS internal market. Mistakes in interpreting the smear tests meant that 345 women were wrongly informed that they were clear, and as many as eight of these women are now believed to have died, though they could have survived if the cancer had been noticed and they had been treated promptly. Twenty-one women, three of whom had yet to start their families, needed hysterectomies as a result of the failure of screening, and 50 women with abnormalities of the cervix have still not been traced. The financial cost in terms of a rescreening programme, legal costs and compensation is expected to be enormous. Meanwhile, new tests are being developed to improve the accuracy of smears and to detect the presence of human papillovirus which is implicated in 95% of cervical cancer cases[33]. The case of *Penney v East Kent Health Authority*[97], the facts of which are outlined in Chapter 2, is an example of a successful claim brought as a result of negligent screening.

An accreditation procedure, which is to be applied to laboratories offering screening for cervical cancer, has also been announced. This process has been designed by Health Services Accreditation, the body established to develop sound standards in healthcare. Forty-eight standards have been set covering training, workload and quality control, and requiring all laboratory staff to pass two proficiency tests each year. Laboratories wishing to be accredited have 15 months within which they must meet the 48 new standards, and they will need to renew their accreditation every two years. Several women have succeeded in obtaining compensation for the illness and injury they have suffered as a result of the errors in the system.

Up to 200 women were recalled for screening in Lincolnshire after errors in interpreting smear tests had been discovered. A study had revealed that a consultant pathologist, who is currently on sick leave, wrongly reported that the women's smear tests were normal. Further problems were identified in Leicestershire in 2001.

In June 2000, the Government announced a pilot scheme for liquid-based cytology and Human Papilloma Virus (HPV) screening, following the appraisal by the National Institute for Clinical Excellence, as part of the cervical screening

---

96   Published in *Health Law*, March 2000, based on a report submitted by the claimant's solicitor.

97   The Times 25 November 1999.

process. The techniques, which are established practice in other screening areas, offer a new way to prepare smear samples for examination in the laboratory. NICE have suggested that introducing LBC into the cervical screening programme could increase the sensitivity of slides, reduce the number of inadequate smears (which currently result in women being recalled for a further smear test) and improve the speed with which cytoscreeners can read slides.

NICE advised that although there is insufficient evidence to justify the introduction of LBC technology across England and Wales at this time, it is likely that LBC will have benefits in cervical screening. The LBC arm of the pilots should be designed to collect information on the effect, costs and practical implications of introducing LBC technology into the cervical screening programme.

Negligence in Other Areas of Healthcare

NHS Direct

The NHS telephone help-line called NHS Direct was established to provide patients with an alternative to conventional medical consultations. However, it was alleged by the journals *Doctor* and *Hospital Doctor* to have experienced serious technical problems over the busy New Year period in 1999, and callers were given instructions to telephone their GPs instead of being given advice over the telephone. Although NHS Direct, which follows an American model, has been promoted strongly by the Government, the BMA has been very critical of the service, suggesting that it interferes with the relationship between doctors and their patients and that the money being spent on it would be better used elsewhere. The service which is now available almost everywhere in the UK, cost £31 million. The telephone advisers are usually nurses who follow strict protocols. However, there is some evidence that many patients consult their GPs after seeking the services of NHS Direct and being directed to take further medical advice.

NHS walk-in centres

In April 1999, the Prime Minister announced the introduction of pilot NHS walk-in centres as part of a series of initiatives to modernise the NHS and improve access to and convenience of primary care services. Each centre offers as a minimum seven days a week opening, mostly from 7am until 10pm no appointment necessary, consultations with an experienced NHS nurse, treatment for minor injuries and illnesses such as strains and sprains, coughs, colds and flu-like symptoms; instant access to health advice and information on other local services and advice on how to stay healthy, local out of hours GP and dental services and local pharmacy services.

Every walk-in centre in the pilot scheme has the full support of its local Primary Care Group. Walk-in centres are intended to provide a service that is complementary to services provided by GPs: they are not intended to replace or duplicate existing primary care services. All walk-in centres will have links with local GP surgeries to assure continuity of care for patients. Potential legal problems lie in the fact that walk-in centres may not have access to all the information required to treat a patient effectively.

Prison doctors

In the last chapter there was some discussion of the possibility that prison doctors may not be required to exercise the same standard of care as doctors in more conventional medical practice. A recent application of the law is to be found in *Zinzuwadia v Secretary of State for the Home Department*[98], the outcome of which depended upon the principles established in the *Bolam* and *Bolitho* cases to a case in which a psychiatrist had failed to diagnose that a prisoner was a potential suicide risk. The claim was brought in negligence by the widow of a man who had committed suicide in prison. The prisoner had been sentenced, on 5 October 1992, to two-and-a-half years in prison for a violent incident in which an imitation firearm had been used to threaten a publican and his wife. In May 1993 the prisoner was seen by a doctor at HM Prison Ashwell, who found that he could not safely be kept at that prison. Accordingly, the prisoner was transferred to HM Prison Leicester, but was transferred back again to Ashwell a few days later, because he had not displayed any indication of mental disturbance during his short stay at Leicester. However, three weeks later there was a violent incident involving the prisoner and a member of prison staff and he was again moved to Leicester on 15 June 1993. At that time there were concerns about his mental state, and the doctor at Ashwell thought that the prisoner was psychotic and was in danger of harming himself or others. He was placed in a single cell at Leicester, was kept under 15-minute observation, and was seen by the psychiatrist. The next morning the psychiatrist concluded that he presented no risk, or no substantial risk, of committing suicide. He found that the man was paranoid, but that his condition was short of schizophrenia, and he prescribed chlorpromazine. On the afternoon before the man died, the prison psychiatrist saw him twice, and though he had not spoken to him, he had not found him distressed. However, he was later found hanging in his cell.

The claimant, the prisoner's widow, submitted that the psychiatrist had been negligent both in coming to the conclusion that he had, and also prescribing the particular level of medication. A psychiatrist for the claimant reported that after the interview with the deceased on the morning of 16 June, the prison psychiatrist should have arranged his supervision either within the prison or by transfer to a hospital, and on evidence from the medical notes, the psychiatrist should have realised that seclusion would have made him worse. The defence psychiatrist gave evidence to the effect that the prison psychiatrist's diagnoses and actions had been correct. The man had assured the prison psychiatrist when interviewed, that he was not a suicide risk and did not need medication. He had even contacted his family and arranged a visit with them for the following day.

The judge found that the prisoner had hidden his suicidal intention from his family and from the doctors and concluded that if a person was determined to commit suicide, he would succeed, and the risk could only be reduced – it could not be eliminated entirely. The standard of care required had been that of a reasonably competent prison psychiatrist applying the standards currently prevailing. Knowledge of what had happened later should not be applied in judging the earlier events, because even with hindsight, the outcome was not of itself proof of negligence. In the case of an error of judgement, no liability could arise unless that error of judgement was such that no reasonable, well-informed and competent member of the profession could have made that decision.

It was held in this case that the prison psychiatrist had made a thorough assessment of the prisoner in question. He had observed him on a previous admission when he had made a spontaneous recovery. The prisoner had showed no sign that he intended to harm himself, and the prison psychiatrist had correctly diagnosed the particular mental health problems. There were two eminent bodies of opinion before the court, and although the judge did not make a choice between them, he found that the prison psychiatrist did not follow an extraordinary course of action and his actions were reasonable and logically defensible. Accordingly, there was judgment for the defendant. In *Orange v Chief Constable of West Yorkshire Police*[99] the Court of Appeal held that although there was a duty to assess prisoners for suicide risks, the duty to protect a prisoner from committing suicide did **not** arise unless the carers knew or ought to have known that the particular prisoner presented a risk of committing suicide.

Nurse Prescribing

A pilot scheme which permitted community nurses and practice nurses to prescribe certain selected medicines has been extended to cover the whole of England from April 1998. Nurse prescribing was first introduced in 1994 in Bolton in eight GP practices. In April 1996 it was extended to the entire district community NHS Trust in Bolton. A further 1,200 nurses in ten trusts were included in the scheme from April 1997. In order to participate in the project, district nurses, practice nurses and health visitors are required to undertake a special training course on prescribing and are able to prescribe products from a nurse prescriber's formulary.

The legal implications of nurse prescribing are significant. The development means that nurses are placed under an additional duty of care to the patients for whom they prescribe and similar rules of law apply to nurses as to doctors in relation to prescribing. There are similarities in the standard of care required of each profession. A nurse would be expected to conform to the professional standards of other similarly qualified nurses. It is hoped that nurses will be aware of these matters and will receive appropriate training in the relevant law.

A consultation paper published in the year 2000 suggests training around 10,000 nurses to prescribe treatment for a broader range of medical conditions, including minor injuries and ailments such as burns, cuts, and hayfever; chronic disease management including asthma and diabetes; palliative care. This consultation is directly relevant for nurses, midwives and health visitors. By early October 2000, nearly 16,000 district nurses and health visitors had already trained to prescribe from the current Nurse Prescribers' Formulary. The consultation follows the Government's acceptance of the main recommendations of the Review of Prescribing, Supply & Administration of Medicines on 13 March 2000. These included extending nurse prescribing, extending prescribing rights to other health professions when Parliamentary time allows and introducing Patient Group Directions. The extension to nurse prescribing is facilitated by the Health and Social Care Act 2001.

Nurse consultants

A further 91 nurse consultant posts have been announced by the Government, and this extension to the responsibility of the nurses concerned also creates the potential for legal claims against them. There will be over 200 nurse consultants in the near future, and over a third will be employed in critical care, and will be in a key position to develop critical care nursing following the announcement of an additional £150 million investment in critical care. The other posts will be spread across nursing expertise in accident and emergency and intermediate care. There will be further nursing, midwifery and health visiting appointments considered for approval later in the year. All nurse consultants will spend a minimum of 50% of their time working directly with patients, ensuring faster, better, and more convenient services. In line with the seniority of these posts, their contribution will be crucial to the development

---

99   The Times, 5 June 2001.

of professional practice, to research and evaluation, and to education, training and development.

Dentists

There are few reported cases in which proceedings are brought against dentists. However, one such case that raises several important issues has recently been reported. In *Appleton and others v Garrett*[100] patients who had suffered damage including pain and suffering, loss of amenity and mental distress when they discovered that their dentists had carried out unnecessary treatment on them, were awarded aggravated damages amounting to 15% of the sum awarded for general damages to cover feelings of anger, indignation and mental distress which they had experienced. For financial gain, between 1981 and 1988 the dentist had carried out treatment which he knew was unnecessary, and had deliberately concealed the truth from the patients in case they withdrew their consent. Not one of the patients had been given any information on which they could have made decisions based on informed consent. This was more than mere negligence because the information had been withheld in bad faith. The defendant had admitted negligence but that left the issue of trespass to the person to be decided. The damages awarded in this case for the cost of immediate and future treatment included all peridontal treatment necessary before crowns could be replaced and any post and core work to be done. They were entitled to have this work carried out by a top dentist with a good reputation in order to secure the best possible remedial treatment. Moreover, this was a case in which aggravated damages could legitimately be awarded on the basis of the criteria set out by Lord Devlin in *Rookes v Barnard*[101] to compensate for the claimant's injured feelings arising from humiliation, distress, insult or pain, where the conduct of the defendant was malevolent, spiteful, insolent or arrogant.

In an out-of-court settlement after an eight-year battle, almost 100 patients of this dentist are to receive a total of almost £2 million. The dentist who was struck off the register in 1989 but reinstated two years later after retraining, admitted negligence and the damages will be paid by the Medical and Dental Defence Union of Scotland.

A dentist, Melvyn Meggitt, who has been struck off the register of the General Dental Council, has also been threatened with legal action by several patients who claim to have been disfigured and traumatised by his incompetent treatment. The President of the Professional Conduct Committee of the General Dental Council has stated that the Committee is satisfied that Mr Megitt had frequently deliberately damaged braces in a sustained course of action in which he had defrauded the NHS. At one time, the dentist was earning in the region of £600,000 per annum by treating patients very fast, allegedly at the rate of 150 a day. More than 130 of his former patients are believed to be bringing claims against him.

Cases involving deaths under dental anaesthesia are outlined in the section covering anaesthetics.

NHS managers

Roylance v General Medical Council (No 2)[102] does not directly concern clinical negligence but it is an important case in that it places responsibility for the Bristol paediatric heart cases on managers as well as clinicians. In this case the Judicial Committee of the Privy Council ruled against Dr John Roylance, former chief

---

100   [1997] 8 Med LR 75.

101   [1964] AC 1129.

102   The Times, 26 March 1999.

executive officer of Bristol Royal Infirmary where several children had died and others had suffered serious injury in the course of undergoing heart surgery. Dr Roylance, who was a consultant radiologist with a background in cardiac surgery, was in a management post as district general manager of the Bristol and Weston Health Authority, and then chief executive officer of the United Bristol Healthcare NHS Trust until he retired in 1995. The incidents that gave rise to concern related to cardiac surgery which had been carried out at Bristol Royal Infirmary between 1990 and 1995. The Professional Conduct Committee of the GMC had found Dr Roylance guilty of serious professional misconduct as a registered medical practitioner for not paying heed to concerns which has been expressed about the high mortality rate of infants at the paediatric cardiac unit, and had ordered that his name be erased from the register of medical practitioners. Dr Roylance appealed on the ground that he had not received a fair hearing, but his appeal was dismissed with costs.

Hospital managers can also be held responsible in criminal law for health and safety offences. Two hospital managers at Princess Margaret Hospital in Swindon are to be prosecuted after serious breaches of the *Management of Health and Safety at Work Regulations 1992* were discovered during a routine inspection. The charge alleged that hospital managers:

'Failed to make appropriate arrangements for effective control of preventive and protective measures to ensure the health and safety of employees and other people likely to be affected by their activities.'

Although no accident had occurred, the alleged breaches of the regulations were so numerous and so serious that Health and Safety inspectors decided to bring the prosecution. Among the allegations are claims that the hospital had no secure unit which could be sealed and fumigated to contain contagious diseases; that there were no appropriate measures in place to prevent violence to nursing and other staff; and that there was no system to ensure that the risks involved in lifting and handling patients had been assessed and catered for. It is very unusual for such a prosecution to be brought without an accident having occurred, and although the Regulations have proved very useful to healthcare staff seeking to bring civil proceedings after they have suffered an injury at work, the original intention behind the legislation was to prevent accidents and to create a safer working environment.

Sports medicine

Sports organisers, doctors and other healthcare professionals are giving considerable responsibility at the scene of sports events, and must suffer legal consequences if they do not meet the required standard of care, *Watson v British Boxing Board Of Control*[103] demonstrates. The British Boxing Board of Control appealed against the decision that it was liable in respect of brain damage suffered by the professional boxer Michael Watson. The trial judge had found that negligence was established and that the Board was liable in full for the injuries sustained. Michael Watson suffered serious brain damage as a result of a title fight with Chris Eubank for the World Boxing Organisation Super-Middleweight title on 21 September 1991. The Board is the sole controlling body regulating professional boxing in the UK, but it argued on appeal that it owed no duty of care to the claimant; if it did owe the duty alleged, it was not in breach of that duty; and the breach of duty alleged did not cause the injuries. The Court of Appeal upheld Kennedy J's decision which had broken new ground in the law of negligence. The Board's duty of care required it to take

---

103   The Times 11 January 2001.

reasonable steps to try to minimise or control the risks inherent in the sport. Concern of the Board about the physical safety of boxers was reflected in its rules and regulations which included rules designed to ensure that a boxer received appropriate medical attention when injured in the course of a fight. It was the claimant's understanding that the Board assumed the responsibility of determining the nature of the medical facilities and assistance to be provided for all boxing contests in the UK. The duty in this case was a duty to take reasonable care to ensure that injuries were properly treated; and it involved making regulations imposing on others the duty to ensure that boxers did not suffer lasting harm through injuries in the ring.

The Court of Appeal concluded that the trial judge's findings on the question of breach of duty had been correct. The issue was simply whether proper care was used in making provision for medical treatment of the claimant, and the ordinary test of reasonable skill and care was the correct one to apply. There should have been a resuscitation facility at ringside. It was the duty of the Board and its medical advisers to seek competent advice as to how a recognised danger could be best combated. Accordingly, the appeal was dismissed.

Psychologist's duty of care

In a ruling which will have far-reaching consequences for people with specific learning problems, it has been held that an educational psychologist owed a duty of care to the local authority which employed her and to the dyslexic child whom she was assessing, through her parents who would act upon the advice they received about the management of their child's condition. In *Phelps v Hillingdon London Borough Council*[104] the claimant had a history of poor performance at the schools which she had attended, and had been referred to an educational psychologist employed by the defendants. The report produced by the psychologist stated that the claimant's problems had an emotional basis and that although her verbal skills were below average, she had no specific learning disabilities and would not require attendance at a special unit. Her educational progress continued to be very poor despite remedial teaching, and further assessments carried out five and six years later concluded that she was dyslexic and would have been dyslexic when she was tested originally. The psychologist who had carried out the tests five years earlier had made errors of judgement, and the fact that the claimant had not been diagnosed and treated earlier meant that the adverse effects of the dyslexia had not been mitigated in time for her to make progress in her education. It was held that the local authority was vicariously liable and the standard of care required of a psychologist is the standard of the ordinarily competent member of that profession.

Pharmacists

It can safely be assumed that pharmacists owe a duty of care to patients for whom they dispense prescriptions either directly or through a friend or relative, and to people they advise and provide with pharmaceutical products over the counter. Most pharmacists receive some legal training and are familiar with the cases in which pharmacists have been found negligent for not noticing prescribing errors made by GPs, for failing to deal adequately with the possibility of drug interactions, and for being careless in reading virtually illegible handwriting on a prescription[105]. Pharmacists have been held liable in negligence for negligently dispensing the wrong drug and the wrong strength of the correct drug.

---

104   The Times 10 October 1997.

105   *Prendergast v Sam Dee Ltd* [1989] 1 Med LR 36, *Dwyer v Roderick* (1983) 127 LJ 806.

Community pharmacists are frequently asked to give over the counter advice about medication, and this involves making a diagnosis and providing advice about matters such as possible alternative treatments and correct dosages. If a pharmacist holds a Patient Medication Record for a particular patient he or she might be found negligent for not cross checking to ensure that the patient will not suffer a drug interaction. The same principles would apply to pharmacists as to doctors in relation to the need to obtain consent to a particular treatment. Community pharmacists face a difficulty that is not usually encountered by doctors. This arises when a person seeks advice on behalf of a friend or relative who is unable to attend the pharmacy. In the event of a legal claim the pharmacist would be judged by the standard of other pharmacists according to the *Bolam/Bolitho* principles.

People who purchase medication over the counter would have remedies in the law of contract under the Sale of Goods legislation if products prove to be unsatisfactory. In addition, under the Consumer Protection Act 1987 a pharmacist who mixes drugs together in the dispensing process would fall within the definition of a *'producer'*, and would be primarily liable to pay compensation to a person injured by a defective product, regardless of fault. However, a pharmacist who sells or supplies a product manufactured or produced by someone else, would only be secondarily liable, and could escape liability by identifying his or her supplier, (s2(3) CPA). This means that batch numbers of products should be routinely recorded and kept in a safe place.

Alternative medical treatment

Shakoor v Kang Situ[106] raises interesting points relating to the standard of care that can be expected of alternative medical practitioners. This claim was brought by the widow of Abdul Shakoor for damages pursuant to the Fatal Accidents Act 1976 and the Law Reform (Miscellaneous Provisions) Act 1934. The defendant was a practitioner of Traditional Chinese Herbal Medicine ('TCHM') but was not qualified or registered as a medical practitioner in the UK. His practice was not subject to licensing or registration but he was a voluntary member of the Register of Chinese Herbal Medicine. The deceased suffered from multiple benign lipomata and had consulted the defendant in 1994, when he was prescribed a course of a Chinese herbal remedy of 12 herbs that was to be mixed with water, boiled for two hours and reduced. The deceased took nine doses before he became ill with loss of appetite, nausea, yellowing of the eyes and skin and heartburn. He was admitted to hospital in January 1995 with acute liver failure, and underwent a liver transplant, but he died a few days later. The claim was based on an allegation that it was negligent of the defendant to prescribe the medicine, or to have done so without warning of the risk of injury. The main issue in dispute was whether the defendant was to be judged by the standards of a reasonably careful Chinese herbal practitioner or by the standards applicable to an orthodox medical practitioner in the UK. The judge took the view that it was necessary to have regard to the fact that a practitioner was practising his *'art'* alongside orthodox medicine. The court would then be required to consider whether the standard of care adopted by the alternative practitioner had taken account of the implications of that fact. *Bolam v Friern Hospital Management Committee*[107] and *Sansom v Metcalfe Hambleton & Co*[108] were considered. It was held that in the present case, the alternative practitioner had to realise he was

---

106   (2001) 57 BMLR 178.
107   1957) 1 BMLR 1.
108   (1997) EGCS 185.

representing himself as competent to practise within a system of law and medicine which would review the standard of care he had given to a patient. Thus, whenever he prescribed a remedy it was not enough to say that the remedy was traditional and believed not to be harmful. The practitioner was also expected to recognise the probability that any person suffering an adverse reaction to a remedy would be likely to find himself in an orthodox hospital with such an incident being reported in an orthodox medical journal.

An alternative practitioner, in prescribing a remedy, was obliged to satisfy himself that there had not been adverse reports on that remedy in journals. The *'relevant literature'* was *'literature read by an orthodox practitioner practising at the level of speciality at which the alternative practitioner held himself out'*. In this case the equivalent orthodox practitioner would have been a general practitioner.

The evidence of letters and articles (especially from *The Lancet*) were equivocal and did not suggest that there was a serious risk in the treatment that had been prescribed. In the circumstances the defendant had not breached his duty to the deceased as he acted in accordance with the appropriate standard of care, and in accordance with the standards required in the UK. The claim was dismissed.

Veterinary treatment

The principles established in the *Bolam* and *Bolitho* cases were applied in *Calver v Westwood Veterinary Group*[109] case in which the Court of Appeal found that a vet had not been negligent where he decided not to administer prophylactic antibiotics.

This was an appeal by the Westwood Veterinary Group concerning the death of a thoroughbred mare which the judge held to have resulted from the appellant's negligence. The mare had aborted and the group's principal surgeon had examined her. He made a decision not to conduct a uterine examination on the mare, and not to administer prophylactic antibiotics. The trial judge had ruled that these decisions were negligent, and had eventually been the cause of the death of the mare from laminitis, resulting from infective metritis, developed after the abortion. The defendant vet, together with the two expert witnesses agreed that the risk of infective metritis was greatly increased if even a small part of the placenta was retained in the uterus following abortion. The defendant's evidence was that, upon careful examination of the placenta, he was satisfied that it was all present, and that none had been retained in the uterus. As he had also found that the mare was otherwise fit and well, he contended that neither uterine examination nor prophylactic antibiotics were necessary or appropriate. His case was that those clinical judgments were reasonably open to him and that the judge had been wrong to find that they were illogical under the principles in the *Bolitho* case. The Court of Appeal held that the crucial difference of opinion between the experts lay in their attitude to the use of antibiotics. The appellant had emphasised that there was a strong body of opinion supported by several parliamentary committees that unnecessary prophylactic use of antibiotics should be discouraged. The respondent's expert argued that all competent vets would be bound to administer antibiotics in any case where, on examination, the vet could not be absolutely certain that the whole of the placenta had been expelled or where there was a possibility that the mare had been aborted more than three hours before her abortion was discovered. Applying the principles established in *Bolitho v City & Hackney Health Authority*[110] the court had to consider whether the judge was entitled

---

109   1 Lloyd's Rep Med 2001.
110   (1997) 39 BMLR 1.

to regard this as one of those rare cases in which one body of veterinary opinion demonstrated that the other was not capable of withstanding logical analysis, or whether it was one of the vast majority of cases where the reasonableness of the opinion was demonstrated by the fact that it was shared by a distinguished expert in the field.

The Court of Appeal ruled that if the approach of the trial judge was correct, there would need to be evidence that there was to be a great deal more prophylactic use of antibiotics in the future than in the past. It was impossible on the evidence to condemn the body of professional opinion represented by the appellant as illogical. There was nothing in the respondent's evidence to justify so extreme a view. Thus there was no possibility here for finding that the vet in question had been negligent. Accordingly, the appeal was allowed.

Conclusion

It has of course been impossible to cover every case decided in recent years on the subject of breach of duty in clinical negligence. However, some of the more interesting cases have been selected in order to provide an overview of the area and to indicate some of the trends in litigation. Readers should bear in mind the fact that the majority of cases are discontinued or settled before they reach trial. The cases outlined here are among the small percentage that reach the courts, and it is on the basis of such cases as these that lawyers acting for the parties, having amassed the evidence, in consultation with medical experts, decide whether to advise their clients to fight, settle or discontinue claims.

Chapter 5

Clinical Negligence and Consent to Treatment[1]

There are several excellent texts dealing with the legal and ethical aspects of obtaining consent to treatment and the circumstances in which a patient can refuse consent[2]. Exceptionally difficult issues surrounding consent and refusal arise in the case of mentally incompetent patients and those who are under the age at which the law considers them to be capable of giving consent. Detailed discussion of all these matters is not possible here. This chapter deals only with the question of how much information should be provided to the patient in the process of seeking consent to medical procedures, as that is where the law of negligence, on which this book is focused, becomes relevant to consent to treatment.

'Consent' in the healthcare context is voluntary and continuing permission given by a patient to a particular treatment, based on adequate knowledge of the purpose, nature and risks of the treatment, the likelihood of its success and any alternatives to it. Consent given under any unfair or undue pressure is not valid. If a doctor treats a patient without seeking consent, or in the face of a refusal by a competent patient to give consent[3], or if the treatment provided goes beyond the scope of the permission given by the patient[4], or is entirely different to that for which consent had been obtained[5], or is obtained by fraud[6], the correct action is for trespass to the person, using the torts of assault, battery and false imprisonment. If a competent patient argues that the treatment was given without sufficient information being provided to allow a reasonably informed decision to be made about whether to go ahead with the treatment, the correct action is for the tort of negligence. It is only this latter area of law, concerned with information provision to competent adults that will be explored here.

---

1   See *Consent: Reference Guide to Consent for Examination or Treatment*, Department of Health 2001 for a detailed document advising on how consent should be obtained.

2   For collected materials on *Consent to Treatment*, see McHale, J, Fox, M, and Murphy, J, *healthcare Law: Text and Materials*, Sweet and Maxwell, London, 1997; Stauch, M, Wheat,K and Tingle, J, *Source Book on Medical Law*, Cavendish Press, London 1998; Kennedy, I and Grubb, A, *Medical Law*, 3rd ed, edited Grubb, A, Butterworths, London 2000. See also Brazier, M, *Medicine, Patients and the Law* Penguin , England 1993 and Mason, K and McCall Smith, S, *Law and Medical Ethics* Butterworths, London, 5th ed 1998, Chapter 10, and Healy, J, *Medical Negligence: Common Law Perspectives*, Sweet and Maxwell, London, 1999.

3   *Re C (mental patient: medical treatment)* (1993) 15 BMLR 77.

4   *Williamson v East London and City Health Authority* (1997) 41 BMLR 85.

5   *Devi v West Midlands Area Health Authority* (1990) CL 44.

6   *Appleton v Garrett* [1997] 8 Med LR 75.

The question of which action is appropriate – trespass to the person or negligence was considered in *Chatterton v Gerson*[7] where Bristow J said:

> '... it would be very much against the interests of justice if actions which are really based upon a failure by the doctor to perform his duty adequately to inform were pleaded in trespass [battery].' ... once the patient is informed in broad terms of the nature of the procedure which is intended, and gives her consent, that consent is real, and the cause of the action on which to base a claim for failure to go into risks and implications is negligence, not trespass. Of course, if information is withheld in bad faith, the consent will be vitiated by fraud.'

Battery is the most common form of trespass to the person. This tort consists of intentionally bringing about offensive contact with the person of another. Assault is the act of putting a person in fear of an immediate battery – for example, approaching a patient, with a syringe in full view and clearly intending to use it. False imprisonment could also be relevant in the healthcare setting as it consists of unlawfully depriving a person of freedom of movement – for example, placing a person under an anaesthetic.

Negligence, Information Provision and Consent to Treatment

Consent should always be sought from all competent adults,[8] if possible, to all forms of medical treatment, though a defence of necessity would be available if a patient was treated without consent in an emergency. Where a patient presents for treatment consent is implied, and this would be sufficient to excuse the defendants of trespass, as long as the treatment that is given is what the claimant was told it would be. When a patient signs a consent form for surgery, he or she is in fact giving permission for the tort of trespass to be carried out – but not of course, the tort of negligence. Consent is a continuing process and can in theory be withdrawn at any time. Any new or additional medical procedure requires fresh consent from the patient. The law concerning consent to medical treatment is built on pragmatic principles, but encompasses to differing extents in different jurisdictions the ethical principle that every individual of sound mind is entitled to determine what is to be done to his own body[9]. In *Re T (Adult: Refusal of Medical Treatment)*[10] Lord Donaldson explained the position as follows:

> 'An adult patient who ... suffers from no mental incapacity has an absolute right to choose whether to consent to medical treatment, to refuse it, or to choose one rather than another of the treatments being offered ... This right of choice is not limited to decisions which others might regard as sensible. It exists notwithstanding that the reasons for making the choice are rational, irrational, unknown or even non-existent.'

Lord Donaldson MR, in *Re W (a Minor) (Medical Treatment)*[11], produced a detailed analysis of the more practical clinical and legal purposes of consent to medical treatment:

---

7   (1980) 1 BMLR 80; [1981] QB 432.

8   In the case of children consent may be provided by a parent or guardian, *Family Law Reform Act 1969*, s8, or if the child is mature enough to satisfy the criteria in *Gillick v Norfolk and Wisbech Health Authority* [1985] 3 All ER 402, by the child herself. There is no space to deal with these matters here.

9   See Lord Goff, *Re F (a mental patient (sterilisation: sterilisation)* [1990] 2 AC 1 reiterating the view of Justice Cardozo in *Schloendorff v Society of New York Hospital* 211 NY 125 (1914).

10   (1992) 9 BMLR 46 at page 50.

11   (1992) 9 BMLR 22, at page 29.

'It [consent] has two purposes, one clinical, the other legal. The clinical purpose stems from the fact that in many instances the cooperation of the patient and the patient's faith or at least confidence in the efficacy of the treatment is a major factor contributing to the treatment's success. Failure to obtain such consent will not only deprive the patient and the medical staff of this advantage, but will usually make it much more difficult to administer the treatment ... The legal purpose is quite different. It is to provide those concerned in the treatment with a defence to a criminal charge of assault or battery or a civil claim for damages for trespass to the person. It does not, however, provide them with any defence to a claim that they negligently advised a particular treatment or negligently carried it out.'

In *Chatterton v Gerson* where the judge explained the appropriate basis for a claim, the claimant was suffering chronic pain at the site of an earlier hernia operation. The defendant doctor suggested that the pain might be relieved by the injection of a solution near the spinal cord to destroy pain-conducting nerves. The claimant explained that she could remember being told the type of pain relief treatment intended, but argued that she had not been warned about the risk of suffering numbness and loss of muscle power. After two sessions of treatment her right leg was left completely numb. She brought a claim in trespass on the grounds that her consent was negatived because the consequences of the treatment had not been adequately explained, and a claim in negligence because the doctor had not explained as he should have under his duty to treat the patient with the degree of professional skill and care expected of a reasonably skilled medical practitioner. Bristow J held that in an action for trespass brought against a doctor on the basis of lack of consent, the patient had to prove that there had been a lack of *real* consent. As soon as the patient had been informed in *'broad terms'* of the nature of the proposed treatment and had given consent, he was not permitted to argue that there had been a lack of real consent. On the question of negligence, Bristow J applied the *Bolam* test. He held that a doctor should, as part of his duty of care in negligence, explain to the patient what he intended to do, and the implications of the proposed procedure as a careful and responsible doctor would have done. If there was a real risk of unpleasant side-effects, or some other danger attached to the procedure, however well it was carried out, the doctor had a duty to warn of such risks. In this case, numbness was not a foreseeable risk of the medical treatment, so there was no duty to warn the claimant about it. He went on to explain that even if the doctor had been in breach of the duty to warn, the claimant had not satisfactorily proved that even if she had been warned, she would have refused to undergo the treatment. This last matter is of course, concerned with the question of causation, proof of which is crucial to the success of any negligence claim, as was pointed out in the *Bolam* case itself[12] where issues surrounding consent to ECT and failure to warn of the risks inherent in it were explained to the jury.

Warnings of risks and side-effects: how much should the doctor tell?

The doctor should provide information to the patient about the nature of the treatment – that is what is going to be done and how the treatment is likely to progress, about alternative treatments and about the risks and side-effects that might be expected[13]. The question is *how much* information the doctor has a duty to provide. For some time the *Bolam* test was considered to be appropriate for determining how much information a doctor should provide about the proposed treatment. The standard required was that of the reasonably competent medical practitioner, in the light of a

---

12   [1957] 1 WLR 582 at page 590.
13   This chapter does not cover consent to clinical trials, for which special requirements are applicable. See EU Directive on good clinical practice in clinical trials.

responsible body of medical opinion, and if there was a contrary body of opinion that would not necessarily invalidate the decision of the particular doctor as to how much a patient should be told[14].

The question came before the House of Lords in the leading case on negligence in the context of information provision and consent to treatment in the UK - *Sidaway v Governors of Bethlem Royal Hospital*[15]. In that case, the claimant complained that she had not been warned of the potential risks of the treatment she was about to undergo. She consented to an operation on her neck intended to relieve pain, but she was not told that the procedure carried a small risk of damage to the nerve roots and spinal column. The outcome of the litigation was inconclusive because the surgeon had died before the trial, the medical records were incomplete, and insufficient evidence was available about what had actually been said. However, the House of Lords discussed and stated the law as it applied in England concerning the extent of the duty to inform. The complexity of the views expressed in the House of Lords means that it is difficult to draw clear guidance from this case. However, what is clear is that the majority of the House of Lords were not prepared to embrace and accept into UK law the principles that had developed in other jurisdictions that favoured patients' autonomy and their right to fully informed consent[16]. Although the House of Lords supported the professional standard as the benchmark for what should be disclosed by a doctor, there are comments in several of the speeches suggesting that there might be situations in which it might be appropriate to apply a modified standard of care. For example, Lord Bridge said that there might be certain circumstances in which a judge might come to the conclusion that:

> *'The disclosure of a particular risk was so obviously necessary to an informed choice on the part of the patient that no reasonably prudent medical man would fail to make it.'*

A similar view was expressed by Lord Templeman, and Lord Scarman gave a strong dissenting speech supporting patient autonomy and the approach taken in the American case of *Canterbury v Spence*. It is Lord Diplock's views expressed in *Sidaway* that have been treated in some later cases, as encapsulating the correct approach to the question of information provision in the context of consent, yet he was not expressing the views of the majority when he said:

> *'To decide what risks the existence of which a patient should be voluntarily warned and the terms in which such a warning, if any, should be given, having regard to the effect that the warning may have, is as much an exercise of professional skill and judgement as any other part of the doctor's comprehensive duty of care to the individual patient, and expert medical evidence on this matter should be treated in just the same way. The Bolam test should be applied.'*

It is difficult to extract a majority view from the *Sidaway* case and the state of the law remained uncertain, and subject to a rash of critical comment[17]. Michael Jones explains the position by stating what, on the basis of *Sidaway* and subsequent case

---

14   See *Chatterton v Gerson*, op cit and *Hills v Potter* [1983] 3 All ER 716; [1984] 1 All ER 1018.

15   (1985) 1 BMLR 132.

16   *Reibl v Hughes* (1980) 114 DLR (3rd) 1; *Canterbury v Spence* (1972) 464 F 2nd 772 (DC Cir); *Rogers v Whittaker* (1992) 109 ALR 625. Dubler N and Schissel A, JAMWA vol 55, No 5, *Women, Breasts and the Failure of Informed Consent*. Despite the North American doctrine of informed consent, it has been suggested that commercial and other factors prevent US doctors from giving patients adequate information.

17   See Brazier, M, *Patient Authority and Consent to Treatment: The Role of the Law?* (1987) 7 LS 169; Jones, M, *Informed Consent and Other Fairy Stories*, (1999) 7 Med L.R. 118; Skegg, P, English Medical Law and *Informed Consent: An Antipodean Assessment and Alternative*, (1999) 7 Med LR 135; Kennedy, I, *Treatment Me Right*, (1991), Chapter 9.

law, doctors are not obliged to disclose. Much of what he catalogues as information doctors need not disclose appears to fall into the category side effects that are common knowledge, based on common sense, such as the everyday risks of surgery[18]. If indeed the law is to take a practical common sense approach the decision in *Davis v Barking, Havering and Brentwood Health Authority*[19] can be justified. There it was held that there is no duty on a doctor to inform the patient of each separate procedure in a proposed treatment such as a blood test or anaesthetic. Since *Sidaway,* it has been decided that there is no distinction between elective treatment and non-elective treatment, nor between therapeutic and non-therapeutic procedures[20], nor does an exceptionally onerous duty fall on the doctor to answer truthfully if the patient asks specific questions about the proposed treatment[21] despite suggestions in *Sidaway* to the contrary.

As result of the *Sidaway* case it was reasonably safe to assume that material risks should normally be disclosed, subject to a *'therapeutic privilege'* to withhold information if the doctor considers that the patient is not capable of accepting the information, or does not want to know. This of course, is based on the somewhat arrogant assumption made by some doctors that *'doctor really does know best'*. Nevertheless there were some cases during the 1990s that indicated a willingness to move away from the strict application of the *Bolam* test in determining how much information a patient should receive. For example, in *Smith v Tunbridge Wells Health Authority*[22] it was held that the failure to inform a 28-year-old male patient that surgery he was about to undergo carried a risk of impotence was negligent, the judge taking the view that the disclosure of that information was the only acceptable course of action despite medical opinion to the contrary[23].

The impact of Bolitho
An important development in the law of clinical negligence is of course the decision of the House of Lords in *Bolitho v City and Hackney Health Authority*[24]. Although Lord Browne-Wilkinson expressly excluded consideration of the question of consent to treatment in that case, the fact that *Bolitho* had a direct bearing on the operation and scope of the *Bolam* test cannot be ignored, nor can the emphasis placed in it on the *'balancing of risks and benefits'* – matters of crucial importance to a patient when deciding whether to undergo medical treatment.

In *Pearce v United Bristol Healthcare Trust*[25] Lord Woolf made it clear that the decision in *Bolitho* is relevant to the question to the issue of how much information should be given to patients when seeking consent to treatment. Mrs Pearce was expecting her sixth child. The expected date of delivery of the baby was 13 November 1991, and on 27 November, she saw her consultant, and asked if labour could be induced or the baby delivered by elective Caesarean section, as she was anxious because the baby was so overdue. The consultant explained the risks attendant upon an induced labour, telling her that there was a longer recovery period required after a Caesarean section than a normal delivery. As he advised her to have a

---

18 *Informed Consent and Other Fairy Stories*, op cit, fn 15 at p112.
19 [1993] 4 Med LR 95.
20 *Gold v Harringey Health Authority* [1987] 2 All ER 888.
21 *Blythe v Bloomsbury Health Authority* [1993] 4 Med LR 151.
22 [1994] 5 Med LR 334.
23 See also *McAllister v Lewisham and North Southwark Health Authority* [1994] 5 Med LR 343.
24 [1997] 4 All ER 771.
25 (1998) 48 BMLR 118.

normal delivery, Mrs Pearce accepted the advice and opted for a natural labour and delivery. She was admitted to hospital on 4 December and the baby was delivered stillborn. Mrs Pearce and her husband brought an action against the defendants but their claim was rejected by the trial judge. They appealed, arguing that Mrs Pearce should have been told that there was an increased risk of stillbirth if the delivery was delayed longer than the 27 November, and that if she had been made aware of the risk she would have opted for an elective Caesarean section as soon as possible.

The Court of Appeal dismissed the appeal. In the case of Mrs Pearce, there was a very small increased risk of stillbirth if the delivery was delayed after the 27 November. This risk was in the order of 1 or 2 in 1,000, and the medical experts indicated that in their view this was not a significant risk. As Mrs Pearce had been in a distressed state at the time she received the advice, this was not a case in which it would be proper for the court to interfere with the opinion of the doctor who treated the patient. The Court of Appeal took the view that even if she had been advised of the risk, Mrs Pearce, on the evidence, would have opted to have a normal delivery.

However, it was held that when deciding how much information to provide to a patient, a doctor must take into account all the relevant circumstances, including the patient's ability to understand the information and the physical and emotional state of the patient. This view was based upon analysis of the speeches in the House of Lords in the difficult and complex *Sidaway* case, and the *Bolitho* case. The Court of Appeal took the view that it will normally be the legal duty of the doctor to advise the patient about any *'significant risks'* which may affect the judgement of a reasonable patient in making a decision about treatment.

There are certain aspects of the Court of Appeal's ruling that are worth noting. First, the *Bolitho* test is likely to be of relevance in consent cases. Second, Lord Woolf indicated in *Pearce* that it is for the court and not for doctors to decide on the appropriate standard concerning what should be disclosed to a patient about a particular treatment. He stated:

> *'If there is a significant risk which would affect the judgement of a reasonable patient, then in the normal course it is the responsibility of a doctor to inform the patient of that risk if the information is needed so that the patient can determine for him or herself as to what course he or she should adopt'.*

This is an indication that there may be a move towards adopting an approach similar to that taken in the Australian case of *Rogers v Whittaker*. There, the Australian High Court ruled in favour of doctors disclosing all material risks which the reasonable patient might regard as significant, taking into account the particular patient. In future UK cases, the crucial issues are likely to centre on what risks are to be regarded as *'significant'* or relevant in the view of a *reasonable patient* to the decision as to whether to agree to the proposed treatment.

However, the law is still evolving and a differently constituted Court of Appeal appeared to take a different approach in the later case of *Burke v Leeds Health Authority*[26]. The case concerned the failure of two consultant oncologists to remind the claimant's parents that the start of treatment could be delayed. In 1989 the claimant, who was then three years old, underwent intense chemotherapy to treat acute lymphoblastic leukaemia, and suffered an encephalopathic episode which resulted in spastic quadriplegia. The risk of this occurring had been regarded by the doctors giving the treatment at that time as only very small. The parents had been

---

26   Court of Appeal, 29 January 2001.

concerned that the treatment would result in such an episode as the claimant had previously suffered an encephalopathic episode following earlier chemotherapy, but as it was recommended by two consultants, the parents had consented. The Court of Appeal held that there was no negligence on the part of the two doctors not to have told the parents that, although from a medical point of view the best approach was an immediate start to treatment of the child, postponement for a few months was a possible option. What a doctor had to tell his patient or the parents of his patient, at what point, and with what force, were matters of clinical judgment for the doctor. Accordingly the appeal was allowed. What appears to have been a deciding factor in this case is that the consultants were experts and their judgment in all other matters had been found by the judge to be entirely correct, and no expert evidence had been called to suggest that such a failure amounted to a breach of the duty of care. The decision might have been otherwise if expert evidence had been presented to the court that undermined the decision of the consultants.

Clearly, how much detail should be given by the doctor depends on the circumstances of the particular case, and there is a rather troubling borderline area between poor communication and negligent failure to inform as the next two cases discussed demonstrate. In *Carver v Hammersmith & Queen Charlotte's Special Health Authority*[27], the issue concerned not so much a positive decision by a doctor to withhold information as a negligently inadequate explanation about a medical procedure, leaving the patient with a mistaken impression about what the treatment involved, upon which she based her consent. It is a case concerning communication failure rather than issues of autonomy, but it is nonetheless instructive. The case involved a claim for damages for the wrongful birth of the claimant's Down's syndrome child. The facts of this case are set out in Chapter 4. As a result of poor communication, the claimant left the consultation with the clear, albeit mistaken, view that the *'Bart's test'* would determine whether or not she had a handicapped child. It was held that the doctor's failure to advise the claimant correctly constituted a breach of duty. This breach of duty was the cause of the wrongful birth.

Similarly, in *Crouchman v Burke and Others*[28] it was held that a communication failure by a gynaecologist when explaining a female sterilisation procedure amounted to negligence and that this caused the claimant to have an unplanned child. The claimant argued that she should have been warned of the risk that she might be pregnant at the time of the sterilisation, and that she was led to believe that if there was a risk of pregnancy it could be effectively removed by a D & C that she was about to undergo. She contended that if she had been warned or not misled she would have discovered the pregnancy and had it terminated when that could still be achieved by D & C or suction.

Causation

When the claimant has established breach of duty he must then go on to establish that the breach caused the damage. It must be proved that if he had been given adequate information he would have rejected that treatment. In *Smith v Barking, Havering and Brentwood Health Authority* the claimant had undergone a hydromyelia operation when she was nine years old. When she was 18 she had a recurrence of her condition and was advised to have a second operation without which she would have been a tetraplegic within nine months. The surgery was regarded as complex, and surgeon

---

27   QBD 25 February 2000.
28   (1998) 40 BMLR 163.

was reluctant to carry it out. However, despite his reluctance he decided that the operation should be recommended. As he did not want to damage the patient's confidence by giving the impression that he did not want to perform the operation, he did not inform her of the risks. She had the surgery and was rendered tetraplegic. Hutchinson J held that the claimant could only succeed on the point of failure to warn if she could prove, on a balance of probabilities that, if she had received proper warning and advice, she would not have undergone that surgery. The burden was not on the defendants to prove that she would not have refused.

As the case of *Carver v Hammersmith* outlined above suggests, it requires strong evidence to convince a judge that the claimant would have taken a different course of action had the treatment been properly explained.

The question of provision of information about the risks of treatment is prominent in cases concerned with failure to warn that sterilisation surgery may become reversed over a period of time by natural processes. Many claims of this kind fail because the claimant is unable to prove, on a balance of probabilities, that he would not have undergone the sterilisation procedure if the risk of natural reversal had been explained. Cases dealing with this matter are discussed in the chapter dealing with causation.

Conclusion

There are cumulative trends suggesting that patient autonomy should be given greater respect by the judiciary. On the basis of these trends Department of Health guidance states: *'The courts will be the final arbiter of what constitutes reasonable practice, although the standards set by healthcare professions for their members will still be influential'*. First, the Human Rights Act 1998 is a factor to be taken into account in future when courts give consideration of the question of consent to treatment[29]. Second, plans to modernise the NHS are ostensibly based on *'patient empowerment'*. Early results from the second national NHS survey of patients confirm patients want to be better informed about their treatment so that they can be more involved in making decisions about their own care. On that basis, the focus for the future is to be on patient care including speed of access, and *'patient empowerment'* delivering fast and convenient care for patients, listening to patients needs and letting them know their rights. The survey was designed to assess NHS quality issues through the patients' eyes and looked at access and waiting times, provision of information and communication between patients and hospital staff, and involvement of patients and their families in treatment decisions. It surveyed 84,300 CHD patients in England who had received hospital treatment. This suggests that in future the question of patient autonomy may be a consideration for judges when they decide cases concerning information provision and consent to treatment. A third example of the drive towards patient autonomy can be found in the conclusions of the independent review group considering the safety of silicone gel breast implants. The Silicone Gel Breast Implant Review Group recommended that women considering having implants should be provided with comprehensive information about the nature of the treatment and all risks attached to it. As a result, a very detailed patient information leaflet, drafted with the assistance of patients, has been produced.

Fourth, very serious concerns were voiced when parents of children who died at the Bristol Royal Infirmary Paediatric Cardiac Unit were not informed at the time that their children's hearts had been removed before burial. The Alder Hey Inquiry

---

29   See Brazier, M, and Miola, J, *Bye-Bye Bolam: A Medical Litigation Revolution*, [2000] 8 Med LR 85.

resulted in recommendations for proper information to be provided to all relatives about what might happen to the organs and tissue removed from their loved-ones after death. This is yet another welcome step towards recognition of a less paternalistic attitude towards patients.

Finally, the GMC Guidance[30] to doctors on obtaining informed consent is also ahead of the law, perhaps for cynical reasons. The guidance is extremely detailed and could provide the basis for legal argument in the event of a dispute concerning information provided to a patient, or the lack of it, by a doctor when seeking consent to treatment[31].

In recent years there has been criticism of the judiciary for supposed failure to be proactive and develop the law in line with changes in moral and cultural attitudes. Even allowing for the fact that judicial development of the common law is classically gradual and incremental, critics argue that any progress towards respecting values such as autonomy has been leaden footed, and behind developments in other jurisdictions. As Sheila McLean[32] suggests, the law in the UK does not currently fulfil a proactive, rigorous or disinterested function. If there is to be revolution in clinical negligence litigation[33], a starting point lies in the *Bolitho* case and its potential developments in relation to consent.

---

30 *Seeking Patients' Consent: the Ethical Considerations*, para 5, GMC, February 1999.
31 Jones, M, *Informed Consent and Other Fairy Stories*, op cit at p133.
32 McLean, S, *Old Law, New Medicine* Pandora Press, London 1999.
33 Brazier, M and Miola, J, op cit.

Chapter 6

Causation and Remoteness of Damage

Once the claimant has established that there has been a breach of duty, the next step is to prove a causal link between the negligent act and the damage that has been sustained. This involves two factors, and the claimant will not succeed unless both can be proved to the satisfaction of the court. The first of these is causation, (cause in fact) and the second, remoteness of damage (cause in law). In strict theory they are dealt with as separate issues, but in practice they frequently merge. To establish causation, the claimant is required to prove that the negligent act caused or materially contributed to the damage complained of. Remoteness of damage is a question of law, the rules of which require the claimant to prove that the damage was of a kind that was reasonably foreseeable. The application of these concepts is essentially policy driven, which can create difficulties for lawyers in evaluating the likely outcomes of cases.

There is much space devoted to the issue of causation in academic texts[1] dealing with the general law of tort, but it is probably in cases involving healthcare negligence that problems concerning factual causation and remoteness of damage arise most frequently[2]. It is in this area of law that many claims fail at the causation stage, in part because of the complexity of scientific evidence and pre-existing medical conditions. The task of deciding causation issues is by no means simple, and scientific matters can sometimes be misinterpreted by judges.

Science and Law: Different Approaches to Evidence

For a scientific theory to be proved and regarded as reputable, it must be published in a peer-reviewed journal. This means that the theory should be based on evidence that is objectively verifiable by scientific methods. The conclusions of a scientific study must be properly drawn and subjected to peer review in which the standards applied are stringent. Evaluation of medical research requires many hours of meticulous work by experts, and probability and certainty are explicitly examined in each case.

As Marcia Angell comments when writing about the controversy concerning scientific evidence in the United States[3]:

---

1. The standard academic text is Hart,L and Honore, T *Causation in the Law*, 2nd ed 1990, Clarenden Press, Oxford. In *Risk and Remoteness of Damage in Negligence*, (2001) 64 MLR No 2, 191-214 Marc Stauch discusses the law of negligence with reference to the work of Hart and Honore. That discussion includes the medical law cases. There is a very useful analysis of the scientific basis of causation in medical cases by Barton, A and MacCrae K, in *Clinical Negligence* ed Powers M, and Harris N, Butterworths, London 2000.

2. See Goldberg R, *Causation and Risk in the Law of Torts – Scientific Evidence and Medicinal Product Liability*, Hart Publishing 1999.

3. Angell, M *Science on Trial: The Clash of Medical Evidence and the Law*, Norton and Co, New York at p97.

'We can rarely absolutely prove a hypothesis, although we can gather enough evidence from enough scientific studies to make the hypothesis so probable that we can say it is true for all practical purposes'.

For the findings of a scientific study to be acceptable as evidence that an outcome is not simply the result of chance, it is usual for a 95% probability to be expected. The law demands no such rigour. Causation must be proved in law only on a balance of probabilities, or on the preponderance of the evidence, so that it is proved to be more likely than not that the negligent act caused the damage. This suggests a mere 51% likelihood, as is confirmed by the cases[4]. The differences of approach have been described by an American judge as *'a cultural chasm'* between the scientific community and those involved in litigation[5].

Personal injury cases, including those involving healthcare negligence, are decided by judges in the UK[6]. In the United States these cases are still decided by juries. There are many examples of US juries falling prey to *'junk'* science and to emotional pleas by claimants and their lawyers[7], and this has worked to the benefit of claimants in some instances. Such cases have drawn the attention of the legal and scientific communities to the fallibility of juries, and the law in the US has recently changed. The previous rule laid down in *Frye v United States*[8] was that scientific evidence would only be admissible if it observed principles and methods *generally accepted* by the scientific community in question (similar to the *Bolam* test in UK law).

However, since 1993, more emphasis is placed on the role of the judges. The case of *Daubert et al v Merrell Dow Pharmaceuticals*[9] laid down new guidelines requiring *judges* to take on the role of gatekeepers of scientific evidence. That was a Supreme Court decision concerning the possible role of a drug in causing birth defects. Judges must, in accordance with the guidance, decide whether the expert scientific evidence is both scientific and relevant. Federal judges must now undertake:

'A preliminary assessment of whether the testimony's underlying reasoning or methodology is scientifically valid and properly can be applied to the facts at issue.'

Such evidence can only be admitted in the course of proceedings if it is founded on the *'methods and procedures of science'*. So US judges now appoint scientific panels to advise and assist them[10].

There is much less opportunity in the UK than in the US for good advocates, claimants and expert witnesses to succeed in claims based on dubious scientific theories. However, even though it is usually possible to rely on our judges to weigh the scientific evidence carefully and to reach balanced conclusions, there are glaring examples of High Court judges being swayed by dubious scientific explanations[11]. The Court of Appeal is very reluctant to interfere with findings of fact by trial judges who have had every opportunity to observe the witnesses and hear their evidence.

---

4   *Hotson v East Berkshire Health Authority* [1987] AC 750.

5   Judge Sam Pointer Jnr cited in Hulka BS, Kerkvliet NL and Tugwell P; *Experience of a Scientific Panel Formed to Advise the Federal Judiciary on Silicone Gel Breast Implants.* New England Journal of Medicine 324: 812-815 (2000).

6   This has been the case since *Ward v James* [1963] AC was decided.

7   Carlsen W, *Jury Awards $7.3 million in Implant Case* San Fransisco Chronicle 14 December 1991, pA13, cited Angell op cit.

8   54 App DC 46, 293F. 1013.

9   509 US 579-601, 1993.

10   Price JM and Rosenburg ES, *The Silicone Gel Breast Implant Controversy : The Rise of Expert Panels and the Fall of Junk Science.* Jo of The Royal Society of Medicine 324:31-34 (2000).

11   *Roe v Minister of Health* [1954] 2 WLR 66; see also the case comment by Goldberg on *Vadera v Shaw* (1998) 45 BMLR 162, in [2000] 8 Med LR No 3; 316 - 328.

Our judges, like juries in the US, are dependent on expert witnesses and the scientific evidence that they present, or omit to present, and it is certainly worth considering whether judges would benefit from the assistance of expert panels similar to those recently established in the United States. Indeed, it has been suggested that clinical negligence claims be decided by panels of people who include a judge and medical assessors, though at present this system is very unlikely to be implemented.

It is hoped that the Civil Procedure Rules will assist judges in their task of deciding causation issues. Judges can now be much more proactive in the conduct of proceedings, including the pre-trial stage[12]. No expert can be used without the permission of the court, and expert witnesses must set out in their reports the substance of their instructions. Experts must meet to identify and as far as possible agree the scientific issues, and the judge has power to order them to do so. The parties are encouraged to use single joint experts if possible, and in certain circumstances the judge can select a medical or other expert from a panel of experts kept by the court if the parties cannot agree between themselves. This, however, is not the usual practice in clinical negligence cases, where there are frequently complex issues to be decided, and the parties are currently given greater freedom to select and use their own experts. The duties of experts are spelled out clearly, and include the warning that experts owe an overriding duty to the court, which has priority over the duty to the party giving the instructions and paying the fee. Experts must sign a declaration acknowledging that duty, and stating that the opinions expressed in their reports are correct, and that the facts stated are true. This cultural change makes it more difficult for unscrupulous scientific experts to be partisan.

Particular difficulties arise in relation to proof of causation involving alleged drug-induced injuries[13] and illnesses caused by medical devices such as implants. Even claims under the Consumer Protection Act 1987 for injuries caused by defective products require proof of causation. An example of the rigorous scrutiny required in a scientific study of causation can be found in the work of the UK's Silicone Gel Breast Implant Review Group that reported in 1998[14]. The group, consisting of eminent medical experts and a lawyer, spent many months reviewing a large body of epidemiological, immunological, legal and other evidence relating to claims by women who believed that the illnesses from which they were suffering were caused by their silicone gel breast implants. The group also took evidence from a range of interested parties, including patient groups, plastic surgeons and other physicians, representatives of the pharmaceutical industry, manufacturers of implants, claimant and defence submissions to the United States review panel and lawyers acting in claims based in the UK. The risks and benefits associated with silicone gel breast implants were considered by the Review Group. The Group concluded that there was no histopathological or conclusive immunological evidence that there is an abnormal immune response to silicone from breast implants in tissue, and no epidemiological evidence for a link between silicone gel breast implants and connective tissue disease. Another of their conclusions was that good evidence for the existence of atypical connective tissue disease or undefined conditions such as silicone poisoning is lacking, though it might be possible that low grade infections of a chronic nature could be responsible for some of the non-specific

---

12   The experience in the US is that despite being given greater discretion as gatekeepers of scientific evidence judges still have problems with scientific evidence of experts. See Kaufman H: *The Expert Witness*. Science and Justice 2001, 41(1): 7-20.
13   Ibid.
14   *Silicone Gel Breast Implants: The Report of the Independent Review Group* July 1998; *www.silicone-review.gov.uk*

illnesses noted in some women who had received silicone gel breast implants. There was no doubt that many of the women who had silicone gel breast implants are suffering from debilitating illness, but the group could find no direct causal link between their implants and those medical conditions. However, in the US there have been successful claims and settlements relating to silicone gel breast implants, where the issues of causation were never properly explored. As a matter of practicality, no court would have time to conduct an in-depth review like that undertaken by the Review Group in the UK, yet judges are expected to draw conclusions about causation in cases concerning the side-effects of treatments such as these.

Proving Causation

The legal burden is on the claimant[15] to prove on a balance of probabilities that the defendant's negligence caused the injury or lack of improvement in the medical condition that is suffered. This, on the face of it, is a simple question of fact, but in practice there is frequently a complex web of possible causative factors to disentangle, and many cases are fought solely on the issue of causation. Over the years several tests have been developed to assist the courts in determining the question of causation. Some of these are discussed in this chapter.

Causation is usually a more significant problem in healthcare negligence cases than in other cases involving personal injuries[16]. In clinical negligence cases the claimant was usually suffering from an illness or injury before receiving the treatment that was alleged to have been negligent. Medical expert witnesses may disagree on the precise course that an illness has taken. It follows that the claimant will frequently be faced with an insuperable problem in establishing that the damage was not merely a consequence of the original illness or medical condition. For example, in *Kay v Ayrshire and Arran Health Board*[17] the claimant failed to prove that an overdose of penicillin caused his deafness, and in *Loveday v Renton*[18] where the claimant, a previously apparently healthy child, suffered brain damage after he was given a vaccination. The claimant did not succeed because it could not be proved on a balance of probabilities that the whooping cough vaccine caused brain damage.

Complex problems arise when clinical negligence was merely one of several possible causes of the final injury, there being one or more medical conditions or other factors which could have caused it, as in *Wilsher v Essex Area Health Authority*[19] the facts of which are outlined below. The various causal factors can be so complex in some cases of alleged clinical negligence that the courts are prepared to accept that the claimant has established causation if it can be proved on a balance of probabilities that the negligent act or omission either directly caused or materially contributed to the injury or disease, or materially increased the risk of that injury occurring.

In cases where a breach has been admitted or is relatively easy to prove because a fairly obvious medical error has occurred, the claimant may be very disappointed and even puzzled when the case fails because causation cannot be established. This was the case in *Bolitho v City and Hackney Health Authority*[20] which was discussed

---

15   *Wilsher v Essex Area Health Authority* (1988) 3 BMLR 37; [1988] 1 AC 1075, which reasserted this principle after the speech of Lord Wilberforce in *McGhee v National Coal Board* [1972] 3 All ER 1008 appeared to have contradicted the rule and to be more claimant friendly.

16   See Jones M, *Medical Negligence*, Sweet and Maxwell 1996.

17   [1987] 2 All ER 417.

18   [1990] 1 Med LR 117.

19   supra.

20   (1997) 39 BMLR 1.

at length in Chapter Three, dealing with breach of duty. There can be few tasks more difficult for lawyers or judges than that of explaining to a claimant that although there has been negligence the case must fail because causation has not been proved. The law reports contain many examples of attempts by judges to sympathise and explain this aspect of the law to disappointed claimants[21].

The Tests for Causation

Several tests have been formulated by the courts to assist judges when they decide whether there is a causal link between an act of negligence and the damage that is alleged to have resulted. For example, the *'but for'* test that is explained below, might be applied. Alternatively, the court might consider whether there is an unbroken chain of causation between an act of negligence and the damage, and might be concerned as to whether there was an intervening act between the act of negligence and the damage. None of these is the definitive test, and different judges favour different approaches to the causation problem depending on the facts of the case before them. As one writer explained, the various tests are:

'... only a smoke screen behind which the judges have all too often in the past retreated to avoid the irksome task of articulating their real motivation'[22].

The 'but for' test

A standard test for causation that is sometimes used in more straightforward clinical negligence cases is the 'but for' test. The judge will ask whether the injury suffered by the claimant would not have occurred but for the negligence of the defendant. If the answer is that the injury would probably not have occurred, then a causal link is established. In *Barnett v Chelsea and Kensington Hospital Management Committee*[23] the claimant was the widow of a man who had died after being sent away from a hospital accident and emergency unit by the casualty officer on duty. The deceased had been taken to the hospital in a distressed state and vomiting copiously. He died soon after leaving the hospital, and a post mortem examination revealed that he was suffering from arsenic poisoning. The widow failed in her claim, because although there had been a breach of duty the court found that her husband would have died even if he had been treated soon after arriving at the hospital. The simplicity of this approach is attractive but the test is inappropriate in complex cases where there are evidentiary difficulties and several possible causes of the damage.

The chain of causation

If there is an unbroken chain of events between the original act of negligence and the damage, the person responsible for the first act will be liable for all the damage. In some situations, especially in cases where the claimant was injured in an accident and then received negligent medical treatment, it can be difficult to trace the various chains of negligent events and establish blame[24]. Sometimes liability may be apportioned between two or more defendants. In other cases the court may be able to identify two or more distinct torts and deal with them accordingly. For example, in *Rahman v Arearose and University College London NHS Trust*[25], the claimant, an employee of the first defendant, a fast food company, was violently assaulted at

---

21 eg *Robertson v Nottingham Health Authority* [1997] 8 Med LR 1; *Tahir v Harringey Health Authority* [1996] discussed by Grubb A [1996] 4 Med LR 92.

22 Fleming, JG, An *Introduction to the Law of Torts*, 1977.

23 [1968] 1 All ER 1608.

24 *Robinson v Post Office* [1974] 1 WLR 1176.

25 [2000] 3 WLR 1184.

work by a gang of people whose activities were known to the first defendant, his employer. The claimant then attended University College Hospital London and underwent an operation that led to the permanent loss of vision in his right eye. He claimed damages from the company on the grounds that it had breached its duty to protect him as an employee, and he also claimed damages for negligence on the part of the hospital. The hospital admitted that the eye surgeon had been negligent. In addition to the eye damage, the claimant suffered very severe psychiatric injury as a result of the physical effects of both the assault and the clinical negligence. The Court of Appeal was called upon to decide upon the interrelation of these events in the causation of the claimant's psychiatric injury. Medical experts agreed that the claimant had suffered post traumatic stress disorder (PTSD) as a result of the assault, but that some symptoms were also related to the negligent surgery. He suffered a severe depressive disorder accompanied by psychosis, largely due to the loss of his eye, and developed a specific phobia of black people as a result of the assault, in addition to a personality change that probably would not have developed if he had not lost his eye.

The first defendant, the employers, argued on appeal that that judge should not have apportioned the damages between the defendants on a percentage basis[26]. They contended that the company should be liable for those losses caused directly by the assault. The Court of Appeal held that the fact that the expert evidence did not distribute causative responsibility for the psychiatric injuries did not necessarily bring this case under the Civil Liability (Contribution) Act 1978. The role of the judge had been to arrive at a fair decision on the evidence as to the respective damage caused by each defendant, even though it might only be possible to do so on a broad-brush basis that was later converted into percentages. The Court of Appeal took the view that this was not a case involving concurrent torts where the liability of the tortfeasors was indivisible. It was a case in which respective torts committed by the defendants were the causes of distinct aspects of the overall psychiatric condition. It was positively established that neither defendant had caused the whole of the claimant's PTSD, and that the torts were divisible rather than concurrent. It was held that it would be unjust for the claimant to recover damages from the hospital for the PTSD or the phobia of black people, which were wholly or largely the result of the assault.

The second question was whether the company should be liable for any loss or damage beyond that which the claimant would have suffered if the eye injury, caused by the hospital's negligence, had not occurred. There was no rule of law to the effect that later negligence always extinguished the causative strength of an earlier tort. Every tortfeasor should compensate an injured claimant in respect of that loss and damage for which he was found liable. The concept of causation was not *'frozen'* into a set of restrictive rules. There had been no *novus actus interveniens* (intervening act) in this case to absolve the company of all responsibility for the continuing effects of the psychological damage, nor was this an *'eggshell skull'* case (see later). Although the second defendant had exclusively caused the eye injury, each tort played a part in the claimant's suffering. Therefore, the Court of Appeal adjusted the awards for past and future losses to reflect the relative responsibility of the defendants as assessed on the facts.

---

26   Civil Liability (Contribution) Act 1978.

Novus Actus Interveniens (An Intervening Act)

If there is an intervening act by the claimant or some other individual, or a new set of circumstances arises, the original wrongdoer may escape liability altogether, or share responsibility for the damage with the claimant, if there has been contributory negligence, or with other people. Where several different individuals are involved in causing the damage, liability may be apportioned between them. Sometimes it is possible to separate the acts of negligence and calculate that only one was responsible for the damage, or to calculate the precise part of the damage for which each defendant was responsible[27].

Even if the claimant was himself careless for his own safety and carried out an intervening act that caused him injury, the original actor might still be liable for a large percentage of the damage if the claimant was acting in a dilemma[28] or was not responsible for his actions because of illness. In *Kirkham v Chief Constable of Greater Manchester*[29] the police were liable for a suicide in prison. A prisoner had been transferred to a remand centre by the police officers who did not warn officers at the centre that he was in danger of committing suicide. This follows the basic principle that if an intervening act, in this case the suicide, is foreseeable, the original actor will usually carry full responsibility for it. There may, however, be a reduction in the damages payable if the claimant was careless for his own safety under principles set out in the Law Reform (Contributory Negligence) Act 1945.

In *Reeves v Commissioner of Police for the Metropolis* the House of Lords ruled that where police had been warned that a prisoner was a suicide risk they had a duty to take reasonable care not to allow him any opportunity to kill himself. The defence of *volenti non fit injuria* (consent) could not apply in cases of this kind where the defendant had accepted responsibility for the claimant and the damage was caused by a deliberate act that the defendant had a duty to prevent. The suicide attempt was foreseeable even though the claimant was not of unsound mind at the time. However, it was held that because the deceased had responsibility for his own life, he had also caused his own death and a finding of 50% contributory negligence could be made[30].

A vivid illustration of a *novus actus interveniens* can be found in the Scottish case of *Sabri-Tabrizi v Lothian Health Board*[31]. The pursuer became pregnant for a second time after a failed laparoscopic sterilisation, and brought a claim for damages. On a preliminary point in an action of reparation the issue was whether the defender could be liable for the consequences of a failed sterilisation operation when the pursuer knew at the time of intercourse that the operation had failed. It was held that the defender could not be liable as the chain of causation had been broken.

More Complex Cases

Simple applications of the standard tests for proving causation do not withstand the complexities of some situations involving cliniical evidence. More scientific approaches than the broad brush pragmatic tests that have been developed by the courts have been recommended. These include the application of the NESS test which

---

27   *Baker v Willoughby* [1970] AC 467; *Performance Cars v Abraham* [1962] 1 QB 33.
28   *Sayers v Harlow Borough Council* [1958] 1 WLR 623 where a woman, locked in a public lavatory through the defendant's negligence, injured herself when she tried to climb out.
29   [1990] 3 All ER 246.
30   See *Grange v Chief Constable of West Yorkshire* (cp cit) 2001.
31   43 BMLR 190.

provides a useful assessment of the causal efficacy of different factors,[32] and the use of Bayes' Theorem.[33]

A concession to the difficulties involved in complex cases lies in the case of *Bonnington Castings v Wardlow*[34] which established the principle that in order to succeed the claimant need not show that the defendant's breach of duty was the cause of damage or even the predominant cause of the injury. Lord Reid explained in that case that it is only necessary to show that it made a *'material contribution'*. The claimant must then go on to establish the causal link[35]. In *Bonnington Castings* the claimant was unable to establish the precise source of his pneumoconiosis, as he had inhaled dust from more than one source. He could not identify the exact source of the *'guilty dust'*. However, his claim succeeded because the court accepted that an inference could be drawn that *'guilty dust'* had made a material contribution to his condition. Thus the court leaned pragmatically in favour of the claimant where the exact cause of the illness could not be established with certainty. However, if there are several distinct potential causes of the damage the court is less likely to find that the negligent act made a material contribution to it[36]. In *Wilsher v Essex Area Health Authority* [37], discussed below, as there were five possible causes of the retrolental fibroplasia suffered by the child, and as it was only one of those causes that the claimant was alleging had been responsible for his condition, he could not sustain a successful argument that this was a material cause.

In *McGhee v National Coal Board*[38] a majority in the House of Lords took the view that a material increase in *risk* amounted to virtually the same thing as a *'material contribution'* to the *damage* – possibly as a way of overcoming the problem presented by a gap in the factual evidence connected with lack of scientific knowledge about the exact way in which the claimant's medical condition had developed. The claimant worked for the defendants in their brick kilns. He contracted dermatitis from brick dust. His employers were not negligent in relation to the hours when he was actually working with the brick dust, but they were held to have been negligent in not providing adequate washing facilities. It was impossible to establish which exposure to the dust – exposure at work, or afterwards on the way home – had caused the claimant's dermatitis. The lack of washing facilities at work could certainly have increased the risk of dermatitis, but in terms of the *'but for'* test, it was impossible to prove that this amounted to a *'material contribution'* to the damage. Nevertheless, the House of Lords took the view that the defendants were liable because the claimant had succeeded in proving that the breach of duty made the dermatitis more likely, so bridging the obvious evidential gap. Here the House of Lords took a sensible pragmatic approach in ruling that the defendants were liable. Lord Salmon explained that approach thus:

> *'In the circumstances ... the possibility of a distinction between (a) having materially increased the risk of contracting the disease, and (b) having materially contributed to causing the disease may no doubt be a fruitful source of interesting*

---

32   See Wright *Causation I Law* (1985) California Law Review 1325.

33   Goldberg, op cit.

34   [1956] AC 613.

35   Per Lord Bridge in *Wilsher v Essex Area Health Authority* (1988) 1 WLR 557.

36   As in *Wilsher v Essex Area Health Authority* (supra).

37   supra.

38   [1972] 3 All ER 1008.

academic discussion between students of philosophy. Such a distinction is, however, far too unreal to be recognised by the common law[39].

The House of Lords was clearly anxious to ensure that the injured workmen received compensation in this case, and judges in later cases recognised the artificiality of the reasoning in *McGhee*[40]. The possibility of a reversal of the burden of proof[41] was implicit in the approach taken by the House of Lords, though this does not appear to have been followed up in later cases.

It appears that the approaches established in *Bonnington Castings* and *McGhee*, which might have been confined to claims relating to dust-related illnesses such as asbestosis, could apply across a wide range of personal injury claims, including claims for psychiatric injury[42].

The reasoning in *McGhee* does not withstand too close a scrutiny and should be regarded as taking what Lord Simon described in the Court of Appeal[43] as *'adopting a robust and pragmatic approach to the undisputed primary facts of the case'*. He continued:

'When the court's knowledge of all the material facts is not complete, on occasion it will be legitimate to ... infer from those facts ... that the defendant's negligence did indeed cause or contribute to the plaintiff's injury'.

Although a broad brush approach is to be welcomed, it is not always possible to predict before a case reaches trial how the judge will deal with the causation question. Alluding the difficulties involved in predicting the policy direction of the court, Kennedy comments[44]:

'Where there is a breach of duty and uncertainty as to what may lead to what, the court has the choice of favouring the plaintiff or defendant. If the court chooses the latter it can merely decide that the "but for" test is not satisfied, and the case is over. If, on the other hand it is thought proper to assist the plaintiff in pursuit of a remedy, once a defendant is judged to have breached his duty the court in effect has two principle policy options.'

These, he explains are first, the reversal of the burden of proof. This is not really an option as it was that approach in the *McGhee* case that was rejected in the circumstances that applied in *Wilsher*. The second option is to use the *'material contribution'* approach to draw appropriate inferences[45].

In *Best v Wellcome Foundation Ltd*[46] the claimant succeeded in a claim for injuries caused by vaccination because the Supreme Court of Ireland was prepared to draw an inference, from the fact of the short interval of time between the vaccination and the development of convulsions, that the claimant's brain damage was caused by the vaccination. In *Wilsher v Essex Area Health Authority*. The House of Lords confirmed the position that it was possible in some circumstances, for a claimant to establish causation by proving that the negligence of the defendant had *materially contributed* to the damage suffered, and reiterated the rule that the burden of proving causation is on the claimant. The claimant, who had been born prematurely, had received an excess of oxygen during early treatment as a result of the negligence of

---

39   at page 1018.

40   Lord Mustill in *Wilsher v Essex Health Authority* [1986] 3 All ER 801 at page 815, for example.

41   See Weinrib (1975) 38 MLR 518.

42   *Page v Smith* (No 2) [1966] 3 All ER 272.

43   *Bolitho v City and Hackney Health Authority* [1993] 4 Med LR 381 CA at page 389 in which Wilsher was also examined.

44   *Principles of Medical Law* Butterworths, London, 1999. Chapter 7.

45   See the Canadian case of *Snell v Farrell* (1990) 2 All ER 475 for an airing of these matters.

46   (1992) 17 BMLR 11.

the team of doctors responsible for treating him. He developed retrolental fibroplasia, which resulted in blindness. However, as there was contradictory expert evidence as to the causes of retrolental fibroplasia, and as the trial judge had not found as a fact that this condition had been caused or materially contributed to by the excess oxygen in the claimant's blood, the case was sent for retrial (though in the event it was never retried as it was settled out-of-court). This case suggests that there may be a distinction between cases in which there is a set of separate causes of the damage (as in *Wilsher*), and cases where there are several cumulative causes that are difficult to disentangle, (as in *McGhee*). The claimant has a better chance of success if the potential causes are inseparable. However, the claimant will usually only succeed in establishing causation, where there are several possible causes of the final medical condition, if it can be proved that the act of negligence in question was sufficiently significant to be taken into account as a potential cause[47].

More recently, in *Holtby v Brigham and Cowan (Hull) Ltd*[48] however, it was held that the defendants were only liable for their material contribution to the damage, and for no more, as it would be unfair to make the defendant responsible for any part of the damage to which he had not in fact contributed. The damages awarded to the claimant, who had contracted asbestosis as a result of working for the defendant, were reduced by 25% to take account of the fact that the material contribution of the defendant did not extend to the full extent of the damages claimed. This approach was confirmed by the Court of Appeal on the basis that the point had not been argued in *Bonnington Castings*. This case could prove crucially important for defendants in future.

In *Miles v Redbridge and Waltham Forest Health Authority,*[49] the decisions in *Bonnington Castings* and *McGhee* were followed. The case concerned a baby who suffered severe brain damage as a result of a series of connected incidents around the time of birth. The defendants were found liable for misdiagnosing foetal death, and as a result of that misdiagnosis, administering the drug Pethidine to the mother to ease her pain, just when she was about to deliver her baby. In addition they were negligent in delaying, for a period of three-and-a-half hours, ventilation to the child to *'blow away'* the hypercarbia (excess carbon dioxide) caused by the Pethidine. The judge held that there had been no negligence in the failure to carry out a Caesarean section, and even if there should have been a Caesarean, the question was whether, in so far as the trauma and bruising suffered by the claimant had caused or contributed to the brain damage, the decision not to carry out a Caesarean was relevant. He took the view that even if the failure to give the mother a Caesarean was negligent, it was not possible to conclude, on the balance of probabilities, that there had been more bruising and trauma as a result of vaginal delivery than there would have been in the case of a Caesarean section.

The doctor was not negligent in failing to locate the foetal heart, but he was negligent to diagnose death without identifying the heart and satisfying himself that it was not beating. He should have proceeded on the basis that the baby was alive. But for that misdiagnosis, Pethidine would not have been given to the mother immediately before the delivery. The result of the injection was depression of the claimant's respiration at birth, which itself led to hypercarbia. If that conclusion was

---

47 This is demonstrated by the victory of the coal miners in protracted litigation concerning the possible causes of chronic diseases of the chest.

48 [2000] 3 All ER 421.

49 QBD 18 February 2000.

wrong, and the defendant was not negligent as to the cause of the hypercarbia, the judge considered that the question remained as to whether the defendant's admitted negligence in delaying ventilation for three-and-a-half hours caused or materially contributed to the brain damage. The judge found that the negligent extension of the hypercarbia as a result of ventilation not commencing within 30 minutes after the onset of the hypercarbia, caused the injury. The brain damage was not caused by the non-negligent period of hypercarbia. Furthermore, in the alternative, the substantial three-and-a-half-hour period of extension contributed substantially to causing the injury.

Causative difficulties, where there is a range of possible causes that are interrelated, might account for the relatively high number of cases that reach trial on the issue of causation, and in those that are settled out-of-court, many settlements are reached on the basis of a reduced sum to take account of the uncertainties faced by the claimant in proving causation if the case were to reach trial. Two examples of cases in which the award was reduced to allow for the causation difficulties are as follows. In the first case, *Boland v Bexley and Greenwich Health Authority*[50] the claimant received the sum of £1,450,000 for the brain damage she suffered at birth as a result of the defendant's alleged mismanagement of her mother's labour. Despite warning signs of foetal distress there had been a delay in delivering her, and the claimant contended that the hospital had been negligent in not taking appropriate steps to respond and deliver her two-and-a-half to three hours sooner. Shortly after her birth a diagnosis of birth asphyxia and meconium aspiration was made. The claimant was severely brain damaged, and her condition was found to be permanent with little prospect of improvement. A compromise figure was agreed between the parties on the basis of full liability with a discount of 9% to reflect the potential difficulties the claimant may have incurred in establishing causation. Similarly, in *Brown v Mid Glamorgan Health Authority*[51] the claimant received £800,000 damages due to the alleged negligence of the hospital where he was born. He suffered hypoglycaemic encephalopathy, which resulted in cerebral palsy with spastic quadriplegia. His life expectancy was reduced and he require constant care for the rest of his life as a result of an alleged negligent failure by the defendants to recognise that his mother was suffering from diabetes when she was pregnant with him. Liability was disputed, and the final award was one-third of the total value, in recognition of the problems that would have been involved in proving causation.

The Standard of Proof: Examples from the Cases

The claimant must prove causation on a *'balance of probabilities'*. This means that it is for the claimant to establish that there was a 51% likelihood that the breach of duty had caused or materially contributed to the injury[52]. The negligent act must have been more likely than not to have caused the damage. Examples of some of the difficulties in proving causation in clinical negligence cases are found in the cases that follow in this section. In *Richardson v Kitching*[53] a widow brought an action against the GP who had treated her deceased husband. He had initially failed to diagnose an acoustic neuroma which had caused deafness. After it had eventually been diagnosed, surgery was performed to remove the neuroma and the patient died as a result of the operation.

---

50   QBD 27 February 1999.

51   QBD 11 January 1999.

52   *Hotson v Berkshire Area Health Authority* [1987] AC 750.

53   [1995] 6 Med LR 257.

His widow argued that the surgery should have been performed earlier, at the time the condition should have been correctly diagnosed, and the patient referred to a consultant. The claim failed. It was found on the facts that the patient had merely raised isolated points on three visits to the GP that led the GP to conclude not unreasonably, that the patient was suffering from a disease of the middle ear. This would not have required urgent referral to a consultant. The appropriate time for the questions about any history of deafness from which the patient had suffered was when he was referred to the hospital, and there was no reason for the GP to have made detailed inquiries into his history. The claimant also failed to prove causation because there was insufficient evidence to establish on a balance of probabilities that the outcome of the surgery would have been different had it been performed earlier.

In *Gates v McKenna*[54], the claimant sought damages for developing schizophrenia, an illness that he alleged he had contracted after the defendant had hypnotised him on stage. In the days following the hypnotist's show, the claimant had behaved in an increasingly odd and disturbed way until he was admitted to a psychiatric hospital suffering an acute schizophrenic episode. He had since suffered further episodes that amounted to permanent schizophrenia, and he lost his job. It was accepted by the defence that the claimant must have suffered from a pre-existing or underlying condition making him vulnerable to schizophrenia, and that the defendant may not have had reason to foresee the nature and extent of the illness. However, the claimant relied on the principle in *Smith v Leech Brain & Co Ltd*[55] (see later in this chapter) that a wrongdoer must take his victim as he finds him, no matter how impossible it is to anticipate the full extent of the injury. The defendant contended that schizophrenia was an organic illness which could not be caused by hypnosis, that the claimant was either already suffering from schizophrenia or was about to do so when he was hypnotised, and that the connection between the show and the manifestation of the illness was a coincidence. The judge held that the claimant had failed to establish a causative link between hypnosis and schizophrenia. The only way in which there could be such a link between the hypnosis and the injury would be to classify the experience as a *'life event'*, the stress of which had triggered the disease. The judge concluded that common sense and reason, based on the evidence, suggested that the claimant's medical condition must already have reached the stage at which it could be easily triggered and would therefore have manifested itself without any triggering event, or would have been triggered by any other life event involving comparable stress. The claimant had therefore failed to establish that his schizophrenia was in any way attributable to his experience of stage hypnotism[56].

In the tragic case of *Vadera v Shaw*[57] the claimant was 22 and soon to be married, so she sought contraceptive advice from her GP, the defendant. On 11 October, she was prescribed Logynon, an oral contraceptive and as a matter of routine good practice, her GP took her blood pressure and found it to be high, at 150/100. The claimant started to take the oral contraception on the following day. On 19 November she suffered a serious brain stem stroke as a result of thrombosis, that left her almost completely disabled with a condition known as *'locked-in syndrome'*. Her medical expert argued that Logynon was the likely cause of this condition as it

---

54   (1998) 10 Lloyd's Rep Med 405: (1999) 46 BMLR 9.

55   [1962] 2 QB 405.

56   But in The Times, 26 May 2001 there was an account of a successful PTSD claim against another stage hypnotist (*Howard v Green*).

57   (1998) 45 BMLR 162.

carries a risk, albeit a very small risk compared with other contraceptive drugs, of thrombosis. Proceedings were brought against the GP, alleging negligence in diagnosing the oral contraceptive in the light of her alleged history of hypertension and migraines, which are contraindicated for Logynon. The trial judge found, on the available evidence, including epidemiological studies, that the claimant was not suffering from hypertension on 11 October. Hypertension is not normally diagnosed after a single reading of blood pressure. In fact doctors routinely take a patient's blood pressure on three separate occasions to establish a true reading. The claimant's medical records contained no note of headaches on the GP notes or the hospital records, nor of an alleged consultation for headache on the 8 October. As the causal connection between the claimant's illness and the contraceptive pill had not been established, either in whole or in part, the claim failed. The Court of Appeal confirmed the findings of the trial judge.

The decision in *Vadera v Shaw* can be criticised[58] on the grounds that the trial judge and the Court of Appeal failed to pay sufficient attention to the scientific evidence and to relate it to the personal circumstances of the claimant. It is unusual for a doctor to prescribe the contraceptive pill to a patient with a single high blood pressure reading without asking her to return on another occasion to establish that the high reading was an aberration, as the pill is contraindicated for women with high blood pressure. The case illustrates the gulf between scientific proof[59] and the proof required in civil claims, in many of which judges rely on intuition rather than science.

In *Brown v Lewisham and North Southwark Health Authority*[60] the Court of Appeal explained that to establish causation in a clinical negligence case it must be shown that the injury suffered by the patient was within the risk from which it was the doctor's duty to protect the claimant. If it was not, the breach was not a relevant breach of duty. The claimant had been admitted to Guy's Hospital in London for a quadruple coronary artery by-pass graft on 19 September 1990. He had been referred there from the Royal Victoria Hospital Blackpool. During surgery he had been given Heparin, an anti-coagulant drug and the operation itself was successful. He was discharged from Guy's and travelled by train to the Liverpool Hospital on 28 September 1990. When he arrived there it was discovered that he had a number of medical problems, including a chest infection and a deep vein thrombosis of the left leg. He was given more Heparin, but it was not widely known at the time that this could cause a very serious adverse reaction in certain patients. Unfortunately, the claimant was one of these patients and in due course a haematologist was consulted when the claimant's condition deteriorated. It was admitted that some of the advice given by the haematologist was negligent, and after gangrene set in the claimant had his left leg amputated. The defendants argued that there was no causal connection between the negligence of the haemotologist and the amputation of the claimant's leg, because by the time he saw him gangrene was inevitable, and was a consequence of the adverse reaction to Heparin.

The trial judge held that in order to succeed, the claimant was not required to prove that the defendant's negligence was the cause, or indeed was the dominant cause, of the ultimate damage, but merely that it had made a material contribution to

---

58   See Goldberg [2000] 8 Med LR No 3; 316-338.
59   Goldberg discusses several scientific studies that were not presented to the court, which would have supported the claimant's case.
60   (1998) Lloyd's Rep Med 265.

that damage. Following *Wilsher*, the claimant must show a causal link between the alleged negligence and the damage. If he would have sustained that damage whatever the defendants had done, the claim would fail. In this case, although there had been negligence on the part of the second defendants, (but not the first defendants), the claimant had failed to establish a causal connection between the negligence of the haematologist and the amputation of his leg which had been an inevitable consequence of his reaction to Heparin.

On appeal the issue was whether the trial judge's finding that the journey from Guy's Hospital to the Royal Victoria Hospital in Blackpool did not contribute to the loss of the claimant's left leg could stand. Had he not been discharged at that particular time, the claimant would have been spared the effect of a long journey between London and Liverpool that involved him sitting for a long time. The claimant argued that had there not been that negligence, he would have remained in hospital and received treatment sooner.

The Court of Appeal held that the trial judge had been correct in finding that there was no causal link established in this case. The judge's very careful analysis of the medical evidence and the inferences he drew were correct, and the only rational decision was that the journey was not an effective cause of the loss of the claimant's leg. The Court of Appeal took the view that for the purpose of analysis it may sometimes be important to be more precise in the definition of the scope of the duty. A doctor is obliged to exercise the care and skill of a competent doctor. For the claimant to succeed, it must be proved that the injury was within the scope of the risk from which it was the doctor's duty to protect him. If it is not, the breach is not a relevant breach of duty. Accordingly the appeal was dismissed.

In *Rosenorn-Lanng v Scunthorpe and Goole Hospitals NHS Trust and Another*[61], the claimant had attended the Accident and Emergency Department of the defendant's hospital having suffered from a prolonged nosebleed. He was examined by a nurse and a casualty doctor and two extremely high blood pressure readings were recorded. The readings were noted by the nurse, recorded, and the record handed to the claimant. He was not admitted to hospital but was advised to contact his own GP in his home town several hundred miles away when he returned there. The claimant did so in due course, and was attended by the second defendant, his GP, who prescribed standard medication. He took the first tablet four days after that, and suffered a stroke the following day. He contended that the first defendant should have admitted him and that, if he had received competent treatment, his stroke would have been avoided. In addition the claimant contended that the second defendant should have arranged for him to be admitted to hospital on returning home. The first defendant accepted that it should have admitted the claimant to hospital in view of the very high blood pressure, but denied causation. The second defendant denied both negligence and causation. It was held that on a balance of probabilities, the claimant was not suffering from malignant hypertension but had suffered a stroke because his hypertension had, over some time, caused degeneration of the walls of the blood vessels. That kind of stroke would not have been delayed for any significant time had the second defendant admitted him to hospital. Causation was not proved.

In *Gray v Southampton and South West Hampshire Health Authority*[62] there was a claim for clinical negligence arising out of events in July 1984, when the claimant

---

61   QBD 18 October 1999.
62   (2000) 57 BMLR 148.

was aged nine. On that date she had undergone surgery for the removal of a brain tumour. One hour after the operation she suffered a fit, even though she had been free from fits for two years prior to the surgery. She was anaesthetised again, and intubated, but soon afterwards she suffered severe and irreparable damage that left her severely disabled and dependent on her parents. The claimant alleged negligence in her post operative management by the anaesthetist. She alleged that the cause of her injury was systemic hypoxia/hypertension. The defence argued that the effective cause was status epilepticus. The judge held that the claimant's condition was caused by a combination of factors, including a certain degree of systemic hypoxia and/or hypotension. However, there was insufficient evidence about the nature and degree of that condition to justify a finding that on a balance of probabilities, it was caused by lack of proper management by the defendant.

There may be a finding by the court that although the damage was caused by negligence, the extent of the damage is more limited than is alleged by the claimant. In *Glicksman v Redbridge Healthcare NHS Trust*[63] the claimant succeeded in establishing negligence on the part of a surgeon in carrying out a hernia operation, but as her disability after the operation was partly the result of her pre-existing medical problems, the appropriate award was only £4,000.

Causation, Omissions and Bolitho

One of the most important recent developments in the law on causation in healthcare negligence cases is the confirmation by the House of Lords in the *Bolitho* case that the practice of a responsible body of doctors, (as modified by the *Bolitho* case) is relevant in determining causation in some cases. The facts in *Bolitho v City and Hackney Health Authority*[64] are set out in Chapter Three. Counsel for the appellant contended in *Bolitho* that the *Bolam* test had no application in deciding issues of causation and that the judge at first instance had misdirected himself in applying *Bolam* when deciding causation. Lord Browne-Wilkinson, giving the judgment of the House of Lords, concluded that he had no doubt that *'in the generality of cases'* the proposition of law was correct, but equally he had no doubt that the trial judge in the *Bolitho* case was not guilty of any misdirection. The primary question, he explained, was one of fact – did the breach of duty cause the damage? However, where what was complained of was an *omission* rather than a positive act to do something which ought to have been done, the factual inquiry is in the realms of hypothesis. The first question therefore was what Dr Horn or Dr Rodger would have done if they had attended the child when they were summoned to give assistance. The trial judge had accepted that neither would have intubated Patrick even if they had attended him. In the view of the House of Lords the *Bolam* test had no part to play at that point. However, in this case, the answer to what would have happened was not determinative of causation. The defendant at the trial had conceded that if the professional standard of care had demanded that *any* doctor seeing Patrick's condition should have intubated him, the claim must succeed.

To summarise the conclusion of the House of Lords on causation in *Bolitho*: the two separate issues in determining causation in this case were first, what would Dr Horn have done if she had attended Patrick, and second, if she would not have intubated, would that have been negligent? The *Bolam* test was not relevant in relation to the first of those questions but was *'central'* to the second. This indicates

---

63   QBD 29 June 2000.

64   (1997) 39 BMLR 1.

that the question of causation is a complex matter. It involves not simply a question of fact, it may also involve an element of evaluation. Having stated the law in terms of *Bolam* their Lordships went on to modify the *Bolam* test. Thus the correct statement of the legal position would now be that in cases involving negligence by **omission** it is relevant to inquire first what the defendant would or would not have done, and second whether that decision would have been logically defensible within the *Bolitho* criterion.

Bolitho v City and Hackney Health Authority was applied in the case of *Brock v Frenchay Healthcare Trust*[65]. The claimant was injured as a result of a fall from his bicycle when he was 16. He had not been wearing a crash helmet, and he suffered a head injury. The ambulance arrived promptly and took him to hospital, by which time he had regained consciousness after a period of unconsciousness of only about four to five minutes. He had a Glasgow coma scale score of 15 (which is normal) on admission to hospital, and as an X-ray appeared to reveal no fracture he was discharged that same day. However, in the early hours of the following morning the claimant became seriously ill, and was returned to hospital by ambulance. The neurosurgical team was called because his Glasgow coma scale score was then only 3. The claimant was ready for the drug Mannitol to be given at 4.15am to relieve pressure around the brain, but the anaesthetist waited for the surgeon to arrive before he administered it. It was administered at 4.30am, and it was contended on the claimant's behalf that it was this short delay that caused him to suffer irreversible brain damage. The Court was asked to consider whether there had been negligence in allowing him to be discharged from hospital when he was, whether there had been any negligence in the treatment which he had received when he was readmitted to hospital the following day, and whether, if there had been any negligence, it had caused or contributed to the brain damage which he subsequently suffered. The trial judge ruled that there had been no negligence on the part of the doctor who had failed to identify the skull fracture from the initial X-ray, and no negligence in discharging him from hospital. However, the judge decided that in failing to give Mannitol at 4.15am, there had been an omission that fell short of acceptable professional standards. The issue was whether this omission had caused the claimant's subsequent condition. Following *Bolitho*, which also turned upon a negligent omission, the trial judge did not accept that the failure to give the drug at 4.15am made any material difference to the injury, and the claim failed on causation. On appeal on the question of causation, the Court of Appeal confirmed the finding of the trial judge and ruled that the claimant would not have gained any benefit from receiving Mannitol earlier.

Loss of a Chance

If the claimant is able to prove to the court that his condition has been worsened by the failure of the defendant to provide adequate treatment, when the *'but for'* test is applied, the claim succeeds. Problems occur, however, when the defence can establish on a balance of probabilities that even if the defendant had not been negligent the claimant's condition would not have improved. The alleged damage is the loss of a chance of the condition improving, even though that chance was less than 50%. The notion of *'Loss of a chance of a successful outcome to treatment'* is not a separate head of damages in clinical negligence cases, however, though there may be

---

65   Court of Appeal 20 May 1999.

a strong case[66] for allowing this head of damages in tort[67], similar to that in the law of contract[68]. Ian Kennedy[69] argues in favour of this and their view is that recovery of damages for loss of a chance of recovery, would ensure equality of treatment as between patients treated privately, who can bring a claim in the law of contract, and those treated on the NHS who are forced to rely on tort, with its less generous approach to this matter[70].

The problem is illustrated by the case of *Hotson v East Berkshire Health Authority*[71] in which the claimant argued that a five-day delay in diagnosing a fracture of his left femoral epiphysis resulted in a 25% loss of the chance of making a complete recovery. The chance of permanent injury as a result of his original injury would have been put at 75% in any event, but he contended that the defendant's negligent failure to make a correct diagnosis made that a 100% certainty. The trial judge accepted this argument and based his award upon it, assessing the damages at £46,000 and reducing that sum by 25% to cover the 25% loss of chance. The Court of Appeal agreed, but unlike the trial judge treated the matter as one of causation rather than simple quantification. However, the House of Lords disagreed, and dealing with the problem as a causation issue, ruled that the claimant had failed to establish negligence. He had not proved on a balance of probabilities that the negligent diagnosis had caused him not to make a full recovery.

Causation in Obstetrics Cases

As in the case of breach of duty, both the parties and the court rely on expert medical evidence in dealing with the question of causation. The problem of proving causation is especially acute in cases involving brain damage allegedly caused by obstetric negligence[72]. The defence may argue that the brain damage was caused by some inherent genetic defect or that there was an unavoidable incident in the womb that occurred through no fault of the doctors caring for the mother[73]. The cases outlined below illustrate some of the difficulties.

In *Robertson v Nottingham Health Authority*[74], the facts of which are set out in Chapter Two, the claim on behalf of an infant who had been brain damaged since birth failed despite the fact that a breach of duty was established, because it was not possible to prove that the negligence of the defendants had caused the injury complained of. In *Faithfull v Wiltshire Health Authority*[75] there was a claim for injuries allegedly sustained during the course of the claimant's birth at the defendant's hospital. The claimant's mother had been admitted to the hospital on 8 May 1981 suffering from severe pre-eclampsia. From 9.10am on 9 May, a hospital midwife was put on constant special duty to watch her. Labour was induced on that day at 10am and by 1pm the dose had been raised. The CTG trace of the foetal heart rate was normal until 1.40pm but it began to reveal abnormalities between 1.58pm

---

66   See Stapleton J, (1988) 104 LQR 389. See also *A v National Blood Authority* TLR 4 April 2001.
67   See Hill *A Lost Chance for Compensation in the Tort of Negligence by the House of Lords* (1991) 54 MLR 511.
68   *Chaplin v Hicks* [1911] 2 KB 786; *Kitchen v Royal Air Force Association* [1958] 1 WLR 563.
69   *Principles of Medical Law* Butterworths, London 1999 at p411.
70   See also Jones Textbook on Torts, Blackstone Press 7th ed 2000 at p217.
71   [1987] AC 750.
72   See Stening, W, *Medico-Legal Aspects of Birth Defects and Early Childhood Disorders* in *Brain Damage – Medico-Legal Aspects*, Blackstone Press Pty Ltd, Sydney 1994.
73   See *Cerebral Palsy – Antenatal or Intrapartum Aetiology* Farkas A Medical Litigation 1999, October, No 10; 9-10 in which the author discusses the current practices for determining causation when a child suffers with cerebral palsy.
74   [1997] 8 Med LR 1.
75   QBD 29 March 2001.

and 3.06pm. The obstetric registrar attended the mother on the ward at 2.25pm and delivered the baby by Caesarean section at 3.30pm. The claimant argued that the baby suffered hypoxic ischaemia in the womb prior to birth, and that this caused brain damage resulting in spastic quadriplegic, cerebral palsy and cognitive disability. It was alleged that these disabilities were caused by the negligence of the midwife and registrar. The judge found that there was no breach of duty on the part of either, and obiter, that the baby would not have suffered the brain damage had she been delivered by 3pm on 9 May. Failure to deliver her by that time caused her brain damage, but that failure was not the result of a breach of duty on the part of medical staff. Causation was proved but not breach of duty, so the claim failed.

In *Boddison v Hughes and Worcestershire Health Authority and Another*[76] there was a claim for damages for alleged negligence at the time of the claimant's birth on Christmas Day 1970, as a result of which she had since suffered from athetoid cerebral palsy. The claimant's mother had one daughter who had been delivered without complications, and she decided to have a home delivery. The pregnancy was uneventful. Breech presentation was not diagnosed though it was agreed that it was not negligent to have failed to diagnose that. Mild contractions began at 6.30am on Christmas Day and hospital records indicated labour commencing at 8am. The contractions subsided in the afternoon and did not return until evening. At 7pm the mother felt a sharp pain. Her sister telephoned for a midwife. The midwife arrived half an hour later and examined the mother. As she was concerned about the possibility of breech presentation, she decided that the mother should go to hospital. About seven minutes later the locum service were told of an obstetric emergency and the need for an ambulance and a bed. The ambulance arrived at about 9pm and left with the mother at 9.04pm. The baby was delivered at hospital at 9.25pm having been born in the ambulance, except for the head. The journey of nine miles was in snowy conditions and may have taken 17 minutes. It was accepted that a reasonably competent midwife in 1970 would have known that a baby's head should be delivered within eight to ten minutes of the umbilicus in a breech delivery, because of the likelihood that cord compression could result in anoxia causing probable death or brain damage after that period of time. The judge held that there was negligence by the midwife in failing to attempt delivery in the house. As there was no evidence of foetal distress before delivery, or any other foetal problem, the probability was that the cerebral palsy suffered by the claimant would not have occurred if the midwife had attempted delivery in the house.

In *Rossiter v Tilsley and Another*[77] a claim was brought by a mother who had sustained injury when pre-eclampsia had not been diagnosed, and on behalf of her baby whose brain damage was allegedly suffered as the result of his premature birth. The claim failed on causation. The first defendant was a locum doctor who found signs of early onset pre-eclampsia on 17 May 1989 but failed to take appropriate steps. That locum admitted a breach of duty. The second defendant was a partner in the GP practice who was called out to examine the mother on 19 May 1989 when she was suffering from abdominal pain. He did not see her antenatal co-operation card because she thought she did not have it with her. He failed to take her blood pressure or test her urine, and did not diagnose pre-eclampsia. However, he did diagnose a urinary tract infection and prescribed antibiotics. He denied that he was in breach of

---

76   QBD 18 September 1998.
77   QBD 15 February 2001.

duty. Pre-eclampsia was diagnosed on 29 May 1989, and the mother was admitted to hospital as an emergency.

The judge noted that it was agreed that the mother's abdominal pain was probably unconnected with pre-eclampsia. It was held that in the light of what the mother had told the GP, pre-eclampsia would not have been foremost in his mind, as the symptoms she complained would not have suggested that condition. If the GP had been reasonable in diagnosing a urinary tract infection, his duty did not extend to repeating antenatal tests, and was not in breach of duty. Unless the pregnancy would have been prolonged until about 15 June 1989, the claim, except for those parts relating to the mother's pain and suffering caused by the delay in diagnosis, would in any event fail on causation. The damage to the baby would probably have been suffered in any case.

Similarly in *Temple v South Manchester Health Authority*[78] it was held that although there was a finding that a child suffering from diabetic ketoacidosis had been treated negligently after being admitted to hospital, the court could not conclude on a balance of probability that cerebral oedema and its consequences would not have occurred even if he had been treated correctly. The scientific evidence was confused, medical opinion was divided and more research was needed before the cause was properly understood.

Failure to Inform: Issues of Causation

It can be exceptionally difficult for the claimant to establish a causative link between the negligent act and the injury when the claim is based on a failure of the defendant to provide adequate information about the risks and side-effects of a treatment regime to enable the claimant to arrive at a decision as to whether to have the treatment in question. The law concerning information provision and consent to treatment is explained in Chapter 5. Proving causation where there has been a failure to provide adequate information necessarily involves proving that if the information had been provided the claimant would have taken some decision or acted on the basis of the information. For example, in *Carver v Hammersmith and Queen Charlottes Special Health Authority*[79] the facts of which are set out in Chapter 4, the claimant was able to convince the judge that she would have insisted on an amniocentesis had she been told the true nature of the Bart's test and would have had a termination of her pregnancy if she had discovered that she was carrying a Down's syndrome baby, as she had worked with handicapped children and was determined not to have a handicapped child herself.

In cases involving the failure to warn that a sterilisation can undergo a natural reversal, the claimant would have to prove that if he had received the information he would have acted on it – by using condoms or some other form of contraception (which would defeat the object of the sterilisation operation), by insisting on regular tests to ascertain whether fertility had been re-established or by not bothering to have the operation at all. In *Lybert v Warrington Health Authority*[80] the claimant brought an action for damages for an unplanned and unwanted pregnancy after the failure of a sterilisation operation where no warnings as to the risk of failure had been given to her or her husband. The couple produced evidence that they would have taken additional contraceptive measures if they had been warned of the risk, but the

78   QBD 19 July 2000.
79   QBD 7 March 2000.
80   (1996) 7 Med LR 71.

claimant refused to have her pregnancy terminated because she considered that it was too late in the development of the foetus. The Court of Appeal confirmed that the trial judge had been correct to find that the defendants were liable.

Remoteness of Damage

The claimant cannot succeed if the damage is, as a matter of law, too remote from the negligent act. In the early days if a defendant was proved to be in breach of duty and it was found that as a matter of fact that the breach caused the damage, the defendant was liable for all the damage that was the direct consequence of the breach[81]. That approach was considered to be unfair to defendants and a new approach was adopted in 1961[82] by the Privy Council which was confirmed in an appeal to the House of Lords in *Hughes v Lord Advocate*[83] soon afterwards. The underlying basis of this more recent test for remoteness is foreseeability of the type of damage that the claimant sustains. In broad terms, the test is *'Was the type of damage reasonably foreseeable to the defendant?'* This test provides the court with a wide discretion by allowing for the judge to define the *'type of damage'* in as broad or as narrow a way as he sees fit in the particular circumstances of the case.

In *Hughes v The Lord Advocate* the House of Lords ruled that the precise nature of the accident, and the way it happens, need not be foreseeable, as long as the type of damage (eg economic loss, personal injury etc) ought reasonably to have been foreseen. However, later decisions of the Court of Appeal in which *Hughes* was distinguished, suggest that it may be necessary for the claimant to establish that the defendant ought reasonably to have foreseen the way in which the accident happened[84]. In *Tremain v Pike*[85] the claimant failed in his action against his employer. He had contracted Leptospirosis as a result of handling farm material on which rats had urinated. The Court held that the employer could have foreseen an illness resulting from a rat bite, or from food contaminated by rats' urine, but not from handling straw. The damage was thus too remote. This is a rather surprising decision as it has been well known for many years that swimmers, boaters and others using rivers, who might come into contact with places where rats have urinated, are at risk of contracting this disease. The degree of precision required by the judge in predicting the way in which the disease was contracted is unacceptable here.

In cases involving psychiatric injury discussed in Chapter 2, where the claimant is a primary victim, the claim will succeed if the claimant can prove that the defendant ought reasonably to have foreseen that he would suffer some kind of personal injury[86]. Where the claimant is a secondary victim the claimant must, in addition to satisfying the other criteria in *Alcock v Chief Constable of South Yorkshire*[87], prove that psychiatric injury was foreseeable[88].

In *Giblett v Murray*[89] it was held by the Court of Appeal that the claimant would have been able to recover damages for a psychiatric condition that made her incapable of having sexual relations, and of having a family as long as physical

---

81   *Re Polemis, Withy and Co* [1921] 3 KB 560.
82   *The Wagon Mound* [1961] AC 617.
83   [1963] AC 836.
84   *Doughty v Turner Manufacturing Company Ltd* [1964] 1 QB 518.
85   [1969] 3 All ER 1303.
86   *Page v Smith* [1995] 2 All ER 736.
87   [1991] 4 All ER 907.
88   *White v Chief Constable of South Yorkshire* [1999] 1 All ER 1.
89   The Times 25 May 1999.

injury in a road accident caused by the defendant was foreseeable. The test to be applied was *'Did the accident, on the balance of probability, cause or materially contribute to or materially increase the risk of the development or prolongation of the symptoms of the pre-existing psychiatric illness?'* This case and others dealing with foresight of psychiatric injury suggest a far less rigorous approach to the type of damage that must be foreseeable than is found in the earlier cases.

The Thin Skull Rule

Once the claimant has established that the damage was not too remote, the defendant *'must take the victim as he finds him'* and is liable for its full extent. This is known as the *'thin-skull'* rule, and it is of special significance in healthcare cases, because the claimant may be in a vulnerable state through ill-health when the injury occurs. As long as the defendant can be proved to have caused the injury and that it was not too remote, he does not have to foresee the full extent of it. For example, if a normal, healthy individual would only have suffered a mild illness as a result of negligent treatment, but the claimant, who is already vulnerable, dies as a result, the defendant is liable. In *Smith v Leech Brain and Co Ltd*[90] the claimant's deceased husband had suffered a minor burn on his lip as a result of a splash injury at work. He was suffering from a pre-cancerous condition at the time, and developed cancer and died. The defendants were liable for the full extent of his injuries (ie his death) even though so drastic an outcome could not have been predicted. In *Robinson v The Post Office*[91] the claimant was injured at work as a result of negligence, and was later given an anti-tetanus injection by a doctor. He suffered a serious allergic reaction to the injection, and the Court of Appeal held that the defendants were liable for his illness even though the serious consequences of the negligence in a particularly vulnerable individual could not have been foreseen[92]. These cases demonstrate that judicial policy plays an important role in the development of the law on remoteness of damage in cases involving personal injury, and this provides a great advantage to the claimant, especially if he or she has an egg-shell personality as in *Page v Smith* where the claimant had a history of failure to hold down satisfactory employment.

Conclusion

The legal rules developed by the courts concerning causation and remoteness of damage are the product of the need to establish legal responsibility for injury. As has been seen, in UK law this is not a scientific process, but a rough and ready way of doing justice, often based on common sense. In many cases it is not difficult to prove causation, but where the facts are complex and the claimant was suffering from a pre-existing medical condition, proving causation can give rise to great difficulties. The legal processes for determining causation in such cases are a very blunt instrument indeed. The decision process involves judges in value judgements, as when deciding issues relating to duty of care and breach of duty, making it difficult for lawyers to predict the outcome of cases and advise their clients accordingly.

---

90   eg *Smith v Leech-Brain* [1962] 2 QB 405.
91   [1974] 2 All ER 737.
92   It should be noted, however, that negligent medical treatment will usually constitute a *novus actus interveniens*.

Chapter 7

Defences to Healthcare Negligence

There are several defences that can apply to exculpate the defendant in whole or in part from liability in healthcare negligence cases. These include consent (or *volenti non fit injuria*), contributory negligence, illegality (or *ex turpi causa non oritur actio*) and limitation of actions. The burden of proof is normally on the claimant, and it follows that if the claimant cannot establish each element of negligence the claim will fail. However, in some cases, the claimant may be successful in proving all the elements of negligence, but may fail to obtain some or all of the compensation claimed because the defendant succeeds in raising a defence. By far the most common defence relied on in healthcare cases is the limitation defence.

Consent (volenti non fit injuria)

The defence of consent applies when the claimant voluntarily agrees to run the risk of injury. This is complete defence to a negligence claim. In the context of healthcare, this does not mean that when a patient signs a consent form or presents himself for treatment he agrees to take the risk of being treated negligently. Consent to medical treatment is in fact consent to bodily interference – the torts of assault and battery, or on occasion false imprisonment.

Consent has been raised as a defence to claims of negligence when people attempt to, or succeed in committing suicide while in the care of public authorities. The defence was used unsuccessfully in *Kirkham v Chief Constable of Greater Manchester Police*[1]. The claimant's husband had committed suicide in prison when the officers responsible for his care were aware that he was suffering from clinical depression. The Court of Appeal rejected the argument presented by the defence that the man had consented, or chosen to kill himself. It appears that if a person is of unsound mind and is not fully responsible for his actions, he is in no position to consent to a risk. In *Reeves v Commissioner of Police for the Metropolis*[2] the facts of which are stated in full below, a prisoner had committed suicide although he was not suffering from a mental illness at the time. The defence of consent failed again, and the House of Lords held that *volenti* could not apply in circumstances where the defendant had a responsibility to prevent the claimant's voluntary act, whatever his state of mind. The deceased was a known suicide risk and the defendants had a duty

---

1   [1990] 2 All ER 346.
2   [1999[3 WLR 363.

of care to prevent him carrying out the very act that he committed. It could not be said that there was any difference between the duty owed to remand prisoners of sound and unsound mind. Any such theory failed to take into account the complexities of human psychology in the context of the stress of imprisonment. It does not appear that the argument based on the mental state of the deceased is valid[3] except in so far as the mental state might affect the issue of contributory negligence.

The fact that the claimant is aware of, and understands the risk does not necessarily mean that he has agreed to it. All will depend upon the particular circumstances[4]. For example, in *Watson v British Boxing Board of Control*[5] the claimant had agreed to accept the rules of the defendants as the governing body for the sport. He had agreed to abide by those rules and had consented to the risk of being injured by his opponent. However, the Court of Appeal held that he had not consented to take the risk of injury caused by inadequate medical treatment being provided by the defendants. He succeeded in his claim for damages based on the negligent failure of the defendants to provide adequate resuscitation facilities at the ring side in accordance with their own regulations[6].

The claimant's consent to run a risk must be given freely in full knowledge of the nature of the risk. The law recognises that employees are sometimes in a difficult position and cannot sensibly refuse to take on particular types of work or hours of work. In *Johnstone v Bloomsbury Health Authority*[7] a junior hospital doctor was required to work excessively long hours, as a result of which he became ill. He brought a claim against his employers for not taking adequate care of his health and safety as the common law required them to do. He had, however, signed a contract of employment that clearly spelled out the hours he would work, and in so doing he had, on the face of it, agreed to the long working hour regime and, the employers argued, to the associated risks. His claim succeeded in the Court of Appeal by a majority of two to one. However, the law remains unclear from the reasoning in this case, as to the extent of the employer's common law duties in the light of the express terms of the contract of employment. It is likely that the employer's common law duty cannot be extinguished by onerous contract terms that appear to make the employee consent[8].

Contributory Negligence

If the claimant is proved to have contributed to the injury by failing to take proper care for his own safety, there may be a finding of contributory negligence. The statute governing this area of law is the Law Reform (Contributory Negligence) Act 1945 which provides:

> '*Where any person suffers damage partly as a result of his own fault, and partly as a result of the fault of any other person or persons, a claim in respect of that damage shall not be defeated by reason only of the fault of the person suffering the damage, but the damages recoverable in respect thereof shall be reduced to such extent as the court thinks just and equitable, having regard to the claimant's share in the responsibility for the damage.*'

---

3   See *Jones M* (1990) 6 PN 107.
4   See *Johnstone v Bloomsbury* (supra).
5   The Times 11 January 2001.
6   This case is discussed in Chapter 4.
7   [1991] 2 WLR 1362.
8   Unfair Contract Terms Act 1977, section 2.

The judge first calculates the full value of the claim and reduces that sum by the amount to which it is found that the claimant contributed to the damage. Unlike the defence of *volenti*, contributory negligence is not a complete defence that exonerates the defendant from all liability. If a claimant's failure to take adequate care of himself is the only cause of the harm, then his conduct cannot be described as *'contributory'* as he is 100% to blame for his suffering.

Contributory negligence can be used to reduce the damages payable even if the claimant died as a result of the injuries, and the beneficiaries of his estate are made to suffer the same reduction even though no blame was attached to them for the deceased's injuries. This approach suggests the defence operates very much to the advantage of defendants and their insurers, and permits judges to exercise their discretion in that direction when assessing the relative contributions of the parties to the damage. In *Reeves v Commissioner of Police for the Metropolis*[9], the deceased prisoner was found to have been 50% to blame for his own death in custody, and only the reduced sum was available to his partner.

The standard of care and causation in contributory negligence
The standard of care required of the claimant in relation to his or her own safety is that of a reasonable person in the position of the claimant. In some cases the fact that the claimant is a child, or elderly, or mentally ill has involved the courts in making more rigorous inquiries about the character and state of mind of the claimant than is usual in an assessment of the defendant's conduct in relation to breach of duty. It appears that a more subjective approach may be acceptable in contributory negligence. Once the defendant has established that the claimant did not take proper care of himself, it must be proved that that lack of care contributed to the injury. The principles applicable in the various approaches to dealing with causation outlined in Chapter 6 are relevant here. One obvious question is *'Did the claimant's own lack of care for his safety make any difference to the damage?'*

Assessing the relative contributions to the injury
As the statute provides that the court must assess the reduction according to what it considers to be *'just and equitable'*, there is a discretion available to the judge to take into account all the relevant circumstances of the case. In the *Reeves* case, the House of Lords considered this aspect of the case carefully. Mr Lynch had hanged himself in a police cell after two previous suicide attempts in custody, one earlier the same day. A doctor examined him soon before his final attempt, but found no evidence of mental illness. Instructions were given that Mr Lynch, the partner of the claimant, was a suicide risk and that he should be kept under special frequent observation. He was checked at 1.57pm and the wicket hatch in his cell door was left open, contrary to instructions. Another officer checked at 2.05pm and discovered that Mr Lynch had hanged himself. He had tied his shirt through the open wicket. He was taken to hospital but he died a week later. The claimant was Mr Lynch's long-standing partner. The trial judge had found that the police had been in breach of the duty of care that they owed to the deceased. As they knew he was a suicide risk, they had a duty of care to prevent him from committing suicide. He also found that the police had been negligent because they had failed to ensure that the wicket hatch was kept shut. However, the judge held that the breach of duty had not caused the death. In the final analysis he took the view that the sole cause of his death was Mr Lynch's own deliberate act. The Court of Appeal overturned the decision of the trial judge, and

---

9   (2000) 51 BMLR 155; [1999] 3 WLR 363.

held that the breach of duty by the police had been the cause of death, but that there had been contributory negligence on the part of the deceased.

The House of Lords explored the questions of duty of care, breach, causation, *ex turpi causa* (discussed later in the this chapter), *volenti* and contributory negligence that were raised in this case. Their Lordships were of the opinion that the police had been under a duty of care to prevent a deliberate act of self-harm by Mr Lynch. His suicide was a foreseeable consequence of their breach of that duty. The fact that Mr Lynch had committed suicide had not prevented the breach of duty on the part of the police from being a cause of death. That did not, however, mean that the deliberate act of suicide was not a cause of the death as well. Following a common sense approach to causation[10]the House of Lords ruled that the police had a duty to take reasonable care not to allow Mr Lynch to have the chance of committing suicide, and their neglect had caused his death. However, as the deceased was of sound mind, he had responsibility for his own life, and he had caused his own death.

Thus their Lordships ruled that both the police and Mr Lynch had been responsible for the death, and an apportionment of the damages was required under the Law Reform (Contributory Negligence) Act 1945. Section 1 of that Act required the court to apportion responsibility, and the definition of *'fault'* in s4 of the Act was sufficiently broad to extend to deliberate acts as well as negligent acts of the claimant. Contributory negligence was a relevant factor where the claimant's careless or deliberate act was the very act that the defendant had a duty to guard against. The fact that a person of sound mind had some responsibility for the damage would reduce the damages recoverable. As Mr Lynch's act had been a substantial causative factor in his death, there should be an apportionment of responsibility *'as the court thinks just and equitable'*. This concept would sometimes require the court to balance the different factors involved. Apportionment of the damages served to recognise that one purpose of the duty of care owed by the police was to demonstrate to society that they have a responsibility to take reasonable steps to prevent prisoners from killing themselves. However, it would be wrong not to attribute some responsibility to the deceased himself. Therefore the responsibility should have been apportioned equally. The appeal was allowed, and a new award was substituted to allow for the 50% contributory negligence.

In addition to applying to the usual tort claims that arise in medical cases, the Act applies in contract cases to make the defence available in claims relating to private medical care. However, if liability depends not on negligence but on strict liability in contract,[11] the defence does not apply. This might be applicable in situations in which the claimant can establish that there was a breach of warranty. Such as the situation that arose in *Thompson v Sheffield Fertility Clinic*[12], though there was no question of contributory negligence in that case. The claimant, who gave birth to healthy triplets, succeeded on her claim in the law of contract against a fertility clinic, where a mistake in procedures had resulted in her being implanted with three embryos rather than two, as she had requested. There had been a breach of the terms agreed between the parties in their contract.

Contributory negligence is an important defence to negligence in motor accident claims and in claims by employees for injuries and illnesses suffered at work. It is of less importance in healthcare claims. Patients do have responsibility for their own

---

10   *Environment Agency v Empress Car Company (Abertillery) Ltd* [1998] 2 WLR 350.

11   eg Under the Supply of Goods and Services Act 1982.

12   QBD 24 November 2000.

health, however, and if a patient unreasonably fails accurately to inform the doctor who is treating him about previous medical conditions, or does not make it clear precisely how serious his condition appears to be, he might be found contributorily negligent. A patient of full mental capacity who does not follow clear instructions about when and how to take medication, or when to return for a check up, may likewise be found to have been contributorily negligent. This theoretical possibility has seldom been tested in UK courts, and contributory negligence is virtually unheard of in the healthcare setting[13] in the UK. There is, however, some scope for the defence to be used more widely in future if patients are given greater responsibility, as is planned, for their medical records, and if they are to be accorded greater autonomy as part of the regime of *'patient-centred care'*. The success of the defence would depend upon a subjective approach by the courts and the inquiry would need to focus on the ability of the particular patient to take responsibility for his or her treatment. Clearly, a patient who is very ill and distressed would bear little, if any, proportion of the blame for failing to follow a doctor's instructions. But if the patient is reasonably well, is interested and well informed, a judge might be prepared to make a finding of contributory negligence in an appropriate case. It would be unfair to doctors if patients were to be given greater autonomy and at the same time were not expected to take greater responsibility for their own health.

Illegality (ex turpi causa non oritur actio)
The defence of illegality rarely applies in the general law of negligence and is very seldom raised in healthcare cases. The defence applies to conduct that is illegal or immoral and it operates as a complete defence to a claim. Although it has been suggested that the defence might apply where a patient or prisoner commits suicide, that argument has been rejected as inappropriate, even if the deceased was not mentally ill – *Reeves v Commissioner of Police for the Metropolis*[14] and *Kirkham v Chief Constable of Greater Manchester*[15].

Limitation of Actions
The rules concerning limitation periods – the time limits within which claims must be brought – are designed to encourage claimants to proceed while the claim is still fresh and evidence is available, and to protect defendants from the fear that claims might be brought too long after the acts or omissions that give rise to them. If a long period of time has elapsed since the alleged act of negligence it can be very difficult for a claimant to prove breach of duty and causation. Witnesses may have died or disappeared, documentary evidence such as medical records and X-ray photographs may have been mislaid, and the recollections of all the people involved in an alleged incident will have faded with the passage of time. It is believed to be unfair that defendants should suffer the stress of a legal claim many years after the event. These factors justify the imposition of time limits within which legal proceedings must be brought. Healthcare negligence cases frequently give rise to limitation problems. It can be many years before a claimant discovers that he or she may have suffered some illness or injury at the hands of a doctor. Even then the basic information may be obtained by chance, perhaps hinted at by another doctor or by a nurse. In some cases patients have even been made aware of the potential for a negligence claim by a

---

13   The defence had succeeded in some Canadian cases, see Picard, E, *Legal Liability of Doctors and Hospitals in Canada* 2 ed 1984.
14   supra.
15   supra.

television documentary[16]. The limitation periods for litigation are considerably more generous to claimants than those applicable under the NHS Complaints System[17], and although there is a notional discretion to handle a complaint outside the time limits, litigation is the only realistic alternative if there has been a long time lapse since the claimant suffered the injury. This discrepancy is unfortunate if the Complaints System is to be used as a means of defusing litigation.

The Limitation Act 1980 governs the time limits within which claims must be made and permits judges to exercise a discretion to extend the statutory time limits in appropriate cases. The detailed provisions of this Act and the complex body of case law which has grown out of it relating to clinical negligence are matters which are well beyond the space available in this review[18]. Nevertheless, it is useful to make some observations on the recent case law. Recent cases involving limitation questions in healthcare negligence claims concern issues surrounding the date of knowledge, the meaning of *'legal disability'* under the Limitation Act 1980, and the factors taken into account when the courts decide whether it is appropriate for exercise of the discretion under s33 to disapply the time limits in *'exceptional circumstances'*. The entire law on limitation of actions has been under consideration by the Law Commission.

The date of knowledge

Section 11 of the Limitation Act 1980 provides that in cases involving personal injuries the limitation period is three years from the date on which the cause of action accrued, or the date of *'knowledge'* of certain matters, if later, on the part of the claimant. The cause of action accrues on the date on which the damage occurs. Most of the litigation turns on issues concerning the date of knowledge – that is the date on which the claimant acquired knowledge, as defined by s14(1) of the Act. Under that section *'knowledge'* means knowledge of the following matters:

1. that the injury was significant;
2. that the injury was attributable in whole or in part to the act or omission which is alleged to constitute negligence (or nuisance or breach of duty);
3. the identity of the defendant;
4. if it was alleged that the act or omission was that of a person other than the defendant, the identity of that person, and the additional facts supporting the bringing of the action against the defendant.

Knowledge that any acts or omissions did or did not as a matter of law, involve negligence ... is irrelevant.

There is seldom any difficulty in healthcare negligence claims in identifying the defendant, even if the precise identity of the particular staff members involved is not known, as the NHS Trust in question is usually vicariously liable for the acts of its employees. In the context of general practice the claimant should have no difficulty identifying the GP, district nurse or health visitor, or discovering the identity of the locum who treated him. In private healthcare situations there may be more of a practical problem, but again the identity of the doctor who was originally consulted will be known and the members of his or her team should also be readily identifiable.

---

16   *Parry v Clwyd Health Authority* [1997] 8 Med LR 243.

17   The normal time limit is six months from the date of the event that gave rise to the complaint or six months from the date when the matter first came to the complainant's notice, providing that is no more than 12 months from the date of the event itself, thought there is some discretion available to extend the time limits in exceptional circumstances.

18   For a full account of this area of law see Jones, M, *Limitations in Personal Injury Actions*, Blackstone Press, London 1995.

The significance of the injury.

An injury is *'significant'* if the claimant would reasonably have considered it sufficiently serious to justify instituting proceedings against a defendant who did not dispute liability and was able to satisfy a judgment. There need not necessarily be any medical symptoms for an injury to be significant. This means that the limitation period starts to run when claimants who have been exposed to dangerous conditions[19], but have not yet developed symptoms, first acquire knowledge of the potential seriousness of the situation. Such situations are not as uncommon as might be supposed, and include cases of claimants who have symptom free changes in the lungs[20], and those who suffer anxiety as a result of learning that they might have been given blood infected with CJD[21] or hepatitis C[22]. If the injury is merely trivial it is a question for the court to determine in each case whether it amounts to sufficiently serious injury to qualify as significant. The Court of Appeal revisited the question of *'significance'* of the injury in *Briggs v Payne and Another*[23] and ruled that the effects of the drug valium including *'zombification'*, drowsiness, lack of concentration, irritability, impaired judgement and night time incontinence, were not short term, and were clearly not *'side effects'* in relation to the determination as to whether the claimant's injuries had been significant.

Causation and limitations

It is not necessary for the claimant to be able to pin-point causation with precision for him to have acquired the necessary knowledge for limitation purposes. As long as there is broad knowledge that the injury was caused by the acts or omissions of the defendant, there is adequate knowledge for time to begin to run. The claimant may be deterred from bringing a claim by an expert's opinion indicating that there is an insufficient causal link between the act and the damage. That is irrelevant, however, if the claimant had originally had sufficient knowledge to initiate a claim. The cases suggest that much depends upon the degree of belief that the claimant actually possessed. This rule can appear to be very harsh, as many claimants are totally dependent upon medical experts for confirmation of their initial concerns that their injuries may have been caused by negligence[24]. However, if the claimant's original suspicions turn out to be mistaken and acts or omissions of the defendant, other than those originally identified, were a potential cause of the injury the claimant will not have acquired adequate knowledge[25] until that later information emerges. Ignorance of the law is not a relevant factor here, as all that is required of the claimant is broad knowledge of causation, based on the conduct of the defendant. These are matters of fact, not law[26].

Actual and constructive knowledge

Clearly knowledge on the part of the claimant may be actual or constructive. Actual knowledge consists of knowledge actually in the possession of the claimant at the

---

19   In the case of cumulative conditions such as those involving inhalation of dust, the claimant can usually be compensated for the whole of the damage, even if it began to accumulate outside the limitation period – *Clarkson v Modern Foundries Ltd* [1958] 1 All ER 33; unless the damage is severable – *Thompson v Smiths Ship Repairers (North Shields) Ltd* [1984] 1 All ER 881.

20   *Patterson v Minister of Defence* [1987] CLY 1194.

21   *N v UK Medical Research Council* (1996) BMLR 85.

22   See Chapter 4.

23   (1999) 46 BMLR 132.

24   *O'Driscoll v Dudley Health Authority* [1996] 7 Med LR 408, discussed below.

25   *Whitfield v North Durham Health Authority* [1995] 6 Med LR 32.

26   See *Hallam-Eames v Merrett* [1996] 7 Med LR 122. For further discussion of this point see Kennedy I and Grubb A, *Principles of Medical Law* Butterworths London 1999.

relevant time. In *O'Driscoll v Dudley Health Authority*[27] the claimant was found to have actual knowledge at the relevant time. She suffered from cerebral palsy as a result of hypoxia at birth, and failed to bring a claim for negligence within three years of gaining knowledge that she should have been delivered by Caesarean section. She was born in 1970, but her family had not been aware of possible medical mismanagement until 1985. The claimant had discussed the matter with her family in 1988 and a solicitor was instructed in 1991. An expert's report confirmed the suspicion of probable negligence in 1993. The writ was issued on 11 May 1994. The Court of Appeal took the view that judges could ask when the claimant first knew that there was a real possibility that her injury was a result of a failure to deliver her by Caesarean section. Whatever way this was considered, that date was more than three years before the writ was issued 1994. The claimant had the requisite knowledge on the 8 October 1991 when she reached the age of 21, which her parents mistakenly believed was the date of her majority. It was likely that the claimant's knowledge was the same when she was 18. The claim failed on the basis of actual knowledge, as this was not a situation involving constructive knowledge, and the appeal was allowed[28].

Section 14(3) deals with constructive knowledge. That section provides that *'knowledge'* includes knowledge that the claimant might reasonably have been expected to acquire:

(a) from the facts observable or ascertainable by him or her, or

(b) from facts ascertainable by the claimant with the help of medical or other appropriate expert advice which it is reasonable for him or her to seek; but a person is not be fixed ... with knowledge of a fact ascertainable only with the help of expert advice so long as he or she has taken all reasonable steps to obtain (and, where appropriate, to act on) that advice.

A series of recent cases underlines the difficulties facing the courts in arriving at the correct approach to the date of knowledge on the part of the claimant. In many of the cases the issue of knowledge is considered along with the question of whether the court should exercise the discretion to disapply the statutory time limit under s33 of the Act. The Court of Appeal has decided a large number of cases on the correct interpretation of the Limitation Act 1980 and a selection of the more important recent decisions will be considered here.

The combined subjective/objective test for knowledge
Although the words used in the Limitation Act suggest that the approach to determining whether the claimant had the relevant knowledge should be objective, some recent decisions indicate that the courts may be moving towards favouring a subjective approach – that is an approach which takes the view that a claimant had the relevant knowledge when he actually knew rather than when he ought reasonably to have known. The test is *'What would a reasonable man of the age, background, intelligence and disabilities of this particular claimant reasonably have known?'*

In *Nash v Eli Lilly and Co*[29] the Court of Appeal favoured what appeared to be a subjective approach. It was decided that in considering whether or not an inquiry by the claimant as to the possibility of negligence would be reasonable, the situation, character and intelligence of the claimant must be relevant. The Court concluded that

---

27   5 Lloyd's Rep Med 210.
28   5 Lloyd's Rep Med 210.
29   [1993] 1 WLR 782.

'knowledge' within the meaning of s14 of the Limitation Act 1980 is a state of mind experienced by the claimant, actually existing, or which might have existed had the claimant, acting reasonably, acquired knowledge from facts observable or ascertainable by him, or knowledge which he could have acquired with such expert help which it was reasonable for him to obtain. The injury in this case, caused by side effects of the drug Opren, first manifested itself in a minor way, but the claimant later discovered that it was considerably more serious, and the Court of Appeal held that time began to run from the date on which the claimants had knowledge that the side effects of the drug were serious. Many commentators understand this approach to be the trend for the future.

However, a different approach was taken in *Forbes v Wandsworth Health Authority*[30] where it was held by the Court of Appeal that the standard of *'reasonableness'* for the purposes of s14(3) was objective and did not take into account the individual character and intelligence of the claimant. On 4 October 1982 the claimant had a third bypass operation on his left leg. The operation was not successful and he required further surgery to repeat the procedure the next day. This repeat surgery was also unsuccessful, and about ten days later the leg was amputated. In June 1991 the claimant saw a solicitor who commissioned a report from a vascular surgeon. The report was produced in October 1992. The claimant then began proceedings alleging that there had been negligence on the part of the defendant doctor in not performing the repeat operation on the evening of 24 October, when there was no pulse in his foot and it was cold to the touch. The writ was issued on 10 December 1992, and at first instance the judge took the view that the claim was not statute-barred because the claimant did not have knowledge within s14 of the Limitation Act 1980 until the report of the expert vascular surgeon in October 1992. The defendants appealed. The Court of Appeal held that although the claimant had no actual knowledge, given the serious nature of the injury and the history of treatment, it would have been reasonable for him to have obtained a second opinion after the accident and he would have had constructive knowledge. The appeal was allowed.

Another case decided in 1996, the same year as *Forbes,* suggests that the mixed subjective/objective test was preferred by the courts. In *Jones v Liverpool Health Authority*[31] the Court of Appeal held that the trial judge had been correct in his approach to s14 of the 1980 Act. In 1974 the claimant had undergone hospital treatment that he later alleged was negligent. He had sought an expert medical report in 1976 and also counsel's opinion, but had no evidence to support his claim. In 1986 he instructed his current solicitors and a writ was issued in 1987 after a second medical expert had been consulted and reported that he had good grounds on which to base a claim. In 1991 the claimant was examined by yet another medical expert, and in 1993 there was a trial of preliminary issues in which the judge ruled that the claim was statute barred on the basis that the claimant had the relevant knowledge in 1977. Agreeing with the trial judge, the Court of Appeal dismissed the appeal, taking the view that it was not necessary for the claimant to have knowledge of a possible cause of action for knowledge to be present for the purposes of s14. The trial judge had been entitled to conclude that the claimant had not acted promptly and reasonably, the period of delay being in the region of ten years. He had had definite opportunity to obtain further and more detailed advice about the adequacy of his treatment, and it was inequitable to allow his action to proceed.

---

30   (1996) 36 BMLR 1.
31   [1996] PIQR 251.

However, the Court of Appeal returned to the subjective test for knowledge in the case of *Coad v Isles of Scilly Health Authority*[32]. This case concerned a nurse who had suffered a back injury at work. It is one of many cases of this kind which are usually supported by the nurses' trade union, as a result of which, combined with the implementation of the EU Directive (the Six Pack Regulations) health and safety conditions at work for nurses are improving. The claimant suffered the injury to her back in 1983, and she alleged that this was caused by the fault of the defendants. However, it was only when her medical condition deteriorated in 1990 that she realised that the injury was serious enough for her not to be able to return to work, and it was at this point that she believed she had a cause of action. She had genuinely believed that she could not bring an action against her employers unless she was so incapacitated that she could no longer work. In considering whether to exercise its discretion under s33(a) and disallow the time limit under s11 of the Limitation Act 1980, the Court of Appeal considered the meaning of that section. The Court of Appeal was of the view that the section requires the Court to take into account the circumstances of and the reasons for the delay, and in particular the length of and reasons for the delay on the part of the claimant. It was held that the words of the Act implied a subjective test, and since the Court accepted the claimant's version of the reasons why she had not brought an action earlier, she was permitted to proceed with her claim.

In the first instance decision of *Parry v Clwyd Health Authority*[33] the judge considered what approach was appropriate, in view of the claimant's level of knowledge and understanding of scientific matters, after a very long time had elapsed. The claimant was born on 21 July 1966 by breech delivery, and she needed to be resuscitated immediately after delivery. When she was about six months old her mother discovered that she had cerebral palsy but this she simply attributed to the breech delivery, and said so when she was asked to explain her daughter's condition when she was about ten years old. On 24 October 1990, after seeing a television documentary programme that aroused their suspicions, the claimant and her mother took advice from a solicitor who began to investigate whether there had been negligence at the time of the birth. A report by a medical expert concluded that the breech delivery had been badly performed and that as a result the claimant had suffered brain damage. The writ was issued on 21 December 1992, and the defendants argued that the claimant was out of time. The judge held that the claim was not time-barred. He considered that following *Nash v Eli Lilly*[6] the test for knowledge should be a qualified objective test, whether or not there was actual knowledge of the facts (s14(1)). The issue was whether the same test applied under s14(3), and considering the question of what knowledge a person might reasonably be expected to acquire for the purposes of s14(3), he looked at the conduct that could be expected of a *'reasonable man of moderate intelligence'*. The judge concluded that the phrase meant *'a person with no more than average public understanding'* of the problems associated with childbirth. The claimant was a woman of reasonable intelligence, and her mind was inquiring, but only to a limited extent. It was not proved that she had any knowledge of biology to provide her with more than a minimum understanding of the hazards of childbirth. The mother also was of no more than average intelligence. It followed that applying an exclusively objective test along the same lines as *Forbes v Wandsworth Health Authority* that accorded

---

32   [1997] PIQR 92.

33   [1997] 8 Med LR 243.

closely with the purpose of the s14(3), the claimant and her mother had accepted her condition as arising from the normal hazards of childbirth, and that knowledge and information could not justify them in embarking upon an inquiry leading to a claim. Therefore the claimant had no actual knowledge until she saw the television programme in October 1992 and the claim was not statute-barred.

In *Smith v Leicestershire Health Authority*[34] the Court of Appeal again examined the law concerning constructive knowledge and stated the test as *'What would the reasonable person have done placed in the situation of the claimant?'* commenting that each case must turn on its own facts. As to the matter of the Court's discretion, it was emphasised that the role of the Court of Appeal was only to interfere if the judge had misdirected himself on the law, taken into account irrelevant considerations or failed to take into account a relevant consideration. In this case the judge had misdirected himself. The defendants would not be unduly prejudiced in a case such as this that turned on x-rays and documents. The defendants' disadvantage in relation to the evidence was not great, as it was still possible for scientific experts to make proper analyses in cases of this kind many years after an alleged act of negligence. The claimant's appeal was allowed. The prejudice to the defence was small in comparison with the potential loss to the claimant.

In *Thomson v Hanson White Ltd*[35] the Court of Appeal confirmed that the correct approach to be taken by the court in determining the date of knowledge was partly subjective – ie whether the claimant considered that the injury was sufficiently serious, and partly objective – ie whether it would have been reasonable for the claimant not to treat the injury as one that was sufficiently serious.

One question that has exercised the minds of the judges on several occasions is how precise the knowledge must be about causation to constitute knowledge for limitation purposes, especially in the light of s14(1)(b) of the Act which states that knowledge that any acts or omissions did or did not, as a matter of law, involve negligence ... is irrelevant. In *Broadley v Guy*[36] the Court of Appeal took the view that broad knowledge that something had gone wrong with the treatment in question was sufficient – detailed knowledge of the precise circumstances is not necessary. In *Dobbie v Medway Health Authority*[37] the Court of Appeal restated that view in a way that operates to the serious disadvantage of claimants. The claimant had undergone an unnecessary mastectomy in 1973. She was told at the time that the treatment was appropriate, because there were no facilities at the hospital to test tissue while the patients were still anaesthetised but that it was better to be on the safe side and remove her breast. It was in 1988 that she suspected that the operation might have been unnecessary and not until 1990 that she received an expert's report confirming that fact. The Court of Appeal ruled that as she had suffered the injury in 1973, even though she did not know that the injury had been inflicted unnecessarily, time started to run from that date.

This decision is somewhat puzzling. Any ordinary person would not consider that the pain, suffering and scars of surgery are *'injuries'* for litigation purposes until such time as they discover that they were unnecessary. If the claimant has what he believes was successful surgery, even if it left a scar, he can hardly be expected to

---

34   QBD 7 November 1997.
35   Court of Appeal 1 December 1998.
36   [1994] 4 All ER 439.
37   [1994] 4 All ER 450.

have knowledge that there has been the infliction of personal injuries[38]. However, where there is an omission to carry out surgery it would be less straightforward to argue that the claimant had the requisite knowledge until a later date[39]. In a more recent case, the Court of Appeal, commenting on the effect of s14 of the Limitation Act 1980 in relation to economic loss[40], appeared to criticise the approach in *Dobbie*, and to take the view that there must be some minimum knowledge on the part of the patient that something had gone wrong during surgery. In *James v East Dorset Health Authority*[41] it was held that the claimant had not acquired knowledge immediately after surgery, even though he began to suspect that something had gone wrong when his condition started to deteriorate. The claimant had allegedly suffered injury in two separate operations five years apart.[42]

In *Fenech v East London and City Health Authority*[43] the claimant had given birth to her first child in July 1960 at the defendant's hospital. An episiotomy was carried out by one of the doctors and for several weeks afterwards she suffered severe pain in the area of the perineum. The claimant suffered pain thereafter, especially during sexual intercourse. However, she did not tell her male GP about the pain. In 1983, she came under the care of a new GP who was female. Then the claimant explained about her pelvic pain and although gynaecological investigations were carried out, the cause of the pain was not discovered. In 1990 she experienced arthritis in her left hip and in April 1991 an x-ray was taken of the claimant's hip and pelvic area. The x-ray revealed a two-inch fragment of a surgical needle lodged in the claimant's perineum, but she was not informed of this until February 1994. She then consulted solicitors and proceedings were issued on 29 January 1997, one month short of three years since the claimant learnt of the existence of the needle. There was a trial of the preliminary issue as to whether the claimant's action was statute-barred, and the judge decided that she had actual knowledge under s14(1) by February 1994. However, he took the view that her knowledge as defined in s14(3) of the Act ought reasonably to have been present some years before 1994 because she had failed to make reasonable enquiries before 1983.

The Court of Appeal agreed, on the basis that there must be a certain amount of objectivity in the determination as to when it would have been reasonable for a claimant to seek advice, or s14 would never apply unless a person acted out of character. The claimant should have sought medical advice much earlier than she did, and it was irrelevant that she was too embarrassed to do so.

Although it is sensible for judges to support the view that patients must seek medical advice at the earliest possible opportunity if they have worrying symptoms, this case does give rise to some problems especially where cultural attitudes can prevent patients of either gender seeking medical advice from doctors of the opposite gender. The problem is exacerbated if access to a doctor of the appropriate gender is not readily available. Although it was not an issue in the *Fenech* case, the application of a strictly objective approach to determining knowledge under s14 could result in the discriminatory denial of access to a fair trial to determine the civil rights of people of certain races and genders[44].

---

38   See Kenney, I, and Grubb, A, *Principles of Medical Law*, Butterworths, London 1999.

39   *Forbes v Wandsworth* [1996] 4 All ER 881.

40   *Hallam-Eames v Merrett Syndicates Ltd* [1996] 7 Med LR 122.

41   The Times, 7 December 1999.

42   Discussed by Lewis, C in *Limitation and the recent case of James v East Dorset Health Authority* Medical Litigation (1999) December No 12 pages 3-4.

43   [2000] Lloyd's Rep Med 35.

44   Human Rights Act 1998, Articles 2 and 14 of the European Convention on Human Rights.

The state of judicial policy in the application of the law and the interpretation of the legislation can appear to work injustice for claimants on the face of s14 of the Act, but relief might be available under s33 which is discussed later in the chapter. For example in *Sniezek v Bundy*[45] it was held that a claimant may have been in possession of the requisite knowledge that he had suffered an injury and that the injury was significant, even if his medical experts advised that no evidence of injury could be found. However, the Court of Appeal explained that if the outcome under s14 was that the claim was statute-barred before evidence was found, relief might be available under s33 of the Act (see later).

The exercise of the judicial discretion under s33

Section 33 of the Limitation Act 1980 allows the judge, in an appropriate case, to exercise discretion in favour of the claimant and allow a claim to proceed even though the statutory time limit has expired. This discretion is not available to a claimant who issued proceedings within the limitation period but failed to proceed with the claim, and then attempted to issue proceedings again.

In deciding whether to exercise the discretion in favour of the claimant, the court must consider whether it is equitable to do so, having regard to the potential prejudice to the claimant in ss11 and 12 of the Act, and to the defendant if the discretion were to be exercised. If the court is asked to exercise its discretion under s33 of the Limitation Act 1980 and to disapply the limitation provisions, it is the task of the claimant to convince the court that this should be done and that it would not be inequitable to the defendants to do so. The court must consider all the circumstances of the case, in particular:

(a) the length of time involved and the reasons for the delay[46] by the claimant;

(b) the extent to which the evidence is likely to be less cogent than if the claim had been brought within the correct time;

(c) the conduct of the defendant after the cause of action arose, including his response to reasonable requests for information by the claimant;

(d) the duration of any legal disability that might have affected the claimant after the cause of action accrued;

(e) the extent to which the claimant acted promptly and reasonably once he realised that he might have grounds for a claim;

(f) the steps, if any, taken by the claimant to obtain legal, medical and other advice, and the nature of such advice.

Other factors such as the availability to the claimant of an alternative remedy are also relevant and can influence the court in its decision. For example, if a solicitor gave the claimant negligent advice about prospects of succeeding, or failed to issue proceedings within the limitation period, the claimant might have alternative remedy against the solicitor for professional negligence.

It follows that if the claimant had a good chance of succeeding on the merits of the case, there is a greater likelihood that the court will exercise the discretion in his favour, as he is likely to suffer greater prejudice should the court decide not to

---

45   Court of Appeal 7 July 2000.

46   the *'Delay'* refers to the time between the expiry of the primary limitation period under s11 or 12 and the issuing of proceedings. But when considering the possible prejudice to the defendant, the court can take into account the entire period of delay, including the primary limitation period.

exercise the discretion and assist him. The converse proposition is also true, and case law demonstrates that judges are aware of this.

Smith v Leicestershire Health Authority[47] illustrates the difficulties that can arise when a patient seeks to bring an action for clinical negligence some forty years or so after the alleged incident took place. The facts of this case are set out in some detail here because they explain how an enormous period of time can elapse before a claim is brought. The claimant was aged 53 years at the time of the action. When she was only nine years old she saw a consultant orthopaedic surgeon who diagnosed spina bifida occulta, and advised that she required surgery to straighten her knee and to elongate her Achilles tendon. She also suffered from a bladder condition. She underwent surgery in November 1953, but this was not a success and in 1954 her bladder condition deteriorated. After further consultation at a paediatric clinic, a radiologist's report identified lumbar scoliosis with congenital deformity of the neural arches. On 3 December 1954 the claimant had further surgery when a bladder repair was carried out, but by June 1955 the problem had not improved, and an x-ray report on 28 June 1955 noted spina bifida and scoliosis. Four further operations were carried out on the claimant between November 1955 and January 1956, still her bladder condition did not improve. On 9 May 1957 an exploratory laminectomy conducted at another hospital revealed that there was a dermoid cyst, the contents of which were removed. However, the claimant's condition continued to deteriorate and she experienced breathing problems. She had a tracheotomy on 12 May 1957 and soon afterwards she became tetraplegic.

It transpired that the dermoid cyst had been growing slowly over a long period of time, and had eventually put so much pressure on the nerves in the spinal cord as to cause leg and bladder problems. The claimant alleged that there had been negligence on the part of the first hospital in not detecting and removing the cyst in 1954/5. If this had been done in time, she argued, she would not have become a tetraplegic. On 28 November 1983 the claimant was admitted to the National Hospital for Nervous Diseases in London and she became aware sometime between that date and the date on which she was discharged, of a possibility that there may have been some error during the 1957 surgery which had cut off the supply of blood to the spinal cord and caused her to be paralysed. The claimant made inquiries through the Spinal Injuries Association in 1984 and was told that the limitation period had expired on the basis of the 1957 surgery, so she made no further attempts to bring legal action. However, in July 1988 she had a chance meeting with a solicitor who advised her that her case was worth pursuing. She instructed his firm and obtained a legal aid certificate on 30 March 1989. Medical reports obtained on 1 November in the same year indicated that the blame lay with the doctors responsible for her treatment, not in 1957, but in the five years before that date.

On 22 July 1992 a writ was issued alleging that negligence had occurred some 42 years previously. The claimant's case was based on the fact that she had not acquired the necessary knowledge of the alleged negligence until 1 November 1990, from which date she had three years to issue a writ, (s14 Limitation Act 1980). Alternatively, she contended, the court should exercise its discretion in her favour under s33 of the Limitation Act 1980. The evidence of a neuroradiologist was that most radiologists at the relevant time would have identified the tumour and that it was causing enlargement of the spinal cord. The claimant also alleged that the

---

47   (1996) 36 BMLR 23.

doctors who treated her in 1954 and 1955 would have been able to interpret the x-ray films and recognise that there was a tumour. It was held that the claimant had established her claim in principle against the radiologist who had taken the x-rays in 1954/5.

The judge decided that the claimant could have been expected to acquire the relevant knowledge with the help of legal advice, and had in fact acquired that knowledge, in 1988. She knew that she had been paralysed as a result of the operation in 1957 and if she were to make a claim she should have taken advice reasonably promptly some time during the 20 years before she went to the National Hospital for Nervous Diseases. Therefore she had constructive knowledge before 1983. The trial judge was not prepared to exercise the discretion under s33 of the Limitation Act 1980. The burden was on the claimant to persuade the court to exercise the discretion in her favour and disapply the limitation provisions. There were some points in the claimant's favour but there were many indications that meant that the defendant would suffer undue prejudice if the claim were allowed. All the people who were involved in the events of 1954/5 were either dead or so old that they could not reasonably be expected to give evidence, and even if the trial had taken place 20 years earlier it was uncertain that the claimant would have succeeded in proving causation. It would therefore be inequitable to disapply the limitation provisions.

The Court of Appeal disagreed, and the decision was reversed on appeal. The Court of Appeal took the view that where the case turned on documentary evidence such as x-rays that were available to the court, the prejudice to the defendants would be small in relation to that suffered by the claimant if the case were not allowed to proceed to trial.

In *Mold v Hayton and Another*[48] the Court of Appeal emphasised that if the judge exercises the discretion under s33 of the Limitation Act 1980, and disapplies the three-year time limit (in this case allowing the claimant to commence proceedings 18 years after the events), he is under a duty to give meticulous reasons for his decision. The Court of Appeal took the view in this case that it was not equitable for such a long extension of time to have been granted. The claim here arose out of the alleged failure of two GPs in late 1979 or early 1980 to carry out a vaginal examination of the claimant which, she argued, would have revealed that she had been suffering from the early stages of cervical cancer. The cancer could have been treated at that early stage with light doses of radiotherapy.

In an important case that highlights the fact that it is essential not to dispose of medical records too soon, the Court of Appeal expressed strong disapproval of the policy of an NHS Trust in destroying patients' x-rays after three years. In *Hammond v West Lancashire Health Authority*[49] the claimant had commenced a clinical negligence action on behalf of his deceased wife's estate more than three years after he knew of the cause of action within s14(1) of the Limitation Act 1980. However, the Court of Appeal ruled that the action be allowed to proceed, on the exercise of the court' s discretion under s33 of the same Act. The trial judge had been critical of the policy of destroying patients' x-rays because it took no account of the time limits under the Limitation Act 1980. The policy was to destroy the x-rays of patients even though a letter before action had been sent requesting them, providing no further letters were received in relation to the claim. He regarded this as wholly

---

48   Court of Appeal 17 April 2000.
49   The Times 5 March 1998.

unacceptable, as it showed a *'cavalier disregard'* for rights of access by patients to their records. His Lordship had also expressed the view that when patients' notes are requested, x-rays should be sent with them[50]. The Court of Appeal upheld the decision of the judge to disallow the limitation period in the claimant's favour.

Meaning of term 'disability' for limitation purposes

If the claimant was under a legal disability when the alleged negligence occurred, he or she will have three years from the date when the disability ended to commence proceedings. Thus for example, a person who was under 18 has three years after reaching the age of 18 years within which to start proceedings. The question of whether the court could exercise its discretion in favour of an extension of time where the claimant had been under a legal disability, arose in *Thomas v Plaistow*[51]. The Court of Appeal held that the term *'disability'* has the same meaning for the purposes of s33(3)(d) of the Limitation Act 1980 as it does under s28 of the same Act. By s28 there is a mandatory extension of time when there is an *'existing'* disability, but the extension is purely at the discretion of the Court if there is a *'supervening'* disability. Section 33(1) states that if it appears to the court that it would be equitable to allow an action ... then an extension of time may be granted. Section 33(3) goes on to state:

> *'In acting under this section the court shall have regard to all the circumstances of the case and in particular to ... (d) the duration of any disability of the claimant arising after the date of the accrual of the cause of action.'*

Interestingly, and perhaps because one of the member of the Court on this occasion, Lord Justice Hirst, had been a signatory to the report, the Court of Appeal referred specifically to the recommendations of the Law Reform Committee's Interim Report on Limitation of Actions in Personal Injury Claims (1974). Their Lordships concluded that the report showed clearly that the word *'disability'* had the same meaning as under s28, namely infancy or being of unsound mind. This somewhat unusual reference to the background of an Act shows that the courts are now more prepared to take on board the fact that careful consideration is given in official Government reports to issues that may later become unclear when embodied in legislation. The Court of Appeal's seeking clarification by reference to a report of this kind is evidence of a growing pragmatism and flexibility of approach to statutory interpretation that is to be welcomed.

Claims in fatal accidents cases

If the action is for loss of dependency under the Fatal Accidents Act 1976 and the deceased died before the expiry of the three-year limitation period, a new limitation period starts to run in favour of the dependents from the date of death, or the date when the dependents acquired *'knowledge'*, whichever is the later – s12 of the Act. The court has a discretion to disapply the limitation period that may be exercised in favour of the claimant even if proceedings are not commenced within the specified time, and even when the deceased's own limitation period had expired before he died. Section 12 of the Act can only be disapplied if the reason why the deceased could not maintain proceedings was the operation of the time limit specified in s12 of the Act.

The rules applicable to claims on behalf of the estate of a deceased person under the Law Reform (Miscellaneous Provisions) Act 1934 are similar to those outlined above in relation to the Fatal Accidents Act 1976.

---

50 It has been claimed, however, that the holding of x-rays by claimants' solicitors interferes with their subsequent treatment. The Times 15 June 2001.

51 The Times 11 May 1997.

Claims not relating to negligence causing personal injury

This book is concerned mainly with claims for clinical negligence resulting in personal injuries to which the rules of law outlined above apply. If however, the negligence claim is brought to recover damages for something other than personal injuries (for example economic loss covering the cost of bringing up a disabled child), the limitation rules are different. The time limit is six years[52] rather than the three years applicable in negligence cases. Similarly if the claim is brought in the law of contract the six-year limit applies[53]. If the claim is for another tort, such as assault and battery, the cause of action accrues on the date the wrong was committed. In *Stubbings v Webb*[54] the House of Lords ruled that actions for trespass to the person (for example where a healthcare professional treats a person against his or her will), must be brought within six years of the date when the cause of action accrues, and the judicial discretion available in relation to accidents caused by negligence under s33 can never be applied. This rule does not, according to the European Court of Human Rights in *Stubbings v UK*[55], contravene the European Convention on Human Rights.

For claims under the Consumer Protection Act 1987 relating to defective products, the usual limitation periods apply but there is a long stop, (ie an absolute bar to commencing proceedings), of ten years from the date when the defective product was put into circulation by the defendant. Thus there is no discretion available to disapply the limitation period. This could give rise to problems if the damage does not become apparent for many years – for example where the claimant suffers a disease such as hepatitis C after being given infected blood, and the illness does not manifest itself until many years later. A claimant in this instance could only bring an action for negligence and seek the exercise of the courts' discretion.

The Law Commission consultation paper

In January 1998 the Law Commission produced a consultation paper[56] and recommendations for reforming the law on limitations generally. The paper is extremely comprehensive and covers all aspects of the law in this area, producing some controversial recommendations, the most radical of which is the abolition of the discretion under s33 of the Limitation Act 1980. A core regime is proposed as a central feature of the reforms, which would apply to healthcare negligence cases. This suggests a limitation period of three years from the date when the claimant knows or ought reasonably to know that there is a cause of action proposed, and a 30-year long stop from the date of the act which gave rise to the claim, beyond which it would be impossible to bring proceedings.

Conclusion

The claimant is more likely to fail as a result of being unable to establish that there had been a breach of the duty of care owed by the defendant, or that the alleged negligence did not cause the injuries, than because the defendant has successfully raised one of the defences outlined in this chapter. There are relatively few reported cases concerning the defences to clinical negligence – though those involving the limitation defence are rather more common. Nevertheless it is important for claimants and defendants to be aware that there are certain defences available and that simply being able to prove negligence may not be sufficient for the claimant to be successful.

---

52   Limitation Act 1980, s2.
53   Limitation Act 1980, s5.
54   [1993] AC 489.
55   [1997] 1 FLR 105.
56   Law Commission Consultation Paper 151.

Chapter 8

Quantum

If the claimant succeeds in convincing the court that the defendant has been negligent and that the negligence caused the injury, the court has the task of calculating how much compensation should be paid unless this has already been agreed between the parties subject to liability. Most healthcare claims involve personal injuries and economic losses arising from them[1], and there are detailed rules for calculating what the injury is worth in money terms. The object of this chapter is to provide an overview of these rules and to discuss some of the recent developments that have led to higher awards to claimants. The damages payable in any individual case depend entirely on its own facts, and most are settled between the parties without the need to consult the court[2]. It is important for lawyers in personal injury practice to be aware of current figures, and these are published and regularly updated in several excellent specialist publications that are essential reference sources.[3] For non-lawyers, these source materials are available in libraries and on the Internet. There is little point in attempting to deal with particular figures in this book, as these require regular updating. The main objective of this chapter is simply to outline the general principles underlying the calculation of damages. However, in the process, some of the figures arrived at in recent cases are examined.

The Law Commission is reviewing the law relating to quantum in personal injury claims[4] and claims arising as a result of deaths. Some of its recommendations have already been implemented, and more changes are likely in the future[5].

The Accuracy and Fairness of the Law

It is impossible to replace lost health or life with money. The calculation of damages for personal injuries and death is by its very nature a rough and ready process, based on established figures in past cases and on predictions about future events. The object is to put the claimant in the same position as he or she would have been in had the negligence never occurred. The aim is to give the claim full compensation for all the losses. Of course, it is relatively easy to calculate the claimant's actual financial losses to the date of the trial, but it is impossible to calculate accurately what the future losses

---

1   Most claims for clinical negligence concern personal injuries and economic losses that arise from them – such as loss of earnings. Only very occasionally do they involve claims for pure economic loss.
2   Infant settlements must be approved by a High Court judge.
3   Such publications and data bases include Kemp and Kemp; The Judicial Studies Board figures, Current Law, LEXIS, the New Law Journal, Quantum; Lawtel Quantum Reports, Medical Law Monitor, PMILL, Health Law and Smith Bernal.
4   The Damages Act 1996.
5   See Law Commission Report No 262 and the draft Bill that accompanies it.

will be, or to translate intangible harm such as pain and suffering and loss of amenity into money. In attempting to do so the court takes into account evidence of the life-style, education, employment, future care requirements and future prospects of the claimant. To assist this process expert medical witnesses and care experts are frequently employed. Detailed schedules of damages are produced and argued over both in and out-of-court, and the claimants are often videoed by inquiry agents employed by the defendants with the aim of proving that they have not suffered as much damage as they claim. Despite this, a retrospective study by Professor Hazel Genn carried out in 1995[6] revealed that many accident victims believe that the compensation they received turned out to be insufficient to cover their needs. The claimant is at a disadvantage in the process of calculating damages, as the burden of proof rests on him or her to convince the court of precisely how much ought to be paid in the award. Many claimants are worn out by the long legal process and lose the will to fight.

The entire compensation is arbitrary and far from fair. To take but one example – bereavement damages[7] for the loss of a loved one are only available to parents who lose a child or children under the age of 18 years and to a spouse. An arbitrary figure fixed by the Lord Chancellor and subject to review, is payable for this type of loss. A widow who hated her husband can benefit from the rule, but not parents who lose a much-loved only child aged 19 years.

Another source of injustice lies in the fact that the compensation system is not egalitarian. Those who are sufficiently articulate to make out a strong case to a charitable institution, and are fortunate enough to receive payments from such an organisation, have no deduction made from their awards. However, occupational sick pay is deducted[8] as are redundancy payments[9]. A rich claimant will receive a higher award of compensation than a poor one suffering the same injury. This is because the award for loss of past and future earnings, (and possibly the award for loss of amenity in some cases) is certain to be higher in the case of high earners[10]. Those who can afford to buy private insurance or good occupational disability pensions do not have payments from these sources deducted from their damages. The courts have traditionally regarded as reasonable a claimant who opts not to make use of NHS facilities *(Harris v Brights Asphalt Contractors[11])* as long as the service provided was not available as readily on the NHS. These principles are in line with the underlying principle that the law of tort compensates accident victims for expenses which are reasonably incurred, so that they may be restored to the pre-accident position in so far as money can achieve this. Also in accordance with this is the rule that if a tort victim receives NHS care, any saving made because he has been kept at public expense in an NHS institution must be set-off against any income lost through injury[12]. Although these principles do have internal logic and consistency, nevertheless in this respect the law appears to discriminate between people who choose NHS treatment and those who decide on private sector care. Although the law may be in need of some short-term amendment in this area,

6   Law Commission Report no 225, 1995.

7   Introduced into the law in England and Wales by the Administration of Justice Act 1982.

8   *Hussain v New Taplow Paper Mills Ltd* [1988] AC 514.

9   *Colledge v Bass, Mitchells and Butlers Ltd* [1988] 1 All ER 568.

10   See Atiyah P *Accidents Compensation and the Law* ed Cane, P, Weidenfeld and Nicholson 1997, passim.

11   [1983] 1 All ER 395.

12   Administration of Justice Act 1982, s5.

perhaps the long-term solution lies in more radical changes than merely tinkering with the provisions of statutes.

Most damages are paid in the form of a lump sum, a particularly inefficient way of compensating someone who is not financially astute. Compared with other systems such as the social security benefits system, the court system is costly and inefficient[13]. Claimants may have to endure many years of poverty, sickness and suffering before the legal process is complete and they receive compensation – always supposing that they succeed in proving fault and causation – both tasks being particularly difficult in healthcare negligence cases[14]. Once the claimant has received the payment he or she is under no obligation to invest in a particular way to provide a regular income, though it would be sensible to do so, and there is nothing to prevent a claimant from spending the entire sum on foreign travel or riotous living and returning to claim state benefits once the money is used up. One way of preventing this is to have a structured settlement approved by the court if both parties agree. These settlements, that allow regular periodic payments, and offer considerable tax advantage through a special concession by the Inland Revenue, are much less popular than might be supposed. Nevertheless, they are encouraged by the National Health Service Litigation Authority.

Special Damages

Strictly speaking, special damages are all pecuniary losses that can be calculated accurately to the date of the trial. However, some lawyers in practice describe all pecuniary losses as *'specials'* because the same principles of assessment apply to both. For the purposes of this chapter, the term *'special damages'* refers only to pecuniary losses to the date of trial. These losses are the simplest to assess, are set out separately from other awards, and can be pleaded. From October 1997 state benefits over the value of £2,500 received over a period of five years are deducted from special damages under the Social Security (Recovery of Benefits) Act 1997. However, some benefits are not recoverable. These include family credit, child benefit, one parent benefit, earnings top-up, housing benefit, maternity allowance, statutory maternity pay, the retirement pension and retirement allowance, social fund payments and widows' benefits. A complex set of rules determines which benefits are recoverable from which heads of compensation. Detailed information on these matters can be obtained from the Compensation Recovery Unit (CRU). Practising lawyers are very familiar with the rules as they deal with them on a day-to-day basis.

Expenses incurred to the date of the trial

The claimant is entitled to recover a reasonable sum to cover expenses incurred as a result of the injury between the date of the accident and the date of the trial. The parties sometimes argue over the minute details of the expenses claimed and are encouraged by the Civil Procedure Rules 1998 to arrive at an agreement before the trial. It is essential for the lawyers concerned to deal with these matters in a sensitive way[15].

Reasonable expenses can include the cost of nursing and medical care, medicines, special equipment and facilities, hospital visits, loss of earnings (including the loss of increments and promotions) to the date of the trial. Section 5 of the Administration of

---

13   Administrative costs of the a negligence claim can reach as much as 85% of the awards paid to victims, while the cost of administering the Social Security system is only about 11% of what it pays out – Pearson Report 1998.

14   See Chapters 2-5.

15   The notion that a woman who lost both legs in a motor accident in which her husband was killed, should be subjected to an inquiry about the fact that she no longer needed to wear tights, is particularly abhorrent – see article by Bill Braithwaite, The Times 22 July 1998.

Justice Act 1982 appears to discriminate between claimants who are treated for their injuries by the NHS and those who are treated under the private healthcare regime. It provides that:

> *'Any saving to an injured party which is attributable to his maintenance wholly or partly at public expense in a hospital, nursing home or other institution shall be set off against any income lost by him as a result of his injuries'.*

People receiving private care and treatment, on the other hand, are able to claim reasonable sums to cover it, and are not treated by the courts as unreasonable in not choosing to make use of NHS facilities. Any insurance payments that have been made to the claimant will not be deducted from the damages. There is a strong case for insisting that claimants are treated on the NHS whenever possible, and if a claimant is injured by negligence in the NHS, this would provide the perfect opportunity for the NHS to make reparation.

If a spouse, partner or friend of the accident victim gives up work to care for him, reasonable expenses can be claimed to cover this, but not for running the victim's business[16].

General Damages

The term *'general damages'* covers all the losses which are not accurately quantifiable and for the purposes of this chapter, includes future pecuniary losses as well as compensation for intangible damage suffered by the claimant, such as loss of amenity.

Pecuniary losses

For claims in this category the court must reach a sum that represents the present value of a future loss. If the claimant is no longer able to work there is a claim for loss of future earnings, and if he or she will continue to need nursing and other care that can also be taken into account. Loss of future earnings are routinely claimed if the claimant had some working life left before the accident, though of course it is virtually impossible to arrive at a satisfactory sum in the case of a young child, unless there are certainties about the child's potential future career (if he or she showed exceptional artistic or musical promise for example). In the case of a very young child a notional sum is awarded for loss of future earnings[17].

Calculating pecuniary losses

The calculation is based on speculation about future events in the light of available evidence about the earnings prospects, the prognosis and future needs of the claimant. A figure is reached by means of devices known as the multiplicand and multiplier. The multiplicand is an annual figure that represents the claimant's net losses over one year, at the date of the trial. The figure is arrived at on the basis of facts about the claimant's losses. The multiplier is a purely notional figure representing the number of years for which the calculation is to be made. Various contingencies are taken into account when an appropriate figure for the multiplier is arrived at. These are designed to take account of interest rates on investments, and future events, such as the perceived tendency of women to have children and give up work and care for them in infancy, and are simple predictions based on generalisations[18]. In *Bordin v St Mary's NHS Hospital Trust*[19] the

---

16   *Hardwick v Hudson and Another*, The Times 20 May 1999.
17   *Gammel v Wilson* [1981] 1 All ER 578.
18   [1998] 3 WLR 329; (1998) 43 BMLR 99.
19   [2000] Lloyd's Rep Med 287.

multiplier relating to future care and lost dependency in a claim under the Fatal Accidents Act 1976 was reduced. This was a claim by a child for the loss of his mother during childbirth, and the reduction was to allow for the possibility that something might happen to the claimant, or might have happened to his mother, or to his parent's marriage had she lived.

It is unusual to see multipliers that are very much higher than 20^{20}, even if the claimant was relatively young at the date of the trial. Points may be deducted from the multiplier to take health matters into account. For example, if the claimant's family has a history of early deaths through heart disease. Once both the multiplicand and multiplier are calculated, a final lump sum figure is reached to compensate for future pecuniary losses. Income tax is taken into account when damages are calculated[21], but there are problems about predicting future tax rates and the Law Commission has expressed concern that the claimant will inevitably either over-compensate or under-compensate as a result.

The use of the multiplicand and multiplier is a very rough and ready method of assessing how much should be paid to the claimant, and there have been calls for a more scientific approach to be taken by using actuarial evidence[22]. However, judges are traditionally very suspicious of this approach[23]. Actuarial evidence is now permitted, and is admissible under s10 of the Civil Evidence Act 1995, and is occasionally adduced, and it has been recommended that the possibility of making greater use of it should be investigated[24]. The use of the Ogden Tables compiled by Michael Ogden QC with the Government Actuary, who headed a working party, were approved in *Wells v Wells*.

The claimant is expected to invest that lump sum and to use the income, as far as possible, to cover living expenses and the cost of future care and treatment. Although the interest paid on investments changes from time to time, the assumption until recently was that the capital sum would yield a notional 4.5% after tax and inflation are taken into account. That approach has now been changed in favour of claimants by the House of Lords, in line with Law Commission recommendations. The assumption now is that claimants will invest in safer Index Linked Government Securities that yield a lower figure of only 2.3% to 3% on capital sums. In conjoined appeals *Wells v Wells; Page v Sheerness Steel, Thomas v Brighton Health Authority*[25], the House of Lords reviewed this area of law, and explained why it was necessary to change the basis upon which the calculation was made. The three appeals raised the same basic question – *what is the correct basis for calculating lump sum awards to cover loss of future earnings and the cost of future care for the claimant?* These appeals focused on arguments concerning the appropriate discount in the light of changes in the financial markets. In order to determine that, it was necessary to consider what would be the appropriate rate at which it could be assumed that the lump sum would be invested. The House of Lords concluded that the multiplier should be fixed by reference to the return that could be expected on investments in Index Linked Government Securities, rather than by the then current approach that assume that the investment would be made in riskier equities and gilts.

---

20   Higher multipliers are more common since the decision in *Wells v Wells*, see below.

21   *BTC v Gourley* [1956] AC 185.

22   eg by the Law Commission. See *Kemp v Kemp*, vol 1, 6-250

23   See the remarks of Oliver J in *Auty, Mills, and Others v NCB* [1985] 1 WLR 784. Also *Spears v Halliday* 1984 TLR 30 June 1984.

24   Law Commission Report, November 1999 op cit.

25   [1999] 1 AC 345.

Thomas v Brighton Health Authority was the one appeal that concerned healthcare negligence, and the claim arose out of a birth injury suffered as a result of the maladministration of a drug to induce labour. The claimant was severely handicapped, suffering from cerebral palsy. He would require constant care and attention for the whole of his life. In the High Court, Collins J had awarded £110,000 general damages and the total award, based on a life expectancy of 60 years, was £1,307,963. The final multiplier was put at an unusually high figure of 23. Like the High Court judges who decided the other two appeals he had not arrived at this figure on the basis of current practice set by previous House of Lords and Court of Appeal precedents[26], which assumed an investment rate of 4.5%. All three judges had ruled that when fixing the discount rate, the assumption should be that the award would be invested in safe Index Linked Government Securities that had been freely available since 1982. The conclusion was reached on the basis that with this investment the lump sums would retain their real value and make more realistic provision for the claimant in the future.

The Court of Appeal had reinstated the previous approach and fixed the multiplier at 17, apparently influenced by the fact that in two of the three cases the money was invested by the Court of Protection that chose to use a spread of equities and gilts and assumed that there was a yield of 4.5%. However, the House of Lords allowed all three appeals by the claimants[27]. In reaching their conclusions their Lordships referred to the views of textbook writers and those of a Law Commission Report on this matter in 1994[28]. Research conducted by the Law Commission suggested that claimants do not normally select risky investments but prefer building societies and other safe investments. The statement in the Law Commission Report that was particularly influential was as follows:

'We share the views of the majority of those who responded to us that a practice of discounting by reference to returns on ILGS would be preferable to the present arbitrary presumption. The 4% to 5% discount rate which emerged from the case law was established at a time when ILGS did not exist. ILGS now constitute the best evidence of the real rate of return on an investment where the risk element is minimal, because they take account of inflation, rather than attempt to predict it as conventional investments do.'

Section 1 of the Damages Act 1996 provides:

'In determining the return to be expected from an investment of a sum awarded as damages for future pecuniary loss in an action for personal injury, the court, in accordance with the rules of the court made for the purposes of this section, can take into account any such rate of return (if any) as may from time to time be prescribed by the Lord Chancellor.'

The decision in these appeals afforded the Lord Chancellor the opportunity to do this in line with judicial thinking. A consultation paper was issued in the spring of 2000 by the Lord Chancellor's Department entitled *Damages: The Discount Rate and Alternatives to Lump Sum Payments*[29], and action on the responses is expected soon.

Thomas v Brighton Health Authority raised two further issues. First, whether a court can reduce a lump sum award to take account of the contingencies of life when

---

26   *Cookson v Knowles* [1979] AC 556.

27   In reaching their decision in this case, the House of Lords overruled a previous decision of its own as it was entitled to do under the Lord Chancellor's Practice Statement issued in 1966, to take account of changed social and economic circumstances.

28   LC Report No 224 (1994) Cmnd 2646.

29   For consideration of the points raised in this document, see McLaren I, *New Law Journal*, Vol 150, No 6932, pages 573-4.

the claimant's life expectancy and other medical matters have already been agreed between the experts for the parties, and second, what the appropriate discount rate would be for the cost of special housing. On the first of these matters, the House of Lords took the view that the trial judge had been in error in reducing the arithmetical multiplier to override the life expectancy calculated by the medical experts and agreed between them. Contingencies such as possible chest infections, accidents and so on that the claimant might suffer had already been thrown into the equation by the experts and if the judge's calculation of the multiplier were allowed to stand the claimant would run out of money when he reached the age of 39, though his life expectancy had been put at 60. The multiplier was increased from 23 to 26.5. On the second point, the House of Lords restored the figure decided upon by the trial judge in relation to housing.

It was inevitable that the decisions of the House of Lords in these three cases would lead to higher multipliers and substantially higher awards of damages than had been seen previously. Claimants' lawyers welcomed the development because it would ensure that claimants could take a more relaxed and realistic view about the returns on their investments. They are no longer expected to beat inflation when investing their lump-sum awards, but merely to keep pace with it by investing in Index Linked Government Securities. Insurance premiums increased across the board for those who use private insurers, and the amount paid by the NHS in damages for healthcare negligence, has led to much criticism of lawyers[30]. Nevertheless, if the Court of Protection decides to invest money on behalf of claimants in equities and gilts that produce higher rates of return, the result is likely to be unfairness to defendants, and in the case of the NHS this could mean that there is less funding available to care for patients.

Further 'record' settlements and awards followed within a short space of time, and it is not unusual to see awards running into millions of pounds in cases in which the claimant will need a large amount of future care. For example, in a cerebral palsy case, *Mansell v Dyfed-Powys Health Authority*[31], the claimant was 11 years old when the settlement was approved by a High Court judge. The claim arose as a result of negligence at birth that left him severely brain damaged, and requiring constant 24-hour care. The long-term prognosis was that his physical condition would never improve. A total award of £3,281,199.10 was made, and the cost of future care for the claimant was estimated at around £100,000 per annum. This case was the first of several which demonstrates that the House of Lords' decision in *Wells v Wells* has had a significant impact on the levels of awards, particularly in cases where the damages would be high in any event to cover the cost of caring for a very seriously injured claimant.

The decision in *Wells v Wells* is merely one factor that has resulted in spiralling awards of damages. As will be seen, sums awarded for pain, suffering and loss of amenity have also increased, after a long period of being reasonably stable, and solicitors and counsel are very meticulous when compiling detailed schedules of damages. Precise details of the sums of money required to provide adequately for the claimant's future care are painstakingly collected, in consultation with numerous experts, who assess in detail what equipment, nursing, medical and other care the claimant is likely to need. Another factor adding to the expense is the development of new technologies that have led to the provision of ever more sophisticated and

---

30   See Frank Dobson, DOH Press Release April 1998.
31   QBD 13 October 1998.

expensive equipment, to enable injured claimants to have a better quality of life, and to communicate their needs to their carers. There was some criticism by the claimant's solicitor in the *Mansell* case because a very long time had elapsed between admission of liability and final settlement of quantum. However, as it happened, the claimant benefited by the fact that this settlement was made after the House of Lords' decision. This was one of many cases which were awaiting settlement on the outcome of *Wells v Wells* in the House of Lords. Fourteen experts[32] were instructed to advise on the care that the claimant would require, and the case illustrates the fact that this exercise is becoming very much more precise. If interim payments can be arranged it is greatly to a claimant's advantage to take as much time as is really necessary to ensure that the prognosis and final calculation of the sums required for future care are as detailed and accurate as possible.

The Lord Chancellor has yet to make a decision on discount rates under s1(1) of the Damages Act 1996, and in *Warren v Northern General Hospital Trust*[33] the Court of Appeal held that it was for the Lord Chancellor using his power under s1 of the Damages Act 1996 to alter the rate of return from the current 3%. That was not a matter for the court. The Court of Appeal noted that the Lord Chancellor had issued a consultation paper on the matter, and that it was expected that a new rate should be decided upon by the Summer Recess of 2000. The claimant in this case had been one of the claimants in *Heil v Rankin*[34], which is discussed later in this chapter. A sum of £2.5 million had been awarded for future loss on the basis of a discount rate of 3%. The appellant argued that the rate of 3% was too high because the Lord Chancellor had failed to set a rate under the Damages Act 1996, and that the court should do so. The appellant also contended that the rate should be reduced because the incidence of taxation on higher awards distorted the rate of return and the appellant would be under-compensated and suffer injustice.

Similarly in *Barry v Ablerex Construction (Midlands) Ltd*[35] Latham J made reference to that fact. There he made an award of damages in a personal injury claim on the basis that it was appropriate to reduce the discount rate applicable in calculating multipliers to 2%. He considered that this case raised the issue of principle as to whether market conditions currently prevailing justified a reduction from 3% to 2%. On the evidence, he ruled that there had been a significant change in market conditions, of the kind envisaged by the majority of the House of Lords in *Wells v Wells* as would justify a change in the rate applied to calculating multipliers for future losses. When *Wells v Wells* was decided, the average gross redemption yields from Index Linked Government Securities suggested a figure of 3%, based on the previous three years. In *Wells v Wells* the House of Lords had indicated that it would be in order for courts, in the future, if the Lord Chancellor took no action, to consider the appropriateness of the discount rate at regular intervals. Courts might consider that it would be appropriate to vary the 3% if there had been a *'marked'*, or *'very considerable change in economic circumstances'*. Latham J considered that a whole percentage point change was sufficiently significant to justify the change, on the basis that the Lord Chancellor would be likely to decide that the rate should be amended in the light of the changed conditions since *Wells v Wells*. He suggested a test, which was to ask whether the Lord Chancellor, following the principle adopted

---

32   It is unlikely that the Court would permit as many experts as this since the Civil Procedure Rules came into being in 1999.
33   [2000] 1 WLR 1404.
34   The Times 24 March 2000.
35   The Times 22 March 2000.

in *Wells v Wells,* could sensibly reach any conclusion other than that 3% was no longer an appropriate rate. The Court of Appeal[36] disagreed, however, and ruled that Latham J had been wrong to hold that the appropriate multiplier should be calculated on a discounted rate of 2%. The appropriate rate remained 3% as set out in the House of Lords' guidelines in *Wells v Wells.*

It is understandable that the Court of Appeal does not wish to commit itself to making recommendations about the appropriate discount rate, for fear of introducing uncertainty into the law. However, claimants might suffer as a result. The view of the Court of Appeal, referring to the House of Lords' guidance in *Wells v Wells,* was expressed in *Barry v Ablerex* by Lord Justice Judge:

> '*While not purporting to provide any immutable or near immutable principle of law, there would have been little point in the House of Lords providing guidance to lower courts unless it was intended that the guidance should be implemented at least for a significant period.*'

In *Wells v Wells*, Stuart Smith LJ had explained that:

> '*The reduction in the ILGS return rate is not a sufficient change of circumstances to justify a change in the discount rate before the Lord Chancellor sets a rate ... The need for certainty to facilitate settlements coupled with the undesirability of extensive evidence from actuaries or economists with a view to persuading courts to change the discount rate militates strongly against any court seeking to do so before the Lord Chancellor has acted under the Act of 1996.*'

The solution would be for the Lord Chancellor to make a decision and to take action on this matter as soon as possible, to avoid unnecessary appeals and to introduce the certainty that is in the interests of all those involved in these claims.

The lost years

Years that have been lost to a claimant with a reduced life-expectancy as a result of the injury, need not be taken into account when the future losses are calculated[37]. Claimants who are still living at the time of trial or settlement can recover damages to cover loss of earnings even for the years that are lost to them, and their dependents will take the benefits of this rule after the claimant dies. However, if the claimant has already died by the time of the trial or settlement his estate cannot take the benefit of this rule. Here is yet another example of the arbitrary nature of the law concerning quantum.

Other financial losses

Most of the expenses likely to be incurred by the claimant in the future have been mentioned in the preceding paragraphs. However, there are other potential future sources of expenditure. For example, the claimant might be prevented by the injury from caring for his or her children and will require the services of a nanny on a long-term basis. Or the claimant might prefer to be given day-to-day care by a relative rather than by a professional carer[38]. These are legitimate heads of damage and there is ample case law to cover a wide variety of situations, including damages for handicap on the labour market[39]. The question of '*loss of a chance*' is usually dealt with as one of the causation issues in the claim, but there have been attempts to

---

36   [2001] EWCA Civ 498.
37   *Pickett v British Rail Engineering* [1980] 136.
38   But see the limitations on this in *Hunt v Severs* The Times 13 May 1993.
39   *Smith v Manchester Corporation* (1974) – see Kemp and Kemp.

claim for this matter within the realm of quantum[40]. Claims can be made for special accommodation for the claimant, aids and equipment, transport, for loss of pension benefits, and future private medical care, including special therapies such as speech therapy and physiotherapy. Details of these can be found in specialist publications.

Failed sterilisation, the cost of bringing up children and claims for surrogacy treatment

Until 1999, the courts had been prepared, after a rather ambivalent start, to award damages to cover the full cost of bringing up a healthy child born as a result of a failed sterilisation operation. Judges recognised that there were problems in awarding damages for what should have been a joyful event – the birth of a child, and attempted to grapple with the difficulties when claims of this kind were first made in the UK in the early 1980s. However, in the Scottish case of *McFarlane v Tayside Health Board*[41] the House of Lords ruled that the cost of bringing up a child born after an unsuccessful sterilisation operation was a pure economic loss that should be handled cautiously in the light of the reluctance of courts to create liability for pure economic loss where there was no closer link between the act and the damage[42]. The facts of this case are set out in Chapter 2 which also sets out details of the reasoning and the sums awarded. It was decided that it would be contrary to public policy to make an award of damages to cover the cost of bringing up a healthy child who was now loved and wanted. The question of whether damages would be available to bring up a child who was damaged in some way was left open in this case, but was decided in the later case of *Rand v East Dorset Health Authority*[43], discussed below.

This approach was confirmed in the distinguishable case of *Rand v East Dorset Health Authority*[44], where the judge held that the claimants could bring a claim based on the principle in *Hedley Byrne & Co Ltd v Heller & Partners Ltd*[45] for financial losses incurred as a result of the admitted negligence of the defendant, but those losses were limited to the consequences flowing from a child's *disability*. The claim for the cost of maintenance and the cost of care for the child was a claim for pure economic loss, as was the claim for loss of profits of the residential care home run by the claimants. Doctors wrongfully failed to inform Mr and Mrs Rand of the results of a scan indicating that Mrs Rand would probably give birth to a Down's syndrome baby. This negligent omission had deprived the couple of the opportunity to terminate the pregnancy. If they had been given the results, Mrs Rand would have had an abortion. The couple could not, however, recover the full cost of bringing up the child, and the award was assessed by calculating the difference between the cost of bringing up a normal child and a child that is disabled. The damages should be limited to the consequences flowing from the child's disability. The judge ruled that a claim for the financial costs of caring for the child was a claim for pure economic loss. Accordingly, damages could only be recovered in respect of losses that were proved to have arisen from the child's disability, rather than from the mere fact of her having been born. The parents could only recover such losses as they had actually sustained, or would sustain in the future, and their own means, as opposed to the

---

40   See *Stovald v Barlows* The Times 30 October 1995 and *Allied Maples Group Ltd v Simmons and Simmons* [1995] 1 WLR 1602 for clarification of the difficult concepts involved here.

41   The Times 12 November 1999.

42   This case is discussed at length in the chapter dealing with duty of care in negligence. See also *Greenfield v Flatter* TLR 6 February 2001 where the Court of Appeal followed *McFarlane*.

43   (2000) 56 BMLR 39.

44   (2000) 56 BMLR 39.

45   [1963] 3 WLR 101.

child's needs, determined this issue. That claim for economic loss did not automatically terminate, as a matter of law, upon the child reaching her 18th birthday. In addition, Mrs Rand, like Mrs McFarlane, had an award for general damages for pain and suffering.

The question of the heads of damage available for wrongful birth also arose in *Hardman v Amin*[46]. The claimant had rubella when she was pregnant with her son Daniel in 1996, but her GP had failed to diagnose the illness and the claimant was denied the opportunity of terminating the pregnancy which she would have done had she known the prognosis for the child. Daniel was seriously damaged as a result of the illness and required constant care, and would continue to do so when he was an adult. The defendant admitted negligence. Henriques J held that damages were recoverable for the pain, suffering and inconvenience of pregnancy and childbirth, and for the claimant's realisation that her child was damaged. Special damages were available to the claimant for the expenses that arose as a result of the pregnancy, including loss of earnings. Distinguishing *McFarlane*, the judge held that the defendant was liable for the economic loss suffered by the claimant, as the economic loss she suffered as a result of giving birth to a disabled child was a foreseeable consequence of the defendant's negligence. Following *Rand*, the damages were assessed according to Daniel's reasonable needs as a disabled person and the defendant was not entitled to limit the award according to what the claimant would have been able to afford. In addition, the claimant could claim for the gratuitous services provided by her to Daniel. The approach taken by the judge in this case will ensure that the parents of disabled children born as a result of the negligence of a healthcare professional will receive adequate compensation to cover the cost of care.

Briody v St Helens and Knowsley Health Authority[47] is another case that demonstrates the power of public policy in influencing the decisions of judges. A court can refuse to make an award if the proposed project is to be contrary to public policy, and the planned use of the money is unrealistic and unlikely ever to be achieved. In *Briody* the claimant, who was infertile as a result of clinical negligence, claimed damages to cover funding a surrogacy arrangement, as well as awards under the usual heads of damages. The claim for surrogacy costs raised a novel issue, as it had never before been claimed as a head of damages. Courts are able to recognise new heads of damages from time to time if necessary. The claimant argued that as the defendants had deprived her of her ability to have a child of her own, and because, compensatory damages should put the victim in the position she would have been in had it not been for the negligence, she should be awarded a sum of money to enable her to have a child. The surrogacy arrangement required treatment in California, and the judge took into account evidence from a range of sources, including that of renowned infertility experts. She reviewed guidelines produced by the Human Fertility and Embryology Authority, the COTS brochure, the views of the British Medical Association and of a series of Family Division cases. Taking the view that it was in order to consider whether the damages would be available to achieve a realistic objective, she concluded that there were very poor prospects of success for a surrogacy arrangement. The chances of success were so low that it would be unfair to expect the defendants to fund the treatment. She expressed the view that it was not the business of the law of tort to

---

46   [2000] Lloyd's Rep Med 498.
47   (2000) 53 BMLR 108. The Court of Appeal confirmed that no damages would be payable in respect of surrogacy treatment that had a very small chance of success.

provide a legal remedy doomed to almost inevitable failure. The judge explained her conclusion in this way:

'Whether one ultimately makes a decision on the basis of distributive or corrective justice, the issue is whether what is sought by way of reparation can be regarded as reasonable, having in mind the particular circumstances of the particular case ... I do not think that the "traveller on the underground" would regard it as the business of the law to provide a remedy doomed to almost inevitable failure and outwith our law[48].'

Taking public policy into account, the judge pointed out that the claimant was attempting to obtain damages to acquire a baby by a method that did not comply with UK law. Although a court could approve an adoption in the interests of a surrogacy child, that could only be done on a retrospective basis. It was impossible for a court to award damages to enable an unenforceable and unlawful contract for surrogacy to be entered into. The claimant did succeed in obtaining some compensation (£80,000) for pain and suffering, covering the psychological distress she had suffered as a result of her infertility, but that did not exceed the amount that had been paid into court by the defendants (£110,000). Thus she became liable for a large portion of the defendant's costs, and her award was virtually cancelled out. Not surprisingly, she felt bitterly disappointed and badly let down by the legal system after her 11 year legal battle.[49]

Interference with consortium

The old head of damage known as *'Loss of Consortium'* available to a husband who had lost the services and society of his wife, was abolished in 1982[50]. Despite this, if a relationship between a couple is impaired, damages may be available for interference with consortium. Children who can no longer adequately be cared for by their mother because she has suffered an injury, but is still alive, may need a nanny or child-minder[51], or their father might decide to give up work to look after them. These losses are essentially pecuniary losses, and the sum required for the care of the family is calculated in the same way as that required for future care of the claimant. However, general damages for the non-pecuniary loss of a mother's care (care that only a mother can give[52]) can also be claimed if she has died[53] and this matter is discussed later in this chapter.

Non-pecuniary Losses

General damages cover non-pecuniary losses suffered by the claimant. Obviously, it is impossible to put a monetary value on human emotions, and feeling such as pain and suffering, and in any case it is impossible to prove precisely how acutely the particular claimant actually suffered. However, there are several heads of damage that deal with these matters and these are not exhaustive, as further heads can be added to from time to time, and the courts are prepared to hear arguments on this matter.

Pain and suffering and loss of amenity

Awards for pain and suffering cover mental and physical anguish, anxiety, stress, and if appropriate, the claimant's awareness of the injury or that his life expectancy has been reduced. If the claimant has scars or other disfigurements as a result of the

---

48   ibid, para 30.

49   See *The Independent*, March 2000, for an article by Jeremy Laurance, the health editor of the newspaper who presents a very different background picture of the defendant to the somewhat critical account of her that appears in the High Court judgment.

50   Administration of Justice Act 1982.

51   See *Heil v Rankin; Kent v Griffiths* (2000) 2 WLR 1173; [2000] Lloyd's Rep Med 203.

52   *Corbett v Barking, Havering and Brentwood Health Authority* [1992] 2 QB 408.

53   *Bordin v St Mary's Hospital* [2000] Lloyds rep Med 287.

accident, these are also features for which compensation can be awarded. A claimant who is unconscious is treated as being free from pain, and a low award is made for pain and suffering, but a higher sum is then awarded for loss of amenity[54]. The award for loss of amenity covers the claimant's inability to enjoy life in the same way as he could before the accident, (and for loss of marriage prospect if they are made less attractive by their injuries). A person who had previously enjoyed playing the piano would be compensated under this head of damages if he or she had lost a hand. Awards for loss of amenity are frequently made to claimants who can no longer enjoy a satisfactory sex life as a result of an accident. Infertility is compensated[55], and in cases of failed sterilisation, a female claimant who becomes pregnant is compensated for the pain and discomfort of child-bearing[56]. In *Thurman v Wiltshire Health Authority*[57] the claimant had lost her unborn child, and was left infertile by the negligence of the defendants. She was awarded damages of £50,000 for permanent infertility and for the physical and psychological pain and suffering she had endured.

These are merely examples of the heads of damages. Detailed lists of cases involving numerous injuries, the various heads of damages and the awards made to claimants, together with tables for updating older sums in line with inflation, are to be found in Kemp and Kemp. The Judicial Studies Board issues guidelines on current figures at regular intervals. However, the difficulties that can arise in attempting to extrapolate from the Judicial Studies Board guidelines are highlighted by the case of *Butters v Grimsby & Scunthorpe Health Authority*[58]. The claimant had suffered considerably as a result of gynaecological problems following the birth of her first child in 1992, when she had undergone surgery to evacuate the retained products of pregnancy from her uterus. During the operation her uterus had been perforated in two places and her endometrium had been damaged. Although she later underwent a laparotomy to repair her uterus the claimant suffered amenorrhoea and continued pain, and after further investigation in 1974 she was given a D&C, hysteroscopy and a further laparoscopy. It was discovered that she had interuterine adhesions and Ascherman's syndrome, which made it unlikely that she would be able to have another child. When she became pregnant later in the same year she suffered a miscarriage. Another hysteroscopy followed in 1995 and she had yet another miscarriage five months later, when a hysterectomy was performed. At first instance the judge awarded general damages of £50,000 under three heads – infertility, physical pain and suffering, and scarring. The Judicial Studies Board guidelines suggested that infertility with associated depression, some anxiety, pain and scarring fell into category (a) of awards in the range of £48,000 to £65,000. Cases of infertility where the claimant already had children and where there were no complications fell within category (b) ranging from £8,000 to £16,250. On appeal the health authority urged the Court of Appeal to accept the argument that damages should fall into the lower category of awards, because the claimant already had a child and there was no evidence that she was suffering from clinical depression. However, since the trial, the claimant had undergone two more operations and her ovaries had been removed. She was still suffering pain and her symptoms were being

---

54   *Wise v Kay* [1960] 1 QB 638.
55   *West and Co v Shephard* [1964] AC 326.
56   *Briody v St Helens and Knowsley Health Authority* (supra).
57   *Allen v Bloomsbury Health Authority* [1993] 1 All ER 651; *McFarlane v Tayside Health Board* (supra).
58   QBD 1996, unreported.

investigated further. The Court of Appeal ruled that the Judicial Studies Board guidelines were insufficiently specific to deal with a case involving so many medical complications. The number of operative procedures was not specified in the guidelines. In this case the most radical surgery was the hysterectomy, and the fact that the claimant was not also claiming for clinical depression was to her credit as she had not succumbed to stress and anxiety. The judge had therefore been right to make an award in the (a) category. An additional sum of £5,000 was awarded for the ongoing pain and surgery.

The Court of Appeal commented upon the status of the Judicial Studies Board guidelines in *Reed v Sunderland Health Authority*[59], in which Sir Christopher Staughton stated that while the title *'guidelines'* might suggest that the guidance issued by the Judicial Studies Board had legal authority, in fact they did not. He explained that the law relating to quantum lay in statutes and decided cases, and the Judicial Studies Board did not have legislative power. Damages awarded to the claimant for negligent diagnosis of a medical condition were reduced from £365,493 to £246,407.40 by the Court of Appeal.

Recent developments in general damages

After a period of uncertainty the Court of Appeal has issued guidance in a series of decisions that are likely to have the effect of increasing awards of general damages. In a series of appeals, *Heil v Rankin: Rees v Mabco (102) Ltd: Schofield v Saunders & Taylor Ltd: Ramsay v Rivers: Kent v Griffiths: Warren v Northern General Hospital NHS Trust: Annable v Southern Derbyshire Health Authority: Connolly v Tasker Court of Appeal*[60], the Court of Appeal gave long and detailed consideration to the question of whether it would be appropriate to change the level of awards for general damages. New guidance was issued on the appropriate levels of damages for pain, suffering and loss of amenity in personal injury and clinical negligence claims worth more than £10,000. The Court of Appeal ruled that awards are to be tapered, the rate of increase rising with the size of the award, up to a maximum increase of one-third on awards at the highest level. The increase was required to bring some awards up to the appropriate standard that was fair, reasonable and just. The eight appeals turned solely on the question of quantum, and the Court of Appeal issued a single judgment that took into account the Law Commission Report No 257[61]. That report contained the recommendation that the level of damages for non-pecuniary loss for personal injuries should be increased, and recommended that in respect of injuries for which the current award for non-pecuniary loss for the injury alone would be more than £3,000, damages should be increased by a factor of at least 1.5, but by not more than a factor of 2. It recommended a tapering of increased awards in the range £2,001 to £3,000 of less than a factor of 1.5. The Law Commission had been of the view that legislation should be avoided if possible, and that the Court of Appeal and House of Lords should lay down guidelines to deal with this matter in a series of cases.

The five member Court of Appeal considered that it was well-equipped to make decisions on the matters in the Law Commission Report. Basic principles should continue to be used in the assessment of damages, but the Court acknowledged that any process of attempting to convert pain suffering and loss of amenity into financial

---

59   The Times 16 October 1998.
60   The Times 24 March 2000.
61   19 April 1999.

damages was artificial and difficult. Changing levels of damages, if they no longer reflected the correct levels, was part of the courts' duty.

Counsel for the defendants argued that it would be wrong, as a matter of principle, for the court to consider the Law Commission's recommendations, and that it would be inappropriate to seek to alter the level of awards by judicial determination. On behalf of the NHS it was contended that a decision to increase damages would have a substantial impact on availability of funds for patient care, and that this was a matter of public policy for Parliament to consider. The defendants submitted that no revision was necessary or appropriate, on grounds of cost, policy, affordability and need.

The Court of Appeal held that consideration of the evidence had led to conclusions which would not radically alter the present approach to the assessment of damages, and it would be inappropriate to increase the levels of awards to the substantial extent recommended by the Law Commission. It was in the case of the most catastrophic injuries that the awards were most in need of adjustment. The scale of adjustment should be reduced as the level of existing awards decreased. At the highest level, awards should be increased in the region of one-third. At the other end of the scale, there was no need for an increase in awards that were below £10,000. Between those two levels the extent of the adjustment should taper, as was illustrated by the decisions in the individual appeals. The starting point of the Court of Appeal in reaching these conclusions was that there was a clear need established for this to be done, and the Law Commission's report assisted the court in reaching that conclusion, but the Commission attached greater significance to the survey which they had commissioned than was considered appropriate by the Court of Appeal[62].

Recent increases in the life expectancy of claimants were also important in considering the appropriate level of awards. The effect of the increases in relation to the higher claims could be very significant. The Court of Appeal noted that the Law Commission had attached minimum significance to the impact of a substantial increase in the level of damages on the level of insurance premiums and on the resources of the NHS. However the opinion of the Court was that this factor should not be ignored. The GDP (Gross Domestic Product) index and the indices dealing with the increases in wage levels supported an increase in awards. It was necessary to take into account the fact that the Judicial Studies Board guidelines had increased substantially above the Retail Prices Index (RPI).

This decision was yet another important victory for claimants in their battle to secure awards that are fair and will ensure that they have sufficient income to give them lives comparable to those that they would have had if they had never been injured by negligence. However, the new rule, along with that in *Wells v Wells* will inevitably mean greater pressure on NHS resources, as the Court of Appeal acknowledged.

Damages on Death

Damages can be claimed under the Law Reform (Miscellaneous Provisions) Act 1934 on behalf of the estate of a deceased person, and these are awarded in addition to any life insurance policy payable on death. Damages under this act are payable on the same basis as if the deceased were still alive, and cover matters such as past pecuniary losses, for example, care to the date of death, and general damages such as pain and

---

62   See Lewis, R, *Increasing the Price of Pain: Damages, The Law Commission and Heil v Rankin* (2001) MLR Vol 64 No 1
       Pages 100-111.

suffering and loss of amenity endured by the deceased between the date of the accident and the date of death. However, if there is a very short period of time between the accident and the death, no award can be made for *'pre-accident terror'*[63]. There can be no award for loss of future earnings for the lost years under the Act.

Dependants of the deceased are entitled to claim on death under the Fatal Accidents Act 1976. The claim is for loss of dependency, and there are now many categories of dependants who are entitled to claim under the legislation[64]. These include a spouse, former spouse, any person who lived as husband or wife with the deceased for two continuous years immediately before the death, parents, other ascendants and people treated by the deceased as parents, children and other descendents, people treated as children of the family, brothers, sisters, aunts, uncles and their issue. To qualify for compensation, it is essential for the claimant under the Act to prove that he or she was dependent on the deceased, or in rare cases was likely to become so[65].

As the claim for loss of dependency is in fact a claim for loss of a breadwinner, the calculation is made on the same basis as that of a living claimant in relation to loss of future earnings, using the multiplicand and multiplier. However, the award is calculated on the assumption that certain claimants, such as children, would cease to be dependent financially once they reach a certain age or complete their education. These are all matters to be proved. Claims can also be made for loss of past support[66]. In the case of spouses or partners, the possibility that the couple might divorce can be taken into account and the multiplier is adjusted accordingly in an appropriate case[67].

However, the possibility of widows remarrying cannot be considered by the court and even if a widow has already remarried a wealthy man, she is entitled to claim under the Act. The same rule does not apply to widowers, nor to children who have lost a father and whose mother might marry. Although the changes in favour of widows are to be welcomed, the discrepancies in the present law are very unfair to children and husbands and out of step with modern thinking.

Non-financial dependency is also compensated. These awards cover domestic services that are no longer available from a parent or other carer, and it is the practice for the judge to calculate the award as if he were a jury, on a mathematical basis[68]. In *Bordin v St Mary's Hospital* a woman had died in childbirth as a result of the negligence of the hospital staff, and an award of £5,000 general damages was made for loss of the child's mother's services – that is the services that only a mother can provide, that are irreplaceable. Travel costs for the grandparents from Spain were included in the award. The financial cost of replacing the mother's services included an allowance to cover paying a nanny with a deduction for what the family would have paid for a professional carer had the mother lived and resumed her career. The judge did not take a broad brush approach to the assessment for lost dependency, and considered whether the sums claimed would have been considered reasonable by a jury if there had been one. This judge as jury approach had been approved by the Court of Appeal in *Hayden v Hayden*[69].

---

63 *Hicks v Chief Constable of South Yorkshire* [1992] 2 All ER 65; (1992) 8 BMLR 70.
64 The Administration of Justice Act 1982 added several categories to the previous list of potential claimants.
65 For example if the accident victim was a promising student who had agreed to support her parents when she qualified as was the case in one of the claims arising from the *Marchioness* disaster; see also *Kandalla v British European Airways Corporation* [1981] QB 158.
66 *Cookson v Knowles* [1979] AC 556.
67 *Martin v Owen* The Times 21 May 1992.
68 *Spittle v Bunney* [1988] 3 All ER 1031.
69 [1992] 4 All ER 681.

In *Day v North Essex Health Authority,*[8] a two-and-a-half-year-old child succeeded in claiming damages for loss of his mother's services on the basis of the decision in *Spittle v Bunney*[9]. The mother had been misdiagnosed as suffering from psychiatric symptoms possibly originating in the misuse of drugs or alcohol. In fact her condition was probably due to a deficiency of vitamin B1 as a result of malnutrition or excessive vomiting. The claimant recovered £35,000.

Bereavement damages

Damages are payable for bereavement, but these are only available to limited classes of individuals explained above.

The Law Commission's reviews

In 1999 the Law Commission produced two reports: *Damages for Personal Injury: Medical, Nursing and Other Expenses; Collateral Benefits* and *Claims for Wrongful Death*[70] in which recommendations were made that are aimed at modernising the existing legislation. The Law Commission had considered that the existing law was out of step with the values of modern society, and needed to be made fairer and more certain. There was criticism of the rule that excludes from entitlement to compensation certain people who were financially dependent on the deceased. The Law Commission recommended reforming the position by adding a generally worded class of claimant to the present fixed list of those who can claim under the Fatal Accidents Act 1976. The report was also critical of the award of bereavement damages only to the deceased's spouse and parents, and recommended extending the list of claimants to include the deceased's children, siblings and long-term partner. There was also a recommendation by the Law Commission that bereavement damages should be raised to £10,000 (with an overall maximum award for any one death of £30,000) and that it should subsequently be adjusted to keep pace with changing economic conditions through index-linking.

Concerned about overcompensation, the Law Commission recommended reform of the law that requires all benefits accruing to a dependant as a result of the death to be ignored, and suggested that the Ogden Working Party, (an expert body of lawyers and actuaries) should consider and explain more fully how actuarial tables now being generally used in the assessment of damages should be applied or amended to produce accurate assessments of damages in wrongful death cases.

Interest on damages

Damages can accumulate interest, though the rate is low, and it is difficult to find a logical basis for the calculation of that interest so the result is arbitrary. Non-pecuniary losses in personal injury claims carry interest at 2% from the time proceedings are issued. Special damages to the date of the trial carry interest from the date of the accident at half the special investment account rate for money paid into court. Future losses, pecuniary and non-pecuniary, carry no interest.

Alternative methods of paying damages

The fact that damages are usually paid in the form of a once and for all lump sum had been criticised by many commentators, including the Pearson Commission which reported in 1978. As the award is based so much on speculation, the result can be unfair to either or both parties, depending on what actually transpires in the years that follow the award. An extreme example is to be found in events arising after the

---

70   Law Commission Report No 262, November 1999.

decision in *Calladine v Nottingham Health Authority*[71]. Publicity given to this case succeeded in focusing public attention on the inequities of the UK compensation system. The claimant, Hollie Calladine, died only days after a long battle to obtain damages in a claim arising out of an error by medical staff during her birth. She suffered brain damage as a result of being deprived of oxygen and was left suffering from quadriplegia, spastic cerebral palsy, blindness and epilepsy. Hollie was nine years old when the case was finally decided in her favour and she received an award of £700,000. However, only a few days later she died, and the health authority indicated that they wished to recoup some of the money because a large proportion of it had been intended to cover the cost of Hollie's future care. When the sum for the child's future care was calculated it was based on an assessment of her projected needs for the future, though it was impossible to predict exactly how long that will be. Medical evidence was adduced in an attempt to estimate the number of years of life which were left to the claimant, and it was open to the defence to challenge that estimate with evidence of its own. However, the case demonstrates that this process is no more than a legal lottery. Inevitably there will also be occasions like that in Hollie Calladines's case when a claimant is overcompensated.

It was a unique event for a defendant to appeal in order to demand the return of a proportion of the compensation, and the inescapable question is whether the health authority would have been equally anxious to offer an additional payment if the claimant had lived longer than the experts had anticipated. In most cases there is no simple solution to this problem in the legal system as it stands. For some claimants, a structured settlement, (see below) tailored to meet the specific needs of the individual, can offer a more advantageous resolution than a lump sum award, but even structured settlements are based on the usual system of calculating compensation. In general the comment of Lord Scarman in *Lim Poh Choo v Camden and Islington Health Authority*[17] still reflects the truth:

> 'There is really only one certainty – the future will prove the award to be either too high or too low.'

When the authority decided to appeal, they based their decision on the belief that they have a *'financial duty and a statutory and moral responsibility to ensure that NHS funds are used to meet the needs of the greatest number of patients'*. Under normal circumstances, an appeal against an award of damages in a civil case of this kind is very rarely allowed even if the relatives of the claimant have received a substantial windfall following the early death of the accident victim. It is only where there are *'exceptional circumstances'* that such appeals succeed. Leave to appeal was granted but the appeal did not succeed.

Structured settlements

In certain instances the problems inherent in lump sum payments of damages can be overcome by the use of a structured settlement[72]. Structured settlements involve the substitution of pensions for lump sum payments. The initial sum payable is calculated in the same way as damages are assessed. Part is paid to the claimant immediately, to cover special damages to the date of the settlement, and the rest is used by the insurer to purchase an annuity for the claimant's benefit. These arrangements are most appropriate in cases involving very high awards (at least five figures) where the claimant does not want the anxiety of managing investments, and

---

71   Unreported.
72   See Lewis R, *Structured Settlements*, Sweet and Maxwell 1996.

claimant's life expectancy is uncertain and there is a large amount of care required. The advantage to the claimant of structuring the damages is a considerable financial saving as a result of significant tax concessions, and the avoidance of the need to invest and manage the money. The defendant also takes the benefit of a tax concession (though in the case of healthcare bodies the position is rather different – see below), and has the added advantage of avoiding the uncertainties presented by the *Calladine* case. However, a significant point is that only larger sums lend themselves to this form of settlement. Both sides must agree to a structured settlement, and this method of paying damages is well worth considering in medical negligence cases involving a substantial period of future care.

The first structured settlement in a healthcare negligence case was in *Field v Herefordshire Health Authority*[73] in which it was agreed that an immediate £59,000 per annum be paid to the claimant on a monthly basis. That sum would increase every year at 5% per annum compound interest, guaranteed for the life of the claimant or ten years whichever was the longer. There would be a deferred sum of £15,315 per annum commencing in five years and payable monthly, increasing at 5% per annum compound interest guaranteed for the life of the claimant or ten years whichever was longer. There would be a further deferred sum of £32,578 per annum and guaranteed for life or five years from the first payment, and a lump sum to be paid at the end of every five years, based on the sum of £50,000 to be increased in line with the retail price index, and only to be paid during the life-time of the claimant.

In 1992 the NHS Management Executive advised NHS Trusts and health authorities that a self financed option directly from the defendant's income would usually represent better value for money and would be more practical than the purchase of an annuity because the payments can be spread over time. Moreover, NHS bodies do not pay tax and can pay the claimant in full without deducting the tax. Since that date there have been several cases in which the NHS has made substantial savings on payments of damages, (see for example, *O'Toole v Mersey Regional Health Authority*)[74].

Structured settlements have not been used as frequently as might be supposed, though their use is encouraged by the NHSLA. One serious disadvantage to structured settlements is that once agreed upon the terms cannot be changed, so it is very important to ensure that the correct arrangements are made at the outset. Another is that claimants might feel under pressure to agree to a structured settlement that they do not really want. Also, even investigating the costs of a structured settlement can be an expensive process. In *Conneely (a minor) v Redbridge and Waltham Forest NHS Trust*[75] it was held that in approving a structured settlement in a clinical negligence case the judge can order that the costs of an investigation be limited to a reasonable set figure. The defendant in this instance sought an order that the costs which the claimant incurred (to be borne by the defendant under standard NHS practice) in investigating whether or not a structured settlement should be arranged, be limited to a reasonable sum. The defendant's argument was that it was normal practice to cap the allowable expenditure for the investigation at £5,000. However, the claimant argued that there should be no cap on allowable expenditure, as the claimant had moved to Eire. The settlement was approved subject to the

73   [1991] PMILL 72.
74   Unreported 1998.
75   QBD 11 January 1999.

defendants' undertaking to pay the claimant's costs of investigating a structured settlement being limited to the sum of £5,000 including VAT. There was to be a reconsideration of this limit, up to a maximum of £7,000 if the sum of £5,000 was reasonably shown by the claimant to have been insufficient.

Another serious disadvantage has recently emerged. The Court of Appeal held in *Beattie v Secretary of State for Social Security*[76] that payments made to a claimant under a structured settlement are income and should be taken into account for the purposes of a claim for income support. The arrangement in place under the settlement was a typical example of an annuity and the only conclusion was that it fell squarely within reg 41(2) of the relevant social security Regulations.

Provisional Awards

The claimant's financial burden may be eased by the payment of provisional damages, authorised under the Administration of Justice Act 1982. There can be an adjustment of the damages at a later date if the prognosis is uncertain and there is a risk of a serious deterioration in his condition at a later date. The claimant must specify what the feared event is likely to be in considerable detail, and the judge specifies the period of time within which the claimant can make an application for a further award if the event materialises – though the claimant can apply for an extension of that time. Further provision is made under the Damages Act 1996 to allow for the situation where death supervenes after the damages have been awarded and before the further award is made. The lifetime award to the claimant in such cases will not prevent the dependants claiming under the Fatal Accidents Act 1976.

Split trials and interim damages

Split trials allow liability to be settled at an early stage so that quantum can be dealt with once the prognosis for the claimant has become clear. After liability has been settled or agreed, the claimant can receive an interim award to ease his difficulties until quantum is finalised[77].

Conclusion

This chapter has covered some of the many problems arising from the arbitrary nature of the way in which damages are assessed in personal injury claims. Developments in relation to funding the growing number of claims will be discussed in the next chapter, together with details of the way in which the defence of claims is handled. The present Government appears to be obsessed with the concept of 'modernisation' in many areas of public life, and it is certainly true that health and legal services have seen a large number of radical changes in recent years, some of them for the benefit of patients, others aimed at reducing the amount of public money that is spent on litigation in healthcare cases. However, it is difficult to see how reform of the long established rules concerning the way in which damages are calculated can be achieved on an incremental basis. The Lord Chancellor's Department and the Law Commission are keeping these matters under review and in time there may be further legislation aimed at bringing about more comprehensive reform of the system than has yet been achieved.

---

76   [2001] EWCA 498.
77   Civil Procedure Rules, 25(1).

Chapter 9

Clinical Negligence and Human Rights

The European Convention on Human Rights was incorporated into English law with the implementation of the Human Rights Act 1998 on 2 October 2000[1]. The Human Rights Act1998 affects both legislation and the common law.

Legislation and Human Rights

The Act provides that wherever possible UK legislation must be interpreted (*'read and given effect'*) in such a way as to be compatible with the European Convention on Human Rights[2]. It is likely that this provision is general in its application, and that it applies to all public authorities such as courts, Government departments, and public bodies, but also to private citizens when they are involved in activities requiring the interpretation of statutes.

Although the incompatability with the Convention has no immediate effect on the continued validity of a statute or statutory instrument, judges in the higher courts have the power to issue declarations of incompatibility if they are satisfied that any legislation is incompatible with the European Convention. Parliament would then be alerted to the need to change the law. However, there is no effect on the position of the parties to the litigation that led to the declaration[3]. Parliament must decide how to respond, and there are fast-track procedures to amend incompatible legislation if necessary[4].

It has been suggested that senior judges should be prepared to appear before Parliament to explain the rationale of their decisions under the Human Rights Act. Such a development would, according to Conor Gearty[5], lead to an American style system with judges appearing at *'confirmation hearings'* before Parliament. He said:

> *'I think senior UK judges will have to be prepared to meet with Parliament, perhaps with a new human rights committee, to explain in general terms what is happening in the courts under the Human Rights Act and to defend general policy developments.'*

---

1 In particular Articles 2 to 12 and Article 14.
2 Section 3(1).
3 A declaration of incompatability was made in *R v Mental Health Review Tribunal, North and East Region, ex parte H*, in relation to ss72 and 73 of the Mental Health Act 1983.
4 It has been judicially decided that some aspects of the Mental Health Act 1983 are incompatible with the Convention. See *Medical Law Monitor*, June 2001.
5 The Times 12 December 2000, p15 reporting the contents of an inaugural lecture at King's College London.

However, it is difficult to envisage such a development in the UK, which has a proud tradition of an independent judiciary.

Common Law and Human Rights

The law relating to clinical negligence is largely common law, having been developed by the courts, and it seldom involves the interpretation of legislation. However, there are some areas of the common law of clinical negligence and other areas of medical law generally on which the Human Rights Act is likely to have a strong impression. An important effect of the Human Rights Act is that courts should interpret and develop the common law in accordance with the Convention. The jurisprudence of the Strasbourg court and the European Commission must be referred to by UK courts when considering human rights law and its application.[6] Failure to act in a way that is compatible with human rights as stated in the Convention may lead to a legal claim, and claimants will not need to go to the Strasbourg Court to enforce human rights, because they can seek remedies from the courts in the UK under the Act. Alleged infringements of Convention rights might form the basis of a stand-alone legal action, or they could be added to existing common law claims such as those for clinical negligence.

Only *'victims'*[7] of alleged infringements have a right to bring a claim, and this term is open to interpretation[8]. Challenges on human rights grounds were possible before the Act and there may be some instances when the term *'victim'* is given a narrower interpretation under the Act than under the pre-existing law. The case law developed by the European Court and Commission suggests that to have standing as a victim a person or organisation must be directly and actually affected by the act or omission in question. This probably means that pressure groups, in what may be their perceived role as public defenders of human rights, would not be able to bring legal challenges merely on the strength of their interest in a particular matter, such as vaccine damage. The challenge would probably need to be brought by a group of individuals who had actually suffered the alleged violation of their rights or by an individual or representative group of individuals within the pressure group[9]. It is predictable that the decisions about the standing of such interest groups will lead to a large body of case law. As Wadham and Mountfield argue[10]:

'The consequence of section 7 will be a series of arcane judgments analysing how far a public interest group is a victim or can in any event rely on the Convention. Further, important breaches of Convention rights may go unremedied because it is not possible to find a nominal applicant.'

This might be the case where violations of Convention rights are alleged in relation to mentally incapacitated people or young children in the context of medical law.

It is believed to be unlikely that UK judges will contemplate radical revision of the common law, and litigants are to be discouraged from raising hopeless issues in their arguments concerning human rights. Indeed, the Government feared that human rights cases could cost the country an extra £60 million, and set aside that sum for

---

6   Section 2(1) of the 1998 Act.

7   Section 7(7).

8   See Wadham J, and Mountfield H, *Blackstone's Guide to the Human Rights Act 1998*, Blackstone Press, London 1999.

9   See Cane P *Standing up for the Public* [1995] PL 276 and Wadham J and Mountfield H, op cit. Note that the Lord Chancellor's Department is currently consulting about the possibility of representative claims in civil cases. This could have a knock-on effect on cases involving human rights. See Chapter 10.

10   op cit page 41.

dealing with the expected flood of claims[11]. Lord Woolf warned in the case of *Daniels v Walker*[12] that judges should be robust in '*resisting inappropriate attempts to introduce arguments based on the Human Rights Act*', but even if human rights arguments form part of common law claims rather than standing alone as is expected, the time spent considering them is likely to add to legal costs. The law surrounding Convention rights must develop gradually, and is subject to interpretation by the UK courts, the European Court of Human Rights in Strasbourg and the Commission. It is essential that Convention rights are interpreted in such a way as to give them a practical and workable effect in modern society.

Public authorities (and this would for many purposes, include their employees) have an obligation to act in a manner that is compatible with Convention rights, unless there is current legislation that makes this impossible[13]. This obligation lies only on '*public authorities*'[14] which are not defined in the Act. The nature of this concept was explained by the Lord Chancellor who asserted that the key issue is whether the body in question has '*functions of a public nature. If it has any functions of a public nature, it qualifies as a public authority*'[15]. The term would include courts, tribunals, coroners, local authorities (which have some responsibilities relating to healthcare) and NHS Trusts. Bodies such as the GMC, Research Ethics Committees, and the Human Fertilization and Embryology Authority (HFEA) would be included, but probably not the BMA, which is a representative body covering the interests of the medical profession[16]. Courts deciding medical law cases would be subject to the requirements of the Act, as would Tribunals inquiring into medical law matters[17].

Private care providers such as residential care homes, private clinics and voluntary sector day centres are '*public authorities*' in relation to the provision of publicly funded care. The Department of Health has emphasised the need for social services departments to '*ensure that contractors and independent providers are made aware of their new duties*'[18]. Chief executives, managers, clinicians, healthcare workers in the NHS and others employed by public authorities would be expected to comply with the Convention in the course of their work when implementing the policies of their employers. Doctors working in private practice would not be acting in a public capacity when treating their patients, but authoritative opinion[19] suggests that all doctors would be regarded by the courts as public authorities in the exercise of NHS functions[20]. Although the doctor-patient relationship is a confidential personal relationship, and therefore in some respects a '*private*' relationship, the NHS is a public service and doctors deliver healthcare in the course of their employment for that service. It has already been judicially decided that doctors and other healthcare professionals act as the agents of their employers when carrying out their duties to patients[21].

---

11   The Times 1 October 2000.

12   The Times 17 May 2000.

13   Section 6.

14   See Bamforth N, *The Application of the Human Rights Act to Public Authorities and Private Bodies* [1999] CLJ 159.

15   Hansard 24 Nov 1997: Column 797.

16   In *Heather v Leonard Cheshire Foundation*, it was held that the Cheshire Foundation is not a public authority.

17   For example the tribunal established under the chairmanship of Professor Ian Kennedy to investigate the events surrounding the deaths of children at the Bristol Royal Infirmary's Paediatric Cardiac Unit.

18   LAC (2000)17; but no equivalent guidance has yet been issued in Wales.

19   Lord Irvin at 583 HL Debate 811 (27 November 1997) cited in Kennedy and Grubb *Medical Law* 2000, Butterworths.

20   Wadham J and Mountfield H, *Blackstone's Guide To the Human Rights Act* Blackstone Presss 1998.

21   *Razzel v Snowball* [1954] 3 All ER 429.

Individuals employed by public institutions should be aware of the rights stated in the Convention and should take account of them in their dealings with patients. If a challenge to a doctor involving a human rights issue came before a court, the court would, as a public body, be required to act in a manner that is compatible with the Convention and apply the law accordingly, so requiring the doctor to act in a manner that is compatible with the Convention[22]. This would affect doctors who undertake private work, and it seems likely that by means of the horizontal effect of the Act, all health disputes will involve a public dimension and attract human rights arguments[23].

It is too soon to predict with certainty which areas of healthcare are likely to result in litigation relating the Convention. However, areas which are most likely to be of concern are:

- duty of care in negligence;
- treatment of minorities;
- fertility treatment and gender reassignment treatment;
- mental health;
- consent to and refusal of treatment;
- allocation of resources;
- the NHS Complaints System;
- the application of the civil procedures rules;
- the activities and recommendations of bodies such as NICE, CHI and the Care Standards Commission.

The Convention rights that are likely to be prominent in argument in medical law cases are:

- the right to life (Article 2);
- the prohibition of inhuman or degrading treatment or punishment (Article 3);
- the right to liberty and security (Article 5);
- the right to a fair trial (Article 6);
- the right to respect for privacy, family life, home and correspondence (Article 8);
- the right to freedom of expression including the right to receive and impart information (Article 10);
- the right to marry and found a family (Article 12);
- the right not to be discriminated against (Article 14).

The relevant provisions of Articles 2, 3, 5, 6 and 8 of the Convention are set out in the appendix to this book. Not all of these are of primary importance in clinical negligence cases, and only the human rights issues that are likely to affect clinical negligence litigation and closely related matters such as the allocation of resources for treatment are covered here. However, there are many other areas of medical law in which the human rights issues are extremely important, such as mental health and abortion.

While articles 3, 12 and 14 of the Convention impose absolute prohibitions on infringements; Articles 2 and 5 allow specific exceptions which require the rights of the individual to be balanced against the rights of others or the rights of society as a

---

22 For discussion about views as to whether the Act has indirect horizontal effect between citizens, see Phillipson G, *The Human Rights Act, Horizontal Effect and the Common Law: A Bang or a Whimper* (1999) 62 MLR 824; and Hunt M, *The Horizontal Effect of the Human Rights Act* [1998 PL 423.

23 Murray Hunt *The Horizontal Effect of Human Rights Law* [1998] Public Law 43.

whole. The jurisprudence of the European Court of Human Rights in Strasbourg and the decisions of the European Commission indicate that when undertaking that balancing exercise between the rights of the individual and the rights of others, UK courts will need to ask whether the alleged infringement is in accordance with or authorised by law; whether it is directed towards a legitimate aim in accordance with the relevant Article, and whether it is necessary in a democratic society (ie whether the limitation to a particular right is proportionate to the legitimate aim being pursued). The European Court is prepared to accept that there is a margin of appreciation, an area of discretion, within which individual States have freedom to implement public policy. Public authorities should consider this balance carefully when deciding whether to take any step which might infringe Convention rights. This should include consideration of other less intrusive options that could achieve the same aim.

Duty of care and human rights

Article 6(1) of the European Convention on Human Rights provides that everyone is entitled to a fair trial in determination of his civil rights and obligations, within a reasonable time by an independent and impartial tribunal established by law. If there is no existing remedy equivalent to a Convention right, the judges would be required, by Article 6, to develop one, and if there has been a previous decision by a UK court providing a defendant with blanket immunity by ruling that there is no duty of care in existence[24], the courts would be required to reconsider the matter.

As has been seen in Chapter 2, consideration of the concept of duty of care is the vital first step in any negligence claim. There are relatively few disputes about whether a duty of care exists in clinical negligence cases, and the Human Rights Act may have the effect of reducing these further, so increasing the number of claims. The leading case, *Caparo Industries plc v Dickman*[25], is the yardstick for judicial determination of the question of duty of care, and the criteria established by the House of Lords in that case are referred to with great regularity in disputes about the existence of a duty when novel cases are presented before the courts. According to the House of Lords, a duty arises when:

- it is foreseeable that the claimant would be affected by the acts or omissions of the defendant;
- there is sufficient proximity between the parties;
- the court considers that it would be fair, just and reasonable to impose a duty in all the circumstances of the case.

Consideration of proximity, and of what is *'fair, just and reasonable'* and the underlying policy issues will now also include human rights issues, and the boundaries of liability may be affected by the Convention rights. In particular, it will not be possible for a court to deny a claimant the right to a fair trial simply by placing a blanket ban on the existence of a duty of care as has happened in the past in relation to public authorities[26]. The cases dealing with public liability are discussed in Chapter 2, and as is explained in that chapter, there have already been some indications that the

---

24 *Palmer v Tees Health Authority and Hartlepool and East Durham NHS Trust* (1999) Lloyd's Rep Med 351.

25 [1990] 1 All ER 568. See Chapter 2.

26 The standard of proof in strike-out cases is higher than the usual standard of a *'balance of probabilities'* – *Royal Brompton Hospital NHS Trust v Hammond*. The Times 11 May 2001.

Court of Appeal[27] and House of Lords[28] are no longer prepared to accept blanket immunities that protect certain classes of defendant without further argument, though human rights issues were not explicitly raised..

Nevertheless, under the principle of the *'margin of appreciation'*, which has been established in the jurisprudence of the European Court of Human Rights, the judges in UK courts are still entitled to consider issues of public policy and morality[29] when dealing with claims to Convention rights. In practice, judges in the UK were prepared to hear arguments about the European Convention on Human Rights even before the Act came into force to ensure that there is consistency between the common law and the Convention, and in those early cases it had become apparent that some of the restrictions of the scope of the duty owed by public authorities would be removed[30] following the decision in *Osman v United Kingdom*[31] where each of the applicants received £10,000 damages in the European Court because the UK courts had denied them the right to bring a civil claim against the police for failing to warn their husband and father when his life was in serious danger.

It is foreseeable that the circumstances in which courts will be required to consider human rights' arguments when deciding whether a duty of care is owed will include the following. This list is of course conjectural.

- A duty on the part of doctors who are aware that an individual, who is not one of their own patients, is in danger of contracting a life-threatening illness (eg HIV or hepatitis) from someone who is one of their patients.
- A duty on the part of healthcare professionals who suspect that a colleague's incompetence is placing patients' lives in danger.
- A duty on the part of occupational health physicians who carry out pre-employment medicals, to the people they examine.
- A duty on the part of people who witness accidents and are able to give medical and other assistance to victims (Good Samaritans)[32].
- A duty on the part of all emergency services.
- A duty on the part of people who cause injury of a psychiatric nature to a wider range of victims than are currently compensated in the UK, as recommended by the Law Commission (see Chapter 2), as long as proximity exists between the parties.

Breach of duty of care in negligence: human rights

Negligent medical treatment gives rise to issues under Article 2 of the European Convention, dealing with the right to life, which imposes a duty not to deprive a person of life intentionally, and Article 3 dealing with inhuman or degrading treatment. Article 2 promotes the duty of a public authority to take positive steps to protect life[33]. Thus the failure of the NHS to undertake a practical and efficient vaccination or screening programme might infringe Article 2, and it is arguable that this principle could be extended to situations in which audit reveals high death rates in a particular hospital, if the NHS Trust takes no steps to investigate and remedy the situation.

---

27   *Kent v Griffiths and The London Ambulance Service* [2000] 2 All ER 474.
28   *W v Essex County Council and Another* The Times 17 March 2000.
29   Established policy arguments are outlined in Chapter 2.
30   *Barrett v Enfield London Borough Council* [1999] 3 All ER 193.
31   [1999] 1 FLR 193.
32   The Commission considered whether Article 3 requires states to enact legislation placing on individuals a general obligation to take prompt action to assist in emergencies – *Hughes v UK* (1986) 48 DR 258.
33   *Naddaf v FRG No 11* 604/85, 50 DR 259 (1986).

In *Association X v UK*[34], parents of vaccine damaged children complained that a state vaccination scheme was inefficiently administered, and that this amounted to a breach of Article 2, in that its deficiencies could lead to serious injury or death in extreme cases. They did not succeed in this argument as the Commission accepted the evidence that the scheme was properly controlled and administered. However, in certain instances it may be possible to establish that there was no proper system of control and supervision of a vaccination scheme, or other public health protection programme, such as a cervical screening service, and that a state had contravened Article 2.

The positive obligation in Article 2 suggests that serious responsibilities are placed on the NHS in relation to the right to life of every individual in its care[35]. This poses particular problems in the case of decisions not to provide particular patients with life saving treatment, or to withdraw essential treatment. The allocation of finite resources within the NHS has always been a difficult and controversial issue, and doctors have a legal and ethical duty to treat their patients according to clinical need. It is possible that the implementation of the *Human Rights Act* could result in resource allocation and treatment decisions being scrutinised under principles closer to the clinical negligence regime, instead of public law principles[36] as they have been in the past[37]. Alasdair McClean[38] takes the view that:

'The shift away from Wednesbury irrationality towards the European principle of proportionality and some modified form of the doctrine of margin of appreciation is likely to increase the applicant's prospects in judicial review.'

One interpretation of the approach of the European Court in *D v UK*[39] is that the decision to terminate treatment when death is the inevitable result could amount to a breach of Article 2 of the Convention. Recent cases highlighted by the media suggest that Do Not Resuscitate decisions were being taken in some NHS hospitals without consulting the patients or the relatives. Clearly, it is desirable to act in consultation with patients and their relatives before making a decision not to resuscitate. Article 2 of the Convention will require healthcare providers to justify any such infringement of patients' right to life.

It is probable that the courts would deal with cases brought on the basis that a health service body or clinician failed to take adequate and appropriate steps to protect a patient's right to life, on the same basis as clinical negligence cases. Cases of this kind could, like clinical negligence cases, be defended on the grounds that a responsible body of medical opinion regards the treatment as logically defensible. This defence would be reinforced if guidelines disseminated by NICE[40] had been followed. This approach is supported by a decision of the European Commission in *Tavares v France*[41] where the Commission rejected a complaint relating to the death of a woman in hospital on the grounds that she could not have died as a result of clinical negligence because the hospital had procedures in place and had followed them as directed.

---

34   (1978) 14 DR 31.

35   Failure to provide adequate treatment to a prisoner who died in custody during an asthma attack was held to amount to a potential breach of Articles 2 and 3 of the Convention – *R v Home Office ex parte Wright*, QBD Administrative Court, 20 June 2001.

36   See Chapter 2.

37   See O'Sullivan D, *The Allocation of Scarce Resources and the Right to Life under the European Convention on Human Rights* [1998] PL 389.

38   *The Human Rights Act 1998 and the Individual's Right to Treatment.* Medical Law International 2000, 245-277 at p263

39   (1997) 24 EHHR 423.

40   See Chapter 3.

41   *Tavares v France Appl* 16593/90 (1991)

There is some evidence indicating that relocating elderly people to a new institution may have an adverse effect on their mental health and life expectancy[42], with some studies suggesting that the increase in mortality rates might be as high as 35%[43]. Department of Health advice recognising this danger on the *'transfer of frail elderly patients to other long stay settings'*[44] in April 1998 takes the human rights issues into account[45].

Article 3, read in the context of Article 1, places a positive obligation on states to take action to ensure that no one suffers from degrading treatment. The European Commission has indicated that inadequate care in the form of negligent treatment received by a patient suffering from a serious illness might amount to a breach of Article 3[46]. It appears, however, that Article 3 would not be engaged unless the circumstances of the complaint were extremely serious[47]. Degrading treatment in the course of medical care could amount to a violation of Article 3[48], but for treatment to be degrading it must be demeaning or grossly humiliating, as in the case of gross ill-treatment of mentally incapacitated patients in institutions. In *Z & others v UK*: 10/9/99 the European Commission Rights unanimously concluded that the UK had violated Article 3 by failing to protect a number of vulnerable children whom it knew to be the victims of ill-treatment and neglect.

Consent to treatment, refusal of treatment and human rights

Cases involving a patient's consent to or refusal of treatment are likely to involve consideration of human rights issues. Failure to provide adequate information before obtaining consent to treatment can amount, in some circumstances[49], to negligence in UK law, and treatment against the patient's wishes would be trespass to the person. There have been several cases decided in the domestic courts in the UK concerning patients who refuse treatment such as blood transfusions[50] and Caesarean sections[51]. Human rights considerations[52] would be raised should similar cases be brought in future. The Convention will have an impact on situations in which patients are not properly involved in decisions about their treatment; including withdrawal of artificial feeding and hydration, and treatment of *'Gillick competent'* minors. Some of these matters do not directly concern clinical negligence, but all are important areas of medical law as a whole. It seems likely from the case of *LVB v UK*[53] that there may, in certain circumstances, be a right to receive advice about medical conditions[54], if a doctor is, or ought to be aware that an individual is at risk of serious illness or injury. This makes the decision of the UK authorities not to inform people

---

42   See, for instance, *International Journal of Geriatric Psychiatry* vol 8, p521 (1993); also see The Times (1994) 7 July, *Elderly patients die within weeks of transfer.*

43   *Relocation of the Aged and Disabled: A Mortality Study Journal of American Geriatric Society*, vol 11, 185.

44   HSC1998/048.

45   Clements, L *Community Care and Human Rights* Open University, 2001.

46   *Association X v UK* (1978) 14 DR 31.

47   *Tryer v UK* (1978) 2 EHRR; *East Africa Asians v UK* (1973) 3 EHRR 76.

48   De Mello suggests that the removal of organs from dead children (as happened in Alder Hey) might be an example of a violation of Articles 3 and 8 and the parents as *'victims'* might be able to pursue the matter as a human rights issue. See De Mello R, *Human Rights and the Public Sector* Informa, London 2000.

49   See *Pearce v United Bristol Healthcare Trust* [1999] 1 PIQR 53.

50   eg *Re E* (1990) 9 BMLR 1.

51   *St George's Healthcare NHS Trust v S, R v Collins ex parte S* (1998) 44 BMLR 160.

52   In *Re O and Re J (children) (blood tests)* 55 BMLR 229, human rights arguments were raised in connection with the taking of blood tests to establish paternity.

53   (1999) 27 EHRR 212.

54   See also *McGinley and Egan v UK* (1998) 27 EHRR 1.

who are known to be at risk of contracting vCJD after receiving contaminated blood, questionable[55]. The issue is *'whether the state had done all that could have been required of it to prevent the applicant's life being avoidably put at risk'*. As there is no cure at present for vCJD, the decision not to inform potential victims is probably safe, but if the medical condition is one which is treatable, as HIV now is, there could well be an obligation on the authorities to inform those at risk.

Inhuman and degrading treatment: anaesthetic awareness cases

There have been several claims brought by people who were conscious (aware) and who experienced pain under general anaesthetic[56]. The question arises as to whether the negligence of the anaesthetists involved in these cases might have resulted in the patient being subjected to inhuman and degrading treatment under Article 3 of the Convention. An argument along these lines could be presented as part of a claim for clinical negligence and/or trespass to the person in an appropriate case. The case law suggests that in each case there must be a minimum level of severity before there is a breach of Article 3, and this would depend upon the duration of the treatment, its effects on the mind and body of the victim and in certain instances, the age, sex and status of the victim.

Anaesthetic awareness cases are just one example of clinical negligence cases that might also involve a breach of Article 3. It could be argued that there is the potential for the breach of Article 3 in certain forms of treatment given to very vulnerable patients who are suffering from severe physical or mental illness, and the Convention rights of these individuals should be uppermost in the minds of those who are caring for them. In *Tanko v Finland*[57], the Commission refused to exclude the possibility that lack of proper medical care when a patient is suffering from serious illness could in some circumstances be contrary to Article 3.

Clinical governance, resource allocation and human rights

As has been seen in Chapter 2, the question of the appropriate allocation of resources for healthcare does not normally involve consideration of the law of negligence, as it is regarded as a public law matter. Healthcare providers are usually left to decide for themselves how to allocate their limited resources, and the courts have seldom been prepared to interfere[58], though they may do so if resource decisions are manifestly unreasonable, or they do not comply with the stated policy of the organisation concerned[59].

However, the positive obligations under Articles 2 and 3 of the Convention may be relied upon to provide a basis for patients to claim that they have a *'right'* to a certain treatment irrespective of what resources are available. This argument could be reinforced by the prohibition on discrimination under Article 14 of the Convention in some instances.

Clinical governance and human rights

When clinical governance was formally implemented, the image presented to the public was that its purpose was the imposition of uniform quality control in order to

---

55 See Chapter 3.

56 eg *Jacobs v Great Yarmouth and Waveney Health Authority* [1995] 6 Med LR 199.

57 Appl 23634/94 unreported, cite in Starmer K, European Human Rights Law, Legal Action Group, London.

58 *R v Secretary of State for Social Services and Others ex parte Hincks* (1980) 1 BMLR 93.

59 *North West Lancashire Health Authority v A,D and G* [1999] Lloyd's Rep Med 399; and *R v North East Devon Area Health Authority ex parte Coughlan* (1998) 47 BMLR 27 – where the claimant's legitimate expectations were held to have been frustrated by the decision of the health authority to break its promise to her of a *'home for life'* In this case, arguments based on Article 3 failed to impress the court, but Article 8 was successfully invoked by the claimant.

raise standards of healthcare throughout the UK. NHS rhetoric spoke of the introduction of formal monitoring of care, the ending of *'post-code'* treatment, continuing professional education and greater accountability in healthcare. Official justifications for clinical governance were reticent about the objective of reducing the NHS drugs bill or the amount spent on litigation in healthcare cases. However, there can be little doubt that dealing with the drugs bill and the litigation explosion were driving forces behind the Health Act 1999 which gave statutory force to clinical governance. The Government, faced with two virtually insoluble difficulties – the finite nature of resources for healthcare and the cost of defending clinical negligence claims – attempted to find the answer by means of one institution – NICE.

The National Institute for Clinical Excellence (NICE) has been given responsibility for appraising existing drugs and treatments, and new technologies and treatments as they become available. It makes recommendations to the Government, and these are almost always accepted. NICE also commissions guidelines on treatment (see Chapter 3). The Commission for Health Improvement monitors the implementation of NICE guidelines and can take drastic action to regulate failing NHS organisations. This process places a convenient distance between the Government and rationing decisions, so taking the issue out of the political arena and reducing any blame that might arise for the failure to make a particular treatment available on the NHS.

NICE and CHI are both public bodies, and are accountable under the Human Rights Act. Sir Michael Rawlins, Chair of NICE, acknowledged that the decisions and recommendations of NICE are not based solely on clinical effectiveness, but also on cost effectiveness, when he explained that there is no point in recommending a therapy if there is not the money available to fund it.

It is possible that NICE guidelines will be challenged by patients who consider that they are being unfairly denied the right to a particular treatment. For example, the decision of a healthcare provider, following NICE guidance, to deny a patient life-saving treatment, such as kidney dialysis[60], because he is elderly[61] or a cigarette smoker, could be challenged under Article 2 of the Convention. Similar challenges could arise in relation to NICE guidelines adopted by the NHS on the provision of drugs, for example beta interferon, that has been recommended for treating multiple sclerosis but only for certain categories of patient, or Relenza for influenza treatment under certain criteria. In *D v UK*[62] the European Court took the view that even if there is no *'right'* to medical treatment provided by the Convention the withdrawal of treatment might amount to a violation of Articles 2 and/or 3.

A patient would be in a stronger position since the Human Rights Act has come into force than under the pre-existing UK law to challenge resource allocation decisions. In *Tanko v Finland*,[63] the Commission expressed the view that the failure to provide adequate medical care to a patient suffering from a very severe illness could amount to a violation of Article 3. The public law remedy of judicial review rather than common law negligence has made it extremely difficult for patients to mount successful challenges to the decisions of healthcare organisations[64]. The courts in the UK have made it clear that they are extremely reluctant to interfere with

---

60   eg *Shortland v Northland Health* (1997) 50 BMLR 255 NZ CA.

61   Article 14 of the Convention would be engaged in this instance.

62   (1997) 24 EHRR 423.

63   23634/94 unreported, cited by Starmer K in *European Human Rights Law*, Chapter 14.

64   See for example, *R v Cambridge Health Authority ex parte B* (1995) 23 BMLR 1.

resource allocation decisions[65], as these are matters of political policy, and judges have taken the view that it is not the business of the courts to make such decisions. Healthcare providers until now, have been permitted to decide, with only minimal interference from the courts, how to allocate their limited resources[66]. In the few UK cases in which there have been successful challenges by patients to resource allocation decisions, the bodies concerned had drafted policies but had failed to follow them[67]. Thus the courts have only been prepared to intervene in the past if resource decisions are manifestly (*Wednesbury*) unreasonable, or they do not comply with the stated policy of the organisation concerned[68]. If however, human rights principles were applied in such cases, the task of the claimant could be facilitated to some extent by the more liberal and balanced approach of the European Court which takes account of the principle of proportionality and the margin of appreciation.

The case law of the European Court of Human Rights indicates that those who make decisions about healthcare are permitted reasonable discretion in determining treatment and funding priorities. Although it is unlikely that the UK courts will adopt a radically different approach in future to questions of resource allocation in healthcare[69], human rights law will mean that they will be required to subject such issues to more detailed scrutiny than ever before. Healthcare organisations are advised to identify objective justifications for decisions that could have the effect of infringing Articles 2 and 3 of the Convention. As May LJ said in *North West Lancashire Health Authority v A, D and G*[70]:

'Health authorities have to make hard and often invidious decisions in the allocation of avowedly inadequate resources. But those decisions must proceed from proper assessments of the conditions competing for treatment.'

In addition to relying on arguments based on the sensible exercise of reasonable discretion in relation to treatment priorities, a healthcare organisation would have a defence if its conduct did not, as a matter of fact, infringe a Convention right. For example, if it could be shown that appropriate alternative treatment was available to a patient to save his or her life, a health authority would be able to argue that although it had not provided precisely the treatment demanded by the patient, it had not denied the patient the right to life, and was not in breach of Article 2.

However, UK courts have already indicated that they will not be willing to hear unhelpful human rights arguments[71] in resource allocation cases, and careful consideration should be given before introducing human rights issues into legal arguments.

Access to records, disclosure of information and human rights

Collection and dissemination of medical data and other information, and the responsible keeping of medical records are essential both for the treatment of patients

---

65   The test for determining that there has been an unlawful decision is the Wednesbury unreasonableness test – a hurdle that is even more difficult than the *Bolam* test for a claimant to surmount.

66   *R v Secretary of State for Social Services and Others ex parte Hincks* (1980) 1 BMLR 93.

67   See fn 59.

68   *North West Lancashire Health Authority v A,D and G* [1999] Lloyd's Rep Med 399; and *R v North East Devon Area Health Authority ex parte Coughlan* (1998) 47 BMLR 27 – where the claimant's legitimate expectations were held to have been frustrated by the decision of the health authority to break its promise to her of a *'home for life'* In this case, arguments based on Article 3 failed to impress the Court, but Article 8 was successfully invoked by the claimant.

69   *North West Lancashire Health Authority v A, D and G* supra, fn 21 in which the judge stated that the courts will not be willing to hear *'unhelpful'* human rights arguments that do not have direct relevance to the case in hand.

70   See fn 16.

71   *North West Lancashire Health Authority v A, D and G* supra, fn 21.

and in the defence of claims for clinical negligence. These matters would be affected by Article 8 (the right to respect for private life) and Article 10 (the freedom to receive and impart information). In *Chare nee Jullian v France*[72] the Commission ruled that collection of medical data and the keeping of medical records would be matters of private life protected by Article 8. In *Gaskin v UK*[73] the European Court did not conclude that there was a general right of access by all patients to their medical records, and recognised that there are many circumstances under UK law when access can be denied[74]. However the Court emphasised the need for reasonable explanation as to why a particular individual should not be permitted to have access to his or her medical records.

The case law of the European Court suggests that disclosure of information about patients without their consent calls for careful scrutiny, and even when a patient makes a claim against a healthcare institution, it should not be assumed automatically that the right to respect for private life has been waived by the patient. In *Z v Finland*[75], the applicant was awarded approximately £22,000 when her HIV status was disclosed and her name was published as part of a court judgment, in breach of Article 8. The Data Protection Act 1998 deals with a wide variety of matters connected with the issue of confidentiality of records, and in the light of that Act, the Caldicott Guardian System, and the Human Rights Act, all healthcare bodies should keep under constant review their procedures and protocols for the handling of patient information, and, in particular, their approach to the disclosure of information without the patient's consent. Whenever any disclosure is made without the patient's consent[76], the health service body concerned must be prepared to document the reasons for disclosure, with reference to the Convention, and such justifications might well include reasons of public safety or the prevention of crime.

Patients already have rights of access to their medical records under current legislation, though these are subject to many exceptions, and it is unlikely that the Human Rights Act will extend these rights significantly. It is possible the statutory exceptions could be questioned under the Human Rights Act, and additionally, there may be circumstances when the NHS should make more information available to patients than at present where a particular risk to health has been identified. The development of telemedicine, and extended electronic record keeping raise further issues in the context of human rights and record keeping in the NHS. The Department of Health has announced that by 2005, every adult will be able to access their own at-a-glance *'electronic health record'* (EHR). These records will hold summarised key data about patients, such as name, address, NHS number, registered GP and contact details, previous treatments, ongoing conditions, current medication, allergies and the date of any next appointments. It is essential that EHRs are securely protected, created with patient consent, with individual changes made only by authorised staff. Pilot studies are already underway to find the best way of allowing patients to access their EHR. Possible options include on-line access via NHS Direct and smart cards for use in information points in GP surgeries, hospitals and walk-in centres. Any option will allow patients to check their summarised and up-to-date health records. The EHR will

---

72   (1991) 71 DR 141.
73   (1999) 12 EHRR 36.
74   Health Records Act 1990; as amended by the Data Protection Act 1998 schedules 15 and 16; Access to Medical Records Act 1998, as amended by the Data Protection Act 1998.
75   (1998) 25 EHRR 371.
76   eg to the police.

have clear benefits for emergency care as important basic information about the patient can be accessed quickly by NHS professionals. All NHS clinical staff will have internet and intranet access including email and on-line information services by the end of 2002, ensuring that they have access to up-to-date information and evidence-bases. Staff will be able to use their electronic network to order tests, and will obtain results more efficiently than at present. A national appointment booking system by 2005, will allow GPS to book hospital appointments online from the surgery. All local health services will have facilities for telemedicine by 2005. This will lead to new ways of working, eg hospital consultants viewing patients in GP surgeries via electronic links or providing an email or phone service for patients to contact their practice nurse or GP for advice. The implementation of all this new technology must be carried out with human rights issues in mind.

The right to a fair trial: the NHS complaints system

The NHS Complaints System, which is outlined in Chapter Seven, was intended to offer patients a simple and inexpensive alternative to litigation when they are dissatisfied about the care they have received in the NHS. The new system was instituted in 1996,[77] and it is clear that there are problems in the way in which it operates. In particular, the system has been criticised for lacking true independence, particularly at the Independent Review stage. Other shortcomings of the system that have been identified are the lack of legal representation for patients and the fact that hearings are held in private[78] and conclusions are not published.

It is possible that the system might be challenged under the Human Rights Act for failing to comply with Article 6(1) of the Convention, which states that:

'In determination of civil rights and obligations everyone is entitled to a fair and public hearing within a reasonable time by an independent and impartial tribunal established by law.'

Such a challenge might be met by a number of arguments along the following lines:

– the system was never intended to set up bodies that were courts or tribunals;
– the system does not involve the determination of *'civil rights and obligations'*;
– there is, in any event, no *'determination'* of issues involved, merely a consideration of grievances.

There could be an answer to each of these arguments based on what is happening *in fact,* in the course of complaints handling. In practice, the system does, at least at Independent Review Stage, allow for a body similar to a tribunal to deliberate upon the issues. A flexible *'two-pronged'* approach is taken by the Strasbourg court in dealing with this point[79]. Independent Review panels do deal with questions of clinical negligence, and in some cases complainants are offered financial compensation in addition to the usual apology if it found that their grievances are justified. The European Court of Human Rights has held that Article 6(1) applies in some cases where the determination of civil rights and obligations is the indirect consequence of other proceedings. However, it is arguable that the procedures will not engage the Article 6 obligation to provide *'independent and impartial'* tribunals because the complaint will not be *'civil'* within the meaning of Article 6.

---

77 Under Directions to NHS Trusts, Health Authorities and Special Health Authorities for Special Hospitals on Hospital Complaints Procedures 1996; Miscellaneous Directions to Health Authorities for Dealing with Complaints 1996; given under s17 NHS Act 1977, Sch 2 para 6(2)(a) NHS&CCA 1990 and the NHS (Functions of Health Authorities) (Complaints) Regulations 1996 SI No 669.
78 See the *Report by the Public Law Project* published in 1999.
79 See Starmer K, *European Human rights Law*, Legal Action Group, London 1999.

No challenge has yet been made to the NHS Complaints System under the Human Rights Act, and it will be interesting to see how a court would interpret the Convention rights in Article 6(1) in relation to these matters.

The right to a fair trial: expert witnesses

In *H v France*[80] the European Court ruled that the requirements of a fair trial apply in proceedings for clinical negligence. One further possible challenge could arise as a result of the way in which medical expert witnesses work since the implementation of the Civil Procedure Rules. Solicitors are reporting that medical experts, who are required to agree on the evidence if possible, are deciding among themselves, in some cases, on the appropriate level at which cases should be settled. Agreement between the experts is, on occasion, allegedly reached late at night over the telephone. This effectively denies the parties the right to have their claim decided by a properly constituted court, and would appear to be contrary to Article 6(1). This is a situation which deserves to be questioned in terms of human rights. However, in *Daniels v Walker* [2000] 1 WLR 1882 the Court of Appeal took the view that it was undesirable for civil proceedings to be complicated by human rights arguments in Article 6. The Clinical Disputes Forum produced guidelines in November 1999 intending them to be incorporated into the Practice Direction for Experts. These were revised in April 2000[81] (though the revised version has not been incorporated as yet) and now provide that:

> *'Unless the lawyers for all parties agree, or the court orders otherwise, lawyers for all parties will attend the discussion of experts. If lawyers do attend such discussions, they should not normally intervene save to answer questions put to them by the experts or advise them on the law'.*

The right to a fair trial: the doctor's dilemma

The public perception is that the Human Rights Act provides protection for the rights of patients. However, the Act and the Convention may also offer a solution to doctors and other healthcare professionals who might suffer injustice as a result of the operation of the Civil Procedure Rules 1999. These Rules regulate the conduct of civil claims in England and Wales and place the court firmly in control over the process of claims. Parties who do not comply with the strict letter of the Rules face heavy penalties. The Civil Procedure Rules, like the Human Rights Act, are endowed with their own principle of proportionality. Under that principle, if the cost of defending a claim is likely to be greatly in excess of the damages payable, the Rules operate in such a way as to penalise a healthcare organisation that proceeds with a defence instead of disposing of the claim sooner by settlement out-of-court at an early stage. The decision to settle a case out-of-court is a business decision to avoid incurring necessary costs in cases where the amount of damages claimed is relatively small, even if there is some likelihood that the claim might fail. The healthcare professional who is accused of negligence, and whose professional reputation may be at stake, is in a very difficult position if he or she feels strongly that it would, as a matter of principle, be desirable to defend the claim. Some doctors believe that they should at least be afforded the opportunity of a court hearing to allow a judge to settle the question of whether they have been negligent. Article 6(1) of the Convention (the right to a fair hearing to determine civil rights and liabilities) might assist in such a situation. It is difficult to convince a doctor that there should be a blame free culture

---

80   (1989) 12 EHRR 74.
81   See *PMILL* Vol 16 No 8, October 2000.

of adverse incident reporting if prospective employers demand details of past and pending claims that have been made against applicants for posts. Even if claims are settled out-of-court on the basis that liability is disputed, the doctors and other defendants will feel that they have been robbed of the opportunity to justify themselves before an independent court. A challenge by a healthcare professional under Article 6(1) can be predicted, though the Lord Chief Justice has asserted that the Civil Procedure Rules cannot contravene the European Convention on Human Rights (*Daniels v Walker*[82]).

Healthcare professions are subject to many established and planned layers of accountability. Among these are the NHS Complaints System, National Confidential Inquiries, audit and monitoring under the clinical governance regime, national league tables, employers' disciplinary procedures, the professional disciplinary procedures of the GMC and other bodies, whistleblowing under the Public Interest Disclosure Act 1998, mandatory critical incident monitoring and the National Clinical Assessment Authority. Each of these forms of regulation must comply with the European Convention on Human Rights.

Access to justice and human rights

Central to the European Convention on Human Rights is the *'universally recognised fundamental principle'*[83] that everyone should be entitled to access to civil justice. In *Airey v Ireland* (1979)[84] the European Court of Human Rights ruled that this could require, in appropriate circumstances, the availability of legal aid. State funding for clinical negligence claims is still available, but only the very poorest members of the community qualify under the Community Legal Service Scheme. Other claimants must rely on the conditional fees scheme or on legal claims insurance, and it is inevitable that some will be deterred by the rule that costs follow the event.

There may be additional problems in relation to human rights challenges against the NHS in the case of those who are mentally ill or mentally incapacitated. Almost half of all complaints made to the European Court in Strasbourg are made by litigants in person, and the vulnerable patient would almost definitely not have this option. Clearly incapacity is not a problem as long as access to a lawyer is available, as it is in relation to detention and treatment decisions under the Mental Health Act 1983. There are numerous procedural obstacles in human rights cases for those who lack full mental capacity. The Civil Procedure Rules state that such a person can only act through a *'litigation friend'* and can only commence proceedings if he lodges a personal undertaking with the court to be responsible for the costs of the proceedings[85]. It surely cannot be easy for vulnerable people to find a person prepared to give a personal guarantee to the costs. Before proceedings can be initiated it is essential to obtain evidence, but access to files and other information is barred in relation to adults lacking capacity. As an incapacitated person is unable to make an informed request to access the information, no one is entitled to do so on his or her behalf. This is the result of a lacuna in the Data Protection Act 1998, which appears to contravene Articles 8 and 14 of the Convention. That fact has been drawn to the attention of the UK Government and the Data Protection Commissioner[86].

---

82   (2000) 1 WLR 1382.
83   *Golder v UK* (1979) 1 EHRR 524.
84   2 EHRR 305.
85   Rule 21.4.3.c, Civil Procedure Rules.
86   See Clements L, *Community Care & the Law* 2nd ed. (2000), para 2.29 et seq: Open University.

Possible defences to a claim invoking human rights arguments

As has been seen, there are some instances when interference with some of the Convention rights might be justified. The following defences could be raised by healthcare institutions:

- The conduct did not, as a matter of fact, infringe a Convention right.

  Convention rights are defined broadly and the Courts are required to interpret the Convention in a variety of different factual situations. It might be possible to raise the argument that conduct of a public authority did not infringe a Convention right at all. For example, if it could be shown that appropriate alternative treatment was given to a patient to save his or her life, a health authority would be able to argue that although it had not provided precisely the treatment demanded by the patient, it had not denied the patient the right to life, and was not in breach of Article 2.

- The conduct complained of falls within a justifiable limitation of the Convention right.

  Although, as has been seen, some Convention rights are absolute, most are subject to qualifications. Circumstances in which infringement of rights may be justified are set out in the Convention. A public authority would be required show that the restriction it placed on the claimant's rights is lawful, in that it was based on existing law, and that the restriction had a legitimate aim, as specified in the Convention, For example, that the restriction was made in the interests of public safety, the protection of public order, health or morals and the protection of the rights of others. It must have been *'necessary in a democratic society'*, based on *'pressing social need'* and it must have been a proportionate response to that need.

  An example might occur if, under the proposed new mental health legislation, a patient's confidentiality was breached by informing a housing officer of his medical condition, in circumstances when the patient posed a threat to the safety of people living on a housing estate. It might be argued that such a breach of confidentiality infringes the right to respect for private life under Article 8. However, the health body concerned would probably be able to show that any such infringement is justified in order to protect of the public, and that it complied with the law.[87]

- The conduct complained of was carried out in accordance with law.

  This *'statutory excuse'* provides protection to public authorities that infringe Convention rights by acting in accordance with existing law of a State. However, the defence will not succeed if the public authority is found to have interpreted the legislation in a manner that does not comply with Convention rights, rather than in a manner that does so comply.

Damages

Awards made by the European Court of Human Rights are generally far lower than awards in negligence cases in the UK courts. Human rights law allows for just satisfaction to be provided to the injured party, but no exemplary damages are payable.

---

87   See the proposals in Part 11 of the *White Paper on Mental Health*, published in December 2000.

Conclusion

It is to soon to assess the full impact of the Human Rights Act on clinical negligence litigation and related law. Healthcare professionals and the huge NHS machine have had enormous power over individual patients. The sick and vulnerable are precisely the kind of people who require the protection that is guaranteed by the European Convention. Although it was possible for challenges to be brought on human rights grounds to the actions and decisions of public bodies before the Human Rights Act was implemented, the formal introduction of fundamental rights into our law by the Act means that the rights enshrined in the European Convention should be foremost in the minds of policy makers and those who implement policies. The judiciary will have the opportunity to develop the common law of clinical negligence consistently with the Convention and to build up a body of case law around it to ensure that individuals are protected from unjustifiable violations of their fundamental rights. However, experience in many cases where human rights arguments have been presented in other spheres suggests that the judges may well react defensively and find that no incompatibility exists. This is analogous to the views of the venerable jurist Blackstone[88] who recognised that positive law was subordinate to natural law but complacently argued that English law in any event conformed to these higher principles.

---

88   Commentary on the Laws of England.

Chapter 10

A Decade of Legal Change

This chapter explores the changes that have been brought about over the past decade (and a little more) in the legal system, in various attempts to provide justice for claimants and defendants. In some instances the legal reforms are directly related to changes in the structure and administration of the healthcare system, and have been introduced as a result of joint consultation with lawyers and healthcare professionals, drawing together the Department of Health and the Lord Chancellor's Department. The legal changes that are discussed here are reforms of funding arrangements for claimants and defendants, changes in the procedures for bringing and defending claims, new rules to guide the use and conduct of expert witnesses, the introduction of the new NHS Complaints System, and attempts to develop alternative forms of dispute resolution. These procedural changes have been accompanied by developments in substantive law, sometimes to the advantage of claimants, as explained in earlier chapters. The changes to the healthcare system are discussed in Chapter 11, and as will be seen, they cover the introduction of greater scrutiny and control by central Government of the entire NHS and its work, accompanied by a series of mechanisms to ensure accountability, and changes in professional regulation.

The Need for Change

The Pearson Commission, which reported in 1978[1], had singled out *'medical negligence'*, as it was then called[2], for special consideration, although the subject was technically beyond its terms of reference. The Pearson Commission concluded that claimants in healthcare negligence cases had a lower chance of success than those in other cases of negligence, such as motor accidents. Payment was made to claimants in only 30%-40% of cases, as opposed to 86% in other personal injury claims. Many of the difficulties for claimants identified by the Pearson Commission stemmed from rules of substantive law, (*Bolam* in particular), and from difficulties connected with proving causation in healthcare negligence cases. However, the Pearson Commission was also critical of the restricted role of the Health Service Commissioner and of the rules that prevented claimants obtaining documentary evidence relating to their claims. A range of options for reform was considered, but the recommendations were rather half-hearted and no radical changes have been achieved. However, as will be

---

1   *Royal Commission on Civil Liability and Compensation for Personal Injury 1978*, Cmnd 7054.
2   The term *'clinical negligence'* appeared with the Woolf reforms in the late 1990s.

seen, some piecemeal reforms have been introduced over the years, through legislation and case law, that answer some of the criticisms in the Pearson Report. For example access to documents such as medical records[3] has been made simpler through legislation, and the *Bolam* test has been modified by the House of Lords[4].

Ten years later, Ham et al, in 1988, reviewed the growing healthcare negligence litigation problem[5] and identified with great prescience, many areas of the litigation system that were in need of reform. The group took the view that it was necessary to increase the accountability of healthcare professionals by adverse incident reporting, and to promote high standards of medical practice by increasing the use of clinical audit, and developing continuing education for healthcare professionals. In relation to the legal system and access to justice, the research group concluded that:

'the key measures worth pursuing are:

- *Providing potential claimants with a means of identifying solicitors with appropriate skills in medical negligence cases.*
- *Giving greater publicity to legal services through advertising and other means in order to increase public awareness of the general possibilities of claiming damages.*
- *Modifying fee-splitting arrangements among lawyers to create greater incentives for solicitors to pass on cases to specialists.*
- *Making access to legal aid easier.*
- *Developing a system to enable health authorities to pool their risk in order to cope with a larger number of successful claims.'*

Since the writing of that paper, litigation concerning healthcare has grown at an alarming rate, but it has taken successive Governments some 12 years to implement many of the suggestions concerning professional accountability, regulation of medical practice and access to justice. An early development was the introduction of NHS indemnity, discussed below, and pooling arrangements through the Clinical Negligence Scheme for Trusts. Specialist firms of solicitors now handle virtually all clinical negligence claims and all defence work, and state funding has been retained for the purposes of healthcare negligence. Conditional fees are being encouraged, as a means of providing claimants with the opportunity of accessing the civil justice system.

There have many criticisms since 1988 of the legal and healthcare systems in the UK and various reviews have taken place at official and unofficial levels. The Civil Justice Review in the late 1980s made several recommendations for changes in the legal system, and in the late 1990s, Lord Woolf undertook another review of the civil justice system[6] that resulted in radical procedural reforms and changes to the role of expert witnesses through the Civil Procedure Rules 1998. The NHS Complaints Review Committee, (the Wilson Committee) reported in 1994 and recommended the introduction of a new NHS Complaints System and extensions to the role of the Health Service Commissioner. These were duly implemented in 1996[7] and their operation is currently under review. During this period of legal change, there were

---

3   Access to Health Records Act 1990.

4   *Bolitho v City and Hackney Health Authority* [1998] AC 232, discussed at length in Chapter 3.

5   Ham, C, Dingwall, R, Fenn, P, Harris, D *Medical Negligence: Compensation and Accountability* 1998.

6   See Woolf, *Access to Justice: the Final Report to the Lord Chancellor on the Civil Justice System of England and Wales* (1996).

7   Health Service Commissioners (Amendment) Act 1996.

many reforms within the NHS, beginning with the restructuring of the NHS in 1990[8] to establish an internal market for healthcare, (which was subsequently abolished), to encourage monitoring and accountability through the use of clinical audit, and culminating in the Health Act 1999. Independent healthcare is currently in the process of being reformed along similar lines to the NHS, to ensure greater accountability[9]. The inquiry into the paediatric heart unit at Bristol Royal Infirmary is still in progress at the time of writing, and is due to publish its report in the Summer of 2001. It is likely that more substantial changes, aimed at ensuring greater accountability and improved professional regulation, will follow. Already, as a result of the Interim Report of the Bristol Inquiry, another Committee was established to inquire into the storage and use of organs taken from dead children at the Alder Hey Childrens' Hospital. Following its report, measures are being taken to prevent further abuses of the healthcare system[10]. There follows an outline of some of these reforms. Changes in substantive law are discussed elsewhere in this book[11].

Funding of Litigation

Various measures have recently been taken to reduce the cost of bringing and defending claims, as public money spent on medical litigation is perceived by the Government to be a diversion of funds out of healthcare and into the legal system[12]. As John Harris points out:

'It is quite implausible to suppose that justice is served by the automatic prioritisation of the claims of successful litigants when this must have the effect of subordinating at least some, perhaps many, more urgent and important claims to healthcare[13].'

In a press release issued on 26 February 1998, entitled *Keeping Lawyers out of Hospital, Keeping Doctors out-of-courts,* the then Secretary of State for Health, Frank Dobson, expressed great concern about the increase in litigation against doctors and the NHS in general. He stated at a Parliamentary Press Gallery lunch that:

'It is not just the cost of lawyer's fees for doctors, patients and the NHS. The harm goes much wider than that. Doctors spend days in court defending themselves or giving expert evidence and even more time preparing a case. While they are doing that they are not treating patients.'

He condemned defensive medical practices and the litigation culture and expressed his determination to change the system by raising standards and providing apologies to patients when mistakes are made. He emphasised the need to make the new NHS Complaints System work as a viable alternative to litigation and as a means of producing feedback that would in turn improve the quality of healthcare. The figures quoted by the Government are interesting – clinical negligence then cost £200 million a year, and that figure has risen annually since 1998[14]. It had risen to an

---

8   National Health Service and Community Care Act 1990.

9   See the Health and Social Care Act 2001 and the Care Standards Act 2000.

10 See Harpwood, V, *Medical Law Monitor*, March 2001.

11 Chapters Two and Three.

12 Michael Jones argues convincingly that far from draining the NHS of funds unnecessarily, *'from the patients perspective the malpractice "crisis" arises from too few successful claims rather than too many'* in *Medical Malpractice in England and Wales – A Postcard from the Edge* (1996) *European Journal of Health Law*, 109.

13 *BMJ* (1997) 384; 1921.

14 But see Mulcahy, L, *The Challenge of Medical Negligence Claims* in *Law and Medicine, Current Legal Issues*, vol 3, 2000, 81 – 105, where the author argues, on the basis of comprehensive research covering claims in participating areas between 1990 and 1995, that the cost of clinical negligence claims is relatively low in the light of the overall NHS budget. This research preceded the decisions of the Court of Appeal and House of Lords that have led to a rise awards of damages – see Chapter 8.

estimated £4 billion by April 2001 when the Audit Commission produced its report for the year. Both the Department of Health and the Lord Chancellor's Department have been attempting to improve the system. The imbalance between the value of claims and the costs they involve was highlighted by Lord Woolf in his final report[15], and the Civil Procedure Rules contain measures to remedy that situation. The Government hopes that by raising standards and providing high quality healthcare, the volume of litigation will be reduced. The National Institute for Clinical Excellence (NICE) and the Commission for Health Improvement have been given key roles in this process. The NHS Litigation Authority has been proactive in its attempts to improve the litigation process in healthcare negligence cases.

It was rather naive of the Government to presume that in *'being more helpful and responsive to patients when things go wrong'*, as Frank Dobson suggested, there would be fewer claims for negligence. We live in litigious times and the present consumer-orientated climate and complaints culture in healthcare are likely to fuel the drive towards litigation. Although the most recent research[16] indicates that in reality the majority of claims are discontinued (up to 78% in one area studied), and a large number are settled out-of-court (around 14%) at some stage, in successful claims that do reach trial, awards of damages can be very high indeed. A single successful award for brain damage suffered at birth can run into millions of pounds. The publicity given to such awards by the media encourages others to claim. The threat of litigation may be more perceived than real[17], but it is a threat that the Government and healthcare professions cannot afford to ignore, and refuse to be reassured on. It can be no comfort to a doctor practising in a high-risk area of healthcare, such as obstetrics, that application forms for posts ask whether there is a claim pending against the applicant. As Linda Mulcahy points out:

> *'The construction of a shared threat to the profession may well serve to increase professional solidarity and demonstrates how a defence of expertise is accomplished on a broader basis.'*

It is undeniable that there is a funding problem in healthcare. This has exercised the minds of ministers in successive administrations, partly because the money spent on litigation is thought to be parted with unnecessarily. For example, the Conservative Government even considered that NHS immunity from liability under the *Health & Safety at Work Act 1974* should be reintroduced so that hospitals would once again be protected from prosecutions. This was one way in which NHS insurance costs could be reduced and the NHS could save as much as £30m each year. New Labour is threatening innovations to deal with the compensation culture in healthcare following the 2001 general election[18].

State funding for claimants

The majority of claims in clinical negligence cases are still brought with the aid of financial assistance from the state[19]. Legal aid provision for healthcare negligence cases rose from £20.6m in 1992/3 to £50.2m in 1995/96, of which the costs recovered in 1992/3 were £9.4m and in 1995/6 £22m, and the Lord Chancellor, Lord Irvine, in 1998 announced a radical restructuring of the way in which legal actions for personal

---

15   HMSO London 1966, p355.

16   See Mulcahy, L, op cit, fn 12.

17   See Mulcahy, L, op cit, fn 12.

18   See *Times Law Supplement* 22 May 2001.

19   This conclusion was reached by AVMA which found that 90% of cases in the final stage of litigation for clinical negligence were legally aided.

injuries generally were funded. Expressing the view that the legal aid scheme was failing to provide adequate access to justice, he warned that it would be drastically curtailed in favour of a large expansion of the *'no-win, no-fee'* (conditional fee) system, previously introduced in a limited way. If the chance of winning is high, the fee will be lower and vice versa.

Healthcare negligence cases were singled out in the Lord Chancellor's consultation paper (para 3.17) for special consideration. Figures quoted in the paper indicate that the cost to the taxpayer of what were then termed *'medical negligence'* cases which were legally aided in what was described as a *'good year'*, 1996/97, was £27 million. Thirty-two cases recovered more than £500,000, and leaving aside these cases, the average cost was £4,122 to recover £4,107 in damages. In only 17% of the cases was £50 or more recovered by claimants.

The Access to Justice Act 1999 removed the availability of state financial support for most personal injury claims caused by negligence[20], but it was retained for the purposes of clinical negligence claims, for personal injuries caused by trespass (eg where a person is treated against his will) and for claims under the Consumer Protection Act 1987[21]. The 1999 Act replaced the Legal Aid Board with the Legal Services Commission, and established the Community Legal Service and the Criminal Defence Service. The aim is that there should be flexibility in the system. The Legal Services Commission is a public body that has the task of developing the Community Legal Service and allocating funds to priority areas, which it must set at both national and local levels.

Most of the detail concerning state funding[22] of claims is to be found in secondary legislation, as the Act is for the most part an enabling Act. As with the legal aid system, claimants have to satisfy a merits test as well as a means test before they can be eligible for funding assistance. Section 7 of the Act permits funding to be provided only to claimants who can satisfy the financial criteria. Claimants who are under the age of 18 years have their means assessed in their own right, without taking into account the income of their parents, so the vast majority of claimants in this group automatically satisfy the means test. In March 2001 the Lord Chancellor's Department issued a consultation paper suggesting revised eligibility limits for funding civil cases. The proposals in that paper should, if implemented, give a larger number of people access to state funding[23].

When the Access to Justice Act was conceived, liability for costs in funded claims was to be reviewed, and there were plans to allow the success fee and insured premiums in conditional fees to be recovered by claimants in appropriate cases. Referring to the intention to continue funding clinical negligence claims, the Lord Chancellor made the following comment in the House of Lords[24]:

> *'We do, however, intend to do what we can to reduce the high failure rate of these cases. It cannot be right that it is only in as few as 17% of all the cases that are supported by a legal aid certificate that more than £50 is recovered in damages ... I have no doubt that part of the reason the failure rate is so high is that lawyers take these cases without the necessary experience. They are therefore, unable to*

---

20 Funding was retained for personal injury claims in trespass or strict liability torts.

21 There is no funding available for coroners' inquests.

22 Section 8 permits a funding code to be made, taking into account certain factors such as conduct of tbe individual concerned and the public interest.

23 The implementation date is set at 1 October 2001.

24 Hansard (HL) 4 March 1998, cols 1203 and 1204.

make timely, informed decisions on the merits of a case, or whether an offer of settlement is appropriate or reasonable in amount.'

The result has been that since 1 August 1999 there has been a drastic reduction in the number of firms of solicitors[25] permitted to act for clients in receipt of state financial support[26]. This has been achieved by means of restricted franchises so that only solicitors who have sufficient experience and expertise represent clients in clinical negligence cases. Around 200 firms have been approved as suppliers of state funded services for clinical negligence claims, and are official members of the clinical negligence franchise panel[27] under the Legal Aid (Prescribed Panels) Regulations 1999[28]. A community legal Service *'quality mark'* system was launched in April 2000 to reassure the public as to the quality of legal services. Defence solicitors will be aware from the early stages of a claim if the claimant is in receipt of state financial assistance, and as the defence is extremely unlikely to recover costs in a state funded case, there is considerable pressure on defendants to settle such claims.

As Lord Irvine announced when clinical negligence franchising was introduced:

'Restricting these cases to a group of highly competent specialists will give people the best possible chance of resolving disputes successfully[29].'

It appears that the strategy has been successful. Arnold Simanowitz of AVMA reports that there is clear evidence that claimants are now being properly served by solicitors who represent them[30]. Defence solicitors are also reporting that standards have improved among firms representing claimants. However, as so much work is now in the hands of so few firms, solicitors who are excluded from the clinical negligence franchise are unable to gain the experience they need to be realistic competitors for future business.

Conditional fee agreements

It is virtually impossible for the average claimant in a healthcare negligence claim who is not supported by state funding, to proceed without using the conditional fee system[31]. Some far-sighted individuals may have taken out, in advance of being injured, legal claims insurance that covers all types of personal injury litigation, but these are unusual. Conditional fee arrangements have been available since 1995 for personal injuries claims[32]. A conditional fee agreement is:

'An agreement with a person providing advocacy or litigation services which provides for his fees and expenses, or any part of them, to be payable only in specified circumstances.'

These agreements come within the umbrella of the Access to Justice Act 1999 and the Orders made under it[33]. Conditional fee agreements allow a lawyer to enter into an agreement with a client under which the solicitor can demand that if the claim

---

25 Only about 5% survived.

26 Firms not officially approved to undertake state funded work for claimants can take on clinical negligence cases, but claimants are advised to inquire carefully about the expertise and experience of a particular firm before seeking advice from one of its solicitors. AVMA can advise on this matter (see its website) and there are several useful websites for claimants such as *www.medical-accidents.co.uk*

27 Membership of AVMA's approved panel as well as that of the Law Society, can suffice.

28 SI 1999/166.

29 October 1998.

30 *Law Society Gazette*, Vol 97/11, 16 March 2000.

31 See Goldrein I, *Conditional Fees – The Litigator's Highwire Act*, NLJ, 11 October 1996.

32 Now covered by s27 of the Access to Justice Act 1999.

33 Conditional Fee Agreements Order 2000 (2000/823); The Conditional Fee Agreements Regulations 2000 (2000/692); Access to Justice (Membership Organisations) Regulations 2000 (2000/693).

succeeds the client will pay an uplift of up to twice the base fee[34], in the form of a success fee[35]. In fact the Lord Chancellor has approved premiums of up to 25% that can be charged by solicitors. This system means that lawyers are unlikely to take on weak cases, as they wish to be assured of success. If the claim fails the client pays nothing to the solicitor, (sometimes called a *'no-win, no fee'* scheme, but also covering schemes where there are speculative fee agreements or discounts). However, there may be other costs, such as experts' fees, that are payable.

The major difficulty is that if the client loses the claim he must usually meet the legal costs of the opposing party[36] – a rule that helps to ensure that weak cases do not reach trial and spurious defences are not raised[37]. This risk can be covered by an *'after event'* insurance policy[38], but premiums can be very expensive for clinical negligence claims, and not all insurers are willing to provide cover for them. Legal costs for clinical negligence claims can be extremely high and in some instances exceed the value of the claim, though the pursuit of such cases to trial is discouraged by the Civil Procedure Rules. The outcome of clinical negligence cases can be difficult to predict and the market is less lucrative for insurers than the ordinary personal injuries market. Nevertheless some insurance is now available. Robert Owen QC gave an example of a clinical negligence case in which he appeared in 1997 where the client had to pay a premium of £15,000 to cover £100,000 of legal costs. This was an extreme example in an expensive case, and more affordable premiums are currently being quoted[39]. Anecdotal evidence from solicitors indicates that insurers are requiring them to carry out a fairly large percentage of work on a case before they are willing to make a decision about insuring the claimant, and not all firms are prepared to do this[40]. However, since 1 April 1999 both the success fee and the insurance premium have been recoverable from the losing party so that if the claimant wins the case the compensation is untouched.

The Lord Chancellor's Department is anxious to promote the use of conditional fee agreements, and lists what it claims are their benefits[41]. The chief benefit is that these arrangements allow access to justice to more claimants who had previously not had the financial means to support a claim. It is possible that the extension of access to justice is one factor that is responsible for the rise in clinical negligence claims so deplored by the Department of Health, and for which Frank Dobson in 1998 blamed lawyers.

Other sources of funding for claimants

Claimants may be funded by Trade Unions, charities, or legal expenses insurance, but all of these sources are unusual in healthcare negligence claims[42]. Very

---

34 The Policy Studies Institute conducted a survey of conditional fees in 1997 and reported an average uplift of 43% and an almost universal voluntary cap of 25% on the amount of the damages that could be taken as part of the uplift. See Yarrow, S, *The Price of Success – Lawyers, Clients and Conditional Fees*, PSI 1997, cited in Powers, M and Harris, N, *Clinical Negligence* Butterworths, London, 2000 by Barton, D.

35 This scheme is a permitted exception to the ancient rule against *'maintenance and champerty'*.

36 Costs are discretionary but the usual pattern is that the loser pays the costs of the winner, as costs follow the event (Civil Procedure Rules 44.3).

37 In *Hodgson v Imperial Tobacco Company Ltd* [1998] 2 All ER 673 the Court of Appeal held that conditional fee agreements are not contrary to public policy and that lawyers representing clients who lose the claim are not personally liable for costs.

38 Section 29 of the Access to Justice Act 1999 allows a court to include in a costs order the premium paid for *any* insurance policy against the risk of incurring a liability in those proceedings.

39 In 1998 the Lord Chancellor quoted an average fee of £3,000.

40 See *Law Society Gazette*, 2000, Vol 97/11, p27.

41 Access to Justice Act 1999, Provisions Coming Into Effect on 1 April 1999, Lord Chancellor's Department website.

42 However nurses are usually supported by their Trade Union in claims against their employers for injuries and illnesses sustained as a result of their work.

occasionally an independent third party may be prepared to fund a claim for a friend, or as a matter of business. *'Litigation Funding Agreements'* are sometimes available whereby third parties agree to fund litigation and take enhanced repayments from the client if the claim succeeds[43]. Occasionally, barristers and solicitors are prepared to act pro bono, but this is far more common in cases involving social security benefits appeals under the free representation scheme than in clinical negligence cases, which tend to be far more complex and time consuming.

Representative claims

Claimants in private law cases must show that they have a legal right that they seek to enforce as individuals or groups of individuals before they can use the courts. The Legal Services Commission does now have the power to approve funding for a claim under the Community Legal Service if it has a wider public interest, and a means test is applied. Despite this, there are situations in which individuals may not be prepared to pursue a matter themselves, and would prefer an organisation to do so. At present, no other person or group of persons (such as a Consumer Group) is able to test a point of law on behalf of other individuals[44]. The Lord Chancellor's Department is carrying out a consultation[45] on the possibility of allowing responsible representatives of organisations to bring representative claims. The consultation paper states:

> *'There will be some situations, for example, the protection of consumer interests or the rights of members of a group or association, where a representative could usefully pursue court action on behalf of those directly affected.'*

Among such groups could be associations representing patients who have experienced common problems in the context of healthcare, and the consultation paper seeks responses concerning procedural matters and possible remedies on representative actions. The proposals would, if implemented, offer an alternative to the stress of an individual claim in private law for sick and distressed people, and access to justice would be enhanced.

Funding the Defence of Claims

General practitioners and doctors and dentists in private practice

The two defence organisations, the Medical Protection Society and the Medical Defence Union, provide advice and assistance to doctors and dentists who are faced with legal problems. These organisations are companies limited by guarantee and have no share capital. They are not insurance companies. In addition to advising on professional matters involving the GMC, and handling the other services the defence organisations provide, they employ specially trained doctors and lawyers to advise members on clinical negligence matters, and to handle the initial steps in the defence of clinical negligence claims before passing on more complex cases to the firms of solicitors that act for them. They also provide a complete indemnity for costs and damages as long as the premium paid covers the particular situation.

As general medical and dental practitioners are not covered by NHS indemnity, (see later), it is essential that they belong to one of the defence organisations. However, many hospital doctors and dentists also belong to one or other of the organisations, as they offer a range of services beyond the provision of indemnity for

---

43   This is made available under s28 of the Access to Justice Act 1999 as a privately financed contingent litigation support fund.

44   In public law, in judicial review cases the courts are willing to allow access, in an appropriate situation, to anyone with a sufficient interest in a matter.

45   Lord Chancellor's Department, *Representative Claims: Proposed New Procedures*, February 2001.

costs and damages in clinical negligence cases, and cover activities of doctors and dentists outside their normal employment, such as *'Good Samaritan'* medical treatment[46]. They also provide assistance on matters such as complaints, inquests, professional discipline etc that are not necessarily offered by NHS Trusts as employers. Professional and emotional support is given to doctors who are at the centre of clinical negligence claims and who are understandably suffering from stress and anxiety.

Doctors and dentists in independent practice make their own arrangements for professional indemnity, and those who are employed by private clinics are usually required by their contracts of employment to sign an indemnity clause. However, there may still be some private practitioners without indemnity cover. Other healthcare professionals, such as private midwives, need to ensure that they have appropriate professional indemnity arrangements. Subscriptions to the defence organisations are used to ensure that there are adequate funds available to meet current and future claims.

The defence organisations have an important function in the provision of education for their members about potential medico-legal pitfalls, and they also give advice on risk management in healthcare, as well as assistance on how to improve the delivery of healthcare[47].

Prompt action is necessary in the event of a claim, and full cooperation is required of the doctor or dentist who anticipates that a claim may arise, as the Civil Procedure Rules 1998 set strict deadlines on the various early stages of litigation. The aim is to establish the facts and to assess the merits and potential value of the claim, usually with the assistance of clinical experts and solicitors, and later if necessary, counsel. Case committees consisting of staff of the defence organisation, clinical and legal experts, meet regularly to analyse potential claims.

Hospital staff

In 1990 NHS Indemnity was introduced[48], and NHS Trusts became responsible for financing and managing clinical negligence claims arising against their staff within their jurisdiction. This scheme applied to existing claims (pre 1990) as well as to new claims. It did not cover GPs or other staff who are not *'employees'* for the purposes of vicarious liability, nor for work carried out by employees outside their normal contractual duties[49]. The scheme only relates to clinical negligence claims, and does not cover inquests, complaints or professional discipline.

The clinical negligence scheme for trusts

The introduction of NHS indemnity meant that instead of the two defence organisations, there were many more organisations handling clinical negligence claims in the NHS. Control of claims handling was removed, in the secondary care sector, from the clinicians and lawyers working for the defence organisations to Trust managers and their lawyers. Some clinicians felt threatened by this shift in responsibility, as they believed that managers were less likely than the defence organisations to protect the interests of doctors. This resulted in a diffusion of knowledge and a lack of focus and overview of the number and variety of claims that

---

46 See Chapter 2.

47 See Palmer, R, *The UK Medical Protection and Defence Organisations* in Powers, M, and Harris, N, *Clinical Negligence* Butterworths, London 2000.

48 HC(89)34 (1989) Department of Health.

49 eg Good Samaritan acts, voluntary work, independent work and the provision of medico-legal services such as report writing for personal injury claims.

were arising. NHS bodies either employed in-house lawyers or used firms of private solicitors to handle claims for clinical negligence, and fragmentation grew. The new NHS Trusts were responsible for allocating funds for patient care, and for funding the defence of claims and paying damages to successful litigants but they were unable to insure against liability with commercial companies, except in the case of employers' liability and public liability claims. As a result of the concerns of finance directors of NHS Trusts, a working party was established to consider how the rising cost of negligence litigation could best be dealt with by a *'pooling'* arrangement. The Government had discouraged NHS Trusts from using commercial insurance because it was not considered good value for money[50]. The working party took the view that a scheme should be established to create new ways of meeting liabilities[51]. On 1 April 1995 the Clinical Negligence Scheme for Trusts emerged, and was administered for the first three years of its life by the Medical Protection Society. This scheme, which was purely voluntary, offered considerable advantages in terms of mutual indemnity and risk management procedures, and was subscribed to by the majority of NHS Trusts. It offers a mutual assurance scheme, and premiums are calculated in accordance with the types of care offered and the scale of operations of NHS Trusts, combined with its risk management procedures.

The NHS Litigation Authority[52]

The National Health Service Litigation Authority (NHSLA) was established in 1995 as a Special Health Authority under s21(3) of the National Health Service and Community Care Act 1990[53] to ensure that claims against NHS organisations are handled effectively and consistently and to deal with the financial consequences of claims, advising the Department of Health on relevant issues and the likely future cost of claims[54]. Initially the function of the NHSLA was the administration of the Clinical Negligence Scheme for Trusts[55], but its remit grew rapidly and it was given an important responsibility in the administration of the Existing Liabilities Scheme covering claims arising before 1 April 1995 for which central funding is available if specified criteria are met[56]. As part of the initiative under which the quality of claims handling is improved, Trusts must meet certain minimum standards of claims handling before they can take the benefit of the Existing Liabilities Scheme[57]. In addition the NHSLA took over from the Secretary of State for Health responsibility for handling a large number of outstanding claims against the former Regional Health Authorities[58].

Born out of financial necessity and sheer pragmatism, the NHSLA now has important duties that include administering schemes to promote high standards of patient care (risk management schemes) and minimise suffering caused by adverse incidents. It advises the Secretary of State on any changes it considers necessary in

---

50   House of Commons written answer, Hansard, 22nd July 1999.

51   Section 21 of the NHS and Community Care Act 1990.

52   For a comprehensive review of the excellent work being undertaken by this body see Walker, S, and Mead, J in Chapter 8 of Powers, M and Harris, N, *Clinical Negligence* op cit.

53   SI 1995/2800.

54   The National Health Service (Clinical Negligence Scheme) Regulations 1996.

55   In Wales, which has a smaller population, fewer NHS Trusts and more manageable claims, the NHS Risk Pool operates under a different arrangement.

56   Details are to be found in SI 1996/685 and in NHS Circular FDL (95) 56.

57   NHS Circular ELS (96) 11.

58   National Health Service Litigation Authority (Transfer of Liabilities) Order 1996.

the light of its experience[59]. Clearly this body has a unique overview of the quality of care in the NHS in England as well as knowledge of the kinds of complaints and claims that arise on a regular basis. In other words it has the insight previously available to the defence organisations whose responsibilities were reduced in 1990. The NHSLA is likely to have a pivotal role in the development of clinical governance and its relationship with litigation. It had an important part to play in devising the Pre-action Protocol for the Resolution of Clinical Negligence Disputes that accompanied the introduction of the Civil Procedure Rules in April 1999. It reduced the number of solicitors handling the defence of clinical negligence claims and ensures that those that remain are highly efficient[60]. This is part of a continuing role in relation to claims handling. Not only defendants but also claimants have benefited from the fresh and rigorous controls exerted over litigation by the NHSLA, as a pro-active approach is encouraged, and claims that are clearly indefensible are settled as soon as is reasonably possible, apologies and explanations are offered to patients if appropriate, and unnecessary expert reports are not commissioned.

The NHSLA plays a crucial role in relation to the implementation of sound risk management procedures in the NHS, and working in conjunction with its professional advisors, Willis Corroon, it helps to ensure that good practice is encouraged through its risk management manual[61]. Accreditation is necessary for Trusts to obtain a discount on their contributions to the CNST.

The NHSLA is accountable to the Secretary of State and its annual corporate plan is reviewable by him. The NHS chief executive must approve the annual business plan of the NHSLA, and each of these measures is required because of the large amount of public money for which the NHSLA is responsible.

More radical proposals on funding

Developments in relation to funding the growing number of claims have been discussed in this section, with an explanation of the way in which the defence of claims is handled. There are some people who would prefer to see the introduction of an NHS-type legal aid system, with salaried lawyers and a system administered by an independent legal services commission. This radical idea has been mooted for many years but such a system is unlikely to be introduced by this, or indeed, any future Government.

Alternatives to Litigation

The high cost of litigation both to the public purse and to individuals has led to arguments in favour of alternatives to the court system as a means of resolving disputes in clinical negligence cases. Among these are the NHS Complaints System and alternative forms of dispute resolution. One objective of the new NHS Complaints System, in operation since April 1996, is to provide a viable means of dealing with complaints about healthcare including some cases of NHS clinical negligence. This new system was seen as a possible means of reducing the incidence of litigation for clinical negligence. The NHS Complaints System is described in detail in Chapter 11, where consideration is given to the suggestion that the system could offer a suitable alternative to litigation.

---

59   Framework Document NHSE Publication 96 FP 0046.
60   From April 1998 only 18 firms form the panel for dealing with claims.
61   CNST, 1996-7.

Alternative dispute resolution

Various forms of alternative dispute resolution (ADR) in clinical negligence cases have been suggested. According to the Lord Chancellor's discussion paper on alternative dispute resolution published in 1999[62], the term ADR refers to arbitration[63], early neutral evaluation, expert determination, conciliation and mediation. These various options are very different in nature. A proposed arbitration scheme for clinical negligence cases was mooted in 1990, based heavily on the litigation model and this received considerable criticism[64]. It was never implemented. In this chapter, it is proposed to focus on mediation, as that is the preferred option for clinical negligence disputes. This has been encouraged by the Lord Chancellor's Department and suggested by the House of Commons Committee that considered the most appropriate way forward for clinical negligence cases.

Mediation as an alternative to litigation in clinical negligence cases[65]

Lord Woolf recommended in his report on the civil justice system that litigants be encouraged to pursue alternative forms of dispute resolution such as mediation. This view was repeated in the Pre-action Protocol for the Resolution of Clinical Negligence Disputes. He envisaged this being discussed at an early stage in case management, and proposed that judges should discuss mediation as a matter of routine with the parties, seeking to discover why they have not chosen to use alternative forms of dispute resolution.

Healthcare negligence cases do not fall happily into the general run of cases in which mediation is a natural alternative to litigation – there are problems concerning prognosis for example, which mean that some delays are inevitable, and there is heavy reliance on expert witnesses so that there are substantial costs incurred at an early stage in claims. Nevertheless, the House of Commons' Health Committee took the view that mediation had great benefits to offer all those concerned with disputes about clinical negligence and that some form of mediation should be introduced as soon as possible. The report of the Committee[66] defined mediation as:

'A private, confidential and without prejudice process in which a neutral person assists the parties in reaching an agreed resolution. In particular:

(a) The mediator is not a judge or arbitrator and cannot impose a solution on the parties;

(b) The confidential forum allows grievances and problems to be aired face-to-face between the people involved;

(c) The process can address both the legal/facutal issues, and the more personal ones which inevitably feature in such disputes. '

Although both parties to litigation usually engage in negotiation towards settlement at some stage in the pre-trial process, in certain instances they involve the services of a third party. At this point negotiation becomes *mediation.* Mediation was defined by the Lord Chancellor's Department as:

'Negotiation with the assistance of a neutral third party. This is a deliberately wide definition that encompasses non-binding neutral evaluation as well as mediation

---

62   *Alternative Dispute Resolution – A Discussion Paper, 1999.* Lord Chancellor's Department.

63   *Arbitration for Medical Negligence in the National Health Service* DOH 1992.

64   See, for example, Jones, M, *Arbitration for Medical Negligence Claims in the NHS* (1992) 2 PN 142.

65   A leaflet, (MD5), for those interested in pursuing this option in London, can be obtained from the Central London Court's Customer Service Counter, 1st floor, 13, Park Crescent, London W!.

66   *Procedures Relating to Adverse Clinical Incidents and Outcomes in Medical Cases* House of Commons.

in the classic sense. Mediation may be delivered as a free-standing service, or an opportunity to mediate – possibly on court premises – may be built into the litigation process[67].'

Mediation is used most commonly in family cases and in neighbour disputes as well as in commercial cases. The largest mediation organisation is Mediation UK, which has about 2,000 mediators. CEDR (Centre for Dispute Resolution) the organisation assisting with the pilot mediation of some clinical negligence cases, has about 400 mediators of whom over 60% are qualified lawyers. A mediation pilot scheme for clinical negligence was endorsed in 1995 by the Department of Health, but as will be seen, this was not well-received by the legal profession.

The mediator is not a judge and normally acts in a facilitative way, being unable to impose solutions on the parties. Mediation may be purely facilitative, involving a neutral stance by the mediator to allow for a constructive dialogue between the parties, or evaluative, which involves value-judgments by the mediator. This latter type of mediation is not popular with lawyers because they consider that the mediator plays too powerful a role in the process. Mediation of clinical negligence cases must be voluntary, and is only possible if both sides agree to participate. However, the outcome is not binding upon the parties until a contractual situation is reached. The process is confidential, avoiding adverse publicity, and any comments are *'without prejudice'* should the mediation process fail and the claim proceed to trial. The most notable features of mediation are that it is flexible and informal, and it is not subject to rules of evidence and procedure. The psychological stress of a formal trial can be avoided in mediation, and this is especially advantageous to claimants who are ill. Mediation can be much faster than litigation and can take into account personal matters, having at times a cathartic effect. It can also offer the advantage of allowing the parties to remain in control and free to abandon the procedure at any time. Processes that seldom take place during litigation, such as explanations and apologies if appropriate, and face-to-face discussions, can take place in the course of mediation if the parties agree. However, it is significant that the Public Law Project research into the NHS Complaints System indicates that many patients are dissatisfied with the informality of complaints procedures, and this may be one factor accounting for the lack of success of the pilot mediation scheme for clinical negligence recently offered in central England[68].

The benefits of mediation were further identified by the House of Commons Health Committee when it heard evidence about the possibility of extending the use of mediation in clinical negligence cases. The advantages of mediation lie in its speed, and potential cost-savings, the facilitation of early settlement of cases and in the reduction in stress for the claimant and witnesses for the defence. There may be a reduction in costs that is worthwhile to claimants who are not legally aided, and who are genuinely only seeking an explanation and apology plus a small award of damages. Despite these advantages, the process of settlement is arrived at in mediation in a similar way to court proceedings, because expert witnesses are involved and lawyers are paid to represent the parties in many cases. Defendant NHS Trusts are reluctant to pay the £3,500 fee estimated for every day spent mediating and the claimant may not feel that the outcome of the mediation process is satisfactory and may still proceed to a court hearing later.

---

67   Lord Chancellor's Department, Review of Civil Justice and Legal Aid, 24 March 1998, para C4.
68   Mulcahy, L, *Mediating Medical Negligence Claims: An Option for the Futur'*, Norwich, 1999.

The Civil Procedure Rules envisage early communications between the parties and the setting of realistic targets for disclosure of records, together with some consideration as to whether a joint medical expert could be instructed in order to identify the crucial issues in the case. Adversarial attitudes by the solicitors for both sides should be positively discouraged at this early stage, and there was some attempt to introduce mediation as an alternative to litigation in clinical negligence cases as long ago as 1996, when research into mediation in general is being conducted at University College, London. A Pilot Scheme for mediation in general civil claims, has been in place at the Central London County Court since March 1996 for claims over £3,000, but it is difficult to reach any firm conclusion as to whether this method of resolving disputes is likely to be successful in clinical negligence cases, since the majority of the mediations in the London study concern commercial matters.

In clinical negligence cases mediation is seen as a means of saving costs and when it was first mooted, lawyers were somewhat resistant to the idea, especially as it appeared to involve handing over valuable work to a mediator. However, as more lawyers are themselves becoming mediators the advantages of the system over litigation are becoming more obvious. Nevertheless, there are problems emerging from the concept of mediation, not least of which is the need for a proper system of regulation of mediators and those who train them. An expensive short course is sufficient to qualify a professional person to act as a mediator, and there is a growing body of training establishments anxious to provide such courses. Another problem is the fact that there seems to be a need for uniform procedures to apply for the sake of ensuring fairness to both parties to mediation, and this in itself is counter-productive to the concept of mediation.

The Pilot Scheme for clinical negligence mediation based in Anglia, Oxford and in North Yorkshire proved rather disappointing in that the take-up rate was lower than expected. CEDR, the mediation facilitators, blamed the lawyers involved, accusing them of scepticism and ignorance. In a report of a study[69], commissioned by the Department of Health, of mediation of clinical negligence disputes, Linda Mulcahy concluded that for the majority of people who believed that they were the victims of clinical negligence, compensation was not the main priority. The three-year pilot study indicated, in line with the evidence to the Wilson Committee that most claimants are seeking an apology, and an opportunity to discuss their concerns and to meet the members of medical staff face to face. The report concluded that 70% of the claimants who took part in the survey were dissatisfied with the outcome even when they had succeeded in obtaining compensation. These findings are interesting, but in view of the continued increase in litigation ever since the implementation of the Complaints System which does offer complainants precisely the opportunities they say they want, one is led to reflect that the majority of people may not wish to admit, when questioned, that what they really desire is money compensation. It appeared that there was little saved in costs through mediation in the few cases in the pilot scheme.

At present the indications are that mediation is unlikely to offer a popular alternative to litigation in clinical negligence cases, despite Lord Woolf's views. It seems that the complexities of clinical negligence cases, and the range of human emotions involved in them do not readily lend these cases to an informal process of alternative dispute resolution.

---

69   Mulcahy, L, *Mediating Medical Negligence Claims: An Option for the Future*, Norwich 1999.

Procedural Change

Lord Woolf's comprehensive review of the civil justice system[70] at the end of the 1990s led to the introduction of new rules of procedure for the conduct of civil claims. The aims of the review were to improve access to justice, to reduce costs, to reduce unnecessary complexity of procedures and terminology, and to remove unnecessary distinctions of practice and procedure. The review had given special prominence to the problems raised by healthcare claims, and concluded that the pre-existing system failed to meet the needs of litigants in several respects. These were identified as:

- the financial imbalance between costs and damages, especially in lower value claims;
- delays throughout the litigation system;
- the pursuit of unmeritorious claims and weak defences over a long period of time;
- the low success rate for claimants;
- the presence of suspicion between the parties;
- the adversarial nature of proceedings;
- problems arising from the system for using expert witnesses;
- lack of proper training for judges hearing clinical negligence cases;
- the inexperience and lack of expertise of some lawyers acting for claimants.

In general terms, the principles upon which reforms were to be based were as follows:

- the system should be just in its results;
- the operation of the system should be fair to all litigants and cases should be treated alike;
- procedures and costs should be proportionate to the nature of the issues involved;
- the system should be reasonably speedy;
- the system should be understandable to all who use it, including litigants in person;
- the system should be responsive to the needs of litigants;
- there should be certainty in the operation of the system;
- the system should be effective and adequately organised and resourced.

Key to the reforms was the need to introduce greater cooperation between the parties, and a more conciliatory approach to dispute resolution, accompanied in clincial negligence cases by a change of culture designed to remove the mistrust that patients appeared to have for the healthcare professions and doctors in particular. A special pre-action protocol designed specifically to deal with the early stages of litigation in clinical negligence cases was drafted in consultation with lawyers who act regularly for claimants and defendants. This document accompanied the Civil Procedure Rules 1998 when they were implemented in April 1999. It was intended to provide a clear framework for all parties to follow, in order to clarify the issues in dispute before the issue of a claim.

---

70 The review was carried out in a remarkably short space of time and involved wide consultation with lawyers in civil practice. The final report was published in 1996.

The Civil Procedure Rules

The Civil Procedure Rules (CPR), have applied since 26 April 1999 to the conduct of civil cases[71]. The new landscape for civil litigation was intended to have the following characteristics:
- the avoidance of litigation wherever possible;
- more cooperative litigation, with a less adversarial atmosphere;
- less complexity in the procedures;
- a shorter timescale;
- more affordable and predictable costs that are proportionate to the value of the claim;
- parties should be able to conduct their cases on an equal footing, even if one was of more limited financial means than the other.

Simpler, more accessible legal terminology was introduced with the rules, along with the simplified procedures. The changes introduced by the new rules were radical, and will by now be familiar to lawyers handling clinical negligence and general personal injury cases. There is no space here to deal with all the procedures in depth, but some general information about them follows, together with an overview to give non-lawyers some insight into the new system and to the philosophy that underpins the structure. The rules themselves can be found on the Lord Chancellor's Department website, and in specialist publications, which also contain detailed commentaries on the rules[72].

The overriding objective of the new system is to produce *'just outcomes'* of civil cases, and the primary purpose of the new procedures is therefore to ensure that, so far as possible, justice is done. Rule 1.1(1) states:

'These Rules are a new procedural code with the overriding objective of enabling the court to deal with cases justly.'

By rule 1.3 *'the parties are required to help the court to further the overriding objective.'*

The rules are to be interpreted purposively rather than literally, with the aim of achieving the overriding objective. Although they are only rules of procedure, as opposed to substantive law, the new code has inevitably had an impact on the advice given by lawyers about how cases should be handled.

Under the new rules, judges rather than the parties as was the case previously, control the progress of litigation, and in so doing judges must follow, and ensure that the parties also follow, so far as is practicable, the following five basic principles:

(a) to ensure that the parties are on an equal footing;

(b) to save expense;

(c) to deal with cases in ways which are proportionate to the amount of money involved, the importance of the case, the complexity of the issues and the financial positions of the parties, (the principle of proportionality);

(d) to ensure that matters are dealt with fairly and expeditiously;

(e) to allot to each case an appropriate share of the resources of the court, while taking into account the need to allot resources to other cases.

To ensure that contested cases are dealt with quickly and efficiently, there are three separate *'tracks'* or types of proceedings. The small claims track is intended for

---

71   Interim arrangements were put in place for dealing with cases already in the pipeline.
72   eg Blackstone's Civil Court Practice, published annually by Blackstone Press.

cases worth under £5,000, except personal injuries claims, where the limit is £1,000. The fast track is intended for cases between £5,000 and £15,000 (or between £1,000 and £15,000 in personal injuries claims). The multi-track is intended for more complex cases, and includes all claims which are not normally within the small claims or fast tracks, and for other cases which would have been in the fast track but for the fact that the trial will probably last for longer than one day. After a case has been allocated to a particular track, guided by the new rules and their overriding objective, the court takes control over the steps to be followed, in order to deal with matters efficiently.

It is hoped that the new rules, which have been embraced whole-heartedly by the judiciary, but about which some lawyers have expressed rather cynical views[73] will mean that claimants are treated on an equal basis with defendants. Heavy penalties are imposed on lawyers who delay inadvertently, and fail to meet deadlines. There are strict rules about disclosure of documents[74], and punitive interest (up to 10% above base-rate) for defendants who refuse offers that are matched if the case goes to trial. The result could be that in many cases settlements can be arrived at much earlier than previously, and that court hearings will be a last resort. As the matters in issue between the parties will need to be identified early, and as fewer expert witnesses will be used, the entire process should be less expensive and much faster. More detailed discussion about the changing role of expert witnesses can be found later in this chapter.

In addition to the new rules themselves, there are Pre-action Protocols that are also intended to regulate the relationship between the parties. Of particular interest to those concerned with healthcare negligence is the Protocol for the Resolution of Clinical Negligence Disputes[75]. This demands greater openness between opponents, early disclosure of documents, and even early meetings between the parties and their experts to identify and narrow down the issues in dispute. The Protocol was drafted by the Clinical Disputes Forum, an organisation that originated in 1997 during Lord Woolf's review. This body consists of a diverse group of people, among them barristers and solicitors with long experience of acting in clinical negligence cases, client groups – patients' and consumers' representatives, doctors, nurses, dentists, judges, operators and funders of the litigation system, members of the GMC, NHS managers and the Lord Chancellors' Department.

The general aims of the Protocol are *'to maintain/restore the patient/healthcare provider relationship and to resolve as many disputes as possible without litigation.'*

The Protocol, which encourages openness, timeliness and awareness of all options available to both sides, contains details about what should be contained in the letter of claim and response, as well as time limits for achieving the various steps, and recommends that alternatives to litigation, such as mediation, and the NHS complaints system be explored by the parties. The Protocol encourages frankness when it is apparent that there has been a mishap of some kind in the treatment of a patient, and gives detailed information about the steps and time limits for permitting the claimant to have access to health records. It provides general guidance on how a new culture of co-operation may be achieved between the parties, and recommends a timed sequence of measures for all those involved in a clinical negligence case to

---

73   eg Brahams, D, *The Impact of the Civil Procedure Rules on Clinical Negligence Claims*, Medico-Legal Journal, (1999),
      Vol 67, Pt 1. Zander M, The *Woolf Report: Forwards or Backwards for the new Lord Chancellor* (1997) Civil Justice Quarterly 208.

74   Detailed guidelines relating to disclosure are set out in the CPR and protocol.

75   Another protocol dealing with general personal injuries claims was produced at the same time.

follow. Its aim is to resolve disputes in ways that are most appropriate for both parties, to reduce delays and costs and to reduce the need for litigation. One of the interesting features of the protocol is its reference to clinical governance in healthcare. Some of the directions in the protocol are concerned with risk and claims management issues, and this is a reflection of the interests of the Clinical Disputes Forum. In fact much of the document is addressed to claims handlers and risk managers and is at least as important to them as it is for lawyers. For example, the protocol states *'Good Practice Commitments'* for healthcare providers, which include advice about training of staff in healthcare law and dealing with complaints; adverse outcome reporting; a sound approach to clinical governance; good systems for storing and retrieving records; and a proper response to complaints, including the offer of compensation where appropriate. Patients and their advisers are urged to voice their concerns as soon as possible, to consider all options available to them, and to inform their healthcare provider as soon as they are satisfied that the matter has been concluded.

The civil justice reform evaluation

The Lord Chancellor's Department published an evaluation of the operation of the Civil Procedure Rules in March 2001[76]. The key findings in the evaluation report applicable to all types of cases are:

- there has been a drop in the number of claims issued;
- the pre-action protocols are successfully working to promote settlement before the issue of proceedings and to reduce the number of ill-founded claims;
- there are more settlements before the hearing date and fewer at the door of the court;
- part 36 of the CPR (dealing with offers to settle) has been welcomed by interested groups and is leading to early settlements;
- ADR is being used more widely;
- the use of single joint experts has led to a less adversarial culture;
- case management conferences are a crucial factor in reducing the complexity of litigation;
- the time between issue of proceedings and trial has been reduced (except in the case of small claims);
- the number of appeals has fallen sharply;
- it is too soon to obtain adequate evidence about the effect of the CPR on costs.

The evaluation does not single out clinical negligence litigation for special comment, so it is difficult to assess the impact of the reforms on claims arising in the context of healthcare. Much of the evidence in the evaluation report is referred to as *'anecdotal'*, and from a research point of view this is very unhelpful. However, a survey carried out by the Association of Personal Injury Lawyers of its members indicated that 48% *'felt'* that cases had been settled earlier, and 33% of cases had avoided litigation. Joint research has been commissioned by the Law Society and the Civil Justice Council to be carried out by the University of Westminster and the Institute of Advanced Legal Studies to discover the impact of the Pre-action Protocols with particular reference to personal injuries and clinical negligence cases. The report on this is due to be published at the end of 2001.

---

76 *Emerging Findings: An Early Evaluation of the Civil Justice Reforms*, Lord Chancellor's Department, March 2001

The increased use of ADR reported in the evaluation report is not based on systematic research and it is very unlikely, in view of the disappointing response to the pilots for clinical negligence cases, that the general success claimed for ADR is applicable to healthcare cases.

Before any definite measure of success can be claimed for the CPR, it will be necessary to study carefully, when they become available, the findings of various research being conducted by Professor Hazel Genn, by Nottingham Trent University and jointly by the University of Westminster and the Institute of Advanced Legal Studies.

There are some aspects of the CPR that give cause for concern in clinical negligence cases. For example, doctors and their legal representatives are concerned that claims are being settled on the basis of the need for proportionality, or as a business decision by claims managers, when there might have been a viable defence. If the damages payable are likely to be small, the cost of defending a complex clinical negligence claim would undoubtedly be out of proportion to the value of the claim. The CPR discourage litigation of such claims, but doctors believe that such cases are not receiving a fair hearing, and that the overriding objective is not being met. There may also be human rights issues involved. This matter is discussed in Chapter 9.

The use of expert witnesses[77]

Expert witnesses are vital in healthcare negligence cases. Without the advice of an expert in the field of medicine under review in a particular case, lawyers acting for claimants would not easily be able to establish in the early stages whether the case is worth fighting[78]. Experts can advise whether a situation which the patient perceives to involve negligence has the potential for a claim, or whether what is involved is an unfortunate medical accident in which it would be difficult to attribute blame to medical staff, or is merely some unusual side-effect of a particular treatment. Before the Civil Procedure Rules were implemented it was estimated that 10% of cases are abandoned after the first interview a claimant had with a solicitor, and that a further 43% were abandoned after the expert reports have been analysed by the claimant's lawyers. It has also been suggested that 75% of claims are abandoned after the patients' medical notes have been read by their lawyers[79].

As a case progresses, expert witnesses may be involved in examining the claimant and reviewing any new evidence that comes to light. Experts produce reports indicating their views on the evidence when it becomes available, and these may be presented in evidence to the court if the case comes to trial. All of this process is now controlled by the Civil Procedure Rules, which means that the court has an important role in approving experts and the use that is made of them. A related area in which it is becoming increasingly common for medical experts to be used (but without the involvement of the court) is the NHS Complaints System. If a complaint reaches the stage of review by an independent panel, expert assessors will be asked for their views on the incident about which the complaint has been made. If the complaint involves a matter of clinical judgement or practice, experts will be required to comment on it.

---

77   Lord Woolf's Interim Report was followed by an Issues paper on Expert Evidence and then by the Final Report. These documents are an invaluable source of information on the current debate about the use of expert witnesses.

78   Note that for the purposes of obtaining state funding the solicitor acting for the claimant must make a recommendation as to the likely success of the claim on the basis of the medical facts. Some firms employ in-house doctors to assist them in this.

79   Health Service Journal, 16 May 1996.

When Lord Woolf made his report, numerous criticisms had been made of the role of expert witnesses in the adversarial system. He had commented that: *'two major generators of unnecessary cost in civil litigation are uncontrolled discovery and expert evidence.'* It was thought that there was an industry of experts, some of whom were believed to be biased because they were paid for their services by the party instructing them. It was alleged that there was too much scope for expert reports to be tailored to meet the requirements of the case. Some doctors were believed to spend almost as much of their time writing expert reports and giving evidence as they did practising medicine, and Health Minister Frank Dobson expressed his concern at the waste of resources that this meant for the NHS as a whole[80].

The entire system of using expert witnesses was considered to add to the cost and delays of litigation. Lord Woolf expressed the view that the system had the effect of exaggerating the adversarial nature of proceedings to the detriment of the parties, and recommended that unless it was absolutely essential there should be no more than one expert in any speciality. Lord Woolf's Final Report recognised that in healthcare negligence cases there was a need for special arrangements concerning expert witnesses. It was accepted that many claimants had difficulties in finding an expert prepared to act for them, as the majority of experts preferred to act for defendants. The result was that there were long waiting lists for claimant's experts. Lord Woolf had proposed in his Interim Report that the pool of experts be expanded and although this point was not covered in the Final Report, there were proposals at that time to establish better training, and approved Codes of Conduct for expert witnesses, and for building up expert witness directories. These improvements have now been achieved.

Lord Woolf recommended there should be a single expert in straightforward healthcare negligence claims of up to £10,000 confined to issues of quantum, uncontroversial medical issues, and condition and prognosis in simple cases. This, he considered, would reduce the adversarial element. Joint instruction of experts in clinical negligence cases should be agreed between the parties if possible, and cannot be imposed by the court. Lord Woolf's Final Report approved the use of experts' meetings, despite the objections by the legal profession, on the grounds of reducing cost. The legal profession was sceptical about the value of such meetings on the grounds that claimants might not be prepared to accept the findings of experts if they are not made in their presence[81].

The duties of expert witnesses are stated in the Civil Procedure Rules, and it is expected the lawyers instructing experts will acquaint them with and remind them of their duties. Since the implementation of the CPR, the basic rule is that expert evidence is restricted to that which is reasonably required to resolve the proceedings[82] and basic guiding principles are applicable to the use of experts since the introduction of the CPR, starting with the assumption that there should be a single expert acting jointly for both sides if possible[83]. At case management conferences the judge can ask questions about the experts that the parties wish to use. If several disciplines are involved, a single expert is appointed from the lead discipline to prepare a report and annex any other relevant reports to it. No party to the proceedings can call an expert witness or present an expert's report without the

---

80   Press release 26 February 1998.
81   See Chapter 9 on human rights.
82   CPR 35 (1).
83   The parties are jointly and severably liable for payment of the expert.

permission of the court and the court has the power to limit the fee payable to a particular expert and the amount recoverable from the other party in connection with the use of an expert[84]. Under the CPR part 35 the court has power to give directions about expert evidence and no expert may give evidence at a hearing without the permission of the court.

It is expected that the judge and the parties will always consider appointing a single joint expert, and if a party instructs an expert without attempting to agree a single joint expert there is a risk that they may not be allowed the costs of that expert. If there are two experts they should meet to discuss the case and decide what is in issue, and then produce a joint report. The court has a discretion to select an expert if the parties cannot agree, and it has become common practice for courts in each area to hold lists of suitable experts. When experts are instructed all letters that have passed between the parties and all documents relevant to the case should be annexed to the instructions by solicitors acting for the parties.

Training courses are available for experts and all are expected to attend. The emphasis during training is on the duties of expert witnesses spelled out in the CPR, duties that mirror those stated in the *Ikarian Reefer* case[85], and all experts who had attended training courses should have been aware of these even before the CPR were introduced. The most significant statement for the guidance of expert witnesses is as follows:

> *'It is the duty of the expert to help the court in matters involving his expertise, and that duty overrides any obligation to the person from whom instructions are received or by whom the expert is paid[86].'*

Experts' reports should give details of the qualifications of the expert, and should, among other matters, include details of any articles, texts or other literature relied upon in the report. If there is a range of opinions on a particular matter in the report, these should be summarised and the expert should explain why he or she supports one particular view[87]. All experts' reports must be endorsed by a statement of truth which is:

> *'I believe that the facts I have stated in this report and that the opinions I have expressed are correct.'*

The court has the power to impose penalties if an expert's report fails to comply with the provisions of Practice Direction 35 or if experts' reports are not disclosed. There are many important and detailed provisions relating to the use of experts, and these can be found in the Civil Procedure Rules and the relevant Practice Directive. For example, there are rules about the putting of written questions to experts and various time limits that apply. Expert witnesses have the important right to apply to the court for directions if any matter is unclear to them.

The success of the new rules for experts

Although there is still only anecdotal evidence available about the use of experts, solicitors are reporting that they are now tending to rely on lower ranking experts in cases of lower value, and as a result costs are being reduced. It is also reported that fewer experts are being used and that fewer appear in court, as most simply produce written reports.

---

84   CPR 35 (4).
85   [1995] 1 Lloyd's Rep 455.
86   CPR 35 (.3).
87   Practice Direction 35, para 1.

The success of the single joint expert system is confirmed in part by data from the *'Trial Sampler'* but there is some anecdotal evidence that solicitors in some firms tend to use shadow experts as well if there is a single joint expert involved. In clinical negligence cases, the need to have separate experts for each side has been recognised and there is greater flexibility in the use of experts[88].

Some lawyers are concerned because they are not permitted to be present at meetings of experts. There are anecdotal reports that experts are, in some instances, not meeting at all, but simply discuss the issues over the telephone, and effectively decide the outcome of cases between themselves, particularly matters of quantum. It could be argued that there is a human rights issue here – that the parties are being denied the right to a fair trial by the operation of the CPR[89]. In the light of this, the Clinical Disputes Forum, in April 2000, drafted new guidelines that provide:

> *'Unless the lawyers for all parties agree, or the court orders otherwise, lawyers for all parties will attend the discussions of experts. If lawyers do attend such discussions, they should not normally intervene save to answer questions put to them by the experts or advise them on the law[90].'*

It is intended that this guidance be incorporated into the Clinical Negligence Practice Direction and Code of Guidance For experts.

Conclusion

The past decade has been interesting for lawyers. Reforms have been produced with almost unprecedented speed, and many of them were clearly necessary. The passage of time and the results of recently commissioned research will indicate whether the reforms discussed in this chapter have resulted in better access to justice and a fairer and more efficient process of litigation for both claimants and defendants, and whether there is a need for still further reform to parts of the system or comprehensive revision of the entire area. The implementation of the Human Rights Act 1998 could well lead to further developments in the common law, as discussed in earlier chapters.

---

88   See Evaluation of Civil Justice Reforms, Lord Chancellor's Office, op cit.

89   See Chapter 9 entitled *Clinical Negligence and Human Rights.*

90   See *PMILL*, October 2000, Vol 16, No 8.

Chapter 11

A Decade of Change: the Healthcare Context

This chapter deals with changes in the delivery and regulation of healthcare over the past decade and a little more. Almost all the reforms over the 1990's were prompted by financial considerations, but successive Governments have been reluctant to acknowledge this, and have introduced their reforms with rhetoric proclaiming the need to benefit patients and to place them at the centre of the NHS. Some of the changes were prompted by the need to reduce errors and expensive claims arising from them. As a result, risk management has become formalized and is now a central feature of the NHS. The need to reform some aspects of independent healthcare in line with NHS changes became apparent towards the end of the decade and is now in train[1]. New technologies involving telemedicine and computerization of healthcare have facilitated some of the reforms, and *'modernization'* is the buzz word[2] of the new millenium in Government propaganda, through its press releases. Some of the new developments have themselves raised concerns, as they produce legal problems of their own.

Media attention has directed the public to high profile cases such as that of Harold Shipman, the GP convicted of murdering several elderly patients, and whose activities had passed unnoticed for many years. That case is the subject of an inquiry at the time of writing, and other serious cases of multiple malpractice have given rise to public inquiries and internal investigations which have yielded numerous recommendations, some of which are currently in the process of being implemented.

Although the NHS came into being with the National Health Service Act 1946[3], the legislation establishing the modern NHS was the National Health Service Act 1977. Part I of this Act deals with hospital and community care services, and Part II with primary care services, which include all general healthcare services, such as those provided not only by GPs but also by dentists, opticians and pharmacists. Treatment and accommodation is free of charge in the NHS unless charging is allowed for by legislation, for example, for prescriptions[4]. The NHS can also make treatment and accommodation available to private patients, who are charged

---

1   See the measures introduced by The Care Standards Act 2000 and the Health and Social Care Act 2001.

2   The NHS Modernisation Authority is being established to implement changes in New Labour's NHS Plan, published in 2000.

3   See Ham, C, *Health Policy in Britain: the Politics and Organisation of the National Health Service* 3rd ed 1993.

4   See also the Road Traffic (NHS Charges) Act 1999 for a recent example – comment by Leech, C, *Recoupment of NHS Medical Costs – Where Will It End? Health Law*, Dec 1999/Jan 2000, Vol 5, Issue 1, p3.

accordingly[5]. Details of this Act are to be found in the explanatory notes to the Health Act 1990, and in various specialist publications[6].

Funding the NHS has proved an endless problem for all governments since it first came into being. During the 1980s the financial crisis deepened. A solution to this was conceived and proposals were set out in the White Paper *Working for Patients* in 1989[7]. Reforms followed very quickly in the National Health Service and Community Care Act 1990 which created an internal market for the delivery of healthcare within the NHS. Funding would continue to be provided by central Government, and collected through taxation. However, self governing NHS Trusts were created for the purpose of running hospitals, ambulance services and other healthcare provision. Health authorities and larger GP practices (fundholding practices) became the purchasers of healthcare on behalf of patients. Although there was considerable opposition to the notion of a *'market'* for the provision of caring services by the BMA, patients' organisations and others, Margaret Thatcher, then Prime Minister, had been determined to carry through the reforms, and responsibility for their smooth implementation lay with the NHS Management Executive. This system was in operation for some nine years. Certain flaws in the NHS structures established by the 1990 Act became apparent in the course of the decade, and after the defeat of the Conservative Government, rationalization was inevitable, in line with the philosophy of New Labour, the Government in office at the end of the decade. It soon became obvious that the complaints systems operating in the healthcare context were out of step with the new NHS structures, and in 1993 the NHS Complaints Review Committee was established to review the existing systems and recommend changes. The new NHS Complaints System was implemented in 1996.

The NHS Complaints System[8]

The new NHS Complaints System has now been in place for several years, and there have been some attempts to evaluate its operation. The changes to the old system were necessary because the diverse ways of complaining before 1996 were slow, inaccessible and over complex. The old systems had been in place for many years before the NHS reforms introduced in the early 1990s and had not kept pace with the modern consumer orientated approach to healthcare. The NHS Complaints Review Committee (the Wilson Committee) established in 1993 to review the procedures which were then used for dealing with complaints, produced its report *Being Heard* in 1994[7]. The new procedures recommended by the Wilson Committee were designed to embody the principles of *'responsiveness, quality enhancement, cost effectiveness, accessibility, impartiality, simplicity, speed, confidentiality and accountability'*. There followed a consultation period after which the Government's response, *Acting on Complaints* was produced in March 1995[8]. This document contained the Government's proposals for new common procedures for handling all NHS complaints and the implementation date was 1 April 1996. On the same date, the new health authorities came into being under the Health Authorities Act 1995. These bodies were responsible for implementing the single set of procedures designed to cover all NHS complaints.

---

5   Section 65 1977 Act and NHS and Community Care Act 1990, Schedule 2. New Labour plans to expand this provision.

6   Ham, C, op cit.

7   See Ham, C, *Management and Competition in the New NHS* 1995.

8   For a series of articles about the NHS Complaints System, see Harpwood, V, in *Health Law*, October 1999, November 1999 and December 1999/January 2000.

The objectives of the new complaints system

The Wilson Committee hoped that some litigation concerning clinical negligence could be avoided by means of the alternative resolution offered by the NHS Complaints System that it proposed. The objectives of complaints procedures were identified by the Committee as satisfaction and redress for complainants, fairness to the parties involved, improvements in quality *and avoidance of litigation.*

The structure of the new complaints system

The new NHS Complaints System, which applies uniformly throughout the NHS, has three stages. The procedures have been introduced by means of directions and regulations[9], and can be amended from time to time if necessary. All three stages in the complaints system are applicable to all NHS complaints – hospitals, GPs, dentists, pharmacists, opticians, nurses, health visitors, receptionists, ambulance services and so on. All NHS organisations must have broadly the same complaints procedures in place (with some minor variations between primary care organisations and hospital care organisations) and must advertise them prominently, providing full information about how complaints can be made. There is also a Government telephone helpline giving information about the NHS Complaints System[10]. There are very restricted time limits[11] within which complaints must be made, though there is some discretion on the part of NHS organisations to allow complaints to be made outside those limits. Designated complaints officers must be appointed to handle complaints. The system is designed to deal with all types of complaint from the most trivial to the very serious, but there are mechanisms in existence that may be more appropriate than the complaints system for dealing with serious incidents where injury or substantial loss has been sustained. These include litigation, mediation, inquests, Inquiries under the NHS Act 1977, the National Confidential Inquiries, hospital inquiries, and action by the National Institute for Clinical Excellence and the Commission for Health Improvement.

Stage one

The first stage in the NHS Complaints process is local resolution. If a complaint falls within article 7(1) of the Directions (where litigation or disciplinary proceedings appear to be likely) it *must* be referred to the complaints manager. If, after a preliminary investigation, the issue is not resolved, the complaint must be put in writing (by the complainant, his or her representative or an employee of the health body) if that has not already been done. A copy of the complaint must then be sent to any person about whom it is made. The chief executive of the Trust or health authority must respond in writing to all written complaints. If a complaint refers to any matters of clinical judgement then the response must be agreed with the clinicians involved. If the complaint relates to medical care, the response must be agreed by the consultant in charge of the patient's care. Reports should contain a written explanation and if appropriate, an apology, with a statement about what is being done to prevent similar incidents occurring in future, and notification of the right to request an independent review within 28 days. Unless local resolution has been made orally on the spot to the complete satisfaction of the complainant, the response is made in a letter. All complaints should be investigated except where the

---

9   eg SI 1996/702.

10   0800 665544.

11   Normally six months from the date of the event giving rise to the complaint, or six months from the date on which the matter first came to the complainant's attention, as long as that is within12 months of the event. There are also time-limits applicable to the later stages in the system.

complainant states the intention of pursuing a remedy by way of proceedings in a court of law; or where disciplinary proceedings are taken or are being considered. If either of these situations arises after the start of an investigation, it may be discontinued.

Stage two

If the complainant is not satisfied with the local investigation and its outcome, there may be an independent review by a panel, access to which is controlled by a non-executive director of the Trust against which the complaint is made. An independent review must be requested within 28 days from the day on which the result of the first stage investigation was sent to the complainant, or from the date on which the result of conciliation was sent to the complainant. The written request for an Independent Review Panel to be established should be made to the convener, a non-executive director of the Trust or health authority specifically appointed to deal with this matter. That person is in a highly sensitive position, and should be aware of the need to remain impartial. An independent review is not automatic, and is only carried out if the convener considers that a panel should be convened. In order to decide whether to convene a panel, the convener must decide what grievances are still unresolved following the local complaints process. A copy of the complainant's statement must be sent to any practitioner involved. The convener must apply criteria in the directions when determining whether to convene a panel. If a panel is to be convened, the convener decides on its terms of reference. However, the convener may decide that it is more appropriate to consider the complaint again locally, or that the complaint has already been fully and properly dealt with. If the convener does not consider that an Independent Review Panel is necessary the complainant must be advised of the right to approach the Health Service Commissioner.

If there is a *prima facie* case for a disciplinary inquiry in respect of a Trust/health authority employee, or primary care practitioner, the matter should be referred to the appropriate person in the relevant disciplinary body, the Trust, health authority or the police. The convener then ceases to take further action in connection with that particular matter unless and until it is decided that no disciplinary action should be taken. All parties to the complaint must be informed in writing of the convenor's decision and the reasons for it. If the convenor refers the complaint back to the local provider for further local consideration, and the complainant remains dissatisfied, there can be a further referral to the convener to reconsider whether an Independent Review Panel is necessary. Independent Review Panels consist of three members, of whom two are nominated by the Secretary of State from a list of people kept for that purpose. The other member is the convener. If the exercise of clinical judgement is involved, at least two clinical assessors, who are experts with particular knowledge of the area of clinical practice under consideration, must be appointed to advise the panel on clinical matters and to produce a written report. Panels produce a report on their findings. This may contain suggestions for improving the quality of service, and may suggest what other action is appropriate, but it may not contain recommendations about disciplinary proceedings. The chief executive of the Trust must write to the complainant informing him of any action to be taken and advising him of his right to take his complaint to the Health Service Commissioner if he is still not satisfied with the outcome.

Stage three

A final resort if a complainant remains dissatisfied with these avenues, is an application for the matter to be considered by the Health Service Commissioner. Any person with a grievance may complain in writing to the Health Service Commissioner. The grievance must concern some *'injustice or hardship'*, but the Health Service Commissioner only has power to investigate matters if he is satisfied that all the appropriate local avenues (ie stages one and two) for complaining have been exhausted, though he does have power to investigate a matter directly, if in the circumstances it would not be *'reasonable'* to expect local procedures to be invoked or exhausted. There is a one-year time-limit on the Commissioner's jurisdiction, but this can be extended at his discretion. Nevertheless, complaints more than 12 months old are rarely investigated, as it is often difficult to obtain adequate evidence. The Commissioner cannot investigate cases if a legal remedy might be available through the courts or a tribunal, unless he does not consider it reasonable for a legal remedy to be pursued. However, he has a discretion to relax this principle, and has done so on many occasions. Nevertheless, if legal action has already been commenced the Commissioner is not permitted to handle the complaint at all.

An extension to the jurisdiction of the Health Service Commissioner came into effect on 1 June 1995 when the Government's Code of Practice on Openness became operational. Members of the public may complain to the Health Service Commissioner about infringements of the Code of Practice after first complaining to the body or person concerned.

In line with Wilson Committee recommendations there have been several important extensions to the role of the NHS Commissioner, implemented by the Health Service Commissioners (Amendment) Act 1996. The Commissioner now has the power to consider matters of clinical judgement, and has jurisdiction over primary healthcare matters. He must allow the body or person about whom a complaint is made to make comments on the matter, and relevant documents, such as medical records, which have not been produced at an earlier stage, may be obtained by or on behalf of the complainant. Investigations by the Commissioner take place in private and the Commissioner decides on the appropriate procedure in each case. He has the power to allow a person to be represented. Although the investigation is usually informal, the Commissioner has the same powers as the High Court in relation to the attendance and examination of witnesses, and he can require the production of documents. A report of the investigation is sent to the complainant and his or her representative, and to the body or person about which the complaint has been made. If an MP has been involved, he or she must also be given a copy of the report.

The Commissioner can comment upon his findings and make recommendations if a complaint is upheld[12]. He may recommend that a decision of a health body be revised or reconsidered, or that variations in administration be made so that other people do not suffer in a similar way in the future. The Commissioner's decisions are final, unless new evidence is produced, when a new investigation may be undertaken. The Commissioner does not have the power to award compensation, but can recommend that ex gratia payments be made to cover out-of-pocket expenses if these would provide a solution for the complainant.

---

12   These recommendations cover a wide range of matters, such as the need for health bodies to provide better guidance to their employees, to review certain practices and to improve complaints handling generally.

The Commissioner is the final stage[13] for all NHS complaints, and is responsible to Parliament[14]. The Commissioner's annual reports are published and laid before Parliament. He has an overview of the entire complaints system, and in many of these reports there are criticisms about the handling of complaints at lower levels. Section 11 of the 1996 Act provides that information may be disclosed to include disclosure to *'any persons'* whom the Commissioner *'thinks fit'* in the interests of the health and safety of patients. Such persons might include professional regulatory bodies and the Commission for Health Improvement.

Flaws in the NHS complaints system

In January 1998 the first statistics about the NHS Complaints System were published by the Government[15]. It emerged from the figures that only two-thirds of complaints were being resolved at local level within four weeks, suggesting that fewer complainants were receiving satisfaction at local level than had been anticipated by the Wilson Committee, who had heard evidence to the effect that the vast majority of complaints would be satisfactorily dealt with at this early stage. Statistics relating to primary care suggested that more complaints were being rejected by Independent Review Panel conveners than was desirable, though some of these may have fallen into the category of complaints referred back to local level and then resolved. As time has passed, further problems have emerged.

They are as follows:

– lack of uniformity at local level;
– the potential for bias at the independent review stage;
– problems with multi-agency issues where it is difficult to pin-point responsibility;
– the lack of feedback to improve the quality of care;
– the relatively narrow scope of the Health Service Commissioner's jurisdiction;
– the use of the complaints system as a route to litigation.

Local systems

It became apparent at a fairly early stage[16] that there was too much flexibility in the design of the new system, allowing for too many different approaches to complaints handling at local level. The new system had not, it appeared, achieved the uniformity that the Wilson Committee hoped would be possible. It is difficult to assess the way in which the many local procedures are being applied, and for that reason it may never be possible to make a definite judgement about the implementation of the new complaints system. The Public Law project commented on this matter (see below). The full results of the first national NHS survey of patients confirms that patients are not all satisfied with the new complaints system in primary care. The GP patient survey was designed to assist the process of making the NHS more responsive and to assess quality through the patient's eyes. The GP survey was administered as a self-completion questionnaire posted to 100,000 people between October and December 1998. A sample of 1,000 people was randomly selected from the Electoral Registers in each of the 100 health authorities in England, and a questionnaire was

---

13   The Wilson Committee was anxious to avoid legal terms and deliberately chose not to view the Commissioner as an appeal court.
14   For details of the role of the Commissioner see Harpwood, V, *The NHS Commissioner: An Extended Role in the New NHS*, *European Journal of Health Law*, spring 1997.
15   *Handling Complaints: Monitoring the NHS Complaints System in England*, Government Statistical Service, January 1998.
16   See Longley, D, *Complaints After Wilson: Another Case of Too little Too Late*, 5 Med Law Rev, No 2 1997.

posted to each of these 100,000 people. The results are based on over 60,000 completed questionnaires.

The GP survey looked at access, waiting times, communication between patients and GPs, out-of-hours care, competence, and helpfulness, and surveyed 60,000 patients. 11% of respondents said that they had felt like making a complaint at least once in the past 12 months, but in only 1% of cases was a complaint made. Half of the respondents who made a complaint reported that the problem had already been satisfactorily resolved, but for 10% of those involved it was too early to say. In 40% of cases the matter had not been resolved to the patient's satisfaction[17].

Criticisms of independent review

It was clear some time ago that the new system for independent review had the potential to attract the same fundamental criticism as the old system – namely, lack of true independence[18]. Non-executive directors of NHS Trusts and health authorities have the role of screening complaints after local resolution in order to ascertain whether they should proceed to independent review. In certain circumstances this could give rise to a conflict of interest, especially when a complaint concerns service provision or purchasing policy in which the non-executive director could well have been involved. The role of convener might prove too sensitive for a non-executive director. It can be a complex task, because independent review is not automatic, and depends upon consultation between the lay chairperson of the panel and clinical advisers. The NHS guidance leaves considerable scope for discretion on the part of the convener who must also set the terms of the review, and identify the matters to be investigated. Once the panel is convened there is still considerable scope for flexibility in the procedures it decides to adopt and this leaves room for a variety of different approaches, rather than encouraging uniformity. Because the panel is a committee of the health authority or Trust there is a danger of bias towards the organisation concerned[19]. Once the review panel has produced its report, the complainant may use that report as he or she wishes, although it is confidential so far as the Trust or health authority is concerned. Details contained in the report sometimes find their way into press reports, or may be used in the course of litigation if the complainant decides to bring a claim using information that comes to light in the course of independent review. Public Law Project researchers who spent some time evaluating this matter, had serious reservations about the independent review stage.

Multi-agency situations

It was also apparent early in the implementation of the new system, that there were problems arising from the complexities of the situation that can arise when several agencies are involved in a complaint. There are no clear boundaries between the provision of care by health and social services in some cases, and great difficulties can arise when dealing with complaints that relate to a variety of different service providers, even if they are within the NHS purview. This situation is even worse if there are also agencies outside the NHS involved in the complaint. The idea that all are expected to liaise with one another is somewhat naive and it is inevitable that there will be considerable passing of the buck.

---

17   This survey was conducted by an independent consortium led by National Centre for Social Research, with Imperial College and Picker Europe Ltd. The survey is published on the Internet: *http://193.32.28.83/public/nhssurvey.htm*

18   *Health Perspectives: the New NHS Complaints Procedures,* Association of Community Health Councils for England and Wales, 1996.

19   Christensen C, *Complaints Procedures: All Change* (1996) 2 Med Law International 247.

The restricted role of the NHS commissioner

Another source of criticism is that although the role of the NHS Commissioner has been extended to cover primary healthcare and clinical complaints, he is unable to deal with cases unless the particular *'hardship or injustice'* arises as a result of maladministration. Nor can he consider the merits of cases involving administrative failures. Thus he is unable to comment on whether a particular administrative decision was good or bad. He can merely decide it was made within the powers given to the organisation that made the decision.

The NHS complaints system – a route to litigation?[20]

There is some evidence that far from operating as means of avoiding litigation, as the Wilson Committee had hoped, in cases of clinical negligence, the NHS Complaints System is actually being used as a basis for litigation. Even before the new system was instituted, the Wilson Committee noted that procedures similar to those which now operate nationally were in place in Wales, and that the system was not infrequently used as a means of *'fishing'* for evidence that could later be used in litigation. The complaints system certainly has the potential to be used to obtain information with a view to bringing legal claims. Such information would be provided at low cost to the complainant, and could form the basis of a decision whether or not to bring a clinical negligence claim. The Wilson Committee had hoped that the new system would result in a reduction in litigation against the NHS. It was seen as the opportunity to allow complainants to air their grievances without going to court or using expensive legal services. Bearing in mind the recommendations of the Clinical Negligence Protocol it seems that it would be a sensible initial step for the claimant to use the complaints system with a view to settling the grievance, and only if that fails, should there be resort to litigation.

The emerging evidence suggests that the complaints system is being used as a cheap alternative to conventional methods of obtaining information for litigation purposes, and that this practice is being recognised and encouraged by some solicitors. An important indicator of this is a procedure adopted by the Legal Aid Board[21], but since dropped. In some areas of the UK, until recently, Legal Aid certificates were not granted to claimants in clinical negligence cases unless they could demonstrate that they had already exhausted NHS complaints procedures. This prerequisite was in accordance with the Legal Aid Guidelines[22].

For patients who are not assisted by state funding there is an even more compelling reason to seek as much information as possible by using the complaints system. Instructing medical experts to give an initial opinion can prove to be extremely expensive. This expense can be avoided if the matter is investigated via a complaint. Anecdotal evidence from solicitors who act for claimants suggests that they are advising them to make a complaint before deciding whether to proceed with a claim. A simple letter of apology in the earliest stage of the complaints process may admit that certain mistakes have been made and provide sufficient basis for a claim. Alternatively the evidence may suggest that there would be little chance of success. If the complainant is advised by a lawyer not to claim on the basis of a report by the Independent Review Panel, the early investigation has cost very little. If the legal advice is to pursue a claim, valuable information will have been accumulated

---

20   Based on an article by the author in *Health Law*, Dec 99/Jan 2000.
21   Now replaced by the Legal Services Commission.
22   General Council of the Bar, Legal Aid Guidelines, para 2.9 1998.

virtually free of charge. However, if the claim proceeds and the patient loses, he or she may be required to pay the costs of the defendant, which could include the cost of investigating the complaint. Under a scheme proposed by the Law Society, the NHS complaints system would be used as part of a *'mediation'* procedure to provide compensation, in deserving cases, of up to £10,000[23]. Already Independent Review Panels sometimes recommend that payments be made to the complainant, though no figures are suggested. In 1996, even before the Civil Procedure Rules were introduced, Practice Direction 49 asked the parties following the issue of proceedings, whether they had attempted some alternative form of dispute resolution and if they had not, it asked for their reasons[24]. It was hoped that this approach would result in earlier settlement of claims.

There is case law supporting the proposition that NHS bodies can refuse to consider complaints which they suspect are merely *'fishing expeditions'*, leading to litigation[25], and some Trusts and health authorities require complainants to sign a declaration that they do not intend to sue after complaining. Such documents are not legally binding and complainants are entitled to change their minds if they are dissatisfied with the response to a complaint. The case of *Hewlett-Parker v St Georges Healthcare NHS Trust*[26], established that once complaints procedures have begun, it is possible to obtain an order for the disclosure of a complaints file with a view to litigation. The Master had made an order for disclosure, but made no order as to costs. The NHS Trust appealed, and it was held on appeal that it was for the Trust to demonstrate that disclosure was not appropriate at this stage, stating that the vital issue was whether the court be of the opinion that discovery was not necessary either for disposing fairly of the cause or matter or for the saving of costs. The judge was of the view that in order to avoid proceedings it was probably necessary for the claimant's legal advisers to see the complaints file, and that if the file were withheld there could be a delay in any such proceedings. He ordered disclosure on that basis. This case should now be read in the light of the Civil Procedure Rules, but in any event, it does illustrate the importance to the claimant of any documentation held in relation to a complaint.

There are probably only two significant advantages to bringing a claim instead of making a complaint. The first is that the amount of compensation payable is very much higher when the claimant uses the courts. The second is the fact that if the patient does not succeed in a legal claim there is no possibility of an action for defamation by staff of the NHS body against which the claim was brought. Statements made during legal proceedings are absolutely privileged, but statements made in the course of a complaint are only covered by the defence of qualified privilege, which is much more limited in scope.

The cost of defending medical negligence cases and paying damages has led the Government to seek advice from the professions and the public about measures which might reduce the number of claims against the NHS. When the Secretary of State for Health, Frank Dobson, asked for suggestions on this issue,[27] he said:

'I am extremely concerned at the level of litigation affecting the NHS – currently around £200 million a year, and rising. Litigation costs the NHS £235 million in

---

23   See Harpwood V, *The Diplomate*, Vol 4 Number 4 December 1997.

24   RL Turner, Senior Master QBD 1996.

25   *R v Canterbury and Thanet District Health Authority ex parte F and W* [1994] 5 Med LR 132.

26   Unreported, February 1998, noted in *Medical Law Monitor* July 1998, p9.

27   Press release, Department of Health 29 April 1998.

1996/97, an increase of around 17%. Figures from the Medical Defence Union show a similar trend. The number of legal actions against their members has been rising by 15% a year worldwide. Every pound that is spent in the courtroom is a pound not spent on patient care.'

One solution might lie with the NHS Complaints System which can be an effective means of handling smaller claims for compensation along the lines suggested by the Law Society in 1997, through mediation or small claims arbitration[28]. It would indeed be a useful possible alternative to the clinical negligence problem if claimants could be offered compensation through the complaints system. This could only be achieved, however, if the suggestions of the Public Law Project researchers concerning independence and more formal procedures were implemented, (see below).

The involvement of lawyers in the complaints system is precisely what the Wilson Committee had sought to avoid but there is growing evidence of lawyers being involved at all stages in the system and by both sides. Lawyers are acting for NHS bodies at an early stage in the complaints procedures to sift letters of complaint and to identify those that might end in litigation, as well as to draft letters of *'apology'* in terms that do not admit liability.

To discourage litigation it is vital to focus on the positive aspects of the NHS Complaints System, which offers clear advantages over litigation. It provides speedy solutions at a low cost to the complainant, and allows insights into what may have gone wrong which are not always available in the course of litigation, since the vast majority of clinical negligence cases are settled out-of-court and grievances in such cases are never fully aired. Complainants frequently state that they require full explanations and reassurances that mistakes will not be repeated in the future. All of this is possible through the complaints system, which has the added advantage of privacy for both parties. For patients there are many disadvantages to pursuing claims through the court system. Litigation is expensive, conditional fee agreements can be confusing and state funding is only available to the very poorest members of the community. There can often be long delays in the judicial process, even after the implementation of the Civil Justice Rules in 1999, and litigation is a lottery. Obviously, not every complaint lends itself to litigation. Some are trivial and can be dealt with at local level to the complainant's satisfaction. The Public Law Project research report indicates that many complainants would prefer a formal quasi-legal approach to the resolution of their grievances. If rapid resolution of complaints could be combined with formal proceedings and a clearly independent process for dealing with grievances, complainants would be deterred from resorting to legal action, particularly if compensation could be awarded in deserving cases. There could well be real possibilities for establishing a system of compensation through the NHS Complaints System.

The Public Law Project research report[29]

A report published in September 1999 by researchers from the Public Law Project explores some of these areas of concern, but is limited to stages one and two of the NHS Complaints System. The research was funded by the National Lottery Charities Board, and the aim of the project was to evaluate the complaints system only from the perspective of health service users, considering issues of fairness and independence,

---

28   See above fn 9.

29   *Cause for Complaint: An Evaluation of the Effectiveness of the NHS Complaints Procedures*, Public Law Project 1999.

and complainant's satisfaction with procedures and outcomes. The objectives of the research are stated in the report as follows:

- *'To explore and describe current practice in complaints management in all sectors of the health service and at all stages of the procedure.*
- *To identify processes which are working well and efficiently, and those which are proving problematic.*
- *To explore complainants' satisfaction with both the handling and outcome of their handling.*
- *To formulate principles of good practice and recommendations for reform of the procedure so that it is better able to fulfil the needs of users.'*

Data was collected between April 1998 and December 1998, and a combination of qualitative and quantitative research methods were used, including a UK-wide survey of community health councils, and equivalent institutions, a national survey of NHS Trusts and health authority convenors and chairs of independent review boards, and 72 interviews with complainants, NHS personnel and health councils in four UK regions.

The report recognises the value of properly conducted local resolution procedures. The merit of an efficient process for dealing with complaints at this early stage is acknowledged, as it provides the opportunity to defuse confrontational situations by providing prompt satisfaction to complainants, without the need for complex procedures. However a series of weaknesses in the local resolution stage were identified as a result of the research. In particular it fails to recognise the imbalance between the position of power of health professionals and complainants who are challenging them, and it lacks impartiality because of the inherent potential for conflicts of interest in the investigation of complaints by the very organisations about which complaints are made. Local resolution also, in the view of the researchers, fails to provide visible public accountability because it is not open to external scrutiny except that of the NHS Commissioner. This was a real cause for concern in the context of primary care providers, because complaints are directed to the very practitioners who are being criticised. The most serious concerns expressed in the report about local resolution related to cases in which questions were raised about the performance, conduct or competence of NHS professionals where patients were at risk. It was in interviews with complainants that the researchers found several accounts that produced serious disquiet about local resolution, especially as none of the complaints in question had gone further than the local resolution stage. The particular concerns focused on the lack of openness and impartiality in the investigation and the need for remedial action not being taken seriously. Early referral of these serious complaints to an independent investigator process might have proved a satisfactory alternative to local resolution.

The convenor's role gave rise to the most serious concerns about the new NHS Complaints System. In the view of the researchers, a very real problem lies in the potential for bias on the part of the convenor, at a stage in the system when impartiality is critical. Convenors who took part in the survey indicated that they felt it was difficult to be truly independent, and some believed that their problems were even more profound because they were obliged to seek advice from the people who were in a position to influence their judgement. The fact that a lay-chairman of the panel had to be consulted was not seen as a reliable safeguard against the possibility of bias. Some conveners thought that many had not gained sufficient experience in the two-year period of dealing with requests for independent review to enable them to have a good overview of the system. Only 52% of NHS Trust conveners had attended a panel meeting, whereas 91% of health authority conveners had had the opportunity to attend such a meeting because their posts cover a larger population. The need to consult with the lay-chairperson was a cause for delays and for dissatisfaction among complainants. These factors led the researchers to conclude that the role of the convenor is in need of reform or modification.

Surprisingly, the research revealed that a flexible, informal approach to dealing with complaints was not suited to the independent review stage. Complainants do not feel that justice is done to their complaints if there is too much informality. Although the Wilson Committee had concluded that procedural informality was to be essential at all stages of the system, it seems that complainants themselves are in favour of a more legalistic approach, and would prefer a system that inspires confidence in holding the NHS to account for its mistakes and those if its staff. They want formality and visible independence from the body about which the complaint is made. Neutral premises and independence from the staff involved in local resolution would be ideal. Panel members, assessors and convenors expressed a preference for clear standards of conduct for panel inquiries and for more obvious or visible independence to demonstrate that the panel procedures are fair and rigorous.

The Wilson Committee intended that the complaints system would be used to improve the quality of healthcare through a process of feeding back into quality-enhancement. However, the researchers found that many of the complainants were sceptical as to whether their own complaints would have any impact on the quality of services. The report concluded that the use of the complaints system to improve the quality of healthcare was hampered by the fact that there is disorganisation in trusts of the various mechanisms for improving quality – such as audit and risk management. In primary care the problem is greater because of problems in the lack of external monitoring. There was also evidence that some respondents lacked confidence in independent review as a means of achieving improvements in services, as panel recommendations are not enforceable, and there was no external body which is formally charged with the task of monitoring the implementation of panel recommendations. This situation could be remedied through clinical governance.

The complaints procedures deliberately separate complaints process from disciplining of staff, but many complainants felt that this resulted in a lack of accountability. The decline in the number of primary care cases going through disciplinary procedures since the introduction of the new complaints system suggests that staff who might be at fault were not being called to account because of the complaints system. Failings in professional performance may now be dealt with through more informal processes of review and retraining and this does not satisfy complainants, who have now no right to know the detailed outcome of disciplinary procedures. Some complainants thought staff who are in error are *'getting away with it'*.

The main recommendations in the report

- Local resolution could be improved by the implementation of national standards of good practice. Measures should be introduced to improve the speed and efficiency of local resolution.
- The Department of Health should reform local resolution procedures in primary care to enable complaints to be made directly to a person independent of the practice concerned.

- There should be a framework for fast-tracking serious complaints, especially where questions are raised about the conduct or competence of a healthcare professional thought to have put patients' lives or health at risk. An independent person should screen these complaints and decide whether to recommend a formal investigation such as independent review, litigation or professional disciplinary procedures.

- Independent review should be restructured to include independent regional complaints centres to deal with complaints not resolved at local level. Conveners should be completely separate from the organisation about which the complaint is made.

- Panel hearings should have special rules of procedure to ensure that complainants are given fair and open hearings. That guidance, which should be drafted by the Department of Health, should advise that hearings should take place in the presence of both parties unless the complainant objects. Any information and documents relevant to the hearing should be accessible to both parties in advance of the hearing.

- Employment contracts of NHS employees should require them to attend hearings if asked to do so.

- Health authorities should have power to monitor complaints in primary care, and practitioners should be required by their terms of service to submit detailed information about complaints made against them.

- Independent review panels should be able to recommend disciplinary action. Disciplinary procedures should be more open, with complainants receiving full information about the outcome of disciplinary hearings.

- New procedures should be introduced for monitoring the implementation of recommendations made by Independent Review Panels.

- Complainants should be given much more support in the complaints process, and resources should be allocated for this purpose.

Some aspects of the recommendations are very radical, and directly contradict recommendations made by the Wilson Committee, which was anxious to avoid formality and the introduction of quasi-legal procedures into the complaints system. However, in the interests of justice, tried and tested legal procedures cannot be avoided, and it seems that complainants would be reassured by them. The report is very clearly written from the complainant's perspective, and the problems presented in it are, for the most part, those of the consumer. The Government has emphasised that the NHS must be consumer-led, and reforms are likely to be introduced with the complainant in mind[30]. The Public Law Project research was confined to a narrow area of the complaints system and a much more detailed report by the Government is expected on a wider area of the system. Any modifications to the system are likely to be introduced in the light of the Government report as well as that of the Public Law Project.

Complaints in independent healthcare

There have been concerns for some time about inadequate regulation of the independent or private healthcare sector. The regulatory system that applied under the Registered Homes Act 1984 had not kept pace with the developments in healthcare over the two decades since it was implemented, and this had been the

---

30   Available from the Public Law Project, Room E608, Birkbeck College, University of London, Malet Street, London WC1 7HL.

subject of much concern. For example, the Silicone Gel Breast Implant Review Group was anxious for there to be better regulation of advertising and promoting cosmetic surgery, and was in favour of introducing uniform controls over independent clinics offering breast implant services. Until the year 2000 there was no uniform complaints system imposed by statute in the independent sector except in the case of privately financed fertility clinics under the Human Fertilisation and Embryology Act 1990[31]. Nevertheless, there were some independent healthcare providers that did have complaints systems in place, because members of the Independent Healthcare Association have been obliged to do so. Complaints about non-clinical matters were handled by provider organisations, and those about advertising by the Advertising Standards Authority.

Complaints about clinical matters could be dealt with by a health authority investigation or by the GMC, otherwise the only avenue for complaining was by means of litigation. In 1999 the House of Commons Health Committee recommended that all independent healthcare providers should have an obligation to provide clear and accessible information to their customers on all avenues for making complaints. They also recommended that:

'As a statutory condition, the provider organisation should be legally responsible for the investigation of all adverse incidents, including those relating to clinical practice, that take place on its premises, and that full medical records should be available at all times to a clinician nominated by the provider as well as to the patient or patient representative. Each provider should be obliged to name and advertise a complaints manager to whom all complaints should be made[32].'

The Committee also considered the case for having a Health Commissioner for the independent healthcare sector. The idea of extending the role of the NHS Commissioner to the independent sector was ruled out by the Committee and they recommended instead a separate healthcare commissioner who should be accountable to Parliament.

Frank Dobson, the previous Secretary of State, had been reluctant to extend the strict regulation operating in the NHS to the independent sector. The new Secretary of State, Alan Milburn, had no such reservations. The Care Standards Act 2000 makes radical changes to the regulation of the independent healthcare sector, and makes provision for any regulations the minister thinks fit to regulate independent establishments offering healthcare services. Section 22(7)(j) of the Care Standards Act states that such regulations may:

'Make provision requiring arrangements to be made by the person who carries on, or manages, an establishment or agency for dealing with complaints made by or on behalf of those seeking or receiving, any of the services provided in the establishment or by the agency and requiring that person to take steps for publicising the arrangements.'

The Act applies to a wide range of independent care providers, including acute hospitals, including those providing IVF treatment and cosmetic surgery, private doctors, abortion clinics, maternity clinics, private mental health clinics and others. Work to produce regulations and standards is currently proceeding, and a core set of regulations is soon to be published. The National Care Standards Authority is working closely with the Commission for Health Improvement to ensure that standards in the independent sector will be as rigorous as those in the NHS. Draft

---

31   HFEA Code of Practice, 1998, 4th ed.

32   *Regulation of Private and Other Independent Healthcare* (5th Report) 1998-99, HC 281-1.

regulations should be available by the end of April 2001, and these will be the subject of consultation for finalisation in October 2001 and implementation in April 2002.[33]

As part of the process of implementation, the National Care Standards Commission has carried out a detailed consultation with representatives of patients' groups to ascertain what problems exist in the independent sector and how these can best be tackled[34]. A workshop was organised to allow the views and interests of patients and their relatives to be taken into account in the preparation of the consultation document. The workshop brought together representation from a wide range of interests with the objective to identify key issues which participants wanted the Department of Health to address through the development of the standards in order to make a real difference to people using the services of independent healthcare providers.

One of the priority areas identified in the workshop was the establishing of complaints procedures in independent healthcare. Some providers have no complaint procedures, and of those that do, most are deficient and unhelpful. There are very few ways in which patients can air their views with an absence of procedures to encourage and protect *'whistle blowers'*. It appears that complaints are frequently met by threatening responses from insurance companies, medical defence organisations and large private providers. There are many alleged instances of falsifying patient notes and records. There were few good advocacy services for patients, who have difficulty gaining access to independent healthcare settings.

One solution suggested was that there should be greater transparency in relation to complaints. It should not be acceptable for providers and insurance companies to conceal from the public on the grounds of commercial confidentiality, information relating to performance, complaints, untoward incidents, suicides and other deaths. Performance data required of independent healthcare providers should be comparable with that required in the NHS and should include data relating to the performance of consultants, whether or not the independent provider directly employs them. There should be procedures for the genuine and on-going involvement of patients and carers in clinical governance – possibly through complaints procedures, as in the NHS.

Information packs should be made available to all patients which explain the range of treatments and interventions undertaken by the service, condition specific information, risks associated with the prescribed treatment, fees charged and what they cover and how to complain[35]. Information should be available in suitable formats, eg appropriate languages, Braille, audio or explanation.

The new standards for independent healthcare should require providers to operate an uncomplicated, accessible and transparent complaints procedure. The procedure must include the early involvement of an independent statutory procedure, lay involvement or advocacy, and a right of access to medical records for complainants and to a second opinion. The procedure should include the means of dealing with the liability of consultants and include a mechanism to deal with cross-sector complaints. Standards should be put in place to ensure that complainants cannot be victimised by the provider or the healthcare staff who work within the service, by insurance companies or by medical defence organisations.

---

33   See *Regulating Private and Voluntary Healthcare: Developing The Way Forward*, Department of Health 2000.

34   See DOH website publication *National Minimum Standards for Independent Healthcare*, Patients Workshop December 2000.

35   The Patient Information Leaflet drafted for people contemplating silicone gel breast implants contains information such as this.

Independent advocacy groups should be developed within each locality through fees levied by the National Care Standards Commission (to include insurance advocacy). These groups should provide a direct service to individuals and their carers as well as providing advice and support to other organisations as appropriate. Advocacy groups should involve patients in monitoring the quality and effectiveness of services and in the development of new services applying for registration.

Patients should be provided with information about procedures and referral to the National Care Standards Commission if the complainant remains dissatisfied, or if the patient does not have faith in the provider to deal with the complaint. Providers should keep records of all complaints, and details of any investigations and action taken. Arrangements must be in place to have this record checked every three months by a senior manager not based within the service.

Effective quality monitoring systems must be instituted to audit and review complaints and untoward incidents. Quality monitoring should include feedback from service users through, eg user satisfaction questionnaires and discharge interviews, and evidence from records. An annual report will be produced setting out the number and the nature of complaints and untoward incidents, together with an indication of action taken, and to be taken.

These developments are an important step forward for patients in the independent sector, and if the recommendations are implemented patients will receive an immediate benefit. Clearly the independent healthcare sector must act quickly to ensure that there are sound complaints procedures in place. The sector is currently consulting the BMA on this matter and it is hoped that independent healthcare sector complaints systems, with the benefit of hindsight, will avoid the pitfall of the NHS Complaints System. A Code of Practice has been produced by the IHA, and is being piloted at present with the intention of a full review being held in 2001. A working group of members of the Clinical Disputes Forum, the body that has been very active in relation to the drafting and implementation of the Protocol for the Resolution of Clinical negligence Disputes (see Chapter 10) has been involved in this process.

Healthcare Reforms at the End of the Millennium

The White Paper, *The New NHS: Modern Dependable*[36], published in October 1997, stated the new Government's intentions for the rationalisation and modernisation of the framework for the delivery of healthcare. The proposals were of major importance for the delivery of healthcare and for the legal framework within which the National Health Service operates into the beginning of the present century. There was much rather unsubtle political rhetoric in the White Paper. Both the foreword by the Prime Minister and the White Paper itself use dramatic language relating back to the creation of the NHS and to its *'historic principle'*, to modernisation and sweeping away *'wasteful and bureaucratic'* competition. However, the reality was that the New Labour Government, like those before it, had the problem of reconciling increasing demands for healthcare with finite resources, and much of the proposed change was concerned with how this need was to be addressed.

In some ways, leaving aside the question of control and regulation, the changes that were proposed by the Conservative Government in *Working For Patients*[37] which had been implemented during the 1990s were far more radical than any proposed in the White Paper. The New Labour Government freely acknowledged that it intended to

---

36   (1997) Cmnd 3807.
37   DOH 1989.

build upon much that had already been set in place by the previous administration, retaining what it regarded as successful aspects and rejecting or modifying those which had not proved successful or which have created manifest inequalities in the delivery of healthcare. Most prominent among these proposed changes was the abolition of GP fund holding that had resulted in some patients receiving quicker and/or more effective treatment than others. Nevertheless, a certain amount of *'modernisation'* was found in the proposals to justify the title of the *'New NHS'*. These features includes the concept of a 24-hour telephone helpline, improved cancer services, and an end to GP fundholding. However, the notion that there would no longer be a *'market'* in healthcare was somewhat misleading. There are still organisations that commission services and other that provide them, and to some extent there will still be competition, since even when Primary Care Trusts work in partnership with NHS Trusts there will be an element of bargaining involved in that process. Healthcare provision will inevitably continue to be *'rationed'* because resources will always be limited and difficult decisions have to be made about prioritising treatment. The mechanisms for containing the unwieldy drug budget outlined in the White Paper and subsequently enacted, are ingenious, and allow for diversion of blame away from the Government for unpopular decisions on rationing.

Accountability and monitoring, which should have the effect of reducing errors and therefore the number of claims, was an important issue addressed in the White Paper, though it did not receive much attention in the popular press. The White Paper and subsequently the Health Act 1999, are greatly concerned with imposing control over healthcare practice through monitoring and regulation. The education system operating in state funded schools and colleges in the UK was already, by 1997, subject to a task force which could move in to solve serious problems of quality and/or efficiency in particular institutions. It appeared that healthcare institutions would, when the Act was implemented, receive similar treatment as a last resort through the operation of the Commission for Health Improvement. There would also be clear sanctions when performance and efficiency were substandard. An important development for lawyers was the emphasis which the White Paper placed on the development of national standards and guidelines through National Service Frameworks which aimed to standardise access to services and quality of care nationally, and through the National Institute for Clinical Excellence, responsible for providing guidelines based on clinical effectiveness. The proliferation of clinical guidelines has the potential for giving the courts clear indications as to what standard of care can be expected in relation to particular treatments. The question of the likely impact of guidelines on clinical negligence litigation has been covered in Chapter 3 and will be discussed again later.

Most of the proposals in the White Paper came to fruition when the Health Act 1999 was implemented. This Act has done more than simply introduce new structures for the delivery of healthcare. It has created and formalized a new culture and way of life within which regulation and accountability have become part of professional practice for healthcare professionals and those responsible for employing and supervising them. The Secretary of State for Health, then Frank Dobson, announced what he described as *'a new phase in the modernisation of the NHS'*, when the Health Act 1999 received Royal Assent on June 30th 1999. Summarising what the Government believes is important about the Act, he said:

> *'The new law we are introducing in the Health Act will sweep away the era of competition and two-tierism in the NHS and replace it with co-operation and quality. The Health Act 1999 gives us many of the tools we need to do the job. As*

well as developing new services, we also want to ensure that the care people receive is of the highest quality – no matter where they live. For some treatments, standards vary unacceptably across the country. That's why the new Health Act establishes a tough new watchdog for monitoring and improving quality – the Commission for Health Improvement. The Government and the NHS will work with the health professions to raise standards and make sure that poor quality services are dealt with quickly and efficiently'.

GP fundholding was abolished by the Act because this was perceived to be one of the reasons for inequality of treatment in the NHS, and the first primary care trusts came into being in April 2000. These bodies herald the introduction of new primary and community care services, including greater use of day surgery in health centres close to people's homes, *'joined up'* healthcare offering treatment and advice, together with services such as physiotherapy and chiropody. There is provision in the Act for partnerships between NHS organisations, and health authorities, special health authorities, primary care trusts and NHS Trusts have a duty under the Act[38] to cooperate with one another. There is now the potential for all-encompassing health partnerships, such as GPs teamed up with dentists, opticians and pharmacists to provide a complete package of health services. This was envisaged as one way of rationalising services and doing away with competition between them. To achieve this there are new arrangements for funding. The funding arrangements between local authorities and NHS bodies have been simplified by ss30 and 31 of the Act.

The controls imposed by the Health Act 1999 will have an impact on areas of care outside the traditional scope of the NHS. The duty of partnership between local authorities and health bodies found in the National Health Service Act 1977, is extended by the Act. The concept of partnership is extended to a duty to secure and advance the health and welfare of the population, and cooperation is required in the commissioning of healthcare, in its delivery, and in strategic planning. This includes areas such as housing, education, environment and social services. There will be a statutory requirement for all health authorities to plan for improving health and healthcare provision for people living in their areas, and a duty for primary care trusts, NHS Trusts and local authorities to take part in this planning exercise[39]. Although each area is expected to develop specialised local plans for health improvement, involving local communities, voluntary bodies, employers, educational establishments etc, the Secretary of State has the power to issue directions which will ensure that effective programmes can be set in place. Provision is also made for health authorities and primary care trusts to transfer monies for health-related purposes to local authorities, for social services, education and housing functions as part of the concept of partnership. There are detailed provisions for the removal of barriers between the various agencies allowing them to pool resources and staff to develop flexible packages of care for particular individuals in need of special kinds of care.

The underlying agenda

Part of the agenda in the Health Act is concerned with controlling the drug budget and dealing with the rising tide of clinical negligence litigation. The Government, through CHI and its partner the National Institute for Clinical Excellence (NICE), established separately by statutory instrument, is attempting to solve these deeply entrenched problems within the NHS.

---

38 Section 26.
39 The Health and Social Care Act 2001 furthers the partnership and develops the potential for public/private care partnerships.

Quality of healthcare

Perhaps the most significant changes introduced by the Act are those dealing with quality and the monitoring of standards in the NHS, which it is hoped will reduce errors and consequent litigation. NHS organisations are now subject to a duty of quality. Section 18(1) states:

> 'It shall be the duty of each health authority, primary care trust and NHS Trust to put and keep in place arrangements for the purpose of monitoring and improving the quality of healthcare which it provides to individuals.'

By s18(3) the Secretary of State may make regulations to extend the duty in this section to special health authorities of any description. By introducing 'Clinical Governance', health authorities, NHS Trusts and primary care trusts are expected to strive to improve the standards of healthcare they provide. Clinical governance should help to ensure that hospitals and other NHS organisations have adequate processes to identify and deal with shortcomings. Clinical governance is defined as:

> 'A framework through which NHS organisations are accountable for continuously improving the quality of their services and safeguarding high standards of care by creating an environment in which excellence in clinical care will flourish'[40].

In the context of healthcare, clinical governance, a risk management system, draws upon business and corporate governance and applies similar principles to the regulation of clinical teams and the management of healthcare services. The word 'governance' is defined in the same context as 'the control and direction of behaviour, with authority'. Clinical governance is both pervasive and structured, imposing monitoring regimes and a framework of accountability, which it is impossible for doctors to evade without incurring penalties for themselves or their organisations.

The requirements of clinical governance, as described by the Institute of Health Service Management, are:

i) The establishing of clear lines of responsibility and accountability for the entire system of care. Chief executives of each NHS Trust have responsibility for ensuring quality of services in their organisations, and a senior clinician will be responsible for establishing systems of clinical governance and ensuring that they are continuously monitored.

ii) The implementation of a comprehensive programme to improve quality in healthcare. Measures include clinical audit, the use of evidence-based medicine, and the implementation of evidence-based clinical guidelines. Participation by all hospital doctors in audit, and in the National Confidential Enquiries will be required, together with the routine application of clinical standards and guidelines which are evidence-based and effectively monitored. Continuing professional development through education, training and updating is routine as part of the package.

iii) The setting up of risk management systems and practical means of identifying and remedying poor performance of healthcare staff. This is a new departure for the NHS and has been facilitated by the GMC[41] in its advice to doctors, and by the Public Interest Disclosure Act 1998.

---

40 *A First Class Service: Quality in the New NHS,* 1998 White Paper.
41 *Duties of a Doctor,* 2000 GMC.

The Department of Health states as the official view that clinical governance is necessary to overcome regional variations in the quality of healthcare throughout the UK, and to prevent healthcare which is *'inappropriate'*. The Government was not satisfied with the level of accountability achieved by pre-existing audit systems, and sees the introduction of a statutory duty of quality as a means of overcoming the problems.

The central concept in the new regime is the standardisation of the quality of NHS care, so that patients should be assured of the same quality of treatment wherever they live. Part of this process is the standardisation of the availability of medicines and an end to *'post code prescribing'*. It is one function of the National Institute for Clinical Excellence, (NICE) to develop the standardisation of treatments throughout the UK.

The National Institute for Clinical Excellence

The National Institute for Clinical Excellence was established by statutory instrument to implement the reforms in the Act. Its three main functions are the appraisal of new and existing health technologies, the development of clinical guidelines, and the promotion of clinical audit and the National Confidential Inquiries.

NICE is a special health authority with direct responsibility to the Secretary of State for Health. It is the mechanism by which standards are set, targeting specific areas of healthcare, using panels of experts drafting guidelines on specified areas of clinical practice. It is a shell organisation that commissions specialists to undertake specific research and produce evidence-based guidelines on the most appropriate treatments for a range of medical conditions. On the basis of this information, NICE advises the Government on the clinical and cost effectiveness of new and existing health technologies, including medicines, diagnostic tests, and surgical procedures. Modern information technology allows details of innovation to be disseminated quickly and effectively, helping to ensure that all health professionals have guidelines available on treatments in particular areas of healthcare.

NICE has already been engaged in the appraisal of a variety of treatments, and its advice has been accepted by the Government in relation to the drugs Viagra and Relenza. The programme to be followed by NICE is announced annually in December. The latest programme (December 2000) includes the brief to produce clinical guidelines which will assist in the treatment of a range of health problems including heart disease, infection control, eating disorders and asthma. It will also appraise the effectiveness of individual treatments for conditions such as arthritis and schizophrenia. It will evaluate smoking control drugs, prophylaxis for pregnant women, Infliximab for Crohn's disease and rheumatoid arthritis, and growth hormone replacement drugs. NICE will develop specific guidelines for heart failure, eating disorders, depression, Caesarean section, asthma care, management of common medical emergencies in primary care, healthcare associated infection and head injury. Additional tasks are also given to NICE from time to time. For example, it has recently been asked to evaluate the clinical and cost-effectiveness of a range of new drugs and treatments currently being used in different parts of the NHS. Their reports will enable a decision to be made as to whether these treatments should be widely available in the NHS as opposed to just certain areas of the health service which have opted to use certain drugs and therapies. The treatments to be appraised are the drug STI-571 for chronic myeloid leukaemia, Caelyx for ovarian cancer, *'clot-busting'* drugs for heart attacks, surgical treatments for obesity, computerised cognitive behaviour therapy for depression and anxiety, photodynamic therapy for age-related macular degeneration, hip resurfacing for younger patients or more active patients with hip disease and ultrasonic devices for locating veins so patients can be fed intravenously or injected. NICE will also consider whether the rheumatoid arthritis drug, etanercept, should be made available on the NHS for children[42].

The object of these and other evaluations is to end the so-called *'post-code'* prescribing lottery. However, NICE as a public body is subject to the Human Rights Act 1998, and must not act in a manner that is incompatible with the rights in the European Convention on Human Rights. It might be open to an individual who considered that a recommendation by NICE denied him the right to life-saving treatment, to bring a challenge under the Act – see Chapter 9.

Evidence-based medicine: standards and guidelines
In keeping with the spirit of the Health Act 1999 and the role of NICE is the trend in medical practice towards greater emphasis on evidence-based medicine as a means of ensuring that high standards are maintained and patients receive the best quality of treatment available within the limit of the resources allocated to healthcare. Sound medical practice based on well-researched evidence, and widely disseminated by means of authoritative guidelines should inevitably lead to higher standards of patient care. Theoretically, this might reduce the number of legal claims against doctors. The result has been the development of protocols and guidelines for use throughout medical practice. However, guidelines have been drafted for doctors for many years and have been proliferating rapidly since the official introduction of audit in 1990. What is still more important is that the Health Act 1999 promotes this process further and that the guidelines produced by NICE have the potential for clarifying and simplifying litigation by acting as objective standards for the purposes of determining whether there has been a breach of duty in healthcare negligence cases.

The focus for legal analysis of the standard of care in clinical negligence is the House of Lords' decision in *Bolitho v City and Hackney Health Authority*[43] which indicates a greater willingness than previously on the part of our judges to accept a more objective approach to the standard of care required of doctors, based on logic and principles of risk management. As explained in Chapter 3, guidelines commissioned by NICE have the potential to determine the standard of care required of healthcare professionals for the purpose of clinical negligence litigation. Solicitors advising claimants obtain and use guidelines in order to assess the strength of claims and defendants are more ready to settle claims if the doctor or other healthcare professional concerned has failed to follow professional guidelines without giving good reason[44]. The status of guidelines varies according to their provenance[45] and guidelines issued by NICE are very close to the top of the hierarchy. It is likely that they will be taken very seriously in the course of litigation because they will define the standard of care in clinical practice in an objective,

---

42   The Government has announced that soon after each NICE appraisal has been published there will be monitoring to track progress of implementation.

43   (1997) 39 BMLR 1. See Chapter 3.

44   See Harpwood, V, *NHS Reform, Audit, Protocols and the Standard of Care in Medical Negligence* (1994) 1 Med Law International, 241-59, Harpwood, V, *The Manipulation of Medical Practice* in *Law and Medicine* Current Legal Issues, op cit; and Teff, H, *Clinical Guidelines, Negligence and Medical Practice* in *Law and Medicine* Current Legal Issues, ed Freeman, M, and Lewis, A, OUP 2000.

45   See Harpwood, V, in *Medical Negligence and Clinical risk: Trends and Developments 1998* Monitor Press, Chapter 9.

logical and rational way. These guidelines are likely to be more reliable than the expert evidence produced in individual cases because they are drafted by the most expert clinicians in each field without the encumbrance of knowing the facts of any individual case where there is a dispute in existence. Under the operation of the Civil Procedure Rules, when experts meet to discuss the evidence at the pre-trial stage, NICE guidelines are likely to be on the table. Sir Michael Rawlins, Chairman of NICE, stated recently[46], that *'NICE guidelines are likely to constitute a reasonable body of medical opinion'*, and that doctors who do not follow them would be wise to record their reasons for divergence. The impact of clincial guidelines has been the subject of speculation for some time, and there are already examples of courts using official guidelines to measure the standard of care[47].

The partner of NICE, the Social Care Institute for Excellence (SCIE) is to be established in the summer of 2001. SCIE is intended to play a key role in raising the standard of social care provision throughout England and Wales. A sum £2 million has been allocated to help establish SCIE this year. SCIE will create a knowledge base of achievable standards in social care and that information will be made available to managers, practitioners and users. It will review research and practice to provide a database of information on methods proven to be effective in social care practice. Like NICE in the context of healthcare, it will use that information to produce guidelines on realistic and achievable best practice. These in turn, will be disseminated across the sector and will be readily accessible to the staff who actually deliver the services. SCIE will help staff implement best practice, ensuring they are equipped with both the knowledge and support needed to bring about an improvement in services offered. The guidelines will feed into the standards set by the Social Services Inspectorate, and ultimately those produced by the General Social Care Council and the National Care Standards Commission, to monitor performance. This will mean users can then be confident that the services they receive have been tested against the best and most up-to-date knowledge in social care. SCIE will also promote the health and social care partnership agenda through its work with NICE and other organisations in the healthcare sector. The creation of SCIE was announced in the Government's Quality Strategy for Social Care in August 2000.

The Commission for Health Improvement

The Commission for Health Improvement (CHI), was established by s19 of the Health Act, and began its work programme in April 2000. The functions of CHI are spelled out in s20. The main functions of CHI are:

- To provide national leadership and develop the principles of clinical governance.
- To provide advice and information on monitoring arrangements and improvements in healthcare.
- To review the implementation of National Service Frameworks and guidance issued by NICE.
- To investigate, advise and report on specific matters concerning the management of healthcare and its delivery, and on clinical problems.
- To conduct national reviews of particular kinds of healthcare.

---

46   Pulse, 29 May 1999.
47   See Chapter 3.

The Commission for Health Improvement has power to visit every hospital to ensure that these standards are being met.

The Secretary of State has the power to draw the attention of health service bodies to advice given by the Commission. If necessary, he may require them to act on that advice. The Secretary of State is able to direct the Commission to deal with specific issues of concern. CHI has oversight of the entire quality system in the NHS, and checks that local systems for monitoring the quality of healthcare are working satisfactorily. The Commission is accountable to the Government through Parliament, and is required to produce an annual report. It falls within the jurisdiction of the Parliamentary Commissioner for Administration. The role of CHI is advisory, but it must also ensure that the statutory duty of quality is adhered to, review the implementation of National Service Frameworks, and investigate and report where shortfalls in standards occur. For example, s20(1)(d) states that one function of CHI is that of:

> *'Conducting reviews of, and making reports on, the management, provision or quality of, or access to or availability of particular types of healthcare for which NHS bodies or service providers have responsibility.'*

The Secretary of State has wide powers to make regulations in connection with the exercise of CHI's functions, and to give directions concerning the exercise of any of them. Section 21 of the Act allows for CHI to request the Audit Commission to join in the exercise of its functions.

The Secretary of State (s21) can make provision for CHI to have comprehensive powers to enter premises, seize, inspect and copy documents. The Secretary of State also has the power to require individuals to produce documents and reports and give explanations to CHI in certain circumstances. Anyone obstructing CHI[48] or failing to comply with requirements under the Act is guilty of a criminal offence triable by magistrates[49]. CHI has reported on specific issues of concern raised by recent events such as the employment of Rodney Elwood as a locum consultant when he was clearly incompetent to practice in the UK. CHI has also reported on the events surrounding the removal of a healthy kidney from a patient by mistake.

The results of the first routine inspections by CHI have been welcomed by the Government as *'progress towards patient protection'*. The reports give the results of three pilot reviews carried out by CHI at hospitals in Southampton, North Derbyshire and Sunderland, and are the beginning of a comprehensive programme of inspections during which CHI will be visiting every hospital and primary care trust in England and Wales within the next four years. The results are available to the public. The reports by CHI were described by a Government spokesman as *'independent, rigorous, challenging and fair'*, and showing strengths and weaknesses at all three trusts. The emphasis is on the so-called *'new culture'*, which the Government claims does not involve naming and shaming, but which represents a new regime of openness in the NHS. Inspections were carried out by multi-disciplinary teams including doctors, nurses, health professionals and lay members[50].

---

48   Section 23.
49   The Act also contains provision for the protection of certain confidential information identifying individuals – s24.
50   The Care Standards Commission undertakes a similar role in relation to the independent sector.

Dealing with fraud in the NHS

The Health Act 1999 also introduced measures to deal with fraud in the NHS including a new financial penalty charge, and a criminal offence of evading NHS charges such as the prescription charge. One hundred and fifty million pounds is lost every year in England by people evading NHS charges. In addition new powers will be given to the NHS tribunal to tackle fraud. An anti fraud helpline has been established.

Regulation of the professions

The Health Act promotes greater opportunity to update the legislation governing the regulation of the healthcare and associated professions. The Government wants to work with the professions to modernise and strengthen professional self-regulation. The Act provides a procedure that will enable the existing Acts regulating professions to be amended and new professions to be regulated more easily, without the need for an Act of Parliament each time. This is being achieved by Statutory Instrument. Further measures to reform the present system of regulation might be recommended by the inquiry being chaired by Professor Ian Kennedy when it produces its report of the inquiry into the deaths of children at the cardiac unit of the Bristol Royal Infirmary. The Health and Social Care Act, which received the Royal Assent in May 2001, provides for changes in professional regulation relating to GPs and other primary care practitioners[51].

Responses to the Health Act

Although it was generally recognised that there should be uniformity of treatment and high quality of care throughout the NHS, there were some doubts expressed about imposing a system of governance, which was originally applied to business, to the NHS. Moreover, some doctors believe that their clinical autonomy is threatened by the introduction of the clinical guidelines approved by NICE[52]. The Annual BMA Conference, which was in session when the Health Act 1999 received the Royal Assent, did not greet the legislation with unqualified approval, though the need for quality systems was acknowledged. Doctors believe that proper funding and planning for clinical governance are essential, and that implementation must be conducted at a measured pace with proper resources, taking account of increased workloads. Conference delegates were told that the MORI and KPMG surveys highlighted an increase in workload on staff which indicates that growth in consultants' hours has risen faster than any other comparable group in society.

Doctors at the BMA's Annual Representative Meeting condemned the Government for implementing the NHS reforms without adequate information, proper piloting or provision of ongoing evaluation. General Practitioners Committee chairman, said: *'There is under-resourcing at every stage, too little money for developing new strategies for clinical governance, and for educating the public about the reforms. Without proper input of investment, it's clear the new infrastructure will not function properly.'*

Beyond the Health Act 1999: New Initiatives

The Health Act 1999 and the new regime that it has imposed is not the only set of measures designed to control and regulate medicine. The Government also has in

---

51 Sections 17 to 25.
52 See Harpwood, V, *The Manipulation of Medical Practice* in *Current Legal Issues, Law and Medicine*, ed Freeman, M, and Lewis, A, OUP 2000.

place a series of disparate mechanisms for discovering what is wrong in the NHS. These include the annual reports of the Health Service Commissioner, the reports of numerous inquiries established to investigate matters of concern, reviews that give details of matters relevant to *'league tables'*, and the gathering of information from *'whistleblowing'* to name but a few. Other monitoring systems are in the process of being established under the Health and Social Care Act 2001. Some of these mechanisms will be discussed here.

Much of the impetus for the recent reforms was initiated by events at Bristol Royal Infirmary's paediatric cardiac unit, where it emerged that there had been an unacceptably high death and serious injury rate over a period of several years among children undergoing heart surgery. This tragedy, which has become known as the *'Bristol case'* is the subject of a major public inquiry and a report is awaited. The Public Inquiry into events at Bristol, established under s84 of the National Health Service Act 1977, is chaired by Professor Ian Kennedy, Professor of Health Law, Ethics and Policy at University College, London. As chairman of the public inquiry, Professor Kennedy had power to require witnesses to attend the proceedings, to give evidence on oath and to produce documents. The inquiry has been very wide ranging, looking beyond the instances of alleged incompetence that had been considered by the GMC in its disciplinary hearings, and covering all aspects of the events at Bristol. It sought to identify any professional, management and organisational failures and will make recommendations to safeguard future patients and their families.

Both accountability and regulation of the medical profession had been the focus of media attention when the Bristol events came to light. The role of the GMC was questioned by Frank Dobson, then Health Minister, in the light of some of its decisions, and when the Bristol inquiry was established, it was believed that its recommendations might have important implications for the future of the current system of regulating the medical profession. The inquiry was also asked *'to reach conclusions from these events and to make recommendations which could help to secure high quality care across the NHS'*.

Various interim measures have been introduced to stem the tide of criticism that accompanied the Bristol case and other reports of medical error, mishap, and mishandling of sensitive issues. Each fresh scandal prompts a new investigation and a further set of recommendations that inevitably mean the imposing of yet more regulation on the practice of healthcare. Even before the Bristol Inquiry has reported a range of new measures have been introduced to deal with public concerns about the quality of healthcare and the accountability of the professions. Some of these are outlined briefly below.

Whistleblowing

Whistleblowing is the term popularly used for informing on colleagues whose competence is questionable. The Bristol case indicated that the *'whistleblowing'* system is far from satisfactory. The system, by which doctors can seek advice when their colleagues appear to be delivering an unacceptable standard of care, is based on parallel guidance issued by the GMC to all doctors that:

> *'You must protect patients when you believe that a doctor's or other colleague's health, conduct or professional performance is a threat to them,'* (Duties of a Doctor: Good Medical Practice, 1995).

Similar advice is offered by the BMA, but it was not supported by adequate practical measures to protect whistleblowers on the one hand, and doctors who are the victims of malicious professional attacks by colleagues on the other. One solution might lie in a comprehensive system of regular independent scrutiny and audit of the work of all doctors, but in addition there are plans to introduce more formal whistleblowing provisions some time in the future. Meanwhile the Public Interest (Disclosure) Act 1998 has come into force. The Government has also introduced a new initiative to assist whistleblowers in an effort to encourage the passing of information about poor practices in the NHS. NHS Trusts and health authorities must appoint a senior manager with responsibility for protecting whistleblowers. These whistleblowing protectors will be given guidelines about how employees can pass on information if they are concerned about the practices of an individual or department. The guidance provides advice on how to ensure that the informants are not labelled as troublemakers, and do not risk damage to their career prospects.

Despite the existence of the Public Interest (Protection) Act 1998 it seems that people are still afraid to come forward with information. This Act, which became law on 2 July 1999, and is enacted by the insertion of a new Part IV A into the Employment Rights Act 1996, provides statutory protection for employees who act responsibly in disclosing information in the public interest. However, despite the obvious need to protect patients from poor practice, there is a culture in many walks of life, starting during schooldays, which results in 'tell-tales' being ostracised by colleagues. It would take a very serious situation involving life and death for some individuals to divulge information about friends and colleagues. No amount of official guidance will assist the process of whistleblowing in a profession in which people are required to cooperate in teams, – a situation which engenders inevitable resistance to what is frequently seen as 'betraying' colleagues. The introduction of compulsory audit and the changes being introduced by the Health Act 1999 are more likely to bring poor practices to light than the proposed system for protecting whistleblowers. The Government has also emphasised the key role of nurses, midwives and health visitors in ensuring that high quality care is established and maintained. The influence of nurses is seen to be crucial if the NHS is to deliver the quality care agenda outlined by the Government – even if that means 'rocking the boat'. A new initiative, The Strategy for Nursing, Midwifery and Health, has been established and a consultation document launched. However, all such initiatives mean an increase in workload on staff.

Greater openness

The drive towards greater openness has led to the publication of league tables of hospital performance, indicating success rates in surgery, levels of cleanliness, length of waiting lists and other matters of public concern. It is hoped that these measures will result in greater care being taken to avoid adverse publicity and that this will reduce errors and claims. Local NHS organisations are required to publish information on the Internet about the performance of their local health and social care services. They also have to provide information about accessing local GPs, pharmacists, dentists, opticians, social services and key voluntary services. National variations in care are also made public. The NHS Performance Indicators setting out NHS performance against 56 different measures, including cancer survival, patient complaints and deaths following surgery have been published. These highlight wide variations in access to and outcomes of NHS care around the country. In some areas virtually all emergency cases in A&E are seen within two hours, but in others it is only 60%. There is a twofold variation in the death rate from all circulatory disease as between the worst and best health authorities. There are five times as many people waiting for treatment in the worst performing health authorities as compared with the best, and in some health authorities 5% of operations are cancelled at the last minute, while in others almost none are[53]. Thus, figures indicating death rates in the NHS suggest that a patient's chances of surviving are much higher in some hospitals than others. However, the indicators used to measure performance in NHS Trusts have been criticised as too rough and ready, because different populations of patients can be expected to produce different outcomes, and the Government has acknowledged that poverty and social background have an important effect on health.

Publication of Clinical Indicators and High Level Performance Indicators marks the development of a national picture of the quality of clinical care in the NHS throughout the UK. The indicators are intended to assist NHS Trusts, health authorities, and primary care groups in monitoring and improving their performance so that patients throughout the UK have access to uniformly high standards of care. This move was made in advance of implementation of measures in the Health Act 1999 for monitoring the quality of healthcare.

Patients are able to have sight of their medical records more readily since the introduction of legislation to facilitate access[54], and are being given the opportunity to carry their medical records with them in some instances[55]. They have a right of appeal to the Health Service Commissioner if the NHS fails to honour its commitment to openness.

The Freedom of Information Act 1999, another piece of legislation that encourages openness on the part of official public bodies, is disappointingly restrictive in scope and is unlikely to offer a sound basis for those who seek information about healthcare policies and the operation of the NHS.

Managing risk through recommendations of inquiries

Events coming to light in the recent past suggest that there continue to be serious problems in the NHS which are likely to result in further litigation by patients who have been injured as a result of errors by doctors. The Ritchie inquiry was set up by the Government to investigate the case of Rodney Ledward. The inquiry, commissioned in 1999 and chaired by Jean Ritchie QC, conducted a comprehensive analysis of the events that led up to the dismissal of Ledward by his employer, the South Kent Hospitals NHS Trust in December 1996, and to his subsequently being struck off the Medical Register by the General Medical Council. Responding to this report, a Government spokesman said:

> 'The Ritchie report has major significance for the NHS. It describes only too clearly the distress and misery caused to women who were unfortunate enough to be the patients of Rodney Ledward. We have made fundamental changes to make hospitals and other parts of the NHS accountable for the actions of their doctors. We are working with the GMC to make sure that action can be taken more swiftly against bad doctors and that when they are struck off, apart from exceptional cases, it is for life. And our new Care Standards Commission will measure the care patients receive in the private sector.'

The Government intends to press forward as quickly as possible with implementation of the proposals set out in the Chief Medical Officer's report *Supporting Doctors, Protecting Patients*. It sets out plans for an assessment and

---

53   Full details of the NHS Performance Indicators are available on: *http://www.doh.gov.uk/nhsperformanceindicators*
54   eg Access to Health Records Act 1990.
55   eg ante natal records and pilot schemes described in Chapter 9.

support service to ensure problems in an NHS doctor's performance are picked up at a much earlier stage, to tackle poor performance swiftly and to ensure that where necessary action is taken. Annual appraisal of all doctors will support plans being drawn up by the GMC to ensure that all doctors are revalidated on a regular basis so that their practice reflects the latest developments in medicine. Doctors on the GMC's medical register will have to prove that they are up to date in their chosen medical field. In future, disciplinary action taken by the GMC against doctors can be taken swiftly, and only in exceptional circumstances will doctors who have been struck off for life be reinstated on the GMC medical register. The GMC is to have a statutory duty to notify employers of doctors whose fitness to practice is being formally considered.

National mandatory reporting system for adverse events

A new national mandatory reporting system is being established by the NHS for logging all failures, mistakes, errors and near-misses in healthcare. It is hoped that the NHS will learn from the aviation industry and other industries with experience of analysing incidents and *'near misses'*[56]. The new system, is to be based on the Government's report entitled *An Organisation with a Memory*. The recommendations made in the report include:

- the introduction of a mandatory reporting scheme for adverse healthcare events and *'near-misses'* based on standardised reporting systems and clear definitions;
- the introduction of a single database for analysing mistakes and sharing lessons to be learned from incidents and near misses, litigation and complaints data will help to identify common factors and consider specific action necessary to reduce risks to patients in the future;
- the encouragement of a new culture, based on questioning and reporting of incidents in which the NHS moves away from *'blame'* and encourages a proper understanding of the underlying causes of failures;
- the improvement of NHS investigations and inquiries, ensuring that their results are fed into the national database which will enable the whole NHS to learn lessons.

Although NHS organisations were previously required to have incident reporting systems, there was very little consistency in these from one area to another, and there was no single system for assessing adverse events and feeding back lessons to the NHS. Research suggests that as many as 850,000 adverse healthcare events may occur annually in the NHS hospital sector, and the Government gave as an example the persistent failure to learn lessons relating to errors in spinal injections. At least 13 patients have died or been paralysed since 1985 because a drug has been wrongly administered by spinal injection. The challenge of learning from failures in healthcare applies across the world, and there are comparisons to be drawn with the initiative launched earlier in the year by the Clinton administration to tackle what they have termed *'medical error'*. The report also recommends that the Department of Health should examine the feasibility of setting specific targets for the NHS to achieve in reducing the levels of frequently reported incidents, as outlined below:

- To reduce to zero by 2001 the number of patients dying or being paralysed by wrongly administered spinal injections.

---

56   See also Alberti, M, *Medical Errors: A Common Problem*. BMJ 2001; 3222: 501-502.

- To reduce by 25% by 2005 the number of instances of negligent harm to patients in obstetrics and gynaecology which result in litigation. Cases in this field currently account for around half the annual NHS litigation bill.
- To reduce by 40% by 2005 the number of serious errors in the use of prescribed drugs. These currently account for 20% of all clinical negligence litigation – to reduce to zero by 2005 the number of suicides by mental health inpatients as a result of hanging from non-collapsible bed – or shower-curtain rails on wards. This is currently the most common method of suicide on mental health inpatient wards.

Chief Medical Officer Professor Liam Donaldson commented that he would work to implement the proposals as speedily as possible.

An Organisation with A Memory[57] was published on 13 June 2000. It was written by an expert group established in February 1999. Its terms of reference were *'to examine the extent to which the National Health Service and its constituent organisations have the capability to learn from untoward incidents and service failures so that similar occurrences are avoided in the future. To draw conclusions and make recommendations'.*

The National Patient Safety Agency
The Government has announced that a new agency is to be set up to help ensure patient safety in the NHS by introducing a national system for reporting failures, mistakes and near misses in the health service. This is another step towards implementing the recommendations in *An Organisation With A Memory*. The Agency will run a mandatory reporting system for logging all mistakes to ensure that lessons are learned when things go wrong. Liam Donaldson explained that it was estimated that 850,000 incidents and errors occur in the NHS each year. He continued:

'While it is an inescapable fact of life that people make mistakes, there is much we can do to reduce their impact and so reduce the risks for patients. The new agency will be a catalyst for this. The agency's system of identifying, recording and analysing and reporting adverse events will be at the heart of the shift to a more blame-free, open NHS, where lessons are shared and learnt.'

The National Patient Safety Agency is to be independent of Government, and is described in a report *Building a Safer NHS for Patients* which includes details of the agency and the progress being made to set up this new system. The same report also highlights other initiatives for improving safety including a review of the safety environment and a review of clinical practice to reduce risk in the NHS.

The creation of the Agency was announced just before the publication of three separate reports in 2001 into the death of an 18-year-old who had been receiving treatment for leukaemia at the Queen's Medical Centre in Nottingham. He had been injected into the spine with the drug Vincristine that should have been injected into a vein. He died an agonising death as a result of this medical error made as a result of a systems failure – a series of mistakes that should never have occurred. The result of the inquiries is that further recommendations have been made for the establishing of safe systems for administering the drug throughout the UK. This was not the first time that deaths had resulted from the failure to use the drug correctly. The coroner at the inquest blamed mistakes in every part of the NHS for the death.

---

57   Copies from the Stationery Office, PO Box 29, Norwich NR3 1GN or from the Department of Health website *http://www.doh.gov.uk*

Use of the Health Service Commissioner's reports and findings from complaints

The Health Service Ombudsman, Mr Michael Buckley, publishes annual reports giving an overview of the NHS Complaints System and drawing attention to the need for improvements in some areas of healthcare. For example, in the report published in the summer of 2000, the Commissioner drew attention to three matters of special concern – out of hours GP cover, removals from family practitioner lists and communications between NHS staff[58]. The Government is considering how these problems might be remedied.

Standard setting outside the Health Act

Standards continue to be set in addition to the work of NICE. For example, *The Essence of Care* sets out standards that nurses and other staff should meet in caring for patients, in ensuring patients have privacy and dignity on the wards or are given food of high nutritional value. The Government has already introduced a wider programme of work in an attempt to improve nursing standards including: raising standards of nursing through increasing the power of ward sisters and boosting career opportunities for nurses; ensuring higher standards of hygiene, cleanliness and care in hospitals, through routine independent inspections by the Commission for Health Improvement and Patient Environment Action Team, and by creating 400 nurse consultants who will be in post in the near future[59].

New procedures are to be announced for dealing with the sensitive issue of obtaining the consent of relatives to the retention and use of organs after the death of loved-ones. The announcement followed the Redfearn report of the inquiry into the retention and use of organs at the Royal Children's Hospital Liverpool, (Alder Hey) which was published at the end of January 2001. The need for this inquiry became apparent when an interim report was published by the Bristol inquiry. The Redfearn report made a series of recommendations aimed at ensuring that large scale mishandling of the same kind should never again occur. Responding to the highly critical report of the Redfearn Inquiry, the Secretary of State for Health, Alan Milburn, made a statement in the House of Commons, in which he pointed yet again to the efforts being made by the Government to protect patients by monitoring standards through the measures introduced in the Health Act 1999, the creation of the National Institute for Clinical Excellence, the work of The Commission for Health Improvement, and reform to self-regulation of the medical profession to make it faster, more open and more accountable. He stated that the Government would be taking steps to implement the recommendations in the Redfearn report.

National Clinical Assessment Authority

The National Clinical Assessment Authority (NCAA) is a new, national body to provide a fast response to concerns about doctors' performance and it began working

---

58   The four Confidential Enquiries are The National Confidential Enquiry into Perioperative Deaths (NCEPOD). NCEPOD began in 1988 and is concerned with maintaining high standards of clinical practice in anaesthesia and surgery, through audit of hospital deaths which occur within 30 days of any surgical or gynaecological operation. The Confidential Enquiry into Stillbirths and Deaths in Infancy (CESDI) which seeks to identify ways in which stillbirths and deaths in infancy might be prevented and to indicate areas where more research is needed. The Confidential Enquiry into Maternal Deaths (CEMD) began in 1951, and aims to assess the main causes of, and trends in, maternal deaths. It identifies avoidable or below standard factors of care, and recommends improvements for professionals and directions for future research. The Confidential Inquiry into Suicide and Homicide by People with Mental Illness (CISH). This was established in 1991 to carry out a national audit of suicide and homicide by people who have had a history of contact with mental health services. The Health Service Ombudsman, Annual Report 1999-2000 HC542. Investigations completed October 1999 – March 2000 HC541 (Parts I and II).

59   The new standards are available via the NHS response line and at *www.doh.gov.uk\essenceofcare*

from 1 April 2001. This body is seen by the Government as being at the centre of a coordinated approach to better protection for patients and better support for doctors. It will provide a central point of contact for the NHS where concerns about a doctors' performance arise and will give extra training and support to doctors where necessary. The NCAA will make recommendations to NHS hospitals and health authorities to enable them to take appropriate action to check poor performance, and to ensure that doctors are practising safely. If necessary, incompetent doctors will be disciplined. The NCAA has been set up following recommendations made in the Chief Medical Officer's report *Supporting Doctors, Protecting Patients*, published in February 2000. The new body is seen by some commentators as yet another layer of regulation in a profession that is already over regulated. The existence of such a body has been described as *'knee-jerk'* reaction to the *Shipman* case. The move has been criticised by the BMA because the NCAA will be responsible for reporting doctors to the GMC, a body which itself has been much criticised recently for failing to take appropriate disciplinary action in some cases[60].

Greater involvement of patients

Patients have been placed at the centre of the NHS since 1990. The concept of a consumer-led NHS is far from new. Patients have long been treated as consumers, and for a short time in the early part of the 1990s, they were described as *'clients'* by some NHS staff. The patient-centred NHS has been blamed as one contributory factor in the increase in litigation in recent years. During the 1990s the Patients' Charter was introduced on the initiative of John Major. The Government has now replaced the Patient's Charter with *Your Guide to the NHS*, a clearer guide to patients' rights, responsibilities and the national standards and services people can expect from the NHS. The guide explains patients' rights at present, and those that will arise in the future under the NHS Plan. The guide also underlines the responsibilities patients have towards the NHS. The guide contains a *'roadmap'* telling patients and the public how to access the NHS. This is a response to the public's requests for clearer information on how to obtain treatment. *Your Guide to the NHS* explains how patients can play their part in supporting the NHS by guiding them to access the health service at the most appropriate point[61]. When the Government announced the publication of the NHS Plan, it reiterated the established rhetoric by stating that it had been published with a view to the creation of a health service *'designed around the patient'*.

Patients are being given the opportunity to make their views about healthcare known through the NHS Complaints System and through patient surveys that are being commissioned by the Department of Health. The results of these surveys are made public and it is intended that responses will be fed into the NHS system to provide a better quality of care[62].

The Government planned, in 1998, to establish a panel of independent experts to advise on NHS changes in order to ensure that any innovation is guaranteed to provide safety and quality in healthcare. Alan Milburn, Health Minister, is on record as saying that public confidence in the NHS will be increased and maintained by greater public involvement and consultation on NHS changes. He said that restoring

---

60   The report detailing current and future progress on *Supporting doctors and protecting patients: Assuring the Quality of Medical Practice* is available on the internet at: *http://www.doh.gov.uk/assuringquality*

61   Copies can be obtained from the NHS Health Literature Line on 0800 555777 8am to 6pm or from the NHS website at *www.nhs.uk/nhsguide*

62   See Harpwood, V, *Medical Law Monitor*, November 1998.

public confidence is key to modernising the NHS and that he wanted to ensure that the NHS was opened up to greater public scrutiny and patient involvement than ever before. The three-point plan is as follows:

- A commitment to publishing information about all aspects of NHS performance, including the findings of the Commission for Health Improvement.
- A new emphasis on patients' views in shaping the future of the NHS through devices such as opinion surveys and citizens' juries.
- More patient representation in the NHS, not only on NHS Trust Boards, but also on key bodies such as the National Institute for Clinical Excellence and the Commission for Health Improvement.

The Health and Social Care Act 2001 contains further provision for patients to be involved in healthcare decisions through consultation.

In theory these proposals provide for democratic consultation and confirm the commitment to openness voiced by the present Government and the previous Conservative administration. However, while patients welcome greater involvement in NHS decision-making, it is difficult to believe that these promises amount to anything more than a public relations exercise aimed at improving the image of the NHS, as there is little evidence that the public will have real power to effect changes of policy.

Regulating independent healthcare: the Care Standards Act 2000
The independent healthcare sector has been giving cause for concern for several years. Fears have grown with the greater involvement of private healthcare providers in NHS treatment and care[63]. While the Government was able to monitor and make accountable practices within the NHS it had no similar powers, in relation to independent healthcare. The Care Standards Act 2000 establishes greater control over the independent sector than has ever been available in the past, along similar lines to the Health Act 1999. One of the most important features of the Act is the establishment of the Care Standards Commission that will take on its statutory tasks in April 2002. Regulations and minimum standards will be developed and established throughout the independent sector and these will be monitored to ensure high quality of care and proper accountability. The aim is to have these ready for implementation by April 2002[64]. Already, new national standards for the elderly in care homes have been published by the Government, following extensive consultation[65]. The question that arises under the new regime proposed by the latest initiatives, is whether failure to meet the prescribed standards could amount to negligence.

The role of the Medical Devices Agency
The monitoring of the safety of medical devices, such as artificial hip joints and various implants used in healthcare is the responsibility of the Medical Devices Agency. This organisation has an overview of the entire range of medical devices in use in the UK and from time to time recommends if necessary that some be withdrawn from circulation. It is yet another cog in the process of regulating healthcare and ensuring the safety of patients.

---

63 See Newdick, C, *The NHS in Private Hands? Regulating Private Providers of NHS Services, Law and Medicine*, ed Freeman, M, and Lewis, A, OUP, 2000.

64 A full account of the operation of the Act and its contents is available on the Department of Health website.

65 *www.doh.gov.uk/nscs*

The Health and Social Care Act 2001, which received the Royal Assent just as this book was going to press, introduces further innovations in healthcare as outlined in the NHS Plan published in 2000. This, like the Health Act 1999, was passed very precipitately, and some would argue, without adequate reflection. The Act introduces changes in the way that primary care practitioners are regulated. It also creates new arrangements in ss60 and 61 for the sharing of information about patients, in anticipation of the development of the NHSnet, and it introduces certain measures to allow patients greater participation in the NHS through public involvement (s11). It makes new arrangements for the funding of healthcare, facilitates public/private arrangements or partnerships and allows local authority scrutiny of health provision (ss7-10). Independent advocacy services are to be provided to assist patients in making complaints, under s12 of the Act. There are special provisions in s13 for intervention by the Secretary of State if health bodies appear to be failing significantly in their functions. These provide the opportunity for yet another layer of regulation in healthcare. Part Two of the Act deals with new arrangements for pharmaceutical services, including the facilitation of remote pharmaceutical services through the internet, home delivery and mail order, and in s63 it gives prescribing powers to a wider range of healthcare professionals. Part four of the Act is concerned with arrangements for the funding of long-term care, under proposals in the NHS Plan for dealing with the increasing problem of providing care for the elderly and other vulnerable people.

The changes introduced by the Health and Social Care Act are being heralded as part of the NHS modernisation programme, but these new developments complicate still further a healthcare system that is already over complex. There is now surely even greater need for rationalisation.

New Routes to Healthcare

In a series of new initiatives the Government plans to create new routes by which healthcare can be sought and delivered. Modern communications technology is making many of the new developments possible. Building on its programme of health improvement, the Government has been seeking the views of various groups of NHS users in order to ascertain whether there may be new ways of providing advice and treatment for patients.

Success is already being claimed for the healthcare helpline called NHS Direct which was announced in the White Paper *The New NHS: Modern, Dependable*, and is now operational. The system aims to provide patients with guidance on health matters such as whether they should call a doctor, go to an accident and emergency unit, wait until morning, or even wait for a routine appointment. Advice is given about queries concerning missed medication, aches and pains, exercise, types of treatment which might be available for specific conditions, and so on. Health service information, such as the location of the nearest late-night chemist and the length of waiting lists in particular areas, can also be obtained over the telephone.

NHS Direct Online provides the public with a gateway to health information on the Internet and public access to the new National Electronic Library for Health. Using the Internet from home, patients can browse information or download information for later use. While this service will be of interest to those who have access to the Internet and are able to use it, there will be many vulnerable people, such as those who are elderly or socially or financially disadvantaged, who will not benefit from the scheme. This is likely to widen the gap that the Government acknowledges to exist between rich and poor in health and quality of life.

NHS Direct Information Points are designed to provide public access points for NHS Direct in surgeries, libraries, pharmacies, post offices, accident and emergency departments and healthy living centres. The first 100-200 were in place during 1999 and 2000, providing instant access to information about health and local health services. It is hoped that this will increase ease of access to health information, and reduce the need for patients to make special visits to a doctor's surgery for information and advice.

NHS Direct Healthcare Guide draws on the experience of the telephone service to provide advice on common ailments and problems about which NHS Direct nurses routinely advise callers. NHS Direct nurses send the Guide to callers when they think it will be helpful and is also be available on request.

NHS Direct Healthcare Programme uses the NHS Direct healthcare Guide as the basis for providing training for the public on basic healthcare issues. It is hoped that this will increase people's knowledge and ability to care for themselves and for their families.

Although the Government is enthusiastic about NHS Direct, and is working hard to *'sell'* the idea to GPs and patients, from a legal point of view it could present problems. Negligent advice could result in claims by patients who believe that they have suffered injury or illness as a result, and telephone advice can seldom be as acceptable as advice given face-to-face. The NHS Complaints System should be explained to people using the helpline, and publicity leaflets should indicate clearly what steps are available to those who are dissatisfied with the service. As suggested by the Protocol for the Resolution for Clinical Negligence Disputes, this type of pre-emptive action could prevent dissatisfaction escalating into legal claims. Telephone medical advice has been available in America for some time. Although the software systems used in America are claimed to be very successful in preventing negligence claims, the flexibility of the systems favoured in the UK suggests that there should be no complacency on the part of providers of NHS Direct. Nevertheless, if the guidelines provided by the software are followed it would be difficult to establish negligence as long as those guidelines are professionally accredited, are logical and consistent. However, there are dangers in introducing NHS Direct on a nationwide basis too rapidly. As with any new product, time should be made available for proper evaluation of the software systems and it is essential that the safety and efficiency of the systems be assured before there is widespread use of the service. Research undertaken so far is generally inconclusive partly because of what are perceived to be flaws in research methodology used, and partly because it has proved difficult to compare the various systems in use[66].

It is encouraging that one research study[67] suggests that so far there is no increase in adverse outcomes for patients using advice provided by NHS Direct when compared with those managed by doctors in the traditional way. This now needs to be supported by further evaluations, as data from the first pilot studies indicates that 80% of people were advised to take different action to what they had intended before making the call to NHS Direct, and approximately a third of callers were told to seek less drastic measures than they had intended, freeing up resource intensive services such as accident and emergency departments[68].

---

66   Crouch R, Dale J *Telephone Triage: How Good Are the Decisions?* Nursing Standard 1998; 12 (vol35) 33-9.

67   Lattimer V, George S, Thompson F, Thomas E, Mullee M, Turnbull J et al. *Safety and Efficacy Of Telephone Consultation in Out of Hours Primary Care: Randomised Control Trial.* BMJ 1998:317:1054-9.

68   See Harpwood V, *Medical Law Monitor* September 1998, Vol 5, Issue 9, 11.

Fast access walk-in centres

The Government has provided £280 million to promote NHS walk-in Centres in High Streets of towns and cities throughout the UK. The centres are open between 7am and 10pm on weekdays and over weekends, and appointments may not be necessary for patients to use them. Although these centres will, to some extent, be seeing patients who would otherwise be consulting their GPs, they are not intended to replace the more personal approach which general practice can offer, but rather to complement GP services. General practitioners, some of whom might well regard the proposals for walk-in health centres as a threat to their own practices, have not been over-enthusiastic in their response to the idea of walk-in centres, and some believe that more Government money needs to be committed to the scheme.

Conclusion

It has only been possible in the limited space available to catalogue a range of changes and initiatives dealing with the structure, delivery and monitoring of healthcare in the past decade. Many more changes and developments are anticipated. Indeed it is possible that the Department of Health is suffering from *'initiativitis'*, as new developments for monitoring healthcare and making the healthcare professions accountable for errors are announced on a regular basis. The rash of new ideas, many of them very sound, has been perpetuated by the policy of the New Labour Government, with its taste for *'spin'*. External assessment of healthcare delivery is being introduced in many countries[69]. What is needed now is some form of rationalisation to enable all forms of regulation to be covered by a single organisation responsible for monitoring and regulation. The GMC has put forward proposals for improving its regulation of the medical profession, and these should be added to the Government initiatives. The report of the Bristol inquiry is likely to contain further recommendations for regulation and reform and it is very important for the Government to seize the opportunity to bring about effective rationalisation and reform as soon as possible after those recommendations have been published.

---

69   See Shaw C, *External Assessment of Healthcare*. BMJ 2001; 322: 851-854.

Chapter 12

Looking Ahead

This book has covered many aspects of reform currently being implemented by the Government in the context of healthcare and legal procedure, and more gradually, on an incremental basis by the judiciary. In this final chapter there will be an evaluation of some recent trends and an attempt to predict future patterns in the delivery of healthcare and the response of the common law. Many of the developments have been considered in much greater detail elsewhere in the book.

The starting point for the discussion is the NHS Plan for the next ten years, published in 2000, and the ambitious programme of so-called *'modernisation'* of the NHS, the attempts to reduce inequality and place patients at the centre of the NHS, which together with technological developments will inevitably give rise to legal problems. The ever-present concerns about healthcare litigation will be discussed, together with potential solutions, in the light of developments since the introduction of the Civil Procedure Rules 1998. Much depends upon the policies of the Government in power[1], of course, but there is unlikely to be any radical departure from the trend towards imposing ever stricter regulatory regimes by central Government over the practice of healthcare[2] during the early years of the twenty first century.

The NHS Plan

Published in July 2000, the NHS plan sets ambitious targets for improving the organisation of the NHS, investing in extra beds and hospitals, recruiting more staff, giving patients greater choice, reducing waiting times for treatment, improving health and setting new clinical priorities to cope with an aging population. With the now familiar Government rhetoric, Alan Milburn proclaimed:

'This is the most fundamental and far-reaching reform programme. For the first time, the Government has faced up to the breadth and depth of problems in the NHS and has addressed them all in turn.'

However, as Michael Jones asserts[3]:

'It is only now, after 15 years of rising medical negligence claims, that hospitals are beginning to take the question of clinical risk management seriously. In other

---

1   For a review of the manifestos of the three main political parties in the UK at the time of the general election in 2001, see Hall G, *Medical Litigation* (2001) May No 5, p12.

2   See Davies, A, *Don't Trust Me, I'm a Doctor: Medical Regulation and the 1999 NHS Reforms*, Oxford Journal of Legal Studies, Vol 20, No 3, 2000, 437-456.

3   In *Informed Consent and Other Fairy Stories*, 1999, Med L Rev, Vol 7, No 2, at page 133.

words, it is only when there are serious financial consequences that the NHS has started to treat the issue of patient safety as worthy of systematic attention.'
The NHS Plan promises:

- 7,000 extra beds and 100 new hospital schemes;
- 7,500 more consultants, 2,000 new GPs, 20,000 more nurses, 6,500 more health professionals, and new GP and consultant contracts;
- an NHS Modernisation Agency, a National Performance Funds and a National Independent Panel to advise on hospital changes;
- changes in cooperation between the NHS and social services, including new Care Trusts;
- better training and greater responsibilities for nurses, midwives and other healthcare professionals;
- greater choice and better protection for patients;
- new relationships between the NHS and the private sector;
- reduced waiting times;
- reduced inequalities in health provision;
- new clinical priorities;
- better standards of care for older people to allow them greater independence.

Some of these measures are already in the process of being developed through the Health and Social Care Act 2001. For example, more nurses are being given prescribing powers, the relationship between the NHS and social services is being restructured and there are new areas of healthcare under review through the activities of NICE (see Chapter 11). The NHS Plan promises extra funding to enable the targets it sets out to be met, but some doctors are sceptical about the Government's promises and the results of a survey carried out by The Times newspaper and published in April 2001 indicate that the NHS Plan does not have the support of doctors many of whom do not believe that there have been any serious attempts to cost its implementation[4]. At the time of writing, it has been reported that urgent talks are being held with leaders of the medical profession in an effort to deal with major staff shortages in the NHS and what has been described as a *'mutiny'* by doctors who believed that the NHS Plan sets unrealistic targets[5].

The Audit Commission expressed concern in April 2000 that much of the extra funding then promised for the NHS would disappear in the process of defending claims for clinical negligence and making payments to claimants. The Government will be anxious to ensure that the funding targeted for NHS reforms in the NHS Plan will not be dissipated in a similar fashion. It is no coincidence that the *British Medical Journal* devoted an entire issue to the question of medical errors[6].

Continued Central Government Monitoring

NICE will, over the next decade, continue to develop its programme of setting standards and issuing guidelines for specific areas of healthcare practice. CHI will continue to review the implementation and operation of recommendations made by NICE, and improvements should be made in the way in which healthcare is delivered and controlled, as envisaged by the Health Act 1999. The next few years will see similar developments in independent healthcare with the implementation of the

---

4   The Times, 19 April 2001.
5   The Times, 23 April 2001.
6   BMJ 2001; 322.

provisions in the Care Standards Act 2000[7]. Standardisation of treatment and equal access for all to good quality healthcare ought to be achievable if the reforms are effective. Challenges to the decisions of NICE on questions of allocation of healthcare resources under the Human Rights Act 1998 are predictable. Compulsory continuing education for members of the healthcare professions will ensure that doctors and other healthcare professionals keep abreast of current developments. One legal implication of this, and of the widely disseminated NICE guidelines, is that it will become increasingly difficult for healthcare professionals to argue, in defence of clinical negligence claims, that they were unaware of new medical developments. There should also be a reduction in the amount of fraud in the NHS as a result of measures being implemented under the Health Act 1999. Currently, it is reported that there are more than 140 doctors under investigation for fraud.

International Standardisation

The next decade is likely to see greater European and international standardisation of the quality of healthcare and medical qualifications[8].

Greater Regional Diversity

Paradoxically, despite New Labour's commitment to uniformity in healthcare provision, devolution is gradually resulting in regional differences in healthcare in Wales and Scotland. In Wales, people under the age of 25 are allowed free dispensing of prescriptions. Health authorities are being abolished in Wales, where Community Health Councils, which are being abolished in England are to be retained. The Welsh Assembly is to take control of its own health responsibilities through a newly created health and well-being council. In England, the number of health authorities is to be reduced from 99 to 30 in an effort to streamline healthcare. In Scotland, unlike England and Wales, there is to be state support for nursing and social care of all elderly patients who require it. This trend towards greater regional diversity is likely to continue, and could cause cross-border difficulties in some instances.

Professional Regulation

As central Government control becomes an increasingly important feature of the regulation of healthcare and of the standards applicable in its practice, so professional control is likely to diminish. There have been very real concerns about the role of the GMC and further critical comment by the Bristol inquiry is expected. The GMC has already drafted its own reforms.

The proposals published in *Supporting Doctors, Protecting Patients*, some of which are now in the process of being implemented, (see Chapter 11), are aimed at protecting patients and improving standards of care, and are designed to help ensure that all NHS doctors provide a high quality service. The NHS disciplinary procedures had long been regarded as bureaucratic[9], legalistic and ineffective, and the proposals should ensure that NHS trusts and health authorities can take action quickly in future to detect emerging problems and resolve them fairly.

---

7   Partnership between independent and state programmes for setting and assessing standards will be essential and has proved effective in the US and Australia.

8   See Shaw C. *External Assessment of Healthcare* BMJ 2001; 322:851-854.

9   Note that some changes have been introduced by the Health and Social Care Act 2001.

Systematic regulatory reform

It is essential that the regulatory reforms outlined in Chapter 11 are rationalised and developed, but preferably under the auspices of a single regulatory regime. If there is to be a successful system within the healthcare professions for reporting of adverse incidents, the Government must ensure that the promised new *'culture'* within which blame is minimised, accompanies this. It is difficult to envisage any way of achieving this new culture when the perceived, or real threat of litigation is ever-present[10]. A solution to the problem of *'multiple medical malpractice'* cases must also be sought. These cases involve injury suffered by a large number of patients as a result of repeated mistakes, incompetence or deliberate harm occasioned by a small number of healthcarers, usually just one individual[11]. In some instances the errors involve equipment failure, or misinterpretation of data. In others there is a history of incompetence, a persistent culture of insensitivity on the part of the medical profession[12], and in rare cases, even of deliberate injury inflicted on patients. In almost all the instances that have been identified, problems are perpetuated because colleagues of the perpetrators do not recognise or report their suspicions until it is too late. In many multiple malpractice situations, managers and others in authority fail to act promptly on reports from staff. Research is required to document incidents of multiple malpractice in the UK, to identify any common features of such incidents, to explore the factors that lead to the recognition of multiple medical malpractice, to consider the responses of victims and healthcarers, and to evaluate proposals for preventing similar situations occurring in the future. There needs to be an evaluation of recent changes. For example, will the Health Act 1999 make a difference in cases of this kind? What is the role of compulsory audit and compulsory participation in the confidential inquiries, clinical governance and risk management. How will the Health and Social healthcare Act 2001 assist?

Telemedicine

In the fullness of time, NHS Direct could prove to be the beginning of a much broader patient system of patient access to healthcare and professional filtering. It could herald a system of telemedicine[13] (medicine practised at a distance) that will create new demands on health providers, health professionals and their legal advisers. Issues such as confidentiality, access to records, training, professional competence, and the viability and security of computer software and hardware will need to be tackled in the coming years. Most of the legal problems that arise in connection with telemedicine can be solved under the present legal framework, but difficulties can be envisaged in connection with medical procedures that are delivered across national boundaries.

Patient-centred care

The Government has promised to place patients at the *'centre of the NHS'* and a consumer-led NHS has been promised. Tony Blair has announced the introduction of a new booking system for hospital appointments at times to suit the convenience of each patient, that will bring the NHS a step closer to being consumer-led. Pilot

---

10   See Mulcahy, L, *The Challenge of Medical Negligence Cases*, in *Law and Medicine*, ed Freeman, M and Lewis, A, OUP 2000, 81-105.

11   For example, the Bristol cases, the *Shipman* case, the *Ledwood. Elwood,* and *Allitt* cases

12   See the Alder Hey Inquiry Report.

13   See Lang J, *Does Telemedicine Mean New Medico-legel Issues? Health Law for Healthcare Professionals*, March 1999 Vol 4, Issue 3, 1.

schemes are underway at present, and it is hoped that there will be less uncertainty about waiting times, and that with the use of computer technology, patients participating will be able to decide, in their GPs' surgeries when they would like to have hospital appointments. The Health and Social Care Act 2001 continues the trend towards greater patient involvement in healthcare.

National survey of NHS patients

There is likely to be a continuing process of surveying patients for their views. A 20-page postal questionnaire was sent in October 1998 to 100,000 adults selected at random from the Electoral Registers. A response rate of 64.5% was achieved after discounting ineligible addresses. The results are based on 61,426 completed questionnaires. Eighty-one per cent (around 50,000) respondents had seen a GP in the last 12 months. The survey was carried out by a consortium of Social & Community Planning Research (SCPR), an independent research organisation together with Picker Europe and the Imperial College School of Medicine. The research focused on patients' experience of NHS general practice, and covered a range of issues including:

– access;
– communications;
– patients' views of GPs and practice nurses;
– quality and range of services including out-of hours care;
– referrals by GPs to hospital.

The results of the survey suggest that there may be some duplication of the tasks carried out by GPs and the services offered by NHS Direct and walk-in health centres. Patients who are dissatisfied with certain aspects of their GP service, such as waiting times for appointments, will have the alternative of seeking advice from a walk-in centre, NHS Direct, or one of its newer satellite services outlined above. However, as the survey revealed, a patient's GP will know his medical history and family background and be at a considerable advantage by being able to provide personal medical attention in the light of the patient's entire background. At present the NHS Direct telephone advice line can only provide advice on the basis of *'snap-shot'* information supplied by the patient over a telephone on a single occasion.

Early results from the second national NHS survey of patients confirm patients want to be better informed about their treatment so that they can be more involved in making decisions about their own care. On that basis, the focus for the future is to be on patient care including speed of access, and *'patient empowerment'*. The provision of detailed information about services is likely to continue as part of the consumer-led approach to healthcare. All local NHS organisations will be required to publish information on the Internet about the performance of their local health and social care services. They will also be required to provide user-friendly information on accessing local GPs, pharmacists, dentists, opticians, social services and key voluntary services.

Patients' access to records

The Government promises that most patients will have easy access to their medical records in the near future, and that there will be a climate of greater openness within teams of NHS staff, so that for example, copies of letters sent to consultants will be sent automatically to the patients concerned. To provide an effective and efficient service to patients those advising them need access to their medical records. Until there is a comprehensive system providing access to patients' medical records to all those needing them NHS Direct can only provide a stop-gap service. When NHSnet is in place, it should be possible to access a patient's records from anywhere in the UK, but this in itself will create legal and ethical problems. Electronic patient records for everyone in the country will eventually become a reality.

Electronic patient records will play a key role in the NHS Information Strategy – *Information for Health*. The Health and Social Care Act 2001 contains provisions which set the stage for developing access by healthcare professionals to all patient-related information. The aim is that every person in the country will have an electronic record by 2005, which will be instantly available to health professionals all over the UK at any time. Once a system of electronic records available to all health workers is in place, it will be essential that clear guidelines are drafted to ensure that confidential information is only used by those who really need access to it. Monitoring of the use of information by means of the Caldicott Guardian[14] system, which has now been implemented in most parts of the NHS, will be essential.

Regulation of independent healthcare

The implementation of the Care Standards Act 2000 will mean better protection for patients in the independent care sector. This is a major development, taking place in the early years of the twenty-first century, and is very welcome. It is essential if there is to be cooperation between the NHS and the independent sector in the provision of healthcare. There should be effective complaints systems operating in the independent healthcare sector in the near future.

NHS complaints

While it is unlikely that there will be a radical reform of the NHS Complaints System it is probable that some restructuring will be required in the near future, and precisely what this will entail will become clear when the Government receives the results of research. It is predictable, on the basis of research carried out by the Public Law Project, that the main changes will be in the area of Independent Review and the role of the convener. NHS complaints should be a valuable source of information for the purposes of risk management, and any reforms should also make provision for some cases that would otherwise have gone on to litigation, to be settled by means of compensation payments.

Legal Developments

There have been several important developments in the law during the closing years of the twentieth century. The long-standing *Bolam* test was modified by the *Bolitho* case in 1997, and the legal rules for the assessment of damages have been modified in favour of claimants. However, the most far-reaching reforms have been effected by means of statutory intervention, to allow patients access to their medical records and to streamline and improve procedures for bringing claims.

Procedural change

As the impact of the Civil Procedure Rules becomes clearer with the publication of the results of research currently being undertaken, there will be scope for developing further the areas of civil procedure reform that are proved to have been successful. As judges exert greater control over the stages of litigation, there should be more efficient handling of healthcare negligence claims which will, it is hoped, lead to just outcomes for all those involved in clinical negligence cases, but these, as is explained

---

14   See HSC 1998/089 and HSC 1999/012 *Caldicott Guardians.*

in Chapter 9, must be achieved in the light of the Human Rights Act 1998. There is also a real possibility of modifying the NHS Complaints System to allow more scope for grievances to be settled by means of financial compensation, but as Lord Woolf pointed out[15]:

> '*I am concerned to see greater harmonisation of the NHS Complaints System with the Protocol. If clinical negligence complaints systems are to be effective they will need to break down the defensiveness and distrust which is so pervasive. Too often complaints become claims because the potential of the complaints system was not exhausted before the claimant felt obliged to pursue an alternative route. Ideally, complaints procedures should resolve disputes, particularly those for relatively low values.*'

No-fault compensation in clinical negligence cases?

In *Nash v Richmond Health Authority*[16] a clinical negligence case, the judge, Sir Michael Davies, made the following statement that reflects the concerns of many lawyers and medical professionals about medical litigation:

> '*Like most medical negligence actions this is a grave and distressing case. If the plaintiff wins it is a black mark against a professional man, here a senior and distinguished consultant; if the defendant wins a wholly innocent person is left without financial compensation for a terrible injury: in my opinion an even unhappier result. However, the court must be and remain totally uninfluenced by such considerations. The sole question is, has the plaintiff on the evidence, in the light of the applicable law, established negligence and causation?*'

This raises the possibility that the introduction of a no-fault compensation system for clinical negligence claims might provide a better alternative solution.

The term '*no-fault compensation*' refers to a system of providing compensation for the victims of medical accidents without the need to prove fault, and without using the courts. The idea of introducing a *no-fault* compensation for clinical negligence cases has been given in-depth consideration on several occasions[17], and there is potential for a variety of different no-fault schemes, one of which might be selected as suitable for use in the UK. For example it might be possible to compensate all victims of medical accidents through the social security system without actually naming the individual who was thought to be responsible for the accident. Another possibility would be a more limited scheme covering only a small range of medical incidents, such as birth injuries.

As the Pearson Commission pointed out in 1978, there are many medical accidents for which no one can be blamed:

> '*An operation might have unexpected consequences. Blood products may be used which contain viruses the presence of which could not be foreseen. There are now 3,000 drugs in use and 10,000 listed drug interactions, both detrimental and beneficial. More will doubtless be discovered[18].*'

The Pearson Commission did not recommend a no-fault scheme for medical accidents, as it would prove too difficult to finance, and there would be further problems raised by the question of whether treatment given by paramedics and others on the fringe of main stream medicine should be covered by such a scheme.

---

15   Lord Woolf, *Clinical Negligence: What is The Solution? Medical Law International*, 2000, Vol 4, no 2 p133-144.
16   (1996) 36 BMLR 123.
17   eg BMA Working Party on No Fault Compensation. Report. London: BMA, 1987. More recently see Esen U. NLJ 151; 837, 8 June 2001 and Mehendia B, NLJ 151; 846, 8 June 2001.
18   Cmnd 7054, 1978 para 1350.

Another difficulty that led the Pearson Commission to reject no-fault compensation for medical injuries lay in the problem of proving causation. However, it was recommended that more research should be conducted into the operation of the no-fault schemes in New Zealand and Sweden.

In their comprehensive article reviewing the need for change in the legal and healthcare systems, Ham et al[19] considered various options for reform and studying the systems in New Zealand and Sweden, the authors argued that:

> *'A no-fault scheme would overcome many of the shortcomings we have identified in the present system. But neither the Swedish, nor the New Zealand Schemes offers a model which could be imported directly into the United Kingdom.'*

They concluded:

> *'Further research would help to clarify the policy choices we have mapped, but even more important is a political commitment to consider carefully ways in which improvements can be brought about to the benefit of all those involved with medical negligence. Above all, what is now required is an informed debate of the issues and the options, a debate which recognises the need both to provide compensation and to promote deterrence.'*

In 1996, in his final report, Lord Woolf paid special attention to clinical negligence litigation[20]. He did not recommend the introduction of a no-fault scheme as a means of solving the problem and instead his recommendations focused on improving the civil justice system.

The arguments against no-fault compensation centre on the many practical and financial problems that have become apparent in the schemes operating in New Zealand and Sweden. A Private Members Bill introduced in December 1990 by Rosie Barnes, intended to introduce a no-fault compensation scheme for medical injuries, foundered at an early stage and never had a real prospect of success. The many arguments for and against such a scheme were set out by Margaret Brazier and Sheila McLean in *Compensation for Damage: An International Perspective*[21].

The question was resurrected by John Harris in 1997 in an article in the *BMJ*[22]. He first pointed out the injustice that arises because the only group of individuals whose demands for NHS resources are met immediately, and without question, are successful claimants in clinical negligence litigation[23]. He proceeded to consider the possibility of a solution through a separately funded no-fault compensation scheme, arguing that:

> *'It would be fairer to victims of medical accidents and avoid the stigmatisation of doctors; whether it would also remove a degree of existing protection from negligent or callous management might depend on whether tort liability was retained alongside a no fault scheme, perhaps with a ceiling on awards and availability only on the instigation of an ombudsman.'*

He concluded that any such scheme would have to be justified in terms of its relative importance to other healthcare funding priorities, but that at least under a no

---

19   Op cit.

20   *Access to Justice: The Final Report to the Lord Chancellor on the Civil Justice System in England and Wales*, (1996).

21   Brazier M. The case for a no fault medical accident scheme. In: McLean S, ed. *Compensation for Damage. A Comparative Perspective.* Aldershot: Dartmouth, 1993:51-74.

22   Harris, J, *BMJ* 1997; 314:1821.

23   This argument would be persuasive if successful claimants were on a level playing field with others demanding NHS funds. The reality of the situation is that they are not. They may already have queued for some time for the negligent healthcare that they received, and in any event, it is surely right that the system that has injured them should consider compensating their injuries a top priority.

fault scheme large amounts of public money would not be wasted on the process of establishing liability.

The Lord Chancellor gave consideration to the possibility of establishing a no-fault compensation scheme in 1998, but no further action has been taken. The proposal arose from a recommendation for a review of the position by Sir Peter Middleton, former permanent secretary to the Treasury, whose review of civil justice and legal aid has just been published. Since much of the funding for clinical negligence claims already comes from public funds, it was argued by Sir Peter that the money might be better deployed in a no-fault scheme than in employing legal professionals. More recently Lord Phillips of Matravers, Master of the Rolls has urged further reconsideration of a no-fault scheme.

In response to Frank Dobson's comments[24] about the drain placed on NHS resources by clinical negligence litigation, the BMA gave further consideration[25] to the problem and to the possibility of no-fault compensation for medical accidents. MP Paul Boateng had ruled out no fault compensation on the grounds that *'a no fault culture could over time diminish clinical accountability'*. No fault compensation would also reduce the need to provide accident victims with the explanations they require[26].

The UK Government has been introducing no-fault compensation on an ad hoc basis over the years, for certain injuries suffered by adverse healthcare events. The Vaccine Damage Payments Act 1979 is one example of this process. The most recent example is the announcement that there are to be payments of £25,000 to families of victims of vCJD, the human form of bovine spongiform encephalopathy (BSE). The no-fault compensation package was announced after the inquiry by Lord Phillips into the BSE crisis. It could be argued that there is no justification for the singling out of certain relatively narrow categories of accident victims for special treatment in this way, as this will inevitably mean that public funds will be denied to others. If there is to be no-fault compensation, it must be evenly distributed and the product of radical statutory change.

Development of the common law

There is scope for incremental development of the common law within the human rights framework, supported by the jurisprudence of the European Court of Human Rights. It is possible that there will be new challenges to the law on medical confidentiality and the prioritisation of resources for healthcare by NICE in its decision-making role as a public body, in which the appropriate approach would be determined by existing European human rights law. Challenges could also be brought by members of the healthcare professions who believe that the Civil Justice Rules may not be offering them a fair trial of the civil rights and obligations[27]. This may happen despite the strong caution given by the Court of Appeal in *Daniels v Walker*[28] (see Chapter 9). The duty of care in negligence could be extended to cover more situations that have been traditionally within its scope in UK law, such as *'Good Samaritan acts'* [29].

---

24   In Evidence to the Select Committee on Procedures Related to Adverse Clinical Incidents and Outcomes in Medical Care, (1998-9) H.C. 549-11, p233.

25   *BMJ* 1998; 316:1540.

26   See Simanovitz A. The Times, Letters, Law Section, 12 June 2001, p9.

27   See Chapters 9 and 10.

28   (2000) 1 WLR 1382.

29   See Chapters 2 and 9.

Any developments in the common law should be considered in the context of changes in the structure and delivery of healthcare. For example, with the implementation of risk management systems and the development of clinical governance it is likely that more arguments will be presented to the courts on behalf of claimants on the basis of *'systems failure'* in addition to those based on vicarious liability and negligence of individual doctors. The result could be an increase in the scope of emergent primary liability of healthcare institutions. Reliance on clinical guidelines developed by NICE and implemented as part of the clinical governance culture should have a role in the standardisation of healthcare and the determination of the standard of care in clinical negligence cases, as explained at various points in this book[30]. *Bolam* could diminish in importance within this new regime[31]. However, as Margaret Brazier and Jose Miola point out[32]:

'The prospect of the English Courts suddenly revising the tradition of decades and actively seeking to arrogate to themselves the making of clinical judgements is remote.'

Changes and modifications are likely to be slow and cautious, in keeping with the common law tradition, but judges will be able to develop the law by claiming reliance on the clinical judgement of doctors through the use of guidelines developed by senior clinicians for use by their colleagues.

Another area ripe for development is that of the non-delegable duty of healthcare institutions alongside the increasing reliance on the independent healthcare sector for treating and caring for NHS patients, especially the growing population of elderly people requiring care. New Labour is committed to developing this partnership between the NHS and the independent sector.

The promotion of a patient-centred approach in healthcare should herald greater respect for patient autonomy that could be reflected in judicial decision-making, especially in relation to the law concerning consent to treatment and access to information. The tide may already have turned in this respect but there is still scope for further development[33]. However, any such trend is likely to be accompanied by increased patient responsibility, and use of principles of contributory negligence.

Conclusion

The start of the new millennium is an exciting and challenging time for the legal and healthcare professions. Genuine efforts are being made to streamline litigation and to improve and standardise the quality of healthcare in the UK. There is every reason, why, given adequate funding, new technologies and improved systems should promote better services for patients and litigants.

Many aspects of medical law that have not been covered in this book. These include genetics, fertility treatment, abortion, euthanasia and clinical trials, which concern complex ethical issues. As the medical and scientific revolution gathers pace there will be a need for further regulation of the delivery of some types of healthcare[34] to deal with the legal and ethical dilemmas posed by advances in treatment and new medical possibilities. It is unlikely that clinical negligence will remain untouched by this revolution.

---

30   See Chapters 3 and 11.

31   Mason, J. K, *Legal Aspects and Implications of Risk Assessment, Medical Law Review*, 2000, vol 8, No 1, 69-84; Brazier, M, and Miola, J *Bye Bye Bolam: A Medical Litigation Revolution?* ibid, 85-112.

32   Ibid, at p112.

33   See Bailey Harris, R, *Patient Autonomy – A Turn in the Tide*, in *Law and Medicine*, ed Freeman M, and Lewis A, op cit, 127-140.

34   See McLean, S, *Old Law, New Medicine*, Pandora Press, 1999.

Appendix I

A rticles 2, 3, 5, 6 and 8 to the European Convention on the Protection of Human Rights and Fundamental Freedoms.

Article 2

Right to Life

1. Everyone's right to life shall be protected by law. No one shall be deprived of his life intentionally save in the execution of a sentence of a court following his conviction of a crime for which this penalty is provided by law.
2. Deprivation of life shall not be regarded as inflicted in contravention of this Article when it results from the use of force which is no more than absolutely necessary:
   (a) in defence of any person from unlawful violence;
   (b) in order to effect a lawful arrest or to prevent the escape of a person lawfully detained;
   (c) in action lawfully taken for the purpose of quelling a riot or insurrection.

Article 3

Prohibition of Torture

No one shall be subjected to torture or to inhuman or degrading treatment or punishment.

Article 5

Right to Liberty and Security

1. Everyone has the right to liberty and security of person. No one shall be deprived of his liberty save in the following cases and in accordance with a procedure prescribed by law:
   (a) the lawful detention of a person after conviction by a competent court;
   (b) the lawful arrest or detention of a person for non-compliance with the lawful order of a court or in order to secure the fulfilment of any obligation prescribed by law;
   (c) the lawful arrest or detention of a person effected for the purpose of bringing him before the competent legal authority on reasonable suspicion of having committed an offence or when it is reasonably considered

necessary to prevent his committing an offence or fleeing after having done so;

(d) the detention of a minor by lawful order for the purpose of educational supervision or his lawful detention for the purpose of bringing him before the competent legal authority;

(e) the lawful detention of persons for the prevention of the spreading of infectious diseases, of persons of unsound mind, alcoholics or drug addicts or vagrants;

(f) the lawful arrest or detention of a person to prevent his effecting an unauthorised entry into the country or of a person against whom action is being taken with a view to deportation or extradition.

2. Everyone who is arrested shall be informed promptly, in a language which he understands, of the reasons for his arrest and of any charge against him.

3. Everyone arrested or detained in accordance with the provisions of paragraph 1(c) of this Article shall be brought promptly before a judge or other officer authorised by law to exercise judicial power and shall be entitled to trial within a reasonable time or to release pending trial. Release may be conditioned by guarantees to appear for trial.

4. Everyone who is deprived of his liberty by arrest or detention shall be entitled to take proceedings by which the lawfulness of his detention shall be decided speedily by a court and his release ordered if the detention is not lawful.

5. Everyone who has been the victim of arrest or detention in contravention of the provisions of this Article shall have an enforceable right to compensation.

Article 6

Right to a Fair Trial

1. In the determination of his civil rights and obligations or of any criminal charge against him, everyone is entitled to a fair and public hearing within a reasonable time by an independent and impartial tribunal established by law. Judgment shall be pronounced publicly but the press and public may be excluded from all or part of the trial in the interest of morals, public order or national security in a democratic society, where the interests of juveniles or the protection of the private life of the parties so require, or to the extent strictly necessary in the opinion of the court in special circumstances where publicity would prejudice the interests of justice.

2. Everyone charged with a criminal offence shall be presumed innocent until proved guilty according to law.

3. Everyone charged with a criminal offence has the following minimum rights:

   (a) to be informed promptly, in a language which he understands and in detail, of the nature and cause of the accusation against him;

   (b) to have adequate time and facilities for the preparation of his defence;

   (c) to defend himself in person or through legal assistance of his own choosing or, if he has not sufficient means to pay for legal assistance, to be given it free when the interests of justice so require;

(d) to examine or have examined witnesses against him and to obtain the attendance and examination of witnesses on his behalf under the same conditions as witnesses against him;

(e) to have the free assistance of an interpreter if he cannot understand or speak the language used in court.

Article 8

Right to Respect for Private and Family Life

1. Everyone has the right to respect for his private and family life, his home and his correspondence.

2. There shall be no interference by a public authority with the exercise of this right except such as is in accordance with the law and is necessary in a democratic society in the interests of national security, public safety or the economic well-being of the country, for the prevention of disorder or crime, for the protection of health or morals, or for the protection of the rights and freedoms of others.

Index